D1496138

CISTERCIAN STUDIES SERIES NUMBER TWO HUNDRED FIFTY-SEVEN

Gregory the Great

Moral Reflections on the Book of Job

Volume 2

Books 6–10 and Book 2.LII.84–LV.92

CISTERCIAN STUDIES SERIES NUMBER TWO HUNDRED FIFTY-SEVEN

Moral Reflections on the Book of Job

Volume 2

Books 6–10 and 2. 2.LII.84–LV.92

Gregory the Great

Translated by

Brian Kerns, OCSO

Introduction by

Mark DelCogliano

Ⲁ

Cistercian Publications
www.cistercianpublications.org

LITURGICAL PRESS
Collegeville, Minnesota
www.litpress.org

A Cistercian Publications title published by Liturgical Press

Cistercian Publications
Editorial Offices
161 Grosvenor Street
Athens, Ohio 54701
www.cistercianpublications.org

A translation of the critical edition by Marcus Adriaen, *Moralia in Iob*, in Corpus Christianorum, Series Latina 143, 143A, 143B.

Biblical quotations are translated by Brian Kerns, OCSO.

ISBN 978-0-87907-357-2 (Volume 2)

1	2	3	4	5	6	7	8	9

Library of Congress Cataloging-in-Publication Data

Gregory I, Pope, approximately 540–604.
    [Moralia in Job. Selections. English]
    Gregory the Great : moral reflections on the Book of Job, vol. 1,
preface and books 1-5 / translated by Brian Kerns, OCSO ;
introduction by Mark DelCogliano.
       pages cm. — (Cistercian studies series ; number two hundred forty-nine)
    Includes index.
    ISBN 978-0-87907-149-3 (hardcover)
    1. Bible. Job I-V, 2—Commentaries—Early works to 1800. I. Kerns,
Brian, translator. II. DelCogliano, Mark, writer of introduction. III. Title.

BS1415.53.G7413 2014
223'.107—dc23   2014015314

Contents

Abbreviations

General

chap.	chapter
diss.	dissertation
ed(s).	editor(s); edition(s)
gen.	genitive
n(n).	note(s)
no.	number, issue
p(p).	page(s)
pl.	plural
s.v.	*sub verbum*
trans.	translator, translated by
vol(s).	volume(s)

Publications: Books and Series

CCSL	Corpus Christianorum, Series Latina. Turnhout: Brepols Publishers, 1954–
CS	Cistercian Studies series. Kalamazoo, MI, and St. John's, MN: Cistercian Publications.
LXX	Septuagint
PL	Patrologiae cursus completus, series Latinae. Ed. J.-P. Migne. 221 vols. Paris.
Praef.	*Praefatio*
SCh	Sources Chrétiennes. Paris: Les Éditions du Cerf, 1942–

Introduction

On the Necessary Intermingling of the Good and the Bad

Mark DelCogliano

In part 1 (books 1–5) of his *Moralia in Job*, Gregory the Great managed to comment through Job 5:2. In part 2 (books 6–10) he picks up where he left off and extends his commentary to Job 12:5. Parts 1 and 2 originated in the oral discourses that Gregory delivered to the small group of monks and clerics living with him in Constantinople in the early 580s when he was serving as papal ambassador to the imperial court. He later revised these discourses upon his return to the monastery of St. Andrew around 586, achieving the form in which we now possess them shortly after Gregory was elected pope in April 591.[1]

In part 2, there is a complete breakdown of the overly ambitious exegetical method with which Gregory began his exposition in book 1 (CS 249:18; *Letter to Leander* 1, CS 249:48–49). His original plan appears to have been to interpret each selection of verses three times: first the historical or literal interpretation, then the typical interpretation (geared toward what Christians believe or need to believe), and finally the moral interpretation (what Christians need to do). He scrupulously followed this scheme in books 1–3. But book 4 begins with

---

[1] See Gregory the Great, *Moral Commentary on Job*, trans. Brian Kerns, vol. 1, CS 249 (Collegeville, MN: Cistercian Publications, 2014), 8–10; hereafter cited as CS 249, with page numbers.

the historical interpretation of Job 3:1-10 (I.1–XII.22) and concludes with the moral interpretation of Job 3:1-19 (XII.23–XXXV.72):[2] he completely skips the typical interpretation, as well as the historical interpretation of Job 3:11-19, and focuses instead on the moral interpretation. Starting in book 5, Gregory generally comments on each selection of verses only once, whether giving the historical, typical, or moral interpretation. In practice, he mostly abandons the historical interpretation, preferring to delve into the allegorical senses, that is, the typical and the moral senses. In a few cases in part 2, particularly in the earlier books, he treats a few verses in two senses, but never in all three, as if he was still unwilling totally to abandon his original plan.[3] But as he advances through Job, such exegetical repetitions become more rare. The preponderance of the moral sense in his commentary starting in part 2 no doubt contributed to the name of the entire exposition, the *Moralia*.

Gregory probably jettisoned his original plan for two reasons. First, the task of commenting on the entirety of Job in such a fashion would have been enormous. In books 1–3, he comments on five, sixteen, and thirteen verses, respectively. Given that there are over 1,050 verses in the book of Job, if he had maintained the threefold interpretation, assuming that he would have commented on an average of fifteen verses per book, he would have needed at least seventy books to complete the exposition on Job—and probably many years added to his life. Second, Gregory surely knew that his audience was more interested in the allegorical senses than the historical. He did not believe his *Moralia* was suited for a general audience, as is evidenced by his dismay upon hearing that Marinianus, the archbishop of

---

[2] Citations of Gregory contain three numbers; the first Arabic numeral indicates the book, the Roman numeral indicates the paragraph according to the Coccian division, and the second Arabic numeral indicates the paragraph according to the Maurist division. For further explanation see my introduction to volume 1 (CS 249:39–42).

[3] For example, in 6.II.3–V.6 he discusses the typical sense of Job 5:3–5, whereas in VI.7–X.12 he discusses the moral sense of Job 5:3-5.

Ravenna, was having the book read in public at Vigils.[4] He intended the historical sense for "the simple" and the allegorical senses for those "learned in the mysteries" of the Word of God (*Letter to Leander* 4, CS 249:53; Introduction, CS 249:19). He could for the most part dispense with the historical sense for his proficient audience of monks and clerics in Constantinople.

Evidence for this new exegetical approach directed to those learned in the mysteries of the Word is also seen in the opening sentence of part 2, where Gregory for the first time in the commentary proposes to set forth a "mystical interpretation" (*mystica interpretatio*) of Job (6.I.1). In part 2 itself he declines to provide a precise explanation of the "mystical interpretation," as he had for the historical, typical, and moral interpretations in the Preface, but he does have this to say: "His [Job's] words, therefore, are not empty of mystery, just as we learn from the end of the story that the interior Judge praises his words. Indeed, his words would hardly still be valid until the end of the world and win so much veneration if they had not been pregnant with mystical understanding" (7.X.10). The "mystical interpretation" seems to be the insight that Job's words give into the mysteries of the Christian faith: the mysteries of Christ's incarnation and redemption, of the divine economy, of prophecy, of Paradise and heaven, of the spiritual life, of the cross, of interior contemplation, and of the divine wisdom and judgment—the list goes on.

This new "mystical interpretation" was clearly on Gregory's mind throughout books 6–10, because he concludes part 2 with these words: "It should be enough that we have now produced these two parts with the Lord's help. Since we cannot master the extended sequence of the

---

[4] "And I have not been at all pleased about what has been reported to me by some people, that my most reverend brother and fellow bishop, Marinianus, is having my commentary on the blessed Job read out in public at Vigils. For it is not a work for the general public, and it produces an obstacle rather than assistance for ill-educated readers" (*Registrum epistularum* 12.6; English translation by John R. C. Martyn, *The Letters of Gregory the Great*, 3 vols., Medieval Sources in Translation 40 [Toronto: Pontifical Institute of Mediaeval Studies, 2004], 811).

holy book with the mystical interpretation by means of a brief exposition, we must reserve it for a future volume, that readers may return more ardently to the study of the book inasmuch as they have rested during the interruption of the reading" (10.XXXI.55). Perhaps also by "mystical interpretation" Gregory means an interpretation that does not systematically include the historical, typical, and moral in a threefold manner, but rather one that delves into whichever of these three senses might provide the greatest insight into the "mysteries." In any event, part 2 marks the definitive abandonment of the original threefold interpretation in favor of mystical interpretations, usually moral in nature, according to the material supplied by the scriptural verses at hand.

One of the exegetical challenges that Gregory faces in part 2 is that often he is not interpreting the words of Job, but the words of Job's friends, Eliphaz, Bildad, and Zophar. In the Preface, Gregory had explained that Job's friends allegorically represent heretics, "who pretend to advise but intend to seduce. . . . They speak to blessed Job as though holding God's place, but God does not approve of them, for all heretics obviously pretend to defend God, whom they actually offend" (Pref. 6.15; CS 249:71). Citing Job 15:3-4, Gregory notes that Job considered his friends "liars and followers of perverse doctrines" (Pref. 6.15; CS 249:71), and citing Job 42:7, he says that God said to the friends, "You have not spoken the truth about me, as my servant Job has" (6.I.2; see 5.XI.26). Gregory devotes book 8.XXXVI.60–XLII.66, which treats the beginning of Bildad's speech in Job 8, to demonstrating how "Bildad's words coincide with the heretics' pilfering" (8.XXXVI.60).

So how can moral and mystical insight be gained from the words of these liars, who are followers of perverse doctrines and speakers of untruths, who represent pilfering heretics? At the beginning of part 2, Gregory responds that not everything they say is to be rejected:

> I have said that blessed Job's friends play the role of heretics, but
> I do not at all always condemn their words. . . . It is perfectly
> obvious that if something is rejected through comparison with
> a more perfect example, it is still not absolutely contemptible.

> They would, in fact, carelessly fall into criticism of him, but they were still this great man's friends, and from this friendship they learned much spirituality. . . . Truth rightly reprehends their words, because however truthful their statement may be, it should not have been made against this holy man. (6.I.2)

Not even heretics are wrong all the time. There is much truth in their words, Gregory admits. For example, Bildad "produced true and solid arguments against hypocrites, and understanding their application to extend to all other evildoers as well, he leaves himself no concern for defense" (9.I.1).[5] But relative to Job, all the words of Job's friends fall far short of the truth.[6] Gregory justifies his positive use of the words of Job's friends by appealing to the example of Paul, who in 1 Corinthians 3:19 quoted Eliphaz's words in Job 5:13 (6.I.2, 5.XI.26). Paul uses the words of Job's friends, explains Gregory, because of their own merit, but God (in Job 42:7) reproves them because they spoke them to Job out of spite. The main problem, then, is not so much the lack of truthfulness in the words of Job's friends (though it is a problem), but the inappropriate manner in which those words were spoken to the blameless Job.[7] And yet they are like heretics, says Gregory, because

> some of their thoughts are certainly correct, but they also have thoughts that merge with the perverse. In fact, it is characteristic of heretics that they mix good with evil so that they may the more easily deceive those who listen to them. If they only spoke evil things, they would more easily be recognized as evil, and

---

[5] Referring in particular to Job 8:11-14, discussed in 8.XLII.67–XLIII.70.

[6] See 5.XI.27: "It is clear . . . that some of their words are true, but compared to better speeches [i.e., those of Job] they fail the test" (CS 249:329).

[7] "Bildad certainly speaks admirable words against the hypocrites, but he turns the sword of the word against himself, since unless he were an imitator of justice in some small way, he would never presume to teach just men so rashly. The words he speaks are admittedly strong words, but he ought to say them to fools, not to a wise man, to deceitful people, not to a righteous man; the one who passes withering gardens to pour water into a stream declares himself to be a fool" (8.XLI.65).

they would then convince no one of their purpose. On the other hand, if they only thought what was right, they would hardly be heretics. The art of deception serves both truth and falsehood, so that evil infects good and good hides evil, and its practitioners are accepted. (5.XI.28; CS 249:330)

Gregory does not attribute outright deception to Job's friends but sees a parallel between them and heretics insofar as good thoughts are mixed with evil thoughts. Thus the issue in drawing moral and mystical insight from the words of Job's friends is distinguishing between their true and false statements. In practice, this means for Gregory determining *in what way*, or rather *in what sense* their words are true, interpreting them typically, morally, or even historically as needed to uncover their truth.

Gregory was fond of the idea of the good being mixed with the bad. One of the central themes of the *Moralia*, and indeed of his entire literary corpus, is the mixture of good and bad people in the church. This is, in fact, the first subject he treats in the *Moralia*, in 1.I.1, in his commentary on Job 1:1, indicating that it is a key topic for him.[8] He discusses the idea that the intermingling of the good and bad in the church is necessary, in ways that are structurally and even verbally similar, five other times in his writings.[9] An investigation of his treatment of this theme, in the *Moralia* and elsewhere in his corpus, allows us to gain manifold insight into Gregory, as a thinker, as a writer, as an exegete, as a pastor, as a biblical theologian, as an ascetic, as a reuser of his own material, and as a recipient of earlier patristic thought.

In 1.I.1 Gregory notes that Job was a good man among the bad: "For it is not very praiseworthy to be a good man living among good men, but to be a good man living among bad men *is* praiseworthy.

[8] The theme is dealt with more globally in Carole Straw, *Gregory the Great: Perfection in Imperfection* (Berkeley, CA: University of California Press, 1988). See also R. A. Markus, *Gregory the Great and His World* (Cambridge, UK: Cambridge University Press, 1997), and Claude Dagens, *Saint Grégoire le Grand: culture et expérience chrétiennes* (Paris: Études augustiniennes, 1977).

[9] I.e., *Moralia* 20.XXXIX.76; *Homiliae in evangelia* 2.38; *Homiliae in Hiezechihelem* 1.9; *Registrum epistularum* 10.15; and *Registrum epistularum* 11.27.

In the same way, it is considered a grave fault not to be a good man when you live among good men. So it is high praise for a man to have been good while living among bad men" (CS 249:77). This is the core of Gregory's teaching on the necessary intermingling of the good and the bad: true Christian virtue is developed and becomes manifest only in the face of vice. Calmly bearing with bad people and their misbehavior both necessitates and cultivates patience and forbearance. The more one does so, the more one develops these key virtues and the closer one comes to the perfection of goodness. In 20.XXXIX.76, Gregory says that the bad put the good to the test and purify them of their imperfections, as gold is refined in a furnace.[10] Employing another metaphor in *Homiliae in evangelia* 2.38, he says, "the iron sword of our soul does not become razor-sharp unless the file of another's depravity grinds it."[11] Only by living patiently among the bad and calmly bearing with them can the Christian reach perfect goodness. Such is Gregory's basic teaching in each of six instances.

While the *Moralia* passages contain Gregory's basic teaching on the subject, in other discussions he nuances and enriches it. In *Homiliae in evangelia* 2.38 he explicitly states that the good and the bad are mixed together in the church. He explains that the intermingled status of the church is transitory, as the separation of good from bad properly belongs to the next life:

> For as long as we live here below, it is necessary that we walk the path of this present age thus intermingled. But we are distinguished when we reach the next life. Now the good are never alone except in heaven and the bad are never alone except in hell. But just as this life lies between heaven and hell and is thus accessible to all, so too it admits citizens from both regions alike. Nonetheless, now the holy church receives them both indiscriminately, but afterwards, after they depart from this life, she will make distinctions between them.[12]

---

[10] *Moralia* 20.XXXIX.76, lines 33–35 (CCSL 143A:1059).
[11] *Homiliae in evangelia* 2.38 [7], lines 184–86 (CCSL 141:367).
[12] *Homiliae in evangelia* 2.38 [7], lines 141–48 (CCSL 141:365).

In this passage, Gregory implies that the church is not equipped to judge its members. While it is clear to all that in the church there are good and bad, the final judgment of individuals within the church must be reserved for God. The bad serve a mere *transitional* purpose for the good since the tolerance of them in this life leads to a *permanent* separation from them in the next life. Gregory's emphasis in this passage is on the benefit that the good receive from being intermingled with the bad; he does not recognize any sort of relationship of mutual benefit or reciprocity between the good and the bad here in this life. It is a relationship considered from what can be called the unilateral perspective.

In *Homiliae in Hiezechihelem* 1.9, Gregory offers further nuance to his teaching. First of all, he directs his comments toward the good who find themselves unwilling to put up with the bad (notice that he includes himself in this category):

> We ought to note that when it is said to the prophet, *Unbelievers and destroyers are with you, and you dwell with scorpions* [Ezek 2.6], we are being offered a comforting remedy, we who often grow weary of living when we do not want to dwell with bad people. Indeed, we complain, "Why aren't all who live with us good?" We make this complaint because we are unwilling to bear the misbehavior of our neighbors. We think that everyone should already be a saint, although we ourselves do not want there to be anything that we have to bear from our neighbors. But the situation is clear: as long as we refuse to bear with the bad, we ourselves will still possess far less goodness. For someone is not entirely good unless he can be good even with the bad.[13]

Here Gregory's audience seems to be the clerics and monks who formed a kind of small community around him. He forces his audience to examine their own consciences and makes a subtle criticism of those who are good but are unwilling to bear with the bad. He implicitly accuses them of a kind of spiritual inertia since they are

---

[13] *Homiliae in Hiezechihelem* 1.9 [22], lines 456–66 (CCSL 142:135).

unwilling to make the arduous effort of being patient with the bad. Gregory seeks to stir them out of their lethargy by reminding them that Christian perfection is impossible without being good among the bad. Untested Christian virtue falls short of perfection.

In the same homily, Gregory also criticizes those who want to absent themselves from the intermingled church by a change of place:

> When we frequently grumble about the life of our neighbors and attempt to change our place and to choose the solitude of a more secluded life, we ignore the fact that if the Spirit is lacking, no place will be of help to us. For although the same Lot about whom we are speaking was holy in Sodom, he sinned on the mountain. Moreover, that places do not protect the mind is proved by the fact that the very first parent of the human race fell in paradise. But by no means are all the things we are saying concerned with earthly places. For if a place had been able to save, Satan would not have fallen from heaven. This is why the psalmist, observing people being tempted everywhere in this world, sought a place to which he might flee, but he could not find a safe place without God. For this reason he even begged for God to become a place for him! It was as he sought this place that he said, *Be for me a protecting God and a safe place, that you might save me* [Ps 30:3]. Therefore, our neighbors are to be borne with everywhere.[14]

Against those seeking to adopt some form of monastic or religious life out of the impure motive of escaping bad people, Gregory argues that one's irritation with living among the bad can only be mollified through living with them. In other words, true growth in Christian virtue demands confronting one's imperfection head-on, not in seeking to escape it. Here Gregory is in line with a long tradition of ascetical theology.[15] Note, too, that Gregory's argument appeals to a

---

[14] *Homiliae in Hiezechihelem* 1.9 [22], lines 473–86 (CCSL 142:136).

[15] As was articulated, for example, in John Cassian's *Institutes*. Gregory here is not arguing against monastic withdrawal but is saying that if one withdraws from

number of scriptural exemplars, including Lot, Adam, Satan, and the psalmist—a method of argumentation we will encounter again below.

Gregory, however, allows for an exceptional case in which one may legitimately avoid the company of the bad: the one who is weak may withdraw from the bad in order to forestall being corrupted by them:

> But there is one reason for shunning the company of the bad. If the bad are perhaps incorrigible, they are to be shunned for fear they even induce others to imitate themselves. If they cannot be changed from their wickedness, they are to be shunned for fear that they may lead astray those who associate with them. This is why Paul said, *Crooked speech corrupts good habits* [1 Cor 15:33]. And it is said through Solomon, *Do not be a friend to an irritable man nor walk with a man liable to rage for fear you inadvertently learn his ways and take a stumbling block to your soul* [Prov 22:24-25]. Therefore, just as perfect men ought not flee their wayward neighbors because they often induce them to uprightness while they themselves are never induced to waywardness, so too the weak ought also to turn from the company of the bad lest the misbehavior they frequently see and cannot correct entice them to imitate it. So then, when we hear the words of our neighbors every day, we take them into our mind, just as we draw air into the body by inhaling and exhaling. And just as the constant breathing of bad air infects the body, so too the constant hearing of perverse speaking infects the soul of the weak, with the result that the soul wastes away because of delight in depraved works and in perpetual iniquitous talk.[16]

What Gregory says here nuances his teaching in a significant way. For this passage reveals that the intermingling of the bad with the good has the additional purpose of allowing the good to induce the bad to convert to a life of goodness. Hence for Gregory there is,

---

a community, whether from the local church or from the monastery, in order to escape those who irritate him, it is a failure to address the real problem—one's own lack of patience and virtue.

[16] *Homiliae in Hiezechihelem* 1.9 [23], lines 488–504 (CCSL 142:136).

in fact, a relationship of mutual benefit between the good and the bad in the mixed body of the church: the good are given the occasion to grow in patience and tolerance and thus to attain the perfection of Christian goodness, while the bad are given exemplars of good behavior and exhortations to goodness, to which they may respond and be converted to goodness: this can be called the bilateral perspective.

In his letters Gregory adapts the teaching for specific individuals in concrete situations requiring pastoral advice, transforming his core teaching in fascinating ways. These letters, therefore, are good examples of how Gregory's teaching could be deployed with flexibility in eminently practical contexts. In *Registrum epistularum* 10.15 from July 600, Gregory writes to Maximus of Salona in the Dalmatian region, an area then being disturbed by Slavs. The stability of the region was compromised,[17] and Gregory admonished Maximus to work on behalf of the poor and the oppressed.[18] In his exhortation, Gregory encourages Maximus to act in order to win the approval of God and not to be discouraged or thwarted by "wicked men" and the "enemies of God" as he strives to care for the poor and oppressed.[19] Gregory says, "Know this with absolute certainty, that no one can please God and wicked men. And so, let your Fraternity consider that you have pleased almighty God just as much as you will learn that you have displeased sinful humans."[20] Maximus's attempts to help the poor and oppressed were apparently being hindered by the activities of the invading Slavs.

Here Gregory is not encouraging Maximus to bear with the bad in the church as a necessary requisite for Christian perfection. Rather, Gregory is exhorting Maximus to continue to do good in the world despite the opposition of the non-Christian Slavs. Gregory's emphasis here, unlike elsewhere, is not on the necessity of patiently tolerating

[17] *Registrum epistularum* 10.15, lines 10–13 (CCSL 140A:842).
[18] *Registrum epistularum* 10.15, lines 14–15 (CCSL 140A:843).
[19] *Registrum epistularum* 10.15, lines 15–36 (CCSL 140A:843).
[20] *Registrum epistularum* 10.15, lines 23–25 (CCSL 140A:843); trans. Martyn, *Letters*, 725.

one's bad fellow Christians in order to reach Christian perfection, but
rather on the inevitable opposition that the Christian encounters from
bad people in the world when attempting to do good. Gregory is advis-
ing Maximus to persevere in doing good in the face of obstacles rather
than to look to his own perfection in Christian goodness. In this letter,
then, Gregory has adapted his teaching on the necessary mixture of the
good and the bad in the church by transposing it to a different context:
the struggles of Maximus to care for the poor and oppressed when his
region is being overrun by Slavs. But this adaptation is in no way inconsistent with the versions of the teaching elsewhere. Gregory has merely
expanded its scope to include the bad who are non-Christians while
deemphasizing tolerating them for one's own perfection in goodness.

In *Registrum epistularum* 11.27, Gregory writes to Theoctista,
the widowed sister of Emperor Maurice and a prominent member of
the imperial household in Constantinople in charge of the emperor's
children.[21] The purpose of the letter is to admonish Theoctista not to
be distressed by the derogatory comments and insults aimed at her by
certain zealots accusing her of heresy. Gregory begins by expressing
amazement (and indulges in a bit of flattery as well) that the words
of her slanderers disturb her, since her heart is fixed in heaven.[22] For
"if we are delighted by praises and are shattered by insults," it shows
that we are living not according to our conscience but according to the
mouths of others.[23] Our conscience should be our sole judge, not others'
praises or insults: "Although all might insult him, yet a person is free
who is not accused by his conscience, because even if all might praise
him, he cannot be free if he is accused by his conscience."[24] Nonetheless, Gregory is certain that Theoctista's sadness from being insulted
is an act of divine kindness: "For not even to his elect had he promised

[21] See also *Registrum epistularum* 1.5 and 7.23.

[22] *Registrum epistularum* 11.27, lines 8–18 (CCSL 140A:902).

[23] *Registrum epistularum* 11.27, lines 19–20 (CCSL 140A:902); trans. Martyn, *Letters*, 763.

[24] *Registrum epistularum* 11.27, lines 29–31 (CCSL 140A:903); trans. Martyn, *Letters*, 764 (slightly modified).

delightful joys in this life, but rather the bitterness of tribulation, so that, as if taking medicine, they may return to the sweetness of eternal salvation through a bitter cup."[25] Gregory here cites Jesus himself—*In your patience shall you possess your souls* (Luke 21:19)—and says patience can only be developed if there is something to endure.[26]

At this point Gregory launches into his teaching on the necessary intermingling of the good and the bad: "I suspect that there is not an Abel who will not have a Cain. For if the good were without the bad, they could not be perfectly good, as they would not be purified at all. And their very association with the evil acts as a purification for the good."[27] Later on in the letter, Gregory concludes, "Since, therefore, we learn through the witness of Scripture that in this life the good cannot exist without the bad, your Excellency should in no way be disturbed by the words of fools, especially because our trust in almighty God is certain when for doing good, some adversity is received in this world, so that a full reward may be reserved in eternal retribution."[28]

And so, in this letter Gregory's focus is both on the purification of goodness in this life and on the eternal reward won by bearing with adversity in this world. Here he deploys his teaching on the mixed church as part of a larger program of action that he advises for Theoctista when dealing with her critics. In so doing he has slightly modified the teaching delivered elsewhere to make it useful and applicable to one engaged in court politics. Such a modification shows that Gregory saw all Christians as bound by the same standards and motivated by the same principles, even if the instantiation of these shared standards and principles varied according to one's state in life.

[25] *Registrum epistularum* 11.27, lines 47–49 (CCSL 140A:903–4); trans. Martyn, *Letters*, 764.

[26] *Registrum epistularum* 11.27, lines 52–53 (CCSL 140A:904); trans. Martyn, *Letters*, 764.

[27] *Registrum epistularum* 11.27, lines 54–57 (CCSL 140A:904); trans. Martyn, *Letters*, 764.

[28] *Registrum epistularum* 11.27, lines 80–84 (CCSL 140A:905); trans. Martyn, *Letters*, 765.

As was mentioned above, the six passages on the necessary inter-mingling of the good and the bad are structurally and at times even verbally similar. An examination of this structure provides insight into Gregory as a thinker and writer. Gregory's discussion of the reason it is necessary for there to be mixture of good and bad people in the church in its fullest form has a schema that consists of five elements, which generally appear in the following order: (1) a basic statement of the teaching, (2) a few examples of people or things able to flourish only when harmed in some way, (3) a series of scriptural exemplars of groups in which good and bad are intermingled, (4) a series of scriptural citations supporting the teaching that the perfection of goodness is only attained in the midst of the bad, and (5) concluding remarks. Not all five elements appear in each instance, or in the same order, but in general Gregory is remarkably consistent in using this schema when discussing the necessary mixture of the good and bad.[29] Clearly Gregory had no qualms about repeating himself and was prone to reusing material.

Because it is found in all six passages, the fourth element seems to constitute the skeleton on which each instance of the discussion of the necessary mixture is built. Gregory consistently cites six verses as having the same basic interpretation in order to support his teaching, or cites at least a subset of them: Job 30:29,[30] Song of Songs 2:2,[31] Ezekiel 2:6,[32] 2 Peter 2:7-8,[33] Philippians 2:15-16,[34] and Revelation

[29] The second and third elements appear in only half of the discussions: *Moralia* 20.XXXIX.76, *Homiliae in evangelia* 2.38, and *Registrum epistularum* 11.27. The fourth element, the scriptural citations, appears in every case, though there are variations in both which passages are cited and what their order is.

[30] *I was the brother of dragons and the companion of ostriches.*

[31] *As a lily among thorns, so is my love among the daughters.*

[32] *Son of man, unbelievers and destroyers are with you, and you dwell with scorpions.*

[33] *And he rescued the just Lot, who was oppressed by sacrilegious men's lawless way of life. For Lot was just in his sight and hearing, dwelling among those who from day to day tortured that just man's soul with unjust works.*

[34] *In the midst of a wayward and perverse people, among whom you shine like lamps in the world, having the word of life.* In some cases, only Phil 2:15 is used; i.e., *having the word of life* is omitted.

2:13.[35] From his pattern of usage we can infer that the core scriptural texts for Gregory were Job 30:29, Ezekiel 2:6, 2 Peter 2:7-8, and Philippians 2:15-16.[36] These verses are more or less simply quoted, except in two cases (*Moralia* 1.I.1 and *Homiliae in Hiezechihelem* 1.9) where Gregory considered 2 Peter 2:7-8 in need of further exegesis in order to clarify its applicability to what he was teaching.[37]

Gregory's consistent association of these six verses, or the four-verse subset, as having the same interpretation shows that his teaching on the necessary intermingling of the good and the bad was fundamentally and consciously rooted in Scripture. Since Job 1:1 had no direct connection to the doctrine of the necessary mixture in Gregory's mind (that is, it was not one of the six associated verses), Gregory's choice to present this teaching at the beginning of book 1 of the *Moralia* as his commentary on Job 1:1 shows his partiality for it and indeed its centrality for him; this fact is further evidenced by the fact that Job 1:1 is never associated with the six verses elsewhere. Thus its appearance in book 1.I.1 is calculated and deliberate.[38]

---

[35] *I know where you dwell, where Satan's throne is; you both hold fast to my name and did not deny my faith.*

[36] Job 30:39 is included in each of the six discussions. Song 2:2 and Rev 2:13 are not found in three discussions: *Homiliae in Hiezechihelem* 1.9 and *Registrum epistularum* 10.15 and 11.27. Ezek 2:6 is omitted only in *Moralia* 1.I.1 and *Homiliae in Hiezechihelem* 1.9, in the latter case because it is the text on which Gregory is commenting; 2 Pet 2:7-8 is omitted only in *Registrum epistularum* 10.15, the most abbreviated form of the discussion. Phil 2:15-16 is included in each discussion.

[37] "For he certainly could not be tortured in any way except by watching and hearing of the wicked deeds of his neighbors. Yet he was called *just in his sight and hearing*, because the evil lives of his neighbors reached his eyes and ears, at which news he felt not pleasure but aversion" (*Moralia* 1.I.1; CS 249:78).

[38] Whenever Gregory encountered a verse from this set of six verses in the course of his exegesis, he repeats the same teaching: *Moralia* 20.XXXIX.76 is his commentary on Job 20:39 and *Homiliae in Hiezechihelem* 1.9 is that on Ezek 2:6. The teaching comes up in *Homiliae in evangelia* 2.38 as the bulk of the commentary on Matt 22:10, the passage in which the servants of the king gathered the good and the bad for his marriage-feast, which Gregory interprets as the present-day church. In these three cases, the repetition of the teaching was triggered by the need to interpret a specific verse related either scripturally (as

We see a similar but less prevalent pattern with regard to the second and third elements, which always appear together: the examples of (mostly) scriptural people or things able to flourish only when harmed in some way, and the series of scriptural exemplars of groups in which good and bad were intermingled. These two elements appear only three out of six times, in *Moralia* 20.XXXIX.76, *Homiliae in evangelia* 2.38, and *Registrum epistularum* 11.27. The second element is virtually identical in *Moralia* 20.XXXIX.76 and *Homiliae in evangelia* 2.38: "For the one whom a Cain does not vex with wickedness refuses to be an Abel. Just as on threshing floors grains are pressed under the chaff, so too do flowers arise among thorns and a fragrant rose grows when a thorn pricks it."[39] In *Registrum epistularum* 11.27, the second element is reduced to "I suspect that there is no Abel who will not have a Cain."[40] Interestingly, the second element in this abbreviated form appears in the *conclusion* of the discussion in *Homiliae in Hiezechihelem* 1.9: "a person cannot become an Abel if a Cain does not vex him with wickedness."[41] So it seems that Gregory could deem the example of Abel and Cain sufficient to make his point that good people need bad people in order to reach Christian perfection, allowing him to omit the additional examples of the grain, flower, and rose.

Indeed, the example of Abel and Cain is far stronger than that of grain, flowers, or the rose. In the case of the grain, flower, or rose, they flourish only by being in some way harmed (by pressing or pricking), while in the case of Abel and Cain, Cain kills Abel. Gregory's preference for the example of Abel and Cain becomes clearer when one

a member of the six-verse set) or thematically to his teaching on the necessary intermingling.

[39] *Moralia* 20.XXXIX.75–76, lines 19–22 (CCSL 143A:1059) and *Homiliae in evangelia* 2.38 [7], lines 151–53 (CCSL 141:365). The only difference between the two is that the former begins *Abel enim* and the latter *Abel quippe*. Note the allusions to Gen 4 and Matt 3:12.

[40] *Registrum epistularum* 11.27, lines 54–55 (CCSL 140A:904); trans. Martyn, *Letters*, 764.

[41] *Homiliae in Hiezechihelem* 1.9 [22], lines 486–87 (CCSL 142:136).

realizes that, for Gregory, Abel was the primary scriptural type of an innocent person unjustly killed and thus a key prefiguration of Christ.[42] This point is made most clearly when Gregory comments on Job 2.7:

> *So Satan left God's presence and struck Job with a painful ulcer from the soles of his feet to the top of his head* [Job 2:7]. There is no man born to this life led by the elect who has not felt the hatred of this enemy of ours. There have been members of our Redeemer's Body, however, ever since the world began, who suffered tortures, even though they lived holy lives. Was not Abel one of his members? Did he not, by his acceptable sacrifice, as well as by his silence before death, prefigure that death of which it is written, *As a lamb is quiet before the shearers, so he opened not his mouth?* [Isa 53:7]. Satan has tried to beat our Redeemer's body ever since the world began. From the soles of his feet to the top of his head he has wounded him, beginning with the first human beings, until in his fierce wrath he even attacked the very Head of the church himself. (3.XVII.32; CS 249:208)[43]

Abel can therefore be Gregory's choice example of Christian perfection because Abel—the "sole" of the Body of Christ—doubly prefigures Christ, both in offering an acceptable sacrifice to God and in being led to an unjust death without complaint. As is the case for every member of the Body of Christ, the sufferings Abel endured from the bad are overcome through the passion, death, and resurrection of Jesus Christ. Christ is, then, the prime example of an Abel who had a Cain. Accordingly, the perfection of goodness achieved by being good among the bad is not merely a matter of growing in patience; on a more fundamental level it is a participation in the redemptive

---

[42] See *Homiliae in evangelia* 1.19 [1], lines 9–12 (CCSL 141:143); *Moralia* praef.6 [13], line 9 (CCSL 143:19); *Homiliae in Hiezechihelem* 2.3 [21], lines 488–90 (CCSL 142:252).

[43] See also *Moralia* 13.XXIII.26, lines 13–17 (CCSL 143A:683), and *Moralia* 29.XXXI.68–69, lines 27–45 (CCSL 143B:1482).

suffering of Christ.[44] Gregory's inclusion of this second element in his discussion shows the radical Christological orientation of his conception of the Christian life.

The third element is the series of scriptural exemplars of groups in which good and bad are intermingled, an element that always appears with the second element. In each case but one, there is one person of the group (which is sometimes only a pair) who turns out to be the single bad person among the rest, who are good. In the other case, there is only one good person among the rest, who are bad. In each of the three instances of this third element, the list of exemplars is slightly different, and what is said about each exemplar varies.

In *Moralia* 20.XXXIX.76, Gregory lists the following groups as exemplars—the sons of Adam, the sons of Noah, the sons of Abraham, the sons of Isaac, the sons of Jacob, and the twelve apostles—and explains why one of the group is bad while the rest of the group is good (or why one of the group is good and the rest bad):

> Now the first man had two sons: one of these was elect, the other was reprobate. The ark held three sons, but while two remained steadfast in their humility, one was quick to mock his father. Abraham had two sons: one was innocent, but the other was the persecutor of his brother. Isaac had two sons: one served in humility, but the other was reprobate even before he was born. Jacob begat twelve sons: one of them was sold on account of his innocence, but the others were the sellers of their brother on account of their wickedness. Twelve apostles were elected in the holy church, but one of them became involved with those who put them to the test by persecuting them lest they remain untested.[45]

Notice that in each case except the first Gregory offers reasons that one of the group was unique, whether elect (good) or reprobate (bad), except for Abel and Cain.

---

[44] Here one can recall the similar theology of the *Regula Benedicti* prologue.
[45] *Moralia* 20.XXXIX.76, lines 22–32 (CCSL 143B:1059).

In *Homiliae in evangelia* 2.38, Gregory lists the same groups as exemplars but adds the first seven deacons. Regarding the sons of Adam, Noah, Abraham, and Isaac, Gregory merely says, without explanation, that one was reprobate while the other or others were elect, while in the two remaining cases he gives more expanded explanations:

> The first man had two sons: one of these was elect, the other was reprobate. The ark held three sons: two were elect, but one was reprobate. Abraham had two sons: one was elect, but the other was reprobate. Isaac had two sons: one was elect, but the other was reprobate. Jacob had twelve sons: one of them was sold on account of his innocence, but the others were the sellers of their brother on account of their wickedness. Twelve apostles were elected: one of them became involved with those who put to the test, but there were eleven who were put to the test. There were seven deacons ordained by the apostles: six remained steadfast in correct faith, but one arose as the originator of error.[46]

The addition of the seven deacons may be due to Gregory's specific audience for the *Homiliae in evangelia*, since the seven deacons do not appear elsewhere as an exemplary group.[47] Here Gregory alludes to the ancient tradition of ascribing the heresy of the Nicolaitans mentioned in Revelation (Rev 2:6, 15) to Nicolaus of Antioch, one of the first seven deacons (Acts 6:5).[48]

The enumeration of exemplars in *Registrum epistularum* 11.27 differs considerably from the two other lists in terms of what groups are listed, and the explanations of the election and reprobation of the members of each group are more detailed than in the other cases, or at

---

[46] *Homiliae in evangelia* 2.38 [7], lines 154–63 (CCSL 141:365–66).

[47] *Homiliae in evangelia* were preached to the clergy and people of Rome during Mass, whereas *Moralia* and *Homiliae in Hiezechihelem* were delivered to smaller groups outside of a liturgical context.

[48] See K. A. Fox, "The Nicolaitans, Nicolaus and the Early Church," *Studies in Religion/Sciences Religieuses* 23 (1994): 485–96.

least significantly different. Here Gregory lists the familiar groups of the sons of Noah, Abraham, Isaac, and Jacob and the twelve apostles but does not include the sons of Adam and the seven deacons. And there is a new group here, David and his son:

> There were three sons in the ark and one of them ridiculed his father. He received an abusive verdict from his son, although he was blessed in himself. Abraham had two sons before he took Cethura as his wife, and yet his carnal son persecuted the son of the covenant. The great teacher explains this, saying: *As he that was born after the flesh persecuted him that was born after the Spirit, even so it is now* [Gal 4:29]. Isaac had two sons, but the one who was spiritual fled before the threats of his carnal brother. Jacob had twelve sons, but ten of them sold the one who was living more righteously into Egypt. In the case of the prophet David, because he had what should have been purified, it was brought about that he endured his son's persecution. . . . Among the twelve apostles there was one who was false, so that there might be one by whose persecution the other eleven might be tried.[49]

Here Gregory offers considerably more detail in his explanation of the election and reprobation of the sons of Noah and Abraham. Gregory even adds a Pauline passage to support his use of Abraham's sons as exemplars of a group in which good and bad were intermingled. The explanation of Jacob and Esau also differs from the other two examples. Note that Gregory improves the accuracy of his explanation for the sons of Jacob by saying that only ten of his twelve sons were bad, rightly excluding Benjamin as well as Joseph. The ellipses in the above quotation indicate where Gregory includes bits of the third and fourth elements of the discussion. Finally, Gregory includes David and his son Absalom as an exemplary group, perhaps motivated by a desire to provide Theoctista, the recipient of *Registrum epistularum* 11.27 and the emperor Maurice's sister, with an example of royalty being vexed by the bad.

---

[49] *Registrum epistularum* 11.27, lines 58–68 and 71–73 (CCSL 140A:904); trans. Martyn, *Letters*, 764–65.

In the second, third, and fourth elements of the discussion of the necessary intermingling of the good and the bad, Gregory adduces scriptural figures, images, and verses in support of the content of the teaching, showing his thoroughgoing rootedness in the Scriptures. And remarkably, not only was Gregory liable to reuse his own material—sometimes with slight changes to fit the situation—but he also repeated the very schema that he used to present his teaching.

The idea that the church is as a mixed body of good and bad people is of course not original to Gregory. But in general it is notoriously difficult to pinpoint Gregory's sources. It is recognized among scholars that his writings are so suffused with the thought of his patristic predecessors that it is difficult to demarcate where their doctrine ends and his begins. He made the preceding patristic tradition his own. He absorbed the teachings of his predecessors and reexpressed them in a way that reflected his concerns as well as those of his audience. He was no mere copyist; he digested the thoughts of others and ruminated on them in the light of his own experience as a pastor, an ascetic, and a contemplative. This experience often led him to transform the ideas of his sources in striking ways. Hence Gregory's writings often contain sentiments that are simultaneously very familiar and very novel. Perhaps it is Robert Gillet who has best expressed the situation: "A reader [of Gregory] who is even slightly familiar with patristic literature constantly feels that he is reading things he has already come across. But what if he searches for the source of what he has just read? It is most often the case that there is no possibility of making a precise comparison. He merely finds himself in the presence of an immense communal ambience."[50] Nonetheless, despite these difficulties in determining Gregory's familiarity with patristic literature, it is certain that he had an intimate knowledge of the Latin fathers, particularly Augustine and John

---

[50] Robert Gillet, "Introduction," in *Grégoire le Grand: Morals sur Job I–II*, ed. Robert Gillet and André de Gaudemaris, SCh 32 *bis* (Paris: Cerf, 1975), 7–133, here 13.

Cassian, and that whatever knowledge of the Greek fathers he had came mostly through Latin translations.[51]

The notion of the church as a mixed body, however, immediately brings to mind the anti-Donatist ecclesiology of Augustine.[52] The Donatists, following an African tradition that extended back to Cyprian, advocated an ecclesiology rooted in priestly purity: a priest had to be without serious sin in order to administer valid sacraments to the members of the church. If a priest was a sinner (for example, if he apostatized), he put himself outside of the unity of the church and rendered himself incapable of administering valid sacraments. Instead of the sacraments' effecting grace, they transmitted the priest's corruption. The Donatists believed that during the aftermath of the Great Persecution, members of the episcopal hierarchy of the catholic church in North Africa were guilty of *traditio* (handing over the Scriptures), a serious enough sin to render them unable to administer valid sacraments. But since they had continued to administer the sacraments, they had passed on their corruption, and the entire church had become complicit in their sin, as was any church throughout the world that was in communion with them. Contagion had infected the catholic church in the early fourth century and thereafter corrupted the entire church, so that it was impure. The Donatists, however, thought of their church as pure and a congregation of the saints, since their hierarchy alone, they claimed, was free from the contagion of *traditio*.

Besides denying that the members of the Catholic episcopal hierarchy were guilty of *traditio*, Augustine developed a new sacramental theology in which the validity of the sacrament was independent of

[51] See Markus, *Gregory the Great,* 35, citing the relevant studies. See also John Moorhead, *Gregory the Great* (London and New York: Routledge, 2005), 31–32.

[52] Representative passages include Augustine, *De baptismo* 1.24–27, 3.22–23, 4.14–22, 6.5–8; *De fide et symbolo* 21; *Epistulae* 87.2–3, 93.9.28–34, and 108.3.10–12. Such passages could easily be multiplied. Of the many studies of Donatist and Augustinian ecclesiology, I refer the reader to the brief summary of the late Gerald Bonner, *St. Augustine of Hippo: Life and Controversies,* 3rd ed. (Norwich: Canterbury Press, 2002), 278–89.

the state of its minister, thereby countering the Donatist claim of impurity's being transmitted by sinful priests.[53] Augustine also argued that the unity of the church superseded any need for its membership to consist solely of the pure. Augustine rejected the Donatist notion that the pure within the church could be infected with the contagion of the impure simply through ecclesial communion; rather, he said, the pure are affected by the sins of the impure only when they consent to their sins. The holiness of the church is not the holiness of its members but rather that of Christ. Accordingly, both the pure and the impure, the good and the bad, can coexist within the unity of the church without detriment to the good.

In addition, Augustine taught that the mixed church was not competent to judge its members here in this life: the separation of the good from the bad was reserved to Christ at the Final Judgment at the end of the age. Still, even if one could not recognize the good and the bad within the church with any certainty, Augustine's ecclesiology of inclusion of the bad within the unity of the church was aimed at securing their amendment and restoration to purity. The good should accept what can be called external communion with the bad and bear with them within the unity of the church lest that unity be broken. Augustine argued that church unity was far more important than church purity, as schism destroys Christian love. The good, however, should not have what can be called internal communion with the bad, that is, to acquiesce to and accept or join in their sins.[54] Rather, the good should pray for the forgiveness of the sins of the bad, admonish the bad to be converted, and provide models of goodness for them to imitate. In this way, the good and the bad could be intermingled within the church without having any negative effect on the good but having a beneficial effect on the bad.

---

[53] On the divergent sacramental theology of the Donatists and Augustine, see Bonner, *Augustine*, 289–94.

[54] Hence for Augustine the purity of the church was invisible, whereas for the Donatists ecclesial purity had to be visible.

Augustine's ecclesiology was here shaped by another factor besides the Donatist ecclesiology of purity: the inevitable mixture of good and bad in the post-Constantinian church. Whatever its other objections, Donatist ecclesiology was seen by Augustine as impractical and as failing to take into account contemporary ecclesial realities. Despite this context, Augustine had to argue against the Donatists that an ecclesiology of church unity was preferable to that of church purity. Given the vitality of the Donatist movement in Augustine's time, an ecclesiology that conceived of the church as a mixed body of the good and the bad could not be taken for granted. The viability of such a model had to be argued for, and Augustine needed to demonstrate that, despite the Donatist claim to the contrary, the good were not necessarily harmed through mere contact by being in communion with the bad.

Gregory thoroughly absorbed Augustine's ecclesiology of church unity and in his reexpression of it transformed it into a principle of perfection in the Christian life. Yet Gregory's treatment of the theme lacks the complexity and profundity of thought that characterizes Augustine's ecclesiology in his polemical anti-Donatist treatises and letters. Rather, Gregory's teaching on the good and the bad in the church bears much more resemblance to the way Augustine presented his ecclesiology in his sermons.[55] In these, Augustine stresses the mixed nature of the church in this life and the fact that the separation of the good and the bad occurs only at the Judgment at the end of the age. He exhorts the good in the church not to seek to be separate from the bad here in this life but rather to tolerate the bad within the church if they themselves want to be judged favorably. The good, however, should not consent to the sins of the bad. The bad are to be accepted into church, because this acceptance gives them the best possible context for repentance. The good play a role in their repentance: they are to pray for the bad, to rebuke and correct the bad, and to be models for the bad to imitate.

[55] Representative texts are *Enarrationes in Psalmos* 10.1, 25(2).5, 34(2).10, 47.8, 61.8, 64.2, 64.9, 95.2, 99.8–13, 119.9, 128.7–8, 138.26–31; *In Johannis evangelium tractus* 50.10; *Sermones* 4.31–35, 5.3, 5.8, 15.3–9, 37.27, 47.18, 63A.1, 73.3–4, 88.19–22, 223.2, 249.2, 250.2, 252.5–6, 259.2, 260D.2, and 270.7.

Augustine teaches that the temporary tolerance of the bad on the part of the good in this life leads to a permanent separation from them in the next life: "be good among the bad now, and you will be good without the bad."[56] This is the very teaching of Gregory in *Homiliae in evangelia* 2.38. But there is a slight difference. In *Homiliae in evangelia* 2.38, Gregory has the unilateral perspective, considering the church only from the perspective of the good and making no mention of how the good can benefit the bad in the church. In his sermons, Augustine's bilateral perspective is explicit: the toleration of the bad within the church is aimed at their moral amendment, in which the good play a major role. At the end of the age, the good are permanently separated only from those bad people who failed to repent.

Gregory places much more emphasis than Augustine on how the good must be mixed with the bad if they are to attain the fullness of goodness. One does find hints of this theme in Augustine, but only rarely. Augustine says that the bad purify the good.[57] Bearing with the bad is also a sign of progress: "If he thinks that because he has made some progress he cannot be expected to tolerate anyone else, his very intolerance proves that he had made no progress at all."[58] But Augustine never makes the tolerance of the bad on the part of the good the *sine qua non* of Christian perfection that Gregory does. For Augustine, remaining in the unity of church as one tolerates the bad is necessary for attaining salvation; Gregory's emphasis is on achieving Christian perfection here and now by tolerating the bad. Gregory is interested in Christian perfection here in this life, while Augustine's focus is on salvation in the next life.

---

[56] Lat: *Inter malos estote boni, et eritis sine malis boni* (*Sermones* 249.2 [PL 38:1162]).

[57] *Sermones* 15.7–8.

[58] Lat: *Si ergo, quia proficit, nullum hominem vult pati, eo ipso quo non vult aliquem hominem pati, convincitur quod non profecerit* (*Enarrationes in Psalmos* 99.9 [PL 37:1276; trans. Maria Boulding, *Expositions of the Psalms 99–120*, The Works of Saint Augustine, Part 3/19 (Hyde Park: New City Press, 2003), 20]).

For Gregory, as for Augustine, it was inevitable that the church was a mixed body, given the context of the church in late sixth-century Italy. Yet Gregory did not need to argue for the validity of such an ecclesiology. It was taken for granted and did not need to be asserted against opponents. More specifically, Gregory, unlike Augustine, did not need to make the anti-Donatist argument that the good were not adversely affected through mere communion with the bad in the unity of the church. This argument of Augustine is essentially negative in that it denies the claim of the Donatists. Rather, Gregory can make a positive argument for the church's being a mixed body by demonstrating that the good are in fact beneficially affected here in this life through communion with the bad in the unity of the church. For Augustine, the benefit that the good procure from intermingling with the bad is reserved for the next life. Therefore, Gregory develops Augustine's notion that the church is an intermingling of the good and the bad: the good do not simply tolerate the bad within the church without detriment to themselves while waiting for the Day of Judgment (as was the case for Augustine), but the presence of the bad within the church is actually beneficial for the spiritual progress of the good. In saying here that Gregory developed Augustine's ecclesiology, I am not claiming that Gregory improved upon Augustine. Rather, because of his ecclesial context, Gregory could push Augustine's ecclesiology in a direction that Augustine's own ecclesial context would not perhaps have allowed. In fact, Gregory goes even further: the presence of the bad is not merely beneficial for the good, but it is necessary if they are to attain the fullness of good. Gregory has taken an ecclesiology that Augustine had argued was preferable to the Donatists' and made it necessary for Christian perfection. All traces of the anti-Donatist context of this ecclesiology have disappeared, and Gregory's emphasis is solely on living the Christian life in all its perfection.

Gregory assimilated Augustine's ecclesiology of church unity so thoroughly that when presenting his own doctrine of the mixed church he incorporated few of the analogies and scriptural passages employed by Augustine. Augustine's favorite analogy for the intermingled church was the threshing floor from Matthew 3:12 and Luke 3:17: the grain (the good) and the chaff (the bad) are now mixed as they lie on the floor of the church before being threshed, but at the end of the age they will be separated, the good gathered into granaries and the chaff burnt.[59] Augustine also uses the analogies of the wheat and the weeds, which cannot be separated from each other before the harvesttime (Matt 13:24-30),[60] the mixed catch of fish (Matt 13:47-48),[61] and gold's being refined in the furnace.[62] In his second element, Gregory employed the image of the threshing floor but preferred that of Abel and Cain to it. Still, Gregory's use of the threshing floor as a metaphor for the church has nothing of the prominence that it has in Augustine, for whom it was the central analogy. Gregory also once used the metaphor of gold's being refined in the furnace.[63] The only scriptural text that Augustine and Gregory have in common is Song of Songs 2:2.[64] But this was not one of the four core scriptural verses for Gregory. Augustine also saw Matthew 22:10, the passage in which the servants of the king gather the good and the bad for his marriage feast, as a metaphor for the present-day church, as Gregory himself did in *Homiliae in evangelia* 2.38, a commentary on this verse.

There is, then, some but very little substantial overlap in the metaphors and scriptural texts used by Augustine and Gregory. In his second and fourth elements, Gregory employs such items as the threshing floor and Song of Songs 2:2 as Augustine did, but not to the extent that Augustine did. The same holds true for the third element, the scriptural exemplars. Augustine on occasion deploys Jacob and Esau,[65] and Judas and the eleven apostles,[66] as types of mixed

---

[59] *Enarrationes in Psalmos* 25(2).5, 34(2).10, 47.8, 99.8, 99.13, 138.26–27; *Sermones* 4.32, 15.9, 63A.1, 88.19–22, 223.2, 252.5–6, and 260D.2.

[60] *Enarrationes in Psalmos* 128.8, 138.27; *Sermones* 5.3, 5.8, 73.3, and 88.22.

[61] *Enarrationes in Psalmos* 138.27 and 138.31.

[62] *Sermones* 15.4 and 15.9.

[63] *Moralia* 20.XXXIX.76, lines 33–35 (CCSL 143A:1059).

[64] *Enarrationes in Psalmos* 47.8, 99.8, 99.12, and *Sermones* 37.27.

[65] *Sermones* 4.31.

[66] *In Johannis evangelium tractus* 50.10.

churches, but not frequently. Augustine prefers the New Testament metaphors such as the threshing floor to illustrate his teaching on the mixed church, while Gregory prefers to use exemplary groups of people drawn from Scripture to illustrate the same teaching.

All in all, then, Gregory's scripturally rich five-part schema owes little to Augustine, though one can detect certain points of contact. Certainly Augustine never presented his teaching on the mixed church with the same consistent, scriptural structure that Gregory did. While Gregory's teaching on the intermingling of the good and the bad in the church is Augustine's (with slight shifts in emphasis), Gregory's schematization of the teaching and the particular metaphors, scriptural texts, and scriptural exemplars he uses are fundamentally his own.[67] In taking up the theme of the necessary intermingling of the good and the bad in the church, then, Gregory has transformed an element of Augustine's ecclesiology that was forged in the heat of the Donatist controversy into a principle of perfection in the Christian life, removing all traces of the earlier polemic. He abandoned Augustine's negative argument for the preferability of the mixed church and formulated a positive argument for the necessity of such a church for Christian perfection.

This investigation of Gregory's teaching on the necessary intermingling of the good and bad in the church in the *Moralia* and elsewhere in his corpus has provided several insights into Gregory. It reveals him to be a thinker who was so organized (and perhaps even rigid) that he used a five-part schema to present his teaching on the subject, a writer who was prone to reuse his own material but in a flexible way as he adapted and nuanced the core teaching in a variety of settings, an exegete and biblical theologian who built the edifice of his teaching on the foundation of a diverse set of scriptural texts, images, and examples that he nonetheless interpreted as inculcating the same basic teaching, a pastoral theologian who developed an ecclesiology

---

[67] The schema is thus a clear example of the radical biblicism that marked Gregory's age in contrast to Augustine's: see R. A. Markus, *The End of Ancient Christianity* (Cambridge, UK: Cambridge University Press, 1990), 225–28.

that responded positively to the lived situation of the church in his era, an ascetic theologian who denied that perfection of true goodness and holiness could only be achieved in ascetic withdrawal, and a disciple of Augustine who used the thought of the bishop of Hippo as the starting point for his own developments.[68] Thus the interpretation of Job 1:1 at the beginning of book 1 of the *Moralia* affords insight into multiple aspects of the work and thought of Gregory. Indeed, this passage of the *Moralia* is a window into his universe.

In this second of a projected six volumes of the *Moralia* to be published by Cistercian Publications, Br. Brian Kerns, OCSO, has once again provided a fine translation that preserves the complexity of Gregory's style without sacrificing clarity and readability. We are grateful to Br. Brian for his dedication to the enormous task of translating the *Moralia* and for the willingness on the part of Cistercian Publications to publish it. A final word of thanks is also owed to Dr. Marsha Dutton, whose attention to detail and meticulous editing has made no small contribution to the high quality of the final product.

> Mark DelCogliano
> Minneapolis, Minnesota
> March 12, 2015
> The 1411th Anniversary of the Death of
> Saint Gregory the Great

---

[68] Gregory held Augustine in very high esteem. In a letter to Innocent, the praetorian prefect of Africa, Gregory writes, "if you desire to be nourished with delicious food, read the little works of Saint Augustine, your countryman, and do not look for our bran, in comparison with his fine flour" (*Registrum epistularum* 10.16; trans. Martyn, *Letters,* 727). And in a letter to Marinianus, bishop of Ravenna, Gregory writes, "I believed it most inappropriate that you should drink despicable water [i.e., Gregory's own homilies on Ezekiel], when it is certain that you regularly imbibe the deep and clear streams from the springs of the blessed Fathers, Ambrose and Augustine" (*Registrum epistularum* 12.16a; trans. Martyn, *Letters,* 821).

BOOK 6

I. 1. I have proposed to set forth a mystical interpretation of the words of blessed Job and of his friends, without departing from the truth of the story. It is obvious, you see, to all educated people, that Holy Scripture carefully foretold the Redeemer of the world by all her proclamations, as she also zealously indicated him by means of all his chosen ones, who are indeed his members. Accordingly, blessed Job also is rendered in Latin as one who suffers that by his name and by his wounds the passion of our Redeemer might be envisioned. About the latter the prophet spoke as follows: *He really bore our weariness, and he took on himself our sufferings.** Having robbed Job of everything, the tempter killed both slaves and sons, because it was not only the Jewish people, slaves of fear, whom he shot with the arrow of faithlessness during his passion but also the apostles themselves, to whom Christ had given new birth by his love.

*Isa 51:4

The body of blessed Job was wounded raw, because our Redeemer did not refuse to be nailed to the painful cross. From the soles of his feet to his head he was wounded,* because the tempter strikes Holy Church, Christ's body, with grievous persecution, not only the last and most remote but even the highest members. Paul too says, *I supply in my flesh what is missing from the passion of Christ.** When Job's wife tries to get him to curse God, she indicates carnal people inside the church, who are the shrewd tempter's allies. She who prompts him to curse symbolizes the life of the flesh. I have already spoken of those who are members of the church but who behave improperly; because by faith they are

*see Job 2:7

*Col 1:24

neighbors of those who do what is right, their behavior causes them anguish. Since they are like the faithful, they cannot be avoided, and the closer they are to the faithful, the more difficult it is to put up with them. As for Job's friends, they came to comfort him, but they spoke excessively to the point of grievous insults; for this reason they play the role of heretics, who try to defend God against good people but offend him instead.

2. I have striven, therefore, to support what I have already written at some length with a briefer spiritual comment, that such repetition may remind my readers that I am devoted in the present work to perception of the Spirit. Nevertheless, when pastoral needs require it, I also zealously discuss the actual story with attention. On the other hand, when it is necessary, I unite the strands so that allegory may develop spiritual offspring, and please notice that the real story has produced that spiritual offspring. I have said that blessed Job's friends play the role of heretics, but I do not at all always condemn their words, even though God pronounces the sentence against them, *You have not spoken the truth about me*, immediately adding, *as my servant Job has.**

*Job 42:7

It is perfectly obvious that if something is rejected through comparison with a more perfect example, it is still not absolutely contemptible. They would, in fact, carelessly fall into criticism of him, but they were still this great man's friends, and from this friendship they learned much spirituality. As I have already said, Paul himself quoted their words, using them as support of his own argument, and so he is a witness that they are a source of truth. Nevertheless, Truth rightly reprehends their words, because however truthful their statement may be, it should not have been made against this holy man. We may now spiritually evaluate Eliphaz's words spoken to blessed Job. He says,

II. 3. *I saw the fool take root, and I immediately cursed his excellence.** The Jewish people were fools because they spurned eternal Wisdom when he was actually present in the flesh. They took root and prevailed, since by taking the lives of the chosen ones in the realm of time, they were victors. Yet Eliphaz spitefully curses them. As I have said, the friends of blessed Job play the role of all heretics, and all the heretics boast of the name of Christ; by so doing they authoritatively reprehend the faithlessness of the Jews. We are told further of the fool,

*Job 5:3

III. 4. *His sons will be remote from safety.** The sons of this fool are all those who are born of the preaching of his faithlessness. They are indeed remote from safety, because even if they live a worldly life free from trouble, the blows of eternal punishment will be harsh. The Lord spoke about the sons of this fool when he said, *Woe to you, Scribes and Pharisees, you frauds, because you travel all over the ocean and the lands just to make one convert, and once that one is converted, you make that one twice the child of hell that you are yourselves.**

*Job 5:4

*Matt 23:15

They will be cut down at the city gate, and there will be none to help them.* Who else should be understood by the words *city gate* but the Mediator of God and humankind, who said, *I am the gate. If anyone enters by me, he will be safe.** The children of the fool, then, who prosper outside the gate, are cut down at the gate, because the depraved offspring of the Jews flourished before the Mediator's coming by observing the law, but in the very presence of our Redeemer they were cast out by merit of their unbelief and fell away from the service of God. So of course there is none to save them, since they tried to kill the Redeemer himself by persecution and therefore cut themselves off from the remedy of salvation that was offered them.

*Job 5:4

*John 10:9

IV. 5. The text continues, *Hungry people eat his har-*
*Job 5:5 *vest, and the armed bandit will seize him.* The harvest
of this fool would have been the crop of Holy Scripture.
The words spoken by the prophets, you see, are like
ears of grain, which the fool kept without eating them,
because the Jewish people indeed kept the law as far as
the words are concerned but fasted from its meaning
through foolish dislike. Accordingly, hungry people
eat the harvest belonging to this fool, since the Gentile
people indeed feed on the words of the law by understanding them, whereas the Jewish people had worked
the crop without understanding it. The Lord foresaw
these people hungry for faith when he said in the gospel,
Blessed are they who are hungry and thirsty for justice,
*Matt 5:6 *because they will be satisfied.* Hannah, too, is said to
have prophesied about these hungry ones, *Those who*
were full before have hired themselves out for bread,
*1 Sam 2:5 *while those who were hungry are full.*

On the other hand, the fool lost out on the harvest,
so we are rightly informed about how the fool perishes
*Job 5:5 in these added words: *The armed bandit will seize him.*
The ancient enemy was armed, and he seized the Jewish people, because he snuffed out the life of faith in
them by the darts of his deceitful suggestions, so that
whenever they thought themselves united with God,
they might resist his orders. Truth himself warns his
disciples about this: *The hour is coming when anyone*
*John 16:2 *who kills you will think he is worshiping God.*
*Job 5:5 V. 6. *Thirsty people will drink up his wealth.* Thirsty
people drink up the wealth of this fool, because the
minds of Gentile converts are refreshed with the running water of Holy Scripture, which the Jewish people
had possessed with pride and ostentation. It is to these
Gentiles that the prophet speaks when he says, *All you*
thirsty people, come to the water; hurry, you who have

no money.* The word *money* means the word of God, as the psalmist testifies: *The word of God is pure: it is silver, tested by fire.** Accordingly, those who have no silver coins are called to the waters, because the Gentiles who had never received the precepts of Holy Scripture are refreshed by the outpouring of God's word, and to the extent that they had long thirsted for it in a state of dryness, they drink of it now all the more avidly. So also that divine word is called both harvest and wealth: harvest because it satisfies the hungry mind, wealth because it clothes us with great moral beauty. The same divine words are said to be eaten and drunk, clearly because when there is anything obscure in them, we only understand them after they are explained, so it is as if we chewed and swallowed them. On the other hand, when we consume anything just as we find it readily comprehensible, it is as though we drank it without chewing; we absorb it without breaking it up.

*Isa 55:1

*Ps 11:7

We have discoursed briefly on these words to clarify the spiritual sense, lest perhaps we should seem to have omitted something. Still, Eliphaz, Bildad, and Zophar could not be blessed Job's friends unless, from a certain point of view, they were also shining examples of moral excellence. It remains for us therefore to study the moral sense behind the meaning of the words they use; in doing this, as we discuss the import of what they say, we will point out the doctrinal content of their words.

VI. 7. *I saw the fool take root, and I immediately cursed his excellence.** The fool is, as it were, planted in the ground, with roots that grow strong, because all the fool's desires are solidly fixed on the love of earthly things. We are told that Cain was the first to build a city on the earth, a fact that clearly demonstrates that he dug his foundation on the earth, he who was an exile from the security of the heavenly fatherland.* When material

*Job 5:3

*see Gen 4:17

prosperity sustains the fool in this world, that fool is, as it were, firmly rooted and elevated. So fools can obtain all their desires, experience no reverses, and prevail against the weaker without resistance; they can gainsay do-gooders influentially, they can gain still greater advantage by means of still worse actions, and by the very means with which they forsake the way of life they can live happily in the present. When weak minds see the evil flourish they shake with fear, and they are troubled within themselves at the prosperity of sinners; their mind within them wavers and falters. The psalmist surely speaks for them when he says, *As for me, my feet almost slipped, my steps almost went astray, because I was envious of sinners when I saw them prosper in their sin.**

*Ps 72:2-3

8. When the virtuous people see the sinners boasting, they instinctively wait for the punishment that follows the boasting; their deep interior thoughts scorn the pride shown by these arrogant people in their self-importance and outward show. These words, then, are true: *I saw the fool take root, and I immediately cursed his excellence.** When we curse fools' excellence, we indeed judge their boasting with deliberate condemnation: the prouder their boast regarding their sins, the more frightfully will they be engulfed in torment, since pride passes but punishment lasts. They who receive honor on the road will be damned when they arrive. It is almost as if they traveled through pleasant meadows to reach the prison; they enjoyed prosperity in the present life only to end up in destruction.

*Job 5:3

But be sure to notice that in Eliphaz's saying that he had cursed the excellence of the fool, he specified "immediately." It is usual, you see, for the weak human mind to change with the nature of the objects it looks upon. The mind's judgment is often led on by the actual form of the object of sense, and bias and sensation are formed according to the appearance of what the mind sees. It often happens, you see, that when people see others honored, they are delighted with certain aspects of that honor and esteem it as something great; then they desire to earn some of it for themselves. On the other hand, when they see famous people suddenly cast down or even killed, they groan and avow that human fame is utterly nothing. Then they say outright, "Look, a person is really nothing." They would speak more correctly if they said it when they saw someone honored; if they then thought of that one's destruction, they would really understand that temporary power amounts to nothing.

Surely, then, human pride is to be evaluated as nothing when people are exalted above their fellows by their success. Then we must consider how the course of happiness flies away when in the eyes of human beings it seems almost permanent. Any weak person who is about to die can think in the very act of dying that worldly honor is nothing. In that hour, of course, even those who love and pursue honor all the way to death count it nothing. So it is well said, *I saw the fool take root, and I immediately cursed his excellence.** Eliphaz might as well say outright, "Confronted with the fool's excellence I did not delay my cursing of him, because once I saw that, I saw also the punishment that follows. I would not curse him immediately, you see, if any pleasure in that glory held me. Nevertheless, I cursed him without hesitation, because I saw the punishment that would abide, so I had no doubt about disapproving his power."

*Job 5:3

On the other hand, the longer their worldly prosperity lasts, the more people the wicked take with them to destruction, so the next words are appropriate: *Let his sons be remote from safety.** The sons of fools are those who are born from imitating them in their ambition for

*Job 5:4

worldly honor; they are surely remote from safety to the same extent that in their acts of injustice they are struck by no faintheartedness. So the sequel is logical:

VII. 9. *They will be crushed at the city gate, and* *Job 5:4 *there will be none to rescue them.* Just as the entrance to a city is called a gate, so is Judgment Day the gate of the kingdom, because by it all the elect enter into the glory of the heavenly fatherland. Accordingly, when Solomon saw the day approach for rewarding Holy Church, he said, *Her husband is honored at the gate, where he sits* *Prov 31:23 *with the princes of the land.* The church's husband is surely the Redeemer of the human race, who shows his honor at the gate; first he was despised and insulted, but on entering the kingdom he will appear in his majesty. He will sit down with the princes of the land, for he will decree judgment together with the saints and preachers of the church, just as he said in the gospel: *You who have followed me, in the new world, when the Son of Man sits on his majestic throne, you also will sit on twelve thrones* *Matt 19:28 *and judge the twelve tribes of Israel.* Isaiah foretold this event long before it happened: *The Lord will come for* *Isa 3:14 *judgment with the elders of his people.*

Solomon again says about this gate, *Give her the* *Prov 31:31 *fruit of her labor; they will praise her at the city gate.* Then indeed will Holy Church receive the fruit of her labor, when the reward of her labor raises her up to heaven's welcome; then will her labors praise her at the gate when her members are told at the very entrance of the Kingdom, *I was hungry, and you gave me something to eat; I was thirsty, and you gave me something to drink; I was a stranger, and you took me in; I was naked, and you dressed me; I was sick, and you visited me; I was* *Matt *in prison, and you came to see me.* As for the children 25:35-36 of this fool, they strut in front of the gate, but at the gate they will be crushed, since the lovers of this world are proud in the present life, but in the very entrance of the Kingdom they will be struck down by eternal censure. So the following comment is appropriate: *There will be none to rescue them.* The Truth indeed in the eternal trial helps those whom he disciplines in temporal prosperity. Those on the other hand who refuse discipline in this life cannot be rescued in the other; since wicked people disdain him as Father and disciplinarian, they do not find him as rescuer and helper in their time of trial.

VIII. 10. *Hungry people will eat their harvest.** The fool's harvest comes when any evil person receives the gift of right understanding. Such people are taught by the statements of Holy Scripture and then speak correctly, but their actions in no way correspond with their words. They speak the word of God but do not love it, praise it with hyperbole and trample upon it in their life. Since therefore fools both understand and speak what is right and yet show by their actions that they hate it, they renounce the harvest. The hungry one, however, eats it, because the one who pants for God with holy desires learns by listening, puts into practice what is learned, and is therefore fed by the correct preaching of an unruly teacher. What else does it amount to but being refreshed by a fool's harvest? Did not Truth himself advise his hungry disciples to eat the harvest of the fool when he told those who were on fire with holy desires, as he gave orders about the Pharisees, *Do what they tell you, but do not imitate their actions?** It was as if to say, "They tend the harvest of the word by speaking, but by their sinful lives they by no means touch it; let this harvest therefore assuage your hunger, since their foolish squeamishness serves your need.

IX. 11. The text continues, *And the armed bandit will seize him.** The ancient enemy, you see, is conquered as if he were unarmed when he openly suggests

*Job 5:5

*Matt 23:3

*Job 5:5

evil actions to the human mind and tries to bring about the ruin of all that is good with one blow. On the other hand, he comes well armed when, leaving some good actions untouched, he secretly ruins others. He often does not attack their intelligence; he does not deny people meditation on the word of God. Rather, he undermines their life in their actions. They are praised for the extent of their knowledge, yet they are totally unaware of the loss of their good actions. Their mind takes pleasure in the favor of humankind while their wounded life is not attended to. Accordingly, the armed enemy seized them while hidden by a ruse and left them alone in one respect but prevailed in another.

*Job 5:5   X. 12. *Thirsty people will drink up his wealth.** Fools often have an interior source of water but do not drink from it; they have received the ability to understand but scorn the knowledge of truthful statements that they might obtain by reading. They know that they could succeed in understanding by studying, yet they loathe study, and they cease from all doctrinal study. The words of Holy Scripture are also the mind's wealth; fools see this wealth with their eyes, but they by no means appropriate it for their own use to distinguish themselves. They indeed consider the words of the law, which they listen to as being something great, yet they expend no labor of love for the understanding of those words. On the other hand, others thirst but have no skill; they set their heart on meditation, but their slowness of perception is against them. It often happens in their study of God's law that they at times understand by application what the smart but negligent do not know.

So then the thirsty people drink up the wealth of the fool when the intelligent people feel distaste for God's precepts and do not know them, but the slow of mind learn them through love. In them the eye of love lights up the darkness of the slow mind; for the slow of mind, thirst opens up what disdain closes for those who are swifter. Therefore the slow of mind have attained the highest level of understanding, because they never disdained the doing of even the smallest thing that they had understood. Their hands help their minds, so they rise above the level of the more intelligent. Accordingly, Solomon was right to say, *A lizard climbs with its hands, but it lives in kings' palaces.*[*] *Prov 30:28

Birds too, held aloft by their wings, sometimes live in thornbushes. Even lizards, though they have no wings for flying, occupy royal buildings by climbing with hands; so of course when intelligent people grow lazy and negligent, they often remain stuck in crooked actions, whereas simple people, unaided by the wings of intelligence, rise up and reach the walls of the eternal Kingdom by virtue of their activity. The lizard, then, climbs with its hands when it lives in kings' palaces, because the simple person by the intention of good works reaches the place to which the intelligent person never ascends. Yet once we have heard these words, a question arises in our hearts: Why, then, is the gift of intelligence given to the negligent person while the one who makes an effort is impeded by slowness of mind? The answer to that question is speedily given, as the text immediately continues:

XI. 13. *Nothing happens on earth without a reason.*[*] *Job 5:6
That is why lazy people are often endowed with an intelligent mind so that they may be more justly punished for negligence, since they scorn the knowledge they could have obtained without effort. Studious people, however, are sometimes impeded by slowness of mind so that they might obtain greater rewards, for the very reason that they expended greater effort in learning. Accordingly, nothing happens on earth without a reason, since

slowness of mind is profitable for the studious person who thereby obtains a reward, and the quickness of lazy people increases their punishment. Sometimes we are taught by laborious effort, sometimes by the pain of punishment, to understand what is right. Therefore, once the writer has said, *Nothing happens on earth without a reason*, he immediately adds,

*Job 5:6

XII. 14. *Pain does not come out of the ground.** It is as if pain did come out of the ground when a person who is made in the image of God is scourged by un-feeling reality. But since severe pains proceed openly through the hidden sins in our minds, it is also true that pain does not come out of the ground, because our malicious senses require that unfeeling reality should strike us down. Open your eyes and see that it is for our correction that the hoped-for rain does not come when the earth is parched, the sky is dark, the air is dry, and the heat of the sun increases. The sea meanwhile gets stormier and stormier, blocking the progress of sailing ships and by its threatening waves denying embarka-tion to those desiring passage. The earth itself not only threatens growth and fruitfulness but it even destroys the sown seed. In all these adversities one fact clearly emerges, namely, the testimony of the wise concerning the Lord: *With him the whole world will fight against*

*Wis 5:20   *the fools.**

The whole world indeed fights with God against the fools when even the elements turn against criminals to punish them. Still in all, pain does not come out of the ground, because only the goad of our own acts incites any unfelt reality to afflict us. Pain does not come out of the ground, because it is not at all the creature that strikes us that metes out punishment to us, but rather beyond any doubt the creature that releases the force of the blow by sinning. But we must by all means be careful to hope urgently for eternity when external events overwhelm us with a burden of sorrow. The more external pains trouble us, the more our minds must reach for the heights. Therefore the sequel is apt:

XIII. 15. *Man was born for trouble and the bird for flying.*[*] It is true that humans were born for trouble, because, of course, we are endowed with reason, and we know very well that it is impossible for us to escape grief in this time allotted to us. That is why Paul, when he listed his struggles for his disciples, added, *You already know that they are our lot.*[*] Yet at the same time as the flesh is scourged and afflicted, the mind is uplifted and desires heaven, as Paul again bears witness: *Although our outer man gets worn out, still our inner man is renewed every day.*[*] Accordingly, humans are born for trouble and the bird for flight, because the mind flies upward even as the flesh struggles intensely here below.

16. The word *man* can also be used to signify the life in the flesh. Paul again says, *When there is envy and strife among you, are you not in the flesh?*[*] Having said this, he later adds, *Are you not men?*[*] In this life, therefore, humankind is born for trouble, because when carnal persons desire passing things, they burden themselves with the weight of their own wishes. It is indeed serious trouble for anyone to seek honors in this present life, sometimes to grasp what is sought and then to keep and guard what is grasped. It is serious trouble to take hold of that with a mighty effort when the one who has taken hold of it knows very well that it cannot long be held.

As for the saints, however, because they do not love passing things, not only do they not have the burden of transitory desires, but also, if any adversity should cross their path, they are not troubled by the stress and weariness

*Job 5:7

*1 Thess 3:3

*2 Cor 4:16

*1 Cor 3:3
*1 Cor 3:4

that accompany it. What is more painful than scourging? Yet when the apostles were whipped, we are told, *They left the Sanhedrin rejoicing that they had been considered worthy to suffer reproach for the name of Jesus.* What trouble was in the minds of those for whom the pain of stripes was no trouble? Accordingly, humankind is born for trouble, because we who avidly desire the pleasures of this world really feel the hardships of this world. Those whose minds are raised up toward heaven keep below themselves whatever external reality militates against them.

*Acts 5:41

Therefore it is then well said, *and the bird for flying.* Why? It is because the soul is out of the way of the pain caused by trouble to the same extent that its hope lifts it up to the heights. Was not Paul like a bird born to fly, Paul, who suffered so many adversities and said, *Our commonwealth is in heaven,* and *We know that, if our earthly house where we live now is destroyed, we have a house from God, a building not made by hands, eternal, in heaven?* Like a bird he had left earth behind: on the wings of hope he had already lifted himself up above the clouds while his body still remained on earth. But since no one can by one's own efforts lift oneself up on high, while bearing visible affliction to ascend to the invisible places, we are immediately informed,

*Phil 3:20

*2 Cor 5:1

XIV. 17. *For this reason I will beseech the Lord, and I will make a speech to God.* He could have said plainly, "I will ask the one who I know can grant my request." If he had thought he could obtain it on his own, he would not have had to ask God.

*Job 5:8

XV. 18. *He does great and inscrutable wonders, which cannot be counted.* No one could adequately examine the marvels done by almighty God, who created everything out of nothing, who arranged the very structure of the world by wonderful divine power, who

*Job 5:9

hung heaven above the air and poised earth above the cavernous deep. Look how the universe is made up of things visible and invisible, how God created humankind, so to speak, as a second creation, a miniature of the first, a rational creation. He formed humankind out of flesh and spirit; yes, breath and clay were mingled by an inscrutable display of power. Of these two elements we know one, and we are the other. Yet we neglect admiration, because marvels are unreachable by investigation and have become habitually cheap in the eyes of humans. Accordingly, if a dead person should rise, everyone would be rapt in wonder; yet people are born every day who did not exist before, and no one wonders at this.

Nevertheless, it is certainly obvious to us all that the creation of something that did not exist before is greater than the remaking of what did. When Aaron's dry rod bloomed, everyone wondered at it, but every day the dry earth brings forth trees and the power of dust turns into wood, and nobody wonders why. Because five thousand were fed with five loaves, everybody wondered how the food multiplied in their teeth; however, every day the seed grain is scattered, full ears of wheat are multiplied, and no one wonders at it. All those who saw the water once changed into wine were rapt in wonder, but every day the water in the ground is drawn into the root of the grapevine and changed into wine by means of the grapes. Nobody wonders about this.

These are all wonderful things that people disdain to wonder about because, as I have said, they grow dull by constant usage. It is correct, then, to add immediately to the words *He does great wonders, and inscrutable.** It would indeed have been a smaller deed to work wonders if the wonders that were worked had been scrutable. It was also correct to add *which cannot be counted,*

*Job 5:9

because their effect would have been less wonderful if
the inscrutable things he had done had been few.

19. On the other hand, it is incumbent upon us to
realize that God's miracles should be both studied and
pondered but never the subject of intellectual debate.
The human mind, you see, often gets sucked into a
whirlpool of doubt when it searches for reasons for
certain things but cannot find them. For example, when
some people consider how the bodies of dead people
turn to dust, since they cannot through reason infer the
power of the resurrection, they lose hope that those
bodies could return to their former state. Accordingly,
miracles must be believed by faith, not investigated by
reason, because if reason did disclose them to our eyes,
they would not be miracles.

When the mind hesitates, however, it is necessary to
recall those things that we habitually know but do not
infer by reason. Let the mind strengthen our faith by the
use of a similar case to the same extent that we find faith
weakening in us as a result of our clever arguments. The
consideration that human flesh is dust does indeed cause
many to be alarmed and to despair: When would the dust
change back to flesh and arrange the configuration of
the members into a revived body? When would that dry
earth live again in its vigorous members and distinguish
itself specifically and formally? It certainly cannot be
understood by reason, but it can still easily be believed
by analogy. Who would believe that a giant tree could
arise from a single grain of seed unless it were held as
proven by experience? In such a small seed with hardly
any dissimilarity within itself, where is the hardness
of wood hidden, where the inmost pith, whether softer
or harder than wood, where the roughness of bark, the
freshness of the root, the savor of the fruit, the sweet
odor, the rich colors, the soft leaves?

Yet because we know all this by experience, we have no doubt that the source of it all is one seed. What is the difficulty, therefore, for dust to be changed back into members of a body, when we see the power of creation every day, which creates wood from seed in a wonderful way and fruit from wood in a still more wonderful way? Then let us say, *He does great and inscrutable wonders that cannot be counted.** The greatness of God's works cannot be questioned as to quality; nor can they be counted as to quantity. So let us go on.

*Job 5:9

XVI. 20. *He sends rain to wet the land and covers everything with water; he raises up the lowly and lifts to safety those who mourn.** Since we believe that blessed Job's friends learned from familiarity with him, it is necessary that we discuss these words of Eliphaz in a mystical sense. Almighty God accordingly sends rain on the earth when he waters the dry hearts of the Gentiles with the grace of heavenly preaching. He covers everything with water, because he disposes the barren minds of the lost to be filled with the Holy Spirit in order to bear fruit. Truth himself spoke of this promise: *He who drinks the water I give him will never be thirsty again.** The word *everything* signifies humankind, in whom is seen the true image and complete participation in all creation.

*Job 5:10-11

*John 4:13

Everything that exists, you see, is either without life, or is living without sensation, or is living with sensation but without intelligence or discernment, or is living with sensation, intelligence, and discernment. Rocks, for example, are not alive. Trees, on the other hand, are alive without sensation. The life of plants and trees is called their ability to spring up, since Paul said about seeds, *You fool! What you sow in the ground does not live again unless it dies first.** Savage beasts, on the other hand, live and have sensation but no understanding. Angels

*1 Cor 15:36

have life, sensation, understanding, and discernment. Accordingly, humankind has being in common with stones, life in common with trees, sensation in common with animals, and discernment in common with angels. Therefore, humankind is rightly named "everything," because in a sense we are universal. That is why Truth said to his disciples, *Go out to all the world and preach the gospel to all creation.** By all creation he obviously wanted only humans to be understood, whom he created with something in common with all creatures.

*Mark 16:15

*i.e., Job 5:10

21. The word *everything* in this passage* can, however, be understood differently. The grace of the Holy Spirit, you see, while it subjects the rich to its authority, does not cast aside the poor; when it casts down the strong, it does not forbid the weak to come to the Spirit; when it gathers the noble, it at the same time also includes the lowly; while it welcomes the wise, it does not spurn the foolish and ignorant. So God covers everything with water, because the gift of the Holy Spirit calls people of all kinds to the knowledge of God.

22. On the other hand, the different kinds of behavior can be represented by the term *everything*. For example, one person is lifted up by pride, somebody else is stooped over with the burden of fear, another is on fire with lust, this one pants with avarice, that one faints from listlessness, the other burns up with anger. Nevertheless, the teaching of Holy Scripture grants humility to the proud, gives confidence to the fearful, washes clean from impurity the dissolute by zeal for chastity, coaxes the avaricious away from their eagerness and obsession by means of self-control, rouses the lax by zeal for rectitude, and restrains the angry from being hastily provoked; in all these ways God covers everything with water. By the influence of his word he moves each person according to the different kinds of

behavior; each one finds in the word of God that which may germinate the necessary virtue.

A certain wise man spoke of this on the subject of the sweet manna: *You offered them bread from heaven, prepared without labor, which contained all sweetness in itself, as well as every pleasant taste.** Manna indeed contained all sweetness and every pleasant taste in itself; in the mouth of spiritual persons, take note, the manna bestowed the taste of pleasure according to the will of the eaters, since the word of God is both agreeable to everyone and true to itself and therefore adapts itself to the condition of the hearer. Yes, each one of the elect in an individual way profitably understands the word of God, as though having eaten manna and transformed it into the taste desired. Since the glory of the reward follows the labor of good works, after the irrigation of humankind by water, Eliphaz rightly adds, *He raises up the lowly and lifts to safety those who mourn.**

*Wis 16:20

*Job 5:11

23. The lowly are raised up, because those who are now disdained for the love of God will then come with God as judges, since that is what Truth promised these same lowly ones, as we have already said. *You who have followed me*, he said, *in the new world, when the Son of Man sits on his majestic throne, will also sit on twelve thrones and judge the twelve tribes of Israel.** Then he will lift to safety those who mourn, because those who are on fire with desire for him run away from prosperity and suffer trials; they bear persecution and torture, and they even discipline themselves, lamenting over themselves. Therefore, they will be lifted all the higher to safety, in proportion to the degree to which they now loyally die to all the joys of this world. That is why Solomon also says, *The heart knows the bitterness of its soul, and no stranger shares its joy.**

*Matt 19:28

*Prov 14:10

The human mind, you see, knows its own bitterness when it is on fire with desires for the eternal fatherland and knows the pain of its exile in tears. On the other hand, no stranger shares its joy, because the one who is now a stranger to the sting of sadness will then be no sharer in the comforting joy. Truth also says in the gospel, *Amen, amen, I tell you that you will mourn and weep, but the world will rejoice; you will be sad, but your sadness will turn into joy.** Again, *Therefore, now indeed you are sad, but I will see you again, and your hearts will rejoice, and nobody will take that joy from you.** The Lord then, we are told, lifts to safety those who mourn, because he comforts those temporarily afflicted for his sake with true salvation. And there is nothing against applying that salvation to his elect even in this life.

*John 16:20

*John 16:22

24. The Lord indeed raises up the lowly, because when they lie prostrate out of humility, they transcend all the things of time by the judgment of their highest thoughts; when they evaluate themselves as unworthy of everything by consideration and reflection on what is right, they trample upon the glory of this world and leave it behind. Let us consider the humility of Paul. Listen to him tell his disciples, *We do not preach ourselves, but Jesus Christ our Lord; we, however, are your slaves through Christ.** See this humble man already lifted up high, who says, *Do you not know we shall judge angels?** Somewhere else he says, *He raised us up together with him, and he made us sit with him in heaven.** Perhaps he was at the time confined externally by chains, but he had been mentally lifted up high, and he already sat in heaven through the certitude of his hope.

*2 Cor 4:5

*1 Cor 6:3

*Eph 2:6

The saints are therefore superficially despised as though without honor, and they endure it all. Nevertheless, they trust themselves worthy of heavenly seats, and they wait for eternal glory with certitude. While they are hard pressed externally in the trials of persecution, internally they fall back to the secure citadel of the mind. From there they look down on all that goes on below them, all that they know their own bodies likewise experience. They fear no threats because they consider contemptible the torment they suffer. That is why Solomon says, *The just man is like a fearless lion; nothing frightens him.** Therefore he repeats, *Nothing that happens to the just man saddens him.** Those who do what is right are secure in the citadel of their intention; in the act of dying they do not sense death. In a wonderful way the darts of the wicked strike them yet do not touch them. The humble ones are accordingly lifted up high, because whenever they despise themselves, they are secure against all danger.

*Prov 28:1
*Prov 12:21

25. On the other hand, the prophet rightly tells the wicked mind in the guise of Babylon, *Get down and sit in the dust, virgin daughter of Babylon; sit on the ground; there is no throne for the daughter of the Chaldeans.** This passage calls the human mind in my opinion not an unspoiled virgin but an unfruitful one. Babylon, you see, is interpreted "confusion," so the mind is rightly called an unfruitful daughter of Babylon when it by no means gives birth to good works and when it is not governed by any regularity imposed by a correct way of life; so it is, as it were, the child of a mother called *confusion.* If, on the other hand, *virgin* means not "unfruitful" but "unspoiled," after she lost the state of salvation she is called what she once was in order to make her confusion all the greater. So the voice of God suitably tells her reprovingly, *Get down.*

*Isa 47:1

The human soul indeed stands up high when it desires heavenly rewards, but it gets down from that state when in shameful defeat it subjects itself to its passing desires for the world. So the prophet immediately adds, *sit in the dust*. She gets down and sits in the dust when she abandons heaven, sprinkles herself with earthly thoughts, and grovels in the very lowest antics. Repeating himself again, he adds, *sit on the ground*. It is as though reproving her openly he should say, "Since you refused to raise yourself up by means of heavenly companionship, grovel in the earthly actions beneath you." It was necessary therefore for the prophet to add, *There is no throne for the daughter of the Chaldeans.* The *Chaldeans*, you see, are interpreted as "wild." They are indeed wild who follow their own will and do not know enough to restrain their own behavior.

Earthly desires are wild because they render the mind stiff and insensible, not only to the commandments of the Creator but often even to the blows of the whip. The daughter of a wild people has no throne, because the mind that is born to love of the world from evil desires and that persists in the same desires insofar as it subjects itself to earthly pleasure loses its judgment seat. Furthermore, she has no throne on which to preside, for the mind is without any ability to consider or distinguish; it is as though it were banished from its own judgment seat because it wanders among superficial desires. It is perfectly obvious that the mind that has lost its internal seat of counsel is dissipated outside itself through innumerable desires. Because such people pretend not to understand what they are doing, they are indeed blind to the point where they really do not know what they do; often by a just judgment they are allowed their own will and turned loose under that laborious worldly ministry that they so anxiously desire.

So we are told next, *No longer will you be called soft and tender; take the millstone and grind flour.*[*] It is certainly true that parents treat their tender daughters gently and do not force them to work at the strenuous chores of slaves. Accordingly, almighty God calls a daughter tender, as it were, when he calls away a beloved soul from the laborious servitude of this world, lest while it is weakened by physical labor it become insensible to interior desires. The daughter of the Chaldeans, however, is not called soft and tender, because the mind given over to evil desires is abandoned to that labor of this world it so anxiously yearns for; it is allowed to serve the world superficially as a slave because it has no interior love whatsoever for God, as would behove a daughter. Therefore it is ordered to pick up the millstone and grind flour. The stone is turned and flour is produced.

Every theater of action in this world is a mill, which collects many concerns and makes people's minds turn as in a circle; it throws out flour from itself because when hearts turn wrong, they keep generating infinitesimal thoughts. Sometimes, however, a quiet person who is supposed to have some merit is unmasked in the course of some action. Therefore the following words are immediately added: *Uncover your shame, bare your shoulder, show us your legs, cross the rivers.*[*] In the management of a project, shame is certainly uncovered when people of mean and cowardly disposition are recognized by their pretentious actions, although they had previously been supposed to be outstanding when they kept quiet.

*Isa 47:2

The mind bares its shoulder when it reveals what it has done that was previously unknown. It shows us its legs when it admits the steps of its desires, by which it yearns after gain in this world. It also crosses the rivers, because it never stops desiring the actions of this world, which keep flowing every day to their end; moreover, it abandons some and follows up others, as though it were going on from one river to another. We have spoken these few words by way of digression in order that we might show how the mind falls out of the throne of a holy intention and lies prostrate. If it stops yearning after those things that are above it, it keeps falling down to those that are below it. If, however, it abandons the love of the things of time, it holds tight the hope of unchangeable eternity and remains steadfastly on its high throne.

26. Eliphaz is therefore right to say, *He raises up the lowly*, and to add appropriately, *and lifts to safety those who mourn.** It often happens that even in this world there are those who rejoice and are elated when they boast of the mere honor of their prosperity. But God lifts to safety those who mourn. Yes indeed, he raises up his afflicted ones to glory by the solidity of true joy. They are elated, yes, but at their safety, not at senselessness. They are installed in good works, and they give thanks for their firm hope in God. There are those, as we have said, who are evildoers and who never stop rejoicing. Solomon talks about them: *They rejoice when they do evil, and they exult in wayward behavior.** And elsewhere, *There are evil men who feel as secure as if they had done deeds of justice.**

Such as these are certainly elated, not because of safety but because of senselessness. They are proud when they ought to be afflicted; for the very reason that these miserable people stoop to elation, good people weep over them. They are like madmen in their behavior, they prevail in senselessness, and they consider it virtue. When their power is greater than that of healthy people, they do not recognize it as sickness. When their life is nearly over on account of the increase of sickness, they think their power has grown. Since they have no perception of reason, they laugh while others weep. The more ignorant of and insensible they are to the evil they

*Job 5:11

*Prov 2:14

*Eccl 8:14

suffer, the more expansive is their loud elation. The Lord therefore lifts to safety those who mourn, because the minds of the elect do not rejoice in the senselessness of the present life; rather, they rejoice in the certitude of eternal salvation. It is appropriate, then, that we should be immediately told about the very destruction of the evil.

XVII. 27. *He foils the plans of the wicked, to keep their hands from completing what they had started to do.** The minds of the wicked are always on the lookout for shady plans, but God's providence often trips them up, even though they do not give up their crooked design when stopped by opposition. Still, God curbs their power lest they should prevail against good people. God's wonderful judgment works against them so that their wicked plans are without effect, and their conscience finds them guilty and delivers them to the just judgment of the Judge. The fact that they plan evil shows forth their doings, but the fact that they cannot carry it out protects those against whom they plot. So Eliphaz appropriately adds,

XVIII. 28. *He catches the wise in their cleverness, and he foils the plots of the wicked.** You often see people boasting about their human wisdom, but when they notice God's judgment going contrary to their wishes, they try to resist it with clever devices. So that they might bend the intentions of God's providence to their own will, they persist in cunning plans and devise schemes of excessive refinement. Yet even as they strive to change God's will, they end up doing it. While they attempt to resist the counsel of almighty God they obey it, because that with which human application frivolously pesters him often fits his design exactly. Accordingly, God catches the wise in their very cleverness when human acts perfectly serve his plans

*Job 5:12

*Job 5:13

even when they resist them. I will demonstrate how this is done more easily if at this point I mention a few historical examples.

29. Joseph had a dream in which the sheaves of his brothers bowed down to his own sheaf; he had another dream in which the sun, the moon, and the stars worshiped him. He guilelessly told his brothers about them, and immediately envy and fear of his future domination struck their hearts. So when they saw him approaching them, their malice took fire, and they said, *Look, here comes the dreamer. Come let us kill him. Let us see what good his dreams will do him.* Since they were afraid of being subjected to his authority, they let the dreamer down into the cistern; then they sold him to the Ishmaelites who were passing. He was taken to Egypt and sold into slavery, and then he was accused of debauchery; although he was condemned, his virtue of chastity helped him; by the judgment of prophecy he was made master of all Egypt. Heavenly wisdom gave him foresight, and he stored up grain; in so doing he avoided the danger of future want. Accordingly, when famine struck the world, Jacob sent his sons into Egypt in his anxiety to provide food. Jacob's sons met the overseer concerned with the distribution of grain, not knowing that he was Joseph. In order that they might be entitled to receive food, they were compelled to prostrate themselves on the ground and adore the one distributing food.*

*see Gen 37:7-9, 19-20, 24-25, 28; 39:1, 17; 41:41, 48; 42:1-2, 6

Now let us consider the history; let us consider how the power of God catches the wise in their craftiness. Joseph was sold by his brothers so that they wouldn't worship him, yet he was actually worshiped after he was sold. They ventured to do the crafty thing so that God's plan might be thwarted, but in trying to turn aside God's judgment, their resistance forwarded it. Where their crafty action had the object of altering God's

will, there precisely they were forced to fulfill it. Just
so, when God's plan is put aside, it is fulfilled. When
human wisdom resists, it is caught. Joseph's brothers
were afraid he might prevail over them; nevertheless, the
avoiding of God's dispositions ends up by forwarding
them. So human wisdom is tripped up by itself when
it intends to resist God's will, and that act brings about
its completion.

30. In the same way, when Saul saw his subject
David grow stronger every day with new successes on
the battlefield, he offered him his daughter as his bride.
As her bridal gift he asked for a hundred Philistine foreskins so that when the soldier* challenged in this way   *David
tried to exceed his own measure he might end his life
in betrayal to enemy swords. We read, *The king needs
no other betrothal present than a hundred Philistine
foreskins, so that he may be avenged on his enemies, but
Saul thought he was betraying David into the hands of
the Philistines.** David's strength, however, came from   *1 Sam 18:25
the intimate favor of Providence; instead of giving the
king a hundred Philistine foreskins, he gave him two
hundred. Saul was of course beaten by the net result of
this deed of valor and caught by God's Providence in
his wise plan. Where he thought he was taking the life
of a successful soldier, he was actually adding to that
soldier's honorable career.*   *see 1 Sam
                                                            18:20-27
31. Even the elect sometimes contrive to discern
something cleverly, so it will not be out of place to
introduce another wise man to you and to show you
the deep internal counsel by which human craftiness is
tripped up. Jonah certainly intended to act wisely and
prudently after he was sent to preach repentance to the
city of Nineveh. He was afraid that if the Gentiles were
chosen, Judaea would be abandoned, so he refused to
fulfill the office of preaching. He chose instead to take

ship and flee to Tarshish. Immediately a storm arose, and the sailors cast lots to find out whose fault it was that the sea was unsettled. Jonah's guilt was discovered, he was thrown into the sea, a large fish swallowed him, and the swimming beast arrived at the very place where he had contemptuously chosen not to go. Look at this fugitive from God: the storm finds him, the lot catches him, the sea receives him, and the beast locks him up. Because he refuses to obey his Creator's voice, the guilty man is carried in his own prison to the very place to which he was sent. God orders a man to minister prophetically, and he refuses; God breathes, and the beast vomits up the prophet. Accordingly, God catches the wise in their craftiness when he turns around for his own purpose and uses the very thing through which the man wanted to contradict him.*

*see Jonah 1:2-4, 7, 15, 17; 2:10

32. Let us now examine the wisdom of the Hebrews and see what that wisdom ruled out by foreseeing it and what wisdom made happen by ruling it out. Surely the faithful crowd rushed to witness our Redeemer's miracles; just as surely the priests of the people burned with envy and announced that the world was going after him. Here is what they said, *You see, we are getting nowhere! Look, the whole world has gone after him.** They wanted to deprive him of the advantage of such a vast concourse of people. Therefore they attempted to put an end to his influence by killing him. They said, *It is expedient that one man die so that the whole nation may not perish.** But the Redeemer's death brought about his union with his body (the church, that is), not the separation from it. So also the law prescribes in the sacrifice of a dove or pigeon (a figure of our sacrifice) that the neck should be cut and the head not completely severed, so that it may still be attached to the body after it is dead. The Mediator of God and humankind, you see, is the Head

*John 12:19

*John 11:50

of all of us and the Sacrifice of true purification; because
he underwent death for us, he clings to us all the more
closely. So after the head of the dove is cut it clings to
its body, because not even the event of death separates
Christ from the church. The persecutors, then, carried
out what they strove to accomplish with pernicious intent and did him to death so that they might deprive
him of the devotion of the faithful. Yet just where the
cruel infidels thought they could extinguish faith, there
faith grew. And when they thought they were rid of his
miracles through persecution, they naturally compelled
themselves unintentionally to increase them. The Lord
therefore catches the wise in their craftiness when he
reduces what human cruelty sets afoot against him to
the service of his kindness.

33. The just and merciful God adjusts the acts of
mortals: some he gracefully overlooks, but others he
grudgingly allows. Those he allows he puts up with
in such a way that he may adapt them for his own use
and counsel. Accordingly, in a wonderful way even
that which happens without God's will is not contrary
to God's will, because evil deeds are turned to a good
purpose, and even when they are oriented against his
plan, they are nevertheless made to act in accordance
with it. That is why the psalmist says, *Great are the
works of the Lord, carefully wrought in all he wills to
do.** Yes, his works are great, so great that through all
the works of humankind his will is sought out, and it is
often done precisely there where it was thought to be
spurned. So the psalmist says elsewhere, *Whatever God
wills he does in heaven and on earth.** Solomon says for
his part, *There is no wisdom, no prudence, no counsel
against the Lord.**

The conclusion therefore is that in all our doings
we must search out the guiding power of God's will;

*Ps 110:2 Vulg

*Ps 134:6 Vulg

*Prov 21:30

once we know that, all our actions must serve that will
with devotion and follow it as we would a guide in our
journey, lest we should be unwilling servants of God
if in our pride we abandoned the search for his will.
The strong counsel of heaven, you see, can never be
sidestepped, but those who curb the self under God's
command make it theirs with great energy, and those
who bear it willingly on the bowed shoulder of their
heart lighten its weight for themselves. We have mentioned persecutors above. We will now point out how
the following words are congruent with the blindness
of persecutors.

XIX. 34. *All day they find darkness; they stumble at*
*noon, as if it were night.** All day they found darkness.
Why? Because they were blinded in the very presence
of Truth by the error of unbelief. Surely we see clearly
in daylight, but at night our eyes are darkened. Accordingly, the persecutors of our Redeemer saw the miracles
of his divine power, yet they doubted his divinity. So
they encountered darkness in daylight, since they had
lost their eyesight in the presence of the light. Therefore
the Light himself warns them, saying, *Walk while you*
*have light, lest the darkness catch up with you.**

Of Judaea also it is written, *Her sun set while it was*
*still daylight.** Another prophet took up again the voice
of penitents in himself, and he says, *We stumble at noon*
as though in the dark; we are in dark places like the
*dead.** In another place he says, *"Watchman, what of*
the night; watchman, what of the night?" The watch-
*man answered, "Morning comes, and night again."**
The watchman comes at night, you see, because the
Protector of the human race also appeared visibly in the
flesh, but Judaea was hemmed in by the darkness of her
unbelief, and she did not recognize him. That is why
the watchman's voice adds the words, *Morning comes,*

*Job 5:14

*John 12:35

*Jer 15:9

*Isa 59:10

*Isa 21:11-12

and night again. His presence, you see, brings in more light, and it brightens the world, but in hearts without faith the old blindness remains.

So Eliphaz was right to say, *They stumble at noon as if it were night.** We grope about and search for that which our eyes do not see. The Jews had seen his miracles clearly enough, but still they groped about in search of him while saying, *How long will you keep us guessing? If you are the Christ, tell us plainly.** The light of miracles was right there in front of them, yet they stumbled in the darkness of their hearts, and they still groped about in search of him. Their blindness soon turned to cruelty and their cruelty to open persecution. The Redeemer of the human race, however, could not be held for long by the hands of his persecutors. Therefore Eliphaz immediately adds these words,

XX. 35. *Rather, he will save the poor man from the sword of their mouth and from the violence in their hands.** Christ indeed is this poor man of whom Paul is speaking here: *For your sakes he became poor, when he was rich.** It was the Jews who accused the Lord and handed him over; when he was handed over, the Gentiles killed him. By *the sword of their mouth* may then be signified the Hebrew tongues that accused him. The psalmist speaks of them: *As for the sons of men, their teeth are spears and arrows, and their tongue a sharpened sword.** About them also the evangelist testifies that they cried out, *Crucify Him! Crucify Him!** As for the violent hands, they express the Gentiles who did the crucifying, since in the Redeemer's death it was the Gentiles who did the bidding of the Hebrew voices. Accordingly, God saved this poor man from the violent hand and from the sword of their mouth. Our Redeemer suffered the power of the Gentiles and the tongues of the Jews when he died in his humanity, yet he overpowered

*Job 5:14

*John 10:24

*Job 5:15

*2 Cor 8:9

*Ps 56:5

*Luke 23:21

them when he arose in the power of his divinity. And
what else occurred in the resurrection but the strengthening of our weakness by the hope of a life to come?
So we are told without delay,

*Job 5:16   XXI. 36. *There will be hope for the indigent.** With
the poor man saved, the indigent are led back to hope,
because the humble people of faith, although struck down
by fear at the Redeemer's death, are strengthened by his
resurrection. They themselves, the first of the poor of his
people, were his chosen preachers, and they were devas-
tated by his visible death, but the revealed resurrection
restored them. The poor man is therefore saved and the
indigent given hope because the Lord's flesh is risen, and
all the faithful are strengthened and assured of eternal life.
Behold, Truth has already come, manifest and revealed; he
has already suffered death in the flesh, already destroyed
death in his resurrection, and already crowned his resurrection with the glory of his ascension. Yet the Hebrew
tongues still do not stop insulting him. He calmly puts
up with their insults in order that he may convert some
and one day more severely punish those who refuse conversion. Only then will unfaithful tongues silence their
unbridled speeches when they see him coming as a just
Judge, him whom now they judge unjustly. So it goes on,

*Job 5:16   XXII. 37. *Injustice will shut its mouth.** At the
present time injustice opens its mouth wide, because
unbelieving tongues never stop insulting the Redeemer
of the human race. Then, however, it will close its
mouth, not through good will but through punishment.
The sentence may on the other hand be taken to refer to
converted persecutors. With the poor man rescued and
the indigent restored to hope, injustice has closed its
mouth and been rendered speechless, because the miracle of Christ's resurrection has enlightened the world.
An immense multitude of unbelievers accepts the faith

and has consequently stopped insulting and wounding its Redeemer. It had opened its mouth in derision against God, but now it has closed its mouth in fear.

38. Leaving aside the application to the Jews, we may read the text in a moral sense and investigate how it may be applied to wicked people in a general way. To be sure, when the minds of unjust people notice the good deeds of their neighbors, they are tormented and stretched on the rack of their own envy. They endure serious pain in their own malice when they resentfully see any good in another person. So Eliphaz is right to say, *All day they find darkness.** When their minds are troubled by someone else's improvement, they are veiled from the ray of light. As often as they look at the obvious good deeds of their neighbors, you see, they search those deeds to see if there is evil hidden in them; they even anxiously question whether they can possibly find something to accuse their neighbors with. They see perfectly well that the body is sound, yet with the eyes of the heart closed they search for a wound by touch.

So we are told the following, *They stumble at noon as if it were night.** The clear day of good works shines out in their neighbors, but they grope about as if it were night because they suffer from the interior darkness of envy. They strive to reach something reprehensible; they search out an entry point for detraction, but they cannot find one, so they blindly go about outside. This fact is well expressed in the case of Lot, the entrance to whose house the Sodomites did not find because of the protecting angels, as it is written, *They pressed most fiercely against Lot and were already near enough to break down the door, but the men put out their hands and pulled Lot inside. They closed the door, and they struck those outside from the least to the greatest with blindness so that they could not find the door.**

*Job 5:14

*Job 5:14

*Gen 19:9-11

What does Lot's being attacked by evil men and pulled into the house and protected mean unless that any righteous person ambushed by evil people retreats to the mind and stays there unperturbed? The men of Sodom, on the other hand, could not find the door of Lot's house, because the seducers of minds who plot against the life of the righteous find no doorway by which to accuse. They are, as it were, struck with blindness and go around the house, because they envy the words and deeds of this one whom they watch so closely. But since the energetic and praiseworthy actions in the life of the righteous meet them everywhere, they grope about and find nothing but the wall. It is well said, *They stumble at noon as if it were night.** Why? Because they are unable to accuse what they see is good, blinded with malice as they are, and they search for the evil that they do not see in order to accuse it.

*Job 5:14

39. The text continues, *Rather, he will save the poor man from the sword of their mouth and from the violence in their hands.** The poor man is indeed anyone who is not lofty in his own eyes. That is why Truth says in the gospel, *Blessed are the poor in spirit, because the kingdom of heaven is theirs.** All are lured to sin in two ways. They are either led by pleasure or overcome by fear. The sword of the mouth is unjust persuasion, whereas the violent hand is the threat of power. But the truly humble person is here called the poor man, and because such people desire no prosperity in this world, they boldly despise even worldly adversity. Therefore it is rightly said, *He will save the poor man from the sword of their mouth and from the violence in their hands.* Eliphaz could say it outright: *God so secures the humble minds in his own protection that neither can soothing arguments entice them to commit sin nor painful torture break them.* Hope, to be sure, raises the

*Job 5:15

*Matt 5:3

soul to eternal life, and that is why the soul feels none of the evils that it encounters exteriorly. Therefore it follows that *There will be hope for the indigent.** And when the poor finally receive the promise of that hope, all pride shuts its mouth, so the passage continues logically, *Injustice will shut its mouth.**

*Job 5:16

*Job 5:16

Now, you see, the evil ones detract good people and their virtuous deeds, whose practice they shun; these latter they never stop slandering and turning into something else. But then injustice will shut its mouth when it knows the greatness of the glorious reward that is in store for the righteous. At that time, you see, no one will be free to speak against good people, because the torments that are the fitting reward of the evil will lock up their tongues. That is why we are told that Hannah prophesied, *He will guide the steps of his saints, but the wicked will be silenced in the darkness.** Nevertheless, in order that all the elect may escape eternal punishment and the poor may rise up to everlasting glory, they must be tested here by constant trials, and to that extent they can be found purified in judgment. We are brought down daily, you see, by the very weight of our weakness unless by the wonderful hand of our Creator we are lifted up by helpful trials.

*1 Sam 2:9

XXIII. 40. *Blessed is the man whom the Lord corrects.** The first virtue is to avoid sin, to keep from committing it. The second is at least to correct those that we have committed. It often happens, however, that not only do we never avoid the sin that threatens but we do not even notice those we have committed. The less we understand how damaging our blindness is, the deeper is the darkness of sin that engulfs the mind. Consequently it is by God's generous gift that punishment often follows hard upon the sin, the pain of which opens the sinner's eyes, which security among vices had blinded.

*Job 5:17

Unquestionably the sleepy soul is touched by compunction so that it might wake up, insofar as those who lost their state of rectitude in security might in affliction consider where they lie.

For this reason, then, the very harshness of correction is the origin of light. That is why Paul says, *Whatever is declared is revealed by the light.* The power of pain, you see, is the declaration of salvation. Therefore Solomon also says, *Care will put a stop to the gravest sins.* Someone else adds, *Him whom God loves he chastises, and he beats every son he receives.* God also tells John through the angel's voice, *Those I love I rebuke and chastise.* Paul again says, *All discipline seems painful rather than pleasant at the time; afterward, however, it bears peaceful fruit of justice for its recipients.* So although pain and happiness cannot cohabit, we are rightly told at this point, *Blessed is the man whom the Lord corrects.* When the sinner suffers the pain of correction, he is led on to that happiness that is not interrupted by pain. The text goes on:

XXIV. 41. *So do not shun the Lord's reproof.* Anyone who is beaten for a fault but who haughtily complains about the beating shuns the Lord's reproof, because he charges that he has borne it unjustly. There are those, on the other hand, who receive blows not for atonement for crimes but to indicate their courage; when they ask why they have been struck, they should not be said to shun the Lord's reproof, because it is quite enough for them to find out what they themselves do not know. In the same way blessed Job lets out frank words between blows of the whip; the more truly he is himself unaware of the reason for his suffering, the more righteously does he in himself question the judgment of the one striking him. Accordingly, because Eliphaz supposed that Job had been struck not in consideration

*Eph 5:13

*Eccl 10:4
*Heb 12:6

*Rev 3:19

*Heb 12:11

*Job 5:17

of being approved but as expiation, when he heard Job speak frankly between blows, he thought Job had shunned God's reproof. We have said that Eliphaz really plays a role as the heretics who make themselves judges and always twist all the righteous activity of the church into the vice of insincerity.

Nevertheless, because Eliphaz is led into speaking by a pure intention but does not take care to distinguish the one to whom he is speaking, he again proclaims the guidance of God's plan and adds the following:

XXV. 42. *God wounds, but he also heals; he strikes, but his hand will cure.** There are two ways in which almighty God wounds those whom he intends to lead back to safety. Sometimes he strikes at the flesh and causes the stubborn mind to relent for fear of him. Accordingly, he wounds his chosen ones and calls them back to safety; he afflicts them externally so that they may live an interior life. He also speaks to us through Moses. He tells us, *I will kill and give life; I will strike down, and I will heal.** He kills, you see, so that he may give life; he strikes down so that he may heal. He wields the whip externally precisely in order to cure the wounds of our sins. There are other times, however, when external trials seem to be at an end while God inflicts internal wounds on us; yes, he strikes at the obstinacy of our minds by means of our desire for him, but it is a healing blow, since the dart of his fear pierces us and brings us back to a sense of righteousness.

*Job 5:18

*Deut 32:39

Our hearts are really not in good health when they are not wounded by God's love, when they do not feel the harshness of exile, when they do not feel the least compassion for any weakness of their neighbor. They are wounded so that they may be healed. God pierces our unfeeling minds with darts of his love and soon renders them sensitive through the fire of his love. That is

*Song 2:5

why the bride says in the Song of Songs, *I am wounded by love.** The soul was not in good health; she was laid prostrate by the blind security of her exile; she neither saw the Lord nor wanted to see him. She was, however, hit by the darts of his love; now she is deeply wounded by her condition of devotion and is on fire with desire for contemplation. In a wonderful way she who previously lay dead in security is now alive because wounded. She is agitated, she pants, and she now desires to see the one she used to avoid. Therefore, after being struck she is led back to safety, and she is called back to security and quieted internally by having her self-love thwarted.

When the wounded mind begins to pant for God, however, when she spurns all the allurements of this world and sets out for the heavenly fatherland in her desire, everything she formerly held pleasant and enticing in this world now becomes a trial to her. Those who formerly loved the sinner become cruel attackers in the sinner's virtuous life. Those who are right with God endure war from their own body, in which they formerly cultivated vices and lolled in pleasure. Their former pleasures return to their memory and afflict their opposing mind with stern battles. Nonetheless, although we are worn out with passing efforts, we are delivered from everlasting pain. So Eliphaz rightly adds,

*Job 5:19

*see Gen 2:2

XXVI. 43. *He will deliver you from six trials, and you will have no trouble with the seventh.** What is meant by the number six followed by seven unless it is the agitation and the course of this present life? God completed all his work on the sixth day and created humankind, and he rested on the seventh day.* The seventh day has no evening, because there is now no end of the repose that follows. When everything is complete, repose follows, because after the good works done in this present life, we will find the reward of eternal rest. Accordingly, God delivers us from six trials lest we encounter trouble in the seventh. Yes, the Lord wears us out by means of our labor in the present life (it is the teaching of his fatherly love); then on Judgment Day he hides us from the whip in order that he may make us just as certain of our salvation then as the whip chastises us severely now. He follows this act nicely by specifying both the trials of the present life and the aid supplied by heavenly guidance.

XXVII. 44. *In time of famine he will deliver you from death, and in wartime from threat of the sword.** Just as famine of the flesh means removal of the support of the body, so mental famine means the silence of God's voice. The prophet rightly says, *I will send famine on earth, not a famine of bread or a dearth of water, but a famine of hearing God's word.** When God's voice abandons the human mind, temptations of the flesh wax strong against her. So Eliphaz continues, *and in wartime from threat of the sword.* Yes, we suffer war when we are attacked by temptations of our own flesh. The psalmist speaks indeed of this war: *Shield my head on the day of war.**

*Job 5:20

*Amos 8:11

*Ps 139:8
Vulg

Accordingly, reprobates become weak from a famine of the word of God, and at the same time they are stabbed by the sword in wartime; as for his chosen ones, God delivers them from death by famine and hides them from the sword in wartime. Yes, he feeds their minds with the nourishment of his word and renders them strong against the temptations of the flesh. There are, however, those who, although they refresh themselves from the table of God's word against the time of internal famine, and although they are equally strengthened against internal battles of temptation by the virtue of continence, are still in dread of the blows of detraction by men. Even as the darts of tongues worry them, they are often strangled in the snare of sin. So we are rightly told next,

*Job 5:21   XXVIII. 45. *You will hide from the tongue's lash.** The tongue's lash is a reproach by one who insults us. Those who make fun of the good deeds of the righteous and persecute them strike them with the tongue's whip. In blaming a good work the tongue often revokes it; like a whip it strikes, and it lacerates the back of a fearful mind. The prophet had noticed how the tongue's lash lay in ambush against the chosen mind when he promised God's help and said, *He will deliver you from the hunter's snare and from the harsh word.** Hunters, you

*Ps 90:3   see, are out for nothing less than our hide, but we are set free from the hunter's snare and from the harsh word when we overcome both the traps set by carnal people and their mocking reproaches by despising them.

Harsh words are certainly theirs who oppose our righteous ways. But we escape these harsh words when we ignore their mocking derision and trample upon it. The holy soul, therefore, is protected from the tongue's lash, because she seeks no honor or praise from this world, and she does not feel insult or detraction. Still, there are those who already scorn detraction, already care nothing for derision, but who nevertheless fear bodily pain and torture. The ancient foe, you see, has many ways of attacking us so that he may turn us aside from our good intentions, so he approaches our temptation sometimes by a famine of the word, sometimes with battle against our flesh, sometimes with tongue lashing, sometimes with the misfortune of persecution. But because when all those who are perfect have overcome their evil habits immediately arm their minds as well against the wounds they suffer, Eliphaz rightly adds,

XXIX. 46. *So you will not fear a disaster when it arrives.** Since the saints take into consideration the fact that their fight is against an adversary with many shapes, they prepare themselves for many different types of warfare. For example, they have the food of God's word against famine; they have the shield of continence against the sword of war; they have patience to protect them against tongue lashing; they have the help of interior love against the losses of exterior disasters. So in a wonderful way it happens that the more numerous the ways in which the sly enemy tempts us, the richer are the virtues with which the shrewd soldiers of God are endowed. And since all the elect while they bravely endure the battles of the present life are preparing salvation for themselves against the fear of coming judgment, Eliphaz rightly adds,   *Job 5:21

XXX. 47. *You will laugh at desolation and hunger.** At that time reprobates will certainly suffer desolation and hunger, when they have been condemned in the final Judgment and cut off from the vision of the eternal Bread. Scripture has it, *Let the wicked be taken out, lest they see God's glory.** The Lord himself says, *I am the living Bread that came down from heaven.** Desolation and hunger would accordingly simultaneously torment those who not only suffer pain externally but even die from internal starvation. Gehenna wreaks desolation through fire, but hunger kills, because the Redeemer hides his face. The wretched ones are rightly rewarded internally and externally, because they failed him by thought and deed. Therefore the psalmist rightly says, *You will make them like a blazing oven at the time when you are present; God will upset them in his wrath, and the fire will burn them up.** The fire that burns them up is external, but the oven grows hot internally. Therefore   *Job 5:22   *Isa 26:10   *John 6:51   *Ps 20:10 LXX all the wicked are made like an oven at the time when God is present, and they are also burnt up in the fire. When the Judge appears, you see, the multitude of unjust people is repulsed from the sight of him, and while their conscious awareness burns them with interior longing, Gehenna tortures their flesh externally.

48. The whip of the tongue may also be understood in terms of that sentence of final condemnation pronounced by the strict Judge upon the unrepentant: *Depart from me, you accursed, into the eternal fire prepared for the devil and his angels.** The just are then hidden away from the whip of the tongue and from the coming disaster, because at the time of such a strict sentence they are reassured by the comforting voice of the Judge, who tells them, *I was hungry, and you gave me something to eat; I was thirsty, and you gave me something to drink; I was a stranger, and you took me in; I was naked, and you dressed me; I was sick, and you visited me; I was in prison, and you came to see me.** These words are preceded by *Come, you blessed ones of my Father, and take possession of the kingdom prepared for you from the beginning of the world.** Accordingly, the just will laugh at desolation and famine, because when the final penalty overtakes the wicked, those who are just will rejoice at the fame of a fitting retribution. Nor will they any longer be compassionate out of a common humanity toward those condemned, because the just are made partakers of divine justice by resemblance, and they are made firm with the unrelenting force of interior rectitude.

No mercy, you see, sways the minds of the elect who have been raised to the glory of heavenly justice, because high beatitude has rendered them strangers to misery. The psalmist has said it rightly: *The just shall see it and be afraid; they shall laugh at him and say, "Here is the*

*Matt 25:44

*Matt 25:35-36

*Matt 25:34

man who did not let God help him."" The just look at the
wicked now and are afraid, but later they will see them
and laugh. Since, you see, they may fail momentarily
by imitating the wicked, they do experience fear here.
But because they cannot help them later when they are
condemned, they have no compassion on them then.
They find in the very Judge's justice, in which they are
blessed, the judgment that there is no mercy available
for those subject to eternal punishment; it is incorrect
to suppose such a thing, but the degree of happiness
that they enjoy would be lowered if, being resident in
the Kingdom, they should wish what can in no sense be
granted. Whoever commit themselves to a rule of life before receiving their eternal reward already taste here on
earth the beginning of the safety to follow in eternity, so
that they may have no fear of the ancient enemy and may
have not the slightest fright before the enemy's violent
attack when the hour of death arrives. The beginning of
the reward of the just is precisely that tranquil mind often
present at their death. Therefore Eliphaz rightly adds,

XXXI. 49. *You will have no fear of any beast of
the earth.** The cunning adversary is surely named a
beast of the earth, because he becomes wild, violent,
and cruel, trying to attack sinful souls at the hour of
death. Those whom he deceived with flattery when they
were alive he attacks ferociously when they are dying.
The Lord promises the church of the elect help against
these attacks, saying through the prophet, *No evil beast
will pass through her gates.** Accordingly, those who in
their life did not fear the Creator's power fear the beast
of the earth at their death. Because the saints subject
themselves to the fear of God from the core of their
heart, they throw off every burden of fear concerning the
adversary's arrival. That is why the psalmist pleads with
God and says, *Let him never attack my soul like a lion.**

*Ps 51:8-9
LXX

*Job 5:22

*Isa 26:10

*Ps 7:3

He says somewhere else, *O God, hear my prayer when I am in trouble; free my soul from fear of the* *Ps 63:2 *enemy.** While they are alive their fear of the Judge is perfect, lest they should be in dread of the accuser when they are dying. So it is wisely said, *You will have no fear of any beast of the earth.* He could have said openly, "Since you were not caught off guard here by the enticements of the foe, you will have no fear of his cruelty later." Still, granted that we live right, our chief worry is that we should hold others in derision while we ourselves boast of our special status. So it is just as well to remember that it is good to live with others, as we are told immediately:

XXXII. 50. *Your treaty is with the stones of the* *Job 5:23 *regions.** The Gentile churches in the world are, as it were, distinct regions. Although united in faith, they are distinguished by languages and custom. How then do we understand the stones of the regions unless they be the chosen ones of the church? They are told in the words of our first teacher, *You are like living stones in* *1 Pet 2:5 *a building.** God promised Holy Church concerning these stones, speaking through the prophet, *Behold, I* *Isa 54:11 *will pave your stones becomingly.** Accordingly, those who live well make a treaty with the stones of the regions, because since they overcome worldly desires, they unite their life beyond any doubt with the example of the saints who lived before them. But because such people separate themselves from worldly actions, evil spirits multiply their attacks against them; yet the more they weaken a person by sadness, the more humble do they render that person before the Creator. Therefore Eliphaz continues,

XXXIII. 51. *The beasts of the earth will be your* *Job 5:23 *peacemakers.** Let us first notice that he did not say that they were peaceful but that they will be your peacemak-

ers; obviously that means not that they will have peace
but that they will make peace. Subtle enemies attack
while lying in ambush. The mind being attacked, however, wants to return to the eternal fatherland the more
earnestly as its life in this inhospitable exile is the more
difficult; the mind humbles herself all the more truly before the grace of her helper as she judges the traps set for
her by the enemy to be the more dangerous. The beasts
of the earth are consequently peacemakers for the elect,
because when the evil spirits array themselves against
good people and oppress their hearts, they impel them
against their will toward the love of God. Accordingly,
where the battle raised against us by our adversary is
fiercest, there our peace with God is made strongest.

52. The beasts of the earth can also be taken to mean
the movements of the flesh. The latter weary our minds
by suggesting irrational conduct, and in this way they
rise up against us after the fashion of wild beasts. But
when our hearts are subject to God's law, even the in-
citements of the flesh are subdued. Then, even if we are
remotely tempted, we do not go all the way to completed
actions, like raging animals who really bite. Who is
there who still abides in this corruptible flesh? Who
completely tames these beasts of the earth? That famous
preacher who was caught up into the third heaven spoke
thus: *I see another law in my body, resisting the law
of my mind and making me a captive of the law of sin
residing in my body.*

*Rom 7:23

It is one thing, however, to notice these beasts raging in the field of action and something else to hold
them growling within the den of the heart. When they
are confined in the cage of self-control, you see, even if
they roar in temptation, they are not free to bite, as we
have said, or to take any forbidden action. Accordingly,
the beasts of the earth are peacemakers, because even

if the emotions of the body actively desire things, they do not really fight us or openly contradict our actions.

By the very fact that these beasts are called peace-makers, they can also be taken in the same sense we have already used concerning the evil spirits. Emotions of the body, you see, make peace for us with God when they resist us by temptation. The minds of the just are directed toward what is above, so they are tired out by the serious war they wage with their corruptible body. When the mind is hindered in its desire for heaven by pleasure in this world, even if that pleasure be relatively small, the mind is impelled by the very conflict of temptation to love with all its heart that which no resistance troubles. Then the person recalls interior silence to the mind and leaves the enticement of the flesh behind, sighing for that silence with pure love.

Temptation, you see, forces us all to consider the place from which we have fallen: after we abandoned God's peace, we found contention in ourselves rising against ourselves. Then we saw more clearly what we had lost, namely, carefree love of God; fallen therefore into ourselves, we discover that we are outraged against ourselves. Accordingly, the beasts of the earth make peace with us, because emotions of the body assail and provoke us, and in so doing they impel us to love interior silence. So we are rightly told next,

XXXIV. 53. *And you will know the peace that lives in your tent.** In Holy Scripture that peace that is called complete is one thing, and that which is only initial is something else. Truth gave his disciples initial peace when he said, *Peace I leave with you; my own peace I give you.** Simeon desired complete peace when he prayed, *Now, O Lord, you let your servant go in peace, according to your word.** Our peace is initiated by desire for the Creator but completed by the revelatory vision. It

*Job 5:24

*John 14:27

*Luke 2:29

will then be complete when our mind is not blinded by ignorance or alarmed by upheavals of the flesh. Since we are now talking about the initiating of peace, however, when we subject either the mind to God or the flesh to the mind, the tent of the just is said to have peace. This is obviously because in the body, where the mind dwells, the perverse excitement of desires is curbed by the guidance of justice. But what use is it to restrain the flesh by self-control unless the mind knows how to expand by compassion in the love of neighbor? There is no such thing as chastity of the flesh unprotected by a pleasant disposition. So after the peace of the tent we are rightly advised,

XXXV. 54. *When you visit your likeness, you will not sin.** The likeness of one person is another person. Our likeness is rightly called our neighbor, because we see in that one what we are ourselves. We reach our neighbor in a bodily visitation by footsteps; in a spiritual visitation, however, we are led not by our feet but by affection. Accordingly those who direct their loving steps to the people whom they see to be like themselves by nature visit their own likeness. Just as they see themselves in the others, so let them gather from themselves the knowledge of how to conform themselves to the weaknesses of the other people. Those who consider themselves in others so that they may remodel the others in themselves visit their own likeness. That is why Truth, in describing events through Moses, intimated what was yet to happen. Here is what he said: *The earth brought forth green plants, bearing their seed according to their kind; there were also trees bearing fruit, each one with its seed according to its kind.**

**Job 5:24

**Gen 1:12

Yes, the tree bears its seed according to its kind when the mind gathers consideration for another from itself and produces the fruit of good works. Thus a certain wise

---

man said, *What you would not want done to yourself, do not do to another.** Thus also the Lord said in the gospel, *As you wish men to act toward you, do you act toward them likewise.** He might have said openly, "Visit your likeness in the other person and find out from yourselves how to conduct yourselves toward others." Thus also Paul said, *I became like a Jew to the Jews, so that I might gain the Jews; to those under the law I became like one under the law although I was not under the law myself, so that I might help those who were under the law; to those outside the law I became like one outside the law, although I was not outside God's law myself, but inside Christ's law.* A little later he said, *I became all things to all men so that I might save them all.**

Now the famous preacher did not break faith so as to become a Jew, nor did he return to the sacrifice of animal flesh so as to be under the law, nor did he exchange the simplicity of his commitment for the variety of error so as to become all things to all men. Rather, he drew near to those without faith by condescension, though not by failing, so as to welcome them all in himself and transform himself into all of them; he wanted to be like them by compassion, in order that he might be what he rightly wished they would become. Thus he would the more truly hasten to the aid of any wanderer all the more effectively if he had learned his way of salvation from consideration of his own case. Accordingly it is well said, *When you visit your likeness, you will not sin.* Then sin is really overcome, you see, when all consider from their own likeness how they expand in the love of their neighbor. When therefore the flesh is restrained from vices, when the mind grows in virtues, it remains for each one to speak and teach that life that his or her example proves. Those who first sow the seed of good works gather abundant fruit from their preaching.

*Tob 4:16 Vulg

*Matt 7:12

*1 Cor 9:20-22

Then comes the follow-up after peace in the tent and visitation of our likeness:

XXXVI. 55. *You will know that you will have many descendants, and your offspring will be like grass on the earth.*[*] Yes, after the peace of the tent and after the visitation of our likeness arise the many descendants of the just one, certainly because after the weakening of the members and the strengthening of moral virtue, the ability to preach the word is granted to him, and it is exceedingly fruitful, because it is preceded in his heart by the preparation of good practice. The person has eloquence and is a good speaker whose heart is enlarged through zeal for correct living, and such a one's conscience does not forbid speaking when life precedes the tongue. That is why the Egyptians at Joseph's direction became public slaves and humbly subjected themselves to the king's discretion; they even had enough grain to sow seed. Even we free people receive the fruits of the earth to eat when we feed on the word of God, and that we also have an appetite for the things of this world appears in our wandering about in search of pleasure. But when we are enslaved we also receive grain for seed, because when we are fully subject to God we are also filled with the word of preaching.

And because a numerous posterity of faithful people follows once the ability to do holy preaching is obtained, after the multiplication of posterity we are told, *Your offspring will be like grass on the earth.* The offspring of the just are likened to the grass on the ground, because the one who is born from their example and who abandons the withering fame of the present life grows up by hope into eternal life. Or at least the offspring of the just grow up like grass, because they demonstrate in life what they assert in preaching, with the result that an uncountable multitude of followers arises. On the

[*] Job 5:25

other hand, anyone who already scorns worldly desires, anyone who goes out of self to perform the acts of an external ministry, is never satisfied with doing great things externally except by being able also to penetrate internal secrets by contemplation. So Eliphaz rightly adds the following verse,

XXXVII. 56. *You will enter the tomb with abundance, as it is accumulated in its time.** What is expressed by the word for tomb unless the contemplative life? The contemplative life buries us away from the world; it receives us from worldly desires and hides us in its deep places. They were dead as far as external living is concerned and even buried through contemplation to whom Paul said, *You are dead, and your life is hidden with Christ in God.** The active life is also a tomb because it hides us when we are dead from evil actions, but the contemplative life is a better tomb because it buries us far away from all worldly works. Accordingly, whoever has already rid the self of the importunities of the flesh still has to exercise the mind in the effort of acts of holiness. Whoever already trains the mind through holy activity still has to extend this training until reaching the mysteries of interior contemplation. The person is no perfect preacher, you see, who either neglects the work that should be done out of eagerness for contemplation or puts off the work of contemplation because of the urgency of labor.

That is why Abraham buried his dead wife in a double tomb.*[1] All perfect preachers, you see, unquestionably bury their souls, which are dead to the desires of the present life, under the covering of good works and contemplation. They do this in order that their souls

*Job 5:26

*Col 3:3

*see
Gen 23:19

[1] The Vulgate text followed by Saint Gregory has *duplici* instead of *Machpelah*, which is a proper noun.

may lie hidden underneath an active and contemplative life, virtually without feelings from concupiscence of the flesh, although previously their souls were sensible of worldly desire and lived a mortal life. Accordingly, the Redeemer of the human race performed miracles in the city during the day, and he spent the night on the mountain in assiduous prayer,* obviously in order to form perfect preachers and teach them never to abandon activity in favor of a love of contemplation or to scorn the joy of contemplation because of excessive involvement in activity. They should rather silently absorb in contemplation what they would pour out in speech when occupied for their neighbors' sake. By contemplation, indeed, we reach the love of God, but by preaching we again profit our neighbor.

*see Luke 5:12-19

So according to Moses, when a heifer is slaughtered and sacrificed, it is prescribed that it be offered with hyssop and cedarwood and scarlet wool dipped twice.* As for the heifer, we certainly slaughter it when we extinguish unbridled pleasure in our flesh. We offer this flesh with hyssop, cedarwood, and scarlet wool, because along with the slaughtering of our flesh we offer the sacrifice of faith, hope, and charity. Hyssop indeed usually cleanses our internal dispositions. With Peter we say, *He cleaned their hearts by faith.* As for the cedarwood, it never decays, because hope in heaven is unending. That is why Peter says again, *He has given us a new birth into a living hope by the resurrection of Jesus Christ from the dead, an incorruptible, unspoiled, and unfading inheritance.*

*see Num 19:6

*Acts 15:9

*1 Pet 1:3-4

Scarlet wool has a flamelike red color, because charity sets on fire the one whom it fills. So also Truth says in the gospel, *I came to set the earth on fire.* Yet we are directed to offer the scarlet wool dipped twice, obviously because our charity should be colored by

*Luke 12:49

the love of God and of neighbor in the presence of our interior judge. As far as that goes, the converted mind should not prefer peace and quiet for the sake of loving God in such a way as to put off caring and doing good for the neighbor. Nor should one be so devoted to one's job for the love of the neighbor as to abandon peace and quiet altogether and put out the fire of the love of God that is within. Those therefore who have already offered themselves as a sacrifice to God, if they want perfection, should make sure that they not only exercise themselves in hard work but also try to reach the summit of contemplation.

57. Nevertheless, these matters urgently require careful consideration, because the various elements are distributed unevenly among different souls. Some people, you see, have such sluggish minds that if they are given a job to do, they barely begin it before they give it up. Some, on the other hand, are so restless that when they have a respite from their work they work all the harder, because the more freely their thoughts range, the more serious are the disturbances their hearts endure. Therefore the mind at rest should not let itself get stirred up for excessive work, nor should the restless mind let itself contract in zeal for contemplation. Calm people, you see, could often engage in contemplation, but because they were forced to engage in activity, they gave it up. On the other hand, those who could have lived a useful life involved in actions for the good of others were stopped by the sword of their own retirement. That is why some restless spirits search out more by contemplation than they understand, and they even go so far as to teach erroneous doctrines; they disdain to be humble disciples of truth and make themselves teachers of error.

So Truth himself has said, *If your right eye scandalizes you, pluck it out and throw it away. It is better for you to enter life with one eye than to be thrown into the fire of hell with two eyes.** When the two lives, active *Matt 18:9 and contemplative, are kept in mind, they are like the two eyes we have in our face. The right eye is the contemplative life, and the left the active. But as we have said, some people simply cannot perceive the highest spiritual realities by discretion, and yet they assume the heights of contemplation. So they fall into the pit of faithlessness, deceived by the error of false understanding. Accordingly, the contemplative life causes them to fall away from the truth, because they took it up beyond their means, but the active life alone could have kept them in their humble state of righteousness. Truth rightly told them what we have already quoted: *If your right eye scandalizes you, pluck it out and throw it away. It is better for you to enter life with one eye than to be thrown into the fire of hell with two eyes.* He could have said more clearly, "When you are unable to live the contemplative life because you lack sufficient discretion, it is safer for you to stick to the active life alone. When you fall away from that which you choose because it is greater, be content with what you count as of lesser value, in order that if you are forced to lose the knowledge of truth gained by living the contemplative life, you might at least enter the kingdom of heaven with one eye through the active life alone."

The Lord says somewhere else, *He who scandalizes one of these little ones who believe in me should have a millstone hung from his neck and be thrown into the ocean.** What is meant by the ocean unless it *Matt 18:6 is the world? What by a millstone but earthly actions? Such actions bind the neck of the mind tightly with stupid desires and thereby fasten the mind to a cycle of labor. Some people, you see, abandon earthly actions and humility as well, and they rise to the effort of contemplation beyond their intellectual ability; in so doing they not only fall into error themselves but also separate some weak souls from the bosom of unity. Accordingly, anyone who scandalizes one of the little ones would have been better dealt with by having a millstone tied to the neck and being thrown into the ocean. In other words, it might have been easier for a vulgar mind to occupy itself with the world and work at earthly tasks than to try itself in contemplation and be free to ruin many people. On the other hand, if the contemplative life were not more fitting for some souls than the active, the Lord would never have said through the psalmist, *Be quiet and see that I am God.*[*]

*Ps 45:11 Vulg

58. Nevertheless we must remember that love often moves slow minds to action and that fear restrains restless minds and holds them in contemplation. Weighty fear, you see, anchors the heart, which is frequently shaken by the winds of thoughts but held fast by the chains of its self-discipline. No, the storm of its own restlessness does not pull the heart to shipwreck, because perfect charity ties it to the beach of divine love. Therefore, those who are in a hurry to apply themselves to contemplation should first ask themselves carefully about the extent of their love. The power of love is indeed the mind's vehicle; it draws the mind away from the world, and in that act it raises it on high.

Such seekers should first solve this question: Do they seek the heights with love? Do they love with fear? Do they know how to understand the unknown by love or to venerate it by fear when they do not understand? If love, you see, does not arouse the mind to contemplation, its lukewarm inactivity depresses it. If fear does not weigh upon the mind, feeling lifts it through vanity to the cloud of error. If the closed door of mysteries later opens for it, it is thrust farther away from that door by very presumption. Because fear wants to break in, it does not find what it seeks. When the mind grows proud, instead of truth it perceives error; then it is like a person who intends to step inside and ends up outside.

That is why when the Lord was about to give the law, he descended in fire and smoke.* He sheds light on the humble people through the glory of his revelation, and he blinds the eyes of the proud through the darkness of error. And so the mind must first have all its longing for present honor and all its desire for pleasure of the flesh wiped away; only then can it be raised to the sphere of contemplation. That is why the people were not allowed on the mountain when they received the law; their minds were still weak, and they desired earthly possessions, so they could not presume to watch the higher realities. Rightly was it said, *If a beast touches the mountain, it will be stoned.** The beast touches the mountain when the mind that is given over to irrational desires tries to reach the high realities of contemplation. It is stoned to death because it does not endure the high places, and the very blows inflicted by the weight of the upper regions kill it.

59. Accordingly, those who try to reach the summit of perfection and want to hold the citadel of contemplation should first prove themselves in the arena of works through practice. They must really know that they inflict no evil on their neighbor anymore, that they calmly bear any evil inflicted on them by their neighbor, that joy at the reception of worldly goods does not weaken their resolution, that excessive sorrow at temporal loss does not dishearten them. Therefore they should consider when they commune with themselves inwardly that

*see Exod 19:18

*Heb 12:20; see Exod 19:12-13

when they concern themselves with spiritual things, they should certainly bring no shred of bodily reality along, or if perchance they do, they should rid themselves of it with their skill at discernment. If they desire to see the unending light, they must cast out all the images surrounding them, and if they long to touch that which is above them, they must stop being what they are. So Eliphaz says right here, *You will enter the tomb* *Job 5:26 *with abundance.* That is so. The perfect one enters the tomb with abundance because of first gathering works in an active life and afterward in contemplation by effectively hiding the bodily senses from this world, since it is then dead. So Eliphaz rightly adds, *as accumulated in its time.*

60. The time for action, you see, comes first, the time for contemplation last. Therefore, all the perfect must first train their mind to virtue; later they may rest their minds in the quiet harvest. That is why the man whom the legion of devils abandoned at the Lord's command sat at his Savior's feet and listened to his teaching; he wanted to leave his own home together with the one responsible for his safety, yet Truth himself, who had saved him, told him, *First go back home and proclaim* *Luke 8:39 *all that God has done for you.* When, you see, we learn something of the knowledge of God, be it ever so little, we do not want to return to human affairs anymore, we refuse the burden of our neighbors' needs, we seek silent contemplation, and we desire nothing else but refreshment without labor. But after he has healed us, Truth sends us back home; he orders us to proclaim what has happened to us, obviously because the mind has first to work at perspiring labor and later to be refreshed in contemplation.

61. That is why Jacob served for love of Rachel and received Leah instead. He was told, *It is not the custom*

*in our country to allow the younger daughter to marry
before the older.** Rachel means "seen beginning," Leah   *Gen 29:26
"laborer." What else can Rachel signify but the contemplative life, or Leah but the active? In contemplation
indeed it is the beginning or God that is sought; in action
there is labor and a heavy burden of needs. So Rachel
is lovely but barren, whereas Leah is bleary but prolific.
Obviously, when the mind desires leisure for contemplation, it sees more but bears fewer children for God. On
the other hand, when it undertakes the labor of preach-
ing, it sees less but bears more.* After embracing Leah,   *children
therefore, Jacob finally gets Rachel, because every perfect person is first united with the fruitfulness of the active life and later embraces the repose of contemplation.
The words of the holy gospel show us that contemplation
is indeed less than action in time but greater in merit.

In the gospel, you see, we are told of the different
behavior of two women. Mary was actually listening
to our Redeemer's words as she sat at his feet, while
Martha was busy with her service. But when Martha
complained about Mary's disengagement, she was told,
*Martha, Martha, you are concerned and troubled a great
deal, but only one thing is necessary. Mary has chosen
the best role, and she will not be deprived of it.** What is   *Luke
meant by Mary, who sits and listens to the Lord's words,   10:41-42
but the contemplative life? What does Martha, who is
occupied with external service, signify but the active
life? Martha's solicitude is not censured, but Mary's
role is praiseworthy. Great indeed is the value of active
life, but contemplation is better, so Mary's role is said
never to be taken away. Whereas the works of the active
life disappear with the body, the joys of contemplation
wax greater with the end of this life.

This truth is well, if briefly, expressed by the prophet
Ezekiel as he contemplates the flying animals and says,

*Ezek 10:8

*The likeness of a man's hand was underneath their wings.** What else can we perceive in the animals' wings but the saints' contemplation, by which saints fly up to the highest heaven? They abandon earth and hover in heaven. And what do we understand by the hands other than work? When our hands are stretched out, you see, for love of our neighbor, they distribute even the material goods with which they abound. But their hands are beneath their wings because by virtue of their contemplation they surpass their works and actions.

62. The tomb can also be taken to mean, besides contemplation in this life of ours, the repose of our eternal and internal reward, which repose is all the more complete the more completely this corruptible life is done away with. The one who is completely dead to human changeability and buried in the secret place of the true light will enter the tomb with abundance after the accumulated works of the present life. So also the psalmist says, *You hide them in the hideout of your face* *Ps 30:2 LXX *from the commotion of men.** This truth receives additional confirmation from the comparison that follows: *as accumulated in its time.* Grain sown in the field is touched by the sun because the human soul in this life is illuminated with respect to the heavenly light. It receives rain because it grows ripe from the word of truth. It is shaken by winds because it is tried by temptations. It has chaff growing with it because it has to bear the more worthless lives of sinners who contradict it every day. When it ends up on the threshing floor, it is pressed by the weight of other sheaves so that it may be relieved of the chaff that clings to it.

Because our mind is subject to the discipline of heaven, when it receives the blows of correction it leaves behind the companionship of carnal people, having itself been cleansed. Having rid itself of chaff, it is brought to the granary, because the reprobates remain outside when the chosen soul is lifted up to the everlasting happiness of the mansion in heaven. So it is wisely said, *You will enter the tomb with abundance, as accumulated in its time.*[*] After their affliction the just receive their reward in the heavenly fatherland; therefore it is as if the grain were being gathered into the barn after threshing. In some other time indeed they felt the threshing, but in their own time they are free of threshing. For a chosen soul the other time is certainly the present life; so to those still without faith Truth said, *My time has not yet come, but your time is always at hand.*[*] Somewhere else he said, *This is your hour and the power of darkness.*[*] You will enter the tomb, then, as the grain is accumulated in its time, because the one who has first felt the threshing discipline here receives eternal rest in order to be relieved of the chaff that must be burned.

*Job 5:26

*John 7:6
*Luke 22:53

Eliphaz has now mentioned in the course of his speech tent, stones, beasts, seed, grass, and tomb. But he has not used these words literally, as he indicates himself when he adds after them all in the same place,

XXXVIII. 63. *Behold, this is true, as we have discovered.*[*] It is perfectly obvious that in these words Eliphaz has said nothing superficial, because what is discussed is not what is before one's face. One who says he has discovered these things shows having sought deep things with ordinary words. Nevertheless, after all that Eliphaz ends up in the stupidity of boasting when he immediately adds,

*Job 5:27

XXXIX. 64. *Now you have heard it; let your mind study it.*[*] With however much doctrine the mind waxes great, it is serious ignorance on anyone's part to want to teach a greater mind. Therefore while Job's friends indeed spoke the truth, what they said is judged unjust by the interior judge. They lose the power of their own

*Job 5:27

truth because they are not adapted to the hearer, since when medicine is applied to healthy limbs it loses its curative power. Accordingly, in all that we say it is necessary to take into account the occasion, the time, and the person; we must know if the truth of the statement corroborates the words, we must know if a convenient time demands the statement, we must know whether the person's merit does not assail both the truth of the statement and the fittingness of the time. A person, you see, shoots an arrow in a praiseworthy manner who first looks at the enemy at whom it is shot. Warriors bend the bow in a wicked manner when they aim the arrow and let it fly to hit a fellow citizen.

BOOK 7

I. 1. Some minds suffer more from beatings than from reproaches. Others, however, smart more from cruel words than from beatings. Harsh words, you see, often hurt us more than any kind of pain; they raise our hackles in self-defense, and thereby they plunge us into the vice of impatience. Accordingly, it was blessed Job's lot that he could not be spared any temptation; not only did physical trials from heaven batter him but even harsher trials afflicted him: blows delivered in conversation with his friends. The holy man's soul was battered from all sides, in order that anger and pride might force him to act and so that whatever was pure in his life might be spoiled by words of obstinacy and pride. But when blows struck him he gave thanks; when they provoked him with words he answered honestly; when he was struck down he made it known how little he valued bodily health.

When he spoke, he also showed how wisely he held his peace. Mixed in with his words were some points that seem to human judgment to go beyond the limits of patience. We will understand them correctly if we weigh the sentence of the heavenly Judge in our consideration of them. He indeed first introduced blessed Job and spoke against the adversary. Here is what he said: *Have you noticed my servant Job? There is none on earth like him. He is a blameless and upright man who fears God and avoids evil.** After Job's acquittal the same Judge accused Job's friends. He said, *You have not spoken the truth before me like my servant Job.**

Accordingly, if Job's speeches cause the mind uncertainty, its only recourse is to guide itself by the beginning

*Job 1:8

*Job 42:7

91

and end of his story in weighing their import. The eternal
Judge, you see, could not praise Job if he were going to
fall, nor could he exalt him if he had already fallen. If
therefore we are caught in the storm of doubt, we study
the beginning and end of the story; then the ship of the
heart is held fast by the rope of its thoughts, as though it
were the prow or stern of a vessel, lest it stray onto the
rocks of error. We are not buffeted by any winds of our
ignorance if we hold the quiet shore of God's judgment.
Behold, Job now says something that moves the soul of
the reader to a serious question. But who would dare say
it is wrong if it sounds right to God?

II. 2. *If only my sins that have earned me wrath
were weighed in the balance, and the misfortune I suffer, they would seem greater than the sand on the seashore.** Whom else does the word *balance* express but
the Mediator of God and humans? He came to weigh
the value of our life, and he brought along justice as
well as mercy; yet he used the scale of mercy more and
by sparing made our sins lighter. He became a balance
with marvelous weights in the Father's hand; on one
side of himself he placed our misfortune, on the other
our sins. In his death, however, he proved that misfortune weighed a great deal, and he showed that sin was
lightweight in the scale of mercy by relieving it.

The first grace he conferred on us was this: that
he made us aware of our penalty. We, you see, were
created for contemplation of our Creator, but our sins
required that we be exiled from that spiritual joy; we
fell into the toil of corruption and accepted the blindness
of exile. We put up with the punishment for our guilt
without knowing it, so much so that we thought exile
to be our native country and rejoiced as much at the
burden of corruption as if it were liberty and safety. But
he whom we had internally forsaken assumed flesh and

appeared externally as God, and when God manifested himself outside, he recalled us, who had been exiled externally, back to the internal world, that we might now see our loss and might now groan at the penalty of our blindness.

Human misfortune therefore showed up heavy on the scale because we only knew of the evil we bore in the presence of our Redeemer. When we knew nothing of the light, of course, we delightedly accepted the darkness of our condemnation. But after we saw what we loved, we understood our sadness as well; we felt our bitter suffering when we knew that what we had lost was sweet. Accordingly the holy man Job was driven out of the prison of silence by the speeches delivered by his friends and filled with the eloquence of a prophetical spirit; let him speak with his own voice, let him say with the voice of the human race, *If only my sins that have earned me wrath were weighed in the balance, and the misfortune I suffer, they would seem greater than the sand on the seashore.** He might as well say outright, "We think our unfortunate condemnation light, because it is weighed without the knowledge of the Redeemer's equity. If only he would come and place the bitterness of our hard exile on the scale of his mercy and then teach us what we should expect after the exile is over."

*Job 6:2

If it should become known, you see, what we have lost, it might be inferred that our sufferings are great. We are right to compare that misfortune of our exile to the sand of the seashore. Why? Because the action of the waves moves the sand out away from the seashore. Likewise the sinful, because they have been easily moved by the waves of temptation, have left their interior selves and gone outside. Yes, the weight of the sand on the seashore is awesome, but human misfortune is said to be heavier than the sand on the seashore because the penalty was shown to have been more severe at the time when the merciful Judge lightened the guilt. Because all who know the Redeemer's grace and all who desire to return to the fatherland know of their exile and groan under its weight, Job adds the following words after having previously expressed his desire that his sins be weighed:

[*]Job 6:3

III. 3. *That is why my words are full of sadness.*[*] One who loves exile instead of the fatherland cannot be sad even in the midst of sadness. Nevertheless, righteous people's words are full of sadness, because as long as they survive the present life, they long for the other life when they speak; they know all the sins they have committed, and in order that they may return to the happy state, they carefully weigh the judgment by which they are afflicted. So Job adds,

[*]Job 6:4

IV. 4. [*Because*] *God's arrows are in me.*[*] The word for arrows sometimes means the words used in preaching, and sometimes it means a judge's sentence. Arrows mean the words used in preaching when they strike a blow against vices and consequently pierce the hearts of those who live evil lives. We are told of these arrows at the coming of the Redeemer, *Your arrows are sharp, O most powerful king; the people's hearts fail before*

[*]Ps 44:6 LXX

you.[*] Isaiah also speaks of these arrows: *I will send some of those who will be saved to the nations by the sea, to Africa, and to Lydia; bearing arrows they shall go*

[*]Isa 66:19 Vulg

to Italy and to Greece.[*] On the other hand, arrows can also mean a judge's sentence. In this sense Elisha said to King Joash, *Shoot an arrow.* After the shot he said,

[*]2 Kgs 13:17

You will strike Syria until you destroy it.[*] The holy man Job therefore sees the hardship of his exile and groans under the blows of God's judgment, so he says, *That is why my words are full of sadness, because God's ar-*

[*]Job 6:3-4

rows are in me.[*] He might as well say outright, "I am

condemned to exile, and I am unhappy. I am subject
to judgment, and I am sad, because I know the finality
of my sentence." There are many, however, who suffer trials but do not amend their lives. They are rightly
targeted by the following words:

V. 5. *Their fury drinks up my spirit.** What else is
the human spirit but the spirit of pride? God's arrows
drink up the human spirit when the blows of God's judgment restrain the despondent mind from indulging pride.
God's arrows drink up the human spirit, because they
find it absorbed in external activities, and they draw it
within itself. David's spirit had been drunk up when he
said, *My spirit is failing within me, but you know my
path.** Somewhere else he says, *I denied comfort to my
soul; I remembered God, and I was distracted. I was in
trouble, and my spirit momentarily failed.** Furious arrows, therefore, drink up the just person's spirit, because
when God's judgment finds sin in the elect, it wounds
them and thereby changes them; this happens in order
that the mind, once pierced, may forsake its stubbornness, and that the blood of confession may run out of
that salutary wound. The just are considering, you see,
the state from which they have fallen; they are considering the complete happiness from which they have
tumbled into this anguish that belongs to their state of
decay. Not only do they groan at their sufferings, but
they also fear the threat of the fire of hell hurled at sinners by the strict Judge.

VI. 6. *Terror rises up against me.** The mind of the
just not only ponders what it endures but also fears what
is to come. It knows its sufferings in this life, and it
worries lest it should have still greater sufferings afterward. It mourns the fact that it has fallen from the joy
of Paradise into its present blind exile; it fears lest eternal death should follow once the exile is left behind. It

*Job 6:4

*Ps 141:4
LXX

*Ps 76:2-3
LXX

*Job 6:4

already therefore endures its sentence of punishment, yet it still dreads the threat of the coming Judge, knowing its guilt. So the psalmist says, *Your wrath has pierced me through, and your terror has made me anxious.** Yes, it is the internal Judge whose wrath pierces through us, and afterward his terror too gives us anxiety. Why? Because we already suffer one evil from condemnation, and we dread still another evil from eternal retribution.

*Ps 87:17 LXX

Accordingly, let the holy man Job ponder the sufferings he endures and say, *God's arrows are in me, and their fury drinks up my spirit.** But since he fears still harsher sufferings in eternity, let him add, *Terror rises up against me.** He could have said clearly, "Yes, I have been struck, and I groan now, but another pain is still worse, namely that even as I am being punished here, I fear eternal retribution." Nevertheless, he desires the intervention of the scales, and he still weighs the evil fortune into which the human race has fallen; although he was born a Gentile, he was endowed with the fullness of the spirit of prophecy. So he shows us how ardently both Jew and Gentile long for the coming of the Redeemer with the following words:

*Job 6:4

*Job 6:4

VII. 7. *Will the ass bray, when it has fodder? Will the ox low, when it stands before a full stable?** What does the ass (or rather the wild ass) signify but the Gentile peoples? Just as nature has bred them away from the civilized stable, so they have continued wandering in the wilderness of their own desires. What is seen in the figure of the ox but the Jewish people? Yoked to God's mastery, they collected proselytes to hope, and they pulled the plow of the law with the hearts they had mastered. But if there is one thing we know from the testimony of blessed Job's life, it is that we should believe that there were many more Gentiles who had waited for the Redeemer's coming. And from Simeon's coming

*Job 6:5

into the temple at the Spirit's urging when the Lord was born we learn how ardently the saints of the people of Israel desired to see the mystery of his incarnation. That is why the Redeemer himself told his disciples, *I tell you, many prophets and just men desired to see what you are seeing, and they did not see it.** *Matt 13:17

The ass's fodder and the ox's grass are this very incarnation of the Redeemer, which satisfies both Jew and Gentile. That is why the prophet says, *All flesh is grass.** The Creator of the universe, you see, took flesh from our own nature; he willed to become grass so that our own flesh might not remain grass forever. Then the ass also found its fodder when the Gentile people received the grace of God's incarnation. Then the ox had no empty stable when the law presented his flesh to the Jewish people, that long-awaited One whom it had prophesied. Accordingly, the Lord was born and laid in a stable, obviously in order to show that the holy animals, which had been known to go hungry so long under the law, might eat their fill of the fodder of his incarnation. At his birth he filled a manger, and he offered himself as food to the minds of mortal men and women. He said, *He who eats my flesh and drinks my blood abides in me and I in him.** *John 6:57

* *Isa 40:6

The longings of the chosen Gentiles had long been deferred, and all the saints of the Hebrew people had also cried out their expectation of his redemption for a long time. So blessed Job also proclaims the mystery of prophecy and suggests the causes of affliction on behalf of both peoples, saying, *Will the ass bray, when it has fodder? Will the ox low, when it stands before a full stable?** He could say outright, "The Gentiles groan for this reason, that the grace of their Redeemer does not yet refresh them; the Jews multiply their groans because they still hold the law, but they do not see the *Job 6:5

Lawgiver, so they stand in front of the stable hungry."
The law, of course, before the Mediator's coming, was
never followed in a spiritual manner but only in a carnal
one, so he is right to add,

VIII. 8. *Can anything unsavory be eaten without*
Job 6:6   salt? * In the law the salt of the letter means the power
of hidden knowledge. Accordingly, anyone who is intent
on carnal observances and refuses spiritual knowledge,
what else does such a person eat but unsalted food?
Truth, when known, sprinkles this salt on food when he
teaches us that the taste of secret knowledge is hidden
in the law. He says, *If you believed Moses, perhaps you*
John 5:46   would also believe me, because he wrote of me. * Again
he says, *Have salt inside yourselves and be at peace*
Mark 9:49   with one another. * Before the Mediator's coming, however, the Jews kept the law in a carnal way; therefore the
Gentiles refused to obey its extreme demands. Thus they
refused to eat unsalted food. They dreaded being forced
into the service of the letter before receiving the spice
of the Spirit. What Gentile would bear the prescriptions
of the law concerning cutting the sons' foreskins for
the sake of religion or the expiation of sinful words by
death? That is why Job adds,

IX. 9. *Can anyone taste that whose taste brings*
Job 6:6   death? * The law, you see, when tasted according to the
flesh, brought death. How? By exposing the evil deeds
of criminals and judging them harshly. Yes, it brought
death, because the precept noticed the guilt and did not
lighten it by grace. Paul testified to this fact, saying, *The*
Heb 7:19   law made nothing perfect. * Somewhere else he says,
After all, the law is holy, and the commandment is holy,
righteous, and good. And later, *That sin might seem to*
Rom 7:12-13   be sin, but that which is good became death to me. * The
Gentiles who converted to Christ know that he speaks
through the words of the law, so although hard pressed

by their desires, they seek him spiritually among carnal precepts, him whom they fiercely love. Therefore the words that are soon to be those of the church follow through the spirit of prophecy:

X. 10. *Those things that previously I refused to touch have now become my food through hardship.** The man who supposes that blessed Job's words recount history alone will certainly fall into error. He is a holy man, supported by rich praise from his Creator; what noteworthy things or, better, what truths would he speak if he had said he could not eat unsalted food? Who had offered him deadly food to eat that he should say, *Can anyone taste that whose taste brings death?** If we understand these words in relation to his friends' conversation, that understanding is derailed by the following sentence, in which he says, *Those things that previously I refused to touch have now become my food through hardship.* When the holy man still enjoyed the relative safety of his class, he certainly would never have despised his friends' words; he himself bore us witness after that, saying that he was meek to his slaves. His words, therefore, are not empty of mystery, just as we learn from the end of the story that the interior Judge praises his words. Indeed, his words would hardly still be valid until the end of the world and win so much veneration if they had not been pregnant with mystical understanding.

11. Accordingly, blessed Job is a member of Holy Church, so let him speak with her voice and say, *Those things that previously I refused to touch have now become my food through hardship.** Yes, the converted Gentile church becomes anxious, warmed by her love, and she hungers for the food of the Old Testament, that food that in her pride she had long despised. *Those things*, however, also fit the mouths of the Jews, if they are attentively considered. Judea indeed had salt, and

* Job 6:7

* Job 6:6

* Job 6:7

that salt was the teaching of the law; it was the knowledge that God is one. She also scorned all the nations and considered them as nothing else but dumb animals. If under the tutelage of the law's prescriptions she disdained the idea of associating herself with Gentiles, what else was she doing but showing her dislike for eating unseasoned food?

Under the threat of death, you see, God's judgment had forbidden the Israelites to make any covenant with foreigners, lest they should corrupt their holy religion. *Can anyone taste that whose taste brings death?** But when these same Jews of the number of the elect turned to faith in the Redeemer, they did all they could to proclaim the light they had seen through the holy apostles to the unbelievers of their own nation. Yet Hebrew pride spurned the service of that preaching. Accordingly, they soon turned and addressed their words of exhortation to the gathering crowd of the Gentiles, as the same apostles testified: *We were bound to speak the word of God to you* first, but since you reject it and show yourselves unworthy of eternal life, we will now go to the Gentiles.*

For this reason Job wisely adds in this place, *Those things that previously I refused to touch have now become my food through hardship.** After all, Judea scorned the life of the Gentiles, and she refused even to touch it for a long time; she would not even associate with the Gentiles. Yet she came to the Redeemer's grace and was rejected by unbelieving Israelites, but she moved out by means of the holy apostles to gather the Gentiles. In so doing she was like a hungry person accepting a food that she had formerly loathed as disgraceful and despised. She who saw her spoken message spurned by the Hebrews bore the hardship of her preaching. Yet, confronted by this hardship, she ate the food that she had held in contempt for so long a time,

*Job 6:6

*Jews
*Acts 13:46

*Job 6:7

and she who had been repulsed by the hard-hearted Jews gladly accepted the Gentiles whom she had despised.

Accordingly, since we have spoken in a figurative fashion, we must now go on to the moral investigation.

12. The holy man desires the coming of the Redeemer when he uses the word for balance. When he opens his eloquent mouth, he teaches us to examine our life. When he tells his own story, he indicates part of ours. When he suggests points in his life that we can recognize, he strengthens our weak and fearful selves to hope. Now certainly we live by faith in the Redeemer; nevertheless, we still endure the harsh blows of internal judgment for the purifying of our vices. Accordingly, after his desire for balance he adds,

XI. 13. *Because God's arrows are in me, and their fury drinks up my spirit.** Yet be careful, as I have already said; yes, we are stricken by the blows of correction from God, but there is something still more serious than that that we should fear: it is terror of the coming Judge and his eternal scrutiny. That is why Job immediately adds, *Terror rises up against me.** The soul must, however, shake off fear and sorrow and focus only on those desires that want the eternal fatherland. Then, you see, we display the honor of our new life, when we love him as Father whom we now fear as Lord with the attitude of slaves. That is why Paul says, *You have not received a spirit of servitude, that you should still live in fear, but you have received a spirit of adoption as sons, whereby we cry, "Abba, Father."** Let the mind of the elect put down the burden of fear; let them practice the virtue of love, let them desire the honor of new life, let them sigh after the likeness of their Creator. As long as they cannot see him, they must be hungry for their eternal life, that is, their interior food, and wait for him. Therefore Job rightly adds,

*Job 6:4

*Job 6:4

*Rom 8:15

XII. 14. *Will the ass bray, when it has fodder? Will* *Job 6:5 *the ox low, when it stands before a full stable?** Who are they who are designated by the name of ass if not those who live among the faithful, although they are not tied by any reins of responsibility? And who are those expressed by the word for ox if not those driven inside Holy Church in order to perform the office of preaching by the yoke of orders that they have received? The ass's fodder and the ox's feed are the interior food of the faithful people. Some of the faithful, you see, like oxen, are kept inside the church by the reins of the responsibility they have been given. Others, like asses, are unfamiliar with the stable of holy orders; instead they live out in the field of their own will.

Anyone, however, who has lived in the world but is inflamed by the desire of the internal vision, who yearns for the food of that interior dinner, who is conscious of fasting and blindness in this pilgrimage, finds refreshment in tears, like an ass that brays when not finding grass. Someone else, again, may work hard at the task of preaching, because of having accepted the responsibility and taken orders; already this one yearns for the food of eternal contemplation but does not yet see the likeness of the Redeemer, so this preacher is like a chained ox lowing at an empty stable.

We therefore are situated far from internal wisdom, and we do not see the green fields of our eternal inheritance; like brute animals we are hungry for the grass we desire. Our Redeemer certainly spoke of this grass when he said, *If anyone enters by me, he will be safe; he will* *John 10:9 *come and go and find pasture.** It often happens that the sinful lives of some people contradict the holy zeal of those who live uprightly, thus making the love of God a trial. When the mind is seized by a desire for heaven and turns its attention toward a good purpose, it is buffeted by the words and behavior of fools who distract it. The attention, then, that had already flown away to heaven on the wings of contemplation, is grounded and girds itself for battle in order to subdue the folly of lawless people. Therefore Job adds,

XIII. 15. *Can anything unsavory be eaten without salt?** Our minds indeed swallow the words and behavior of carnal people like food, that they may be digested in the belly of contentment. But none of the elect eats unsalted food; no, they see through evil words and actions and spit them out of the mouth of their heart. Paul would not allow unsalted food to be given for the consumption of the mind. He told his disciples, *Let your speech always be gracious and seasoned with salt.** To the psalmist also the words of the reprobate had an unsalted taste in the mouth of his heart when he said, *The wicked told me lies, O Lord, contrary to your law.** It often happens, however, that rude words force themselves insolently on our ears and give rise to battles of temptation in our hearts. However valiantly the reason rejects them, and even the tongue censures them, they are only laboriously overcome in the heart, no matter how authoritatively they are condemned externally. It is necessary, therefore, that whatever the vigilant mind turns away from the entrance of thought should not even come to the ears. Since the saints pant with the desire for eternal life, they live on such a high plain of reality that they henceforth consider the hearing of coarse, worldly words as an intolerable burden for them. In fact, they consider anything that does not reflect their interior love too vulgar to be borne.

16. It often happens that the mind is already taken up to the heights by desire; it is already completely cut off from the foolish conversation of worldly people. Nonetheless, it is not yet ready to endure the suffering

*Job 6:6

*Col 4:6

*Ps 118:85

of the present life for love of truth. It already desires
heaven, it already feels contempt for the stupidity of
earthly activities, yet it does not yet prepare itself to
bear adversity. Therefore Job adds,

*Job 6:6
XIV. 17. *Can anyone taste that whose taste brings
death?* It is indeed bitter medicine to desire that which
crucifies, to seek that which hates life. Yet the mind of the
just person often tries to reach such a lofty peak of virtue
that it is lord over its own inner domain of reason and by
forbearance transforms the folly of those outside it. With
regard to those, you see, whom we attempt to persuade
to adopt a firmer attitude, we must tolerate their weaknesses, because only those who bend their own righteous
approach by compassion will raise those who fall. When
we have compassion on someone else's weakness, we are
also strengthened against our own. By love of the future
life the mind should prepare itself for present adversity
and should expect those sufferings of the body that it used
to worry about. When its desire for heaven grows greater,
the body is straitened, and when it considers the intense
sweetness of the eternal fatherland, it ardently desires
bitterness in the present life for the sake of that sweetness.

Therefore, having written about the aversion for
unseasoned food and the impossible taste of death, Job
continues,

*Job 6:7
XV. 18. *Those things that previously I refused to
touch have now become my food through hardship.*
As the just person's mind makes progress, you see, it
becomes stronger. Previously it cared only for itself
and avoided the knowledge of others; when it had less
compassion for others, it could not overcome adversity.
Once it forced itself to bear its neighbor's weaknesses,
however, it found the strength to overcome adversity.
Then its desire to suffer in the present life for the love of
truth was as strong as its former dislike of its neighbor's

weaknesses. By bending the mind rises, by attracting it expands, by compassion it is strengthened. And when it goes out of itself to love the neighbor, it is as though it derived from meditation all the power with which it rises to its Maker. It is charity, you see, that humbles us and strengthens compassion, then lifts us higher to the peak of contemplation; already strong charity warms us with still greater desires and pushes us even through bodily torments until we reach spiritual life.

Therefore, what previously Job had refused to touch later became his food in adversity. Scarcely containing his desires, he now loves the pain he had feared so long for the sake of his heavenly fatherland. When the mind seeks God, you see, with a firm intention, whatever tasted bitter to the man in this life now tastes sweet, and all his afflictions become repose; he desires to go away and die so that he may obtain life in its fullness. His whole wish is to cease to exist to what is below so that he may the more truly rise to what is above. Yet concerning the soul of any just person and concerning the mind of Job himself I would be a liar if he did not add these words about himself:

XVI. 19. *Who will grant me my petition? Will God give me what I am waiting for? Will he who started it finish me off himself? May he let loose his hand and cut me off; let this be my consolation, that he who infects me with sorrow should spare me not.** Do you suppose it is perversity that makes him plead thus, or that because he wants to be completely annihilated, he blames the One who strikes him for injustice? Hardly. He shows us, you see, in what sense he makes this petition in the words that follow: *I will not contradict the words of the Holy One.** Accordingly, by no means does he murmur about the injustice of the One who strikes him, when he even calls him holy amid the blows which he is striking.

*Job 6:8-10

*Job 6:10

It is important for us to know, however, that sometimes it is the adversary and sometimes God who cuts
us down. When the adversary breaks our defenses, we
fall away from virtue; when God knocks us down, on
the other hand, we are strengthened in virtue and forsake vice. Such a blow is what the prophet foresaw
when he said, *You will rule them with an iron rod, and*
Ps 2:9   you will break them like a potter's jar. The Lord rules
over us and breaks us with the rod, because while the
sturdy domination of his providence refreshes us inside,
it knocks us down outside. At the same time as he reduces the power of the flesh, he empowers the spirit's
purpose. That is why this very breaking is compared to
a potter's jar. Paul also speaks of it: *We carry this trea-*
2 Cor 4:7   sure in earthen vessels. Paul also speaks of both the
breaking and the ruling: *Although our outer man gets*
2 Cor 4:16   worn out, still our inner man is renewed every day.
Let the holy man therefore who desires to draw near to
God, even by means of blows of the whip, say through
his humble attitude,

XVII. 20. *Will he who started it finish me off him-*
Job 6:9   self? The Lord often starts, you see, to bring about
in us the destruction of vices, but when the mind advances from that beginning and exalts itself, boasting
as though it were already virtuous, it opens itself up to
the ferocity of its adversary. So the enemy gets inside
the heart, ruins whatever zeal he finds there for the good
beginning, and obliterates it all the more furiously the
more intensely sad he is at the mind's advance, however
slight. The gospel is our witness when Truth tells us
about the empty house of the consciousness, to which
one spirit returned with seven companions, having left
see   it alone. Lest, therefore, after the beginning of God's
Matt 12:44-45   correction, the ancient enemy should steal the soul and
drag it away for the breaking up of its virtues, the holy

man prays fittingly, *Will he who started it finish me off?* He might as well say, "What he began in me, let him not hesitate to finish by a blow, lest he desert and deliver me up to the adversary for my ruin." Therefore he rightly adds,

XVIII. 21. *May he let loose his hand and cut me off.** Habitual prosperity makes us proud, you see, and we frequently strut and parade our self-reliance. When the Creator notices how we exalt ourselves, he does not immediately express his love for us by disciplining us; rather, he binds his hand and holds it aloof from striking out at our vices. Do you think he did not bind the hand of his affection when he told his sinful people, *I will no longer be angry with you,** or *My wrath has left you?** That he should let loose his hand means, "Let him show his affection." He is right to add, *and cut me off.* You see, when a sudden painful misfortune or a temptation in a moment of weakness strikes us who thought ourselves secure and were proud of our abundant virtues, the result is immediate: our pride is undercut, and we fall from our high position. The mind then dares to undertake nothing of itself; it has been felled by a blow from its own weakness and asks for a hand to lift it up.

When the saints are respected for God's special care of them, they become very much more afraid of prosperity itself, want to be tempted, and desire trials. Indeed fear and pain should train the careless mind, lest when the foe breaks out of his place of ambush on this pilgrim's road, the mind's very security should prove to be it's undoing to its hurt. So the psalmist says, *Prove me, O Lord, and try me,** and again *I am ready for trials.** The minds of the saints, you see, are aware that the wound with which they are stricken is not without rottenness, so they willingly betake themselves to the physician's hand for surgery, so that the poison of sin

*Job 6:9

*Isa 54:9
*Ezek 16:42

*Ps 25:2
*Ps 37:18
LXX

that was wreaking destruction inside the uncut skin may leave the open wound. So Job again adds,

XIX. 22. *Let this be my consolation: that he who* *Job 6:10 *infects me with sorrow should spare me not.** When the chosen ones know they have done wrong but learn by intensive searching that they have suffered no adversity for the wrong they have done, they pine away because of the fearful terror they suffer; they shake with fear, they are excited by the sinister doubts that trouble them, lest grace should forsake them in eternity because no retribution dogs them in the present life for the evil they have done. They worry that the deferred vengeance made heavier might overtake them in the end, so their desire is that God should strike them with fatherly blows; they consider the pain of a wound to be the ointment of salvation.

So now Job is right to say, *This will be my consolation: that he who infects me with sorrow should spare* *Job 6:10 *me not.** He might as well say plainly, "He who spares some people here so that he may strike them forever, let him strike me unsparingly now so that he may spare me in eternity. My affliction is my consolation, because I know the rottenness of human corruption, so I am certain to get back my hope of salvation after being wounded." This he said not out of pride but out of humility, as he makes clear, as I have said, in his next words:

XX. 23. *I will not contradict the words of the Holy* *Job 6:10 *One.** God's words to us are often not spoken sounds but the effects of acts. He speaks to us, you see, in what happens silently. Blessed Job would therefore contradict God's words if he murmured against his blows. But he tells us his feelings about the deliverer of these blows when, as we have already said, he calls him holy whose blows he sustains.

XXI. 24. *What strength do I have to endure? What* *Job 6:11 *is my fate? Why should I keep up my patience?** What we must remember is that the endurance of the just is one thing and the endurance of the wicked is something else. The endurance of the just means victory over the flesh, denial of one's own pleasures, annihilation of delight in the present life, love of harsh treatment in the world for the sake of the eternal reward, contempt for the caresses of prosperity, and overcoming the fear of adversity in the heart. What endurance means to the wicked is as follows: the unceasing love of transitory things, impassively enduring trials sent by the Creator, not even in adversity giving up the love of temporal things, winning worthless honor even with detriment to life, desiring to increase one's malice, attacking the life of the just not only by words and behavior but also with the sword, placing all one's hope in oneself, and daily committing evil without any decrease of desire.

As for the chosen ones, the psalmist tells them, *Act like a man and strengthen your heart, all you who hope in the Lord.*[*] On the other hand, the prophet tells the wicked, *Woe to you who are strong enough to drink wine, you valiant men who get drunk.*[*] That is why Solomon says that all the saints look on internal rest without any weakness of desire: *Behold the couch of Solomon carried by sixty warriors from among the strongest Israelites.*[*] Furthermore the psalmist impersonates the Redeemer in his passion and reproves the wicked, saying, *Behold, they take my life; powerful men attack me.*[*] Isaiah again includes both senses of fortitude when he says, *Those who trust in God exchange their courage.*[*] Since he does not say that they take but rather that they exchange, he certainly clearly indicates that one courage is dropped and another taken up.

25. Are not bad people strong as well? Do they not race with all their strength for the sake of desire for the present life? Do they not boldly oppose themselves to

*Ps 30:25 LXX

*Isa 5:22

*Song 3:7

*Ps 58:4 LXX

*Isa 40:31

danger? Do they not freely bear insults for the sake of gain? Indeed they are beaten by no obstacle; nay, they bounce back and are not kept from their violent appetites. They survive blows, and they endure disasters in the world for the world's own sake, so to speak; in their search for joy they lose it, and yet even when they lose it, they do not give up. That is why Jeremiah adopts humankind's voice and says, *He has made me drunk with wormwood.**

*Lam 3:15

Drunk people really do not know their sufferings. Accordingly, they are drunk with wormwood who, in love with the present life and out of touch with reason, count it as light when they suffer anything for the world's sake; they do not know that the trouble they endure is bitter, obviously, because they are led on in enjoyment to all those things that wear them out in chastisement. The just, however, try to be unable to bear the world's risks for the sake of the world; they have their eye on their goal. They know very well how transitory the present life is, so they refuse to suffer external troubles for its sake; they have overcome its internal delights.

Accordingly, blessed Job can say with his own voice and with the voice of all the just, even while pressed in by the adversities of the present life, *What strength do I have to endure? What is my fate, that I should keep up my patience?** It is as if he boldly spoke up, saying, "I cannot endure misfortune in the world for the world's sake, because I am no longer strong with its desire. When I see the end of the present life, why do I carry the world's burden, the desire for which I tread underfoot?" Since therefore all the unjust people, as I have said, bear the world's misfortunes all the more bravely the more avidly they enjoy its pleasures, he rightly speaks again about this very courage of the wicked and says,

*Job 6:11

XXII. 26. *My courage is not the courage of stones, nor is my flesh made of bronze.** What is meant by stones and bronze in this line, if not the hearts of the unfeeling? They often receive blows sent by God, and yet no stroke of discipline softens their hearts. On the other hand, the prophet says about the chosen ones, concerning the Lord's promise, *I will remove your stony hearts and give you a heart of flesh.** Paul too says, *If I speak with the tongues of men and angels, but have no love, I have become like sounding brass or a tinkling cymbal.** As you know, when stones are struck, they cannot yield a clear sound, but when bronze is struck, it gives forth a very melodious sound. Like stones, however, bronze has no life in it, so its sound has no sense in it.

*Job 6:12

*Ezek 36:26

*1 Cor 13:1

There are also people who are like stones insofar as they have hardened themselves against the commandments of dutiful conduct; when God's notice strikes them, they by no means give forth the sound of a humble confession. There are those on the other hand who differ in no way from the metal of bronze, and when the blows of the divine whips are felt, they do give forth the sound of dutiful confession. Still, they do not emit a humble voice from the heart, and when they are led out to the status of salvation, they do not know what it is they have promised. Accordingly, the former are like stones and have no voices when they are struck; the latter do not hide their imitation of bronze, so when they are struck they speak good words that they do not understand. The former refuse respect to the one who strikes the blows; the latter promise what they do not fulfill, so their cries are lifeless.

Let the holy man, therefore, avoid the hardness of the wicked when he is struck and say, *My courage is not the courage of stones, nor is my flesh made of bronze.**

*Job 6:12

He might as well confess in these words: "I avoid imitating the wicked when I am struck and disciplined, because I have not become hard like stones to the point of
silencing the duty of confession under the pain of beatings. Nor, like bronze, have I sung out my confession
while ignoring the meaning of the voice." But because
the courage of the wicked is weak against blows but
the chosen are without courage but strong, blessed Job
affirms that his strength is not that of senseless excess,
but at the same time he serves notice that his state of
salvation gives him courage. Let him then tell us where
he has acquired the courage, lest he should arrogate
the strength he has to himself and thereby efficaciously
hasten his own death. The strength we have, you see,
often kills us more surely than if it were absent. How?
It instigates the mind to self-confidence, and thereby it
pierces the mind with the sword of pride. Yes, virtue, in
the act of strengthening the mind, gives it life, but then it
raises it and kills it. Obviously it entices it to its own ruin
when it tears it away from faith in its interior strength
through hope in itself. Blessed Job, however, abounds
in power, and he has no self-confidence; he is a strong
weakling, so to speak, and therefore he fittingly adds,

*Job 6:13   XXIII. 27. *There is no help for me inside myself.** It
is already clear where the soul of the stricken man runs
for hope, since he denies that there is any help for himself inside himself. Since he insinuates that he is weak
in himself, let him add that he is also abandoned by his
neighbors, so that he may deserve a yet higher power:
*Job 6:13   *Even my friends have run away from me.** Yet behold how
he who is scorned externally presides internally on the
throne of justice. He asserts that he has been abandoned,
you see, and then he immediately pronounces judgment:
      XXIV. 28. *He who robs his friend of mercy aban-
*Job 6:14   dons the fear of God.** Who is indicated in this verse by

the word *friend* if not any of our neighbors joined with us by faith, insofar as once they have received good service from us in this present time, they effectively help us in our quest of the eternal fatherland afterward? Indeed there are two commandments of love, love of God and love of neighbor; love of neighbor is born from love of God, and love of God is nourished by love of neighbor. Those who neglect the love of God certainly do not love their neighbor; we will make real progress in the love of God only if we are first nursed by love of neighbor in the very lap of that love.

Because the love of God gives birth to the love of neighbor, God, who was going to say in the law, *You must love your neighbor** prefaced it by saying, *You must love the Lord your God.** He did so in order that he might first plant the root of his love in the ground of our heart, inasmuch as brotherly love would later sprout in the branches. On the other hand, love of God grows to fullness out of love of neighbor. John is our witness when he upbraids his disciples: *How can anyone who does not love his brother whom he sees love God whom he does not see?** This divine love is born from fear, but as it grows it changes into affection.

29. Almighty God often arranges everything in a wonderful way so that he may reveal how far each person fails in the love of God and neighbor or makes progress in that love, so that he inflicts trials on some whereas he supports others with prosperity. While he temporarily deserts some, he reveals to others how much evil lies hidden in their hearts. The very ones, you see, who once showed us unequaled respect in our good fortune often persecute us in our misery. When a person who is prosperous is loved, it is always in doubt whether that person is loved or his prosperity. The loss of prosperity, on the other hand, puts the question to

*Lev 19:18;
Matt 22:19;
Mark 12:31

*Deut 6:5;
Matt 22:37;
Mark 12:30;
Luke 10:27

*1 John 4:20

the strength of anyone's love. And so a certain wise
man put it very well: *The friend is not known in good
fortune, nor is the enemy hidden in misfortune.** No indeed, prosperity does not point out a friend, nor does
adversity hide an enemy, because the first is usually
hidden by respect for our good fortune, and the second
is made plain by assurance of our adversity. Let the just
person who has fallen into adversity therefore say, *He
who robs his friend of mercy abandons the fear of God.**

*Sir 12:8

*Job 6:14

Obviously the one who despises a neighbor's adversity is revealed as the one who did not love that neighbor
when prosperous. Almighty God, you see, precisely
strikes down certain ones in order that he might teach
them once they are struck down; by the same token he
offers those not struck the opportunity of performing a
good work. Anyone therefore who despises someone
who has been struck down throws away an opportunity
of virtue. Such people are more wicked adversaries of
the Creator, because they consider him less devoted to
their own welfare and less just in hurting someone else.
On the other hand, it is noteworthy that blessed Job
speaks of his own situation in such a way that the life
of the whole people of God might also be symbolized
through him. He is, after all, a member of that people, so
when he recounts his own suffering, he also announces
what happens to the people. So he says,

XXV. 30. *My brothers have passed me by like a
brook rapidly flowing in the valley.** The base mind loves
only the present existence. Therefore, in the present
the reprobate person often escapes hostile blows and
to that extent remains hereafter an exile from the inheritance. The proud mind scorns the righteous people
whom God's fatherly sternness mercifully afflicts. The
reprobate, however, often hold that same faith by which
we live; they receive the same sacraments of faith, and

*Job 6:15

they participate in the unity of the same religious ob-
servance, yet they are strangers to its deep compassion,
and they are unaware of the power of love with which
we burn toward God and neighbor. Rightly, therefore,
are they called brothers as well as passersby, because
they have come forth out of the same mother's womb
as we have by faith, but they are not held in the grip of
that one eager love for God and neighbor.

That is why they are also compared to a brook rapidly passing through the valley. The brook, you see,
runs down from the highlands into the valley; after the
winter rain accumulates, the heat of summer dries it
up. Accordingly, those who love the things of earth and
forsake their hope in the eternal fatherland are those
who, as it were, leave the mountains and go in search
of the valleys. The winter of this present life increases
the number of these seekers, but the summer of eternal
judgment dries up their flow, because when the sun of
heavenly strictness grows hot, it turns the joy of the
reprobates into dust. So it is well said, *rapidly flowing in
the valley.** For a brook to pass by rapidly in the valley   *Job 6:15
is equivalent to the minds of the reprobate descending to
their lowest desires without any obstacle or difficulty in
their path. Every ascent means effort, and every descent
means pleasure; yes, our steps advance to a higher level
by means of pressing on, whereas we fall back to a lower
level because of giving up.

It costs much effort to carry a rock to the top of a
mountain, but to let the same rock fall to the foot of
the mountain from the top costs no effort at all. That
which was brought to the very top with great exertion
obviously hurtles to the bottom without delay. A crop is
planted laboriously and fed by daily sunshine and rain,
yet it is consumed by a sudden spark. A house is built up
to its proper height little by little, but it is leveled to the

ground suddenly by an accident. A sturdy tree grows up toward the sky by slow increases in height, but however long a time it remains tall, it falls all at once. Ascent therefore means labor, and descent means pleasure, so Job is right to say, *My brothers have passed me by like a brook rapidly flowing in the valley.** All this, however, can be understood in yet another way.

*Job 6:15

31. If we consider the valley as the lowest level of punishment, all the wicked are passing by rapidly like a brook to the valley, because in this life that they desire so ardently they can never stay for long. They get as many days of life as the steps by which they daily approach its end. They desire to lengthen their life, but even what has been granted cannot stand still, because whatever extension of life they obtain they lose from the length of that life. The moments of time that they follow they run away from, and as soon as they receive them they lose them. They rapidly pass on to the valley; they indeed keep prolonging their desires and pleasures, but they are quickly led away to the prisons of hell. Even if this time is extended somewhat by a long life, it is closed by an end, so it is not long; miserable fools learn at the end that life was short that they held by losing. Therefore Solomon was right to say, *Even if a man should live many years and be happy in all of them, he ought to remember dark times and the many days which will come and inflict vanity.** When the fool-ish mind suddenly encounters evil that never passes away, it understands by undergoing its endlessness that what could pass away was vanity. What we must know, however, is this: many people desire to do what is right, but many things in this present life oppose their weak intentions. Since they fear the suffering of adversity in small things, they are out of step with God's righteous judgment. Therefore Job is right to add,

*Eccl 11:8

XXVI. 32. *Those who are afraid of frost will be
buried in snow.** Frost indeed rises from the ground,
whereas snow rushes down from the sky. It often happens that when some people are afraid of times of adversity, they expose themselves to the severity of eternal
judgment. The psalmist in fact tells us, *They shook from
fear, when there was nothing to fear.** Certain people
now desire to defend the truth openly, yet in their very
desire they shake with fear of arousing the wrath of
human power. And when they fear people on earth, contrary to truth, they are subject to the wrath of that same
truth from heaven.

    Others, aware of their sins, now want to bestow their
possessions on the needy, yet they are worried lest they
themselves should be in need of the goods bestowed. So
they fearfully reserve support for their bodily needs and
thereby deprive their soul of the nourishment of mercy;
afraid to suffer want on earth, they cut themselves off
from the eternal abundance of heavenly food. Accordingly, Job was right to say, *Those who are afraid of frost
will be buried in snow.** Those who fear here below what
they should trample upon, you see, will suffer on high
what they ought to fear; when they refuse to pass up
what they could have trampled upon, they will be judged
from above with a judgment they can hardly bear. Yet
in acting thus they are honored in this world. What then
are they going to do when they are called, when they
fearfully abandon all those things at once that they kept
here on earth with such concern? So Job rightly adds,

XXVII. 33. *On the day of their discomfiture they will
perish.** Those, you see, whose life is subjected to the
cares of the present world are discomfited by loss. Then
they will also perish externally who internally perished
long ago by neglecting eternal realities. Job adds the following words concerning them: *Just as they grow warm,*

* Job 6:16

* Ps 13:5

* Job 6:16

* Job 6:17

*Job 6:17 *they are toppled from their place.** Whenever wicked people grow warm, they are toppled from their place, because when they draw near the judgment of internal severity and already begin to feel the heat, knowing the punishment due, they are loosened from the pleasure of the flesh to which they had clung so long.

This is exactly what the prophet reproaches sinners with when he says, *Nothing but harsh treatment will* *Isa 28:19 *make them hear and understand.** They obviously do not understand eternal reality until they are punished for their works in life, but now without hope of amendment. Then the mind grows warm and burns with the fire of fruitless penitence. Such people are afraid of being led to punishment; they cling to the present life by desire, but they are toppled from their place, because they lose delight in the flesh, whose solidity is broken by punishment.

But now, since we have heard what all the wicked suffer when they are taken away, let us hear something more of their lot during the time while they are still free:

XXVIII. 34. *Their footsteps are turned around in the* *Job 6:18 *path.** Whatever is turned around repeats itself. There are people who are determined to use all their willpower to resist the vices that seduce them, but when a temptation actually attacks them, they do not carry through their determined intention. Some people, let us say, are swollen with the depraved boldness of pride, but, seeing that great esteem is accorded to humility, they rise up against themselves and cut off a growth, as it were, of intense haughtiness, proposing to display their humility against whatever insults are offered them. As soon as a single word causes a wound, however, such people immediately return to their habitual bearing of pride, and its growth continues to such an extent that they have no memory whatever of their previous desire for the profit of humility.

Others are on fire with avarice and frantically seek to increase their property. When they realize that all things speedily pass away, they focus their minds, which were straying at will, and determine to give up any further wishes except to keep what they have, exercising restraint and careful management. Yet once they see something they want, their minds are quickly seized by desire, and they do not restrain themselves; rather they seek opportunities to grasp what they want. The self-control they had settled upon is forgotten, and instead they are excited by their thoughts and acquisitive desires.

Still others are spoiled by the vice of licentiousness; they are held captive by habits of long standing. They know very well, however, how wholesome chastity is, and they find it shameful to be overcome by the flesh. So they determine to restrain their open pursuit of pleasure, and they get ready to oppose their habits with all their strength. But either some form has caught their eye or a sudden temptation has reminded them of it; in any case they are quickly turned aside from their first determination. They who had lifted the shield of determination against the flesh now lie transpierced by the javelin of pleasure, and licentiousness has rendered them so powerless that it is as if they had never armed themselves with determination against it.

Others again are inflamed with anger and so lose control that they insult their neighbors. But when nothing happens to anger them, they consider how important a virtue meekness is and how noble is patience, and they patiently govern themselves even to the point of accepting insults. But when some small chance occurs to excite them, they are immediately incited to exclamations and insults from their very marrow, so that not only is the promised patience forgotten, but the mind does not even recognize itself or its own violent reproaches.

And when the mind has completely vented its wrath, it returns to its state of rest as though after physical exertion. Then only does it gather itself into the chamber of silence, not when the patient tongue reins it in but when the fullness of her bold revenge cries "enough!" And hardly even then does it restrain itself after giving free rein to insults, just as foaming horses in full gallop are not stopped by the hand holding the reins but by the end of the course. What has been said, then, about the reprobate is true: *Their footsteps are turned around in the path.** They desire, you see, and determine to do what is right, yet they always repeat themselves and return to their evil habits. Those who indeed want to do good but never abandon their evil ways are, as it were, straining to get outside themselves, yet they circle around and return to themselves. They want to be humble but without contempt, to be satisfied with their own possessions but without urgency, to be chaste but without suffering in their bodies, to be patient but without being insulted. So when they want to attain virtues but avoid the struggles required for virtues, what else do we have but people who have no experience of the battlefield and yet want to join the triumph in the city for victory in war?

35. Despite what I have just written about how the wicked turn around in the path, the text can be understood in yet another way. It often happens, you see, that some people devoutly prepare themselves for battle against certain vices, but they neglect to overcome others. Since they do not rise up against these latter vices, even those former ones that they have overcome turn against them. Somebody has already tamed the flesh and freed it from lust but has not yet restrained the mind from avarice. So when such a person leads a worldly life for the sake of practicing avarice and is not restrained from worldly actions, a chance occasion

quickly emerges, and that person also falls into lust, which had seemed to be already overcome. Somebody else has overcome the obsession with avarice but has not even begun to oppose the urge of lust. So when that person prepares to buy what is needed to satisfy lust, he also bends the neck of the heart for the yoke of avarice, which had earlier been shaken off.

Somebody else has already overthrown the rebelliousness of impatience but has not yet overcome vainglory, and when vainglory makes her a partaker of worldly honor, she is trapped by the strength of inducements and taken captive by impatience. Vainglory raises her hackles to defend herself, so she is trapped into accepting impatience, which she had overcome. Somebody else has already overcome vainglory but has not yet beaten impatience; by means of impatience he utters many threats against those who oppose him, but he is embarrassed for not carrying out his threats, so he again bears the yoke of vainglory; overcome by one enemy, he bears the other, which he had boasted of overcoming completely. In this way, accordingly, the vices help each other to grasp this fugitive slave. As though he had already been missed, they lead him back by right of ownership; they turn him over, one to the other, for punishment. They are perverse indeed whose footsteps are turned around in the path, because even if they lift a foot after defeating one vice while the other is still at bay, even that foot gets turned around by the vice they had beaten.

36. On the other hand, it does happen with those whose footsteps are turned around in the path that they overcome no fault, and at the same time they commit one fault through another. For example, we often deceitfully deny a theft, and the crime of deceit is often made worse by the guilt of perjury. Any sin can often be

committed by means of presumption and boldness; often too, and this is worse than any sin, we are even proud of a sin we have committed. Now it is true that we are usually proud of a virtue, but sometimes a foolish mind boasts about a crime the person has committed. But when one sin joins another, what else do we have but the footsteps of reprobate sinners turned around in the path and tied with double chains? Accordingly, Isaiah rightly speaks against the sinner's mind in the shape of Judaea when he says, *She will be a bed for dragons and a pasture for ostriches; demons will meet onocentaurs,*[1] *and one satyr will cry out to another.**

*Isa 34:13-14

What is meant by dragons but malice? What by ostriches but hypocrisy? The ostrich, you know, looks as though it can fly, but it cannot, and the hypocrite projects an image of holiness to all onlookers but cannot lead a holy life. The dragon, too, lies down in the sinner's mind, while the ostrich grazes; malice, in other words, lies down and covers itself with cunning. It presents a pretense of goodness to the onlookers' eyes.

As for the word *onocentaur,* what does it convey except that the people in question are figuratively lewd and proud? *Ονοσ* means "ass" in Greek, and the word *ass* conveys lewdness, as the prophet bears witness: *Their*

---

[1] Saint Gregory, no doubt, read *onocentauris* in the Vulgate, which transliterated it from the Greek Septuagint. Any classical scholar will say that no such word exists either in Latin or in Greek; thus Saint Gregory attempts to take it apart in order to make sense out of it. The Douai translates it as "monsters," which makes sense in the context. However, since Saint Gregory attempts to explain it through its hypothetical component parts, it is necessary to leave it untranslated. Briefly, a centaur is a mythological creature, half horse and half man; with *ono* in front of it (ονοσ, "ass, donkey"), the impression is that an ass replaces the horse.

flesh is like that of asses.* The word *taurus* ("bull"), on
the other hand, conveys the sense of a proud neck,[2] since
God's voice speaks of proud Jews through the psalmist
who said, *Fat bulls surrounded me.** Accordingly, onocentaurs are those who are captives of the vice of lewdness and who stiffen their necks when they ought to be
humble. They are enslaved to pleasure of the flesh, and
they have long ago rid themselves of shame; not only are
they unrepentant at the loss of righteousness, but they
also actually rejoice in the very fact of such disorder.
Demons meet the onocentaurs because the evil spirits
zealously serve the desire of the people whom they see
rejoicing at the very fact that should make them weep.

 So the text continues, *and one satyr will cry out to
another.** Who do these creatures called satyrs represent if not those whom the Greeks call πανασ and the
Latins *incubus*? Their bodily form indeed begins with a
resemblance to the human, but it ends up as unmistak-
ably that of a wild beast. By the word *satyr*, therefore,
we understand the harsh sense of any sin, which indeed,
although it begins with the possession of reason, nevertheless has a strong propensity for irrational impulses.
As the person ends up as a beast, so a sin begins with
a semblance of reason but trails along all the way to
the effect devoid of reason. For example, the delight in
food is often gluttony's slave, although it pretends to
serve a need of nature; so when it expands the stomach
to gluttony, it also sets up the limbs for lasciviousness.
One satyr cries out to another; the evil that has been
done provokes more evil to be done, and it is as though

*Ezek 23:20

*Ps 21:13

*Isa 34:14

---

[2] Again, Saint Gregory takes the word *onocentaur* apart. After
having dealt with *ono-* ("ass"), he now deals with *-taur* (Latin
taurus). Apparently he is not acquainted with the word *centaur*
or the mythology behind it.

when one sin has already been committed the voice of thought cries out for another sin to be committed.

As we have indicated, gluttony often says, "If you don't feed your body with more than enough nourishment, you will not be able to do any useful work." Then, when it inflames the mind through desires of the flesh, lust also adds words of its own prompting, saying quickly, "If God would not have human bodies united with each other, he should not have made the members so easy to unite." When lust suggests such things to the mind as though reasonably, it entices the mind to unbridled lust. When the mind is caught, it often enlists the defense of deceit and denial, thinking its innocence is preserved if it can save itself by lying. One satyr cries out to another when by some pretense of reasoning a sin, following the occurrence of a previous sin, ensnares the perverse mind. So when harsh and bitter sins engulf the soul, it is as though the satyrs agreed to congregate and take control, and it is again a graver instance of one's footsteps being turned around in the path; one sin joins another in the reprobate mind and binds it.

37. Nevertheless, we must also realize that it sometimes happens that the eye of the understanding is the first to grow tired; after that happens, the soul is imprisoned and wanders among aimless desires. So when the mind is blindfolded, it knows not where it is led and it gives itself up freely to the enticements of the flesh. On the other hand, it is sometimes the desires of the flesh that first become effervescent; after they have long been active in unlawful deeds, the eyes of the heart are darkened. The mind, you see, often discerns what is right, but it does not exert itself and decide boldly against bad action; its resistance is overcome because its very action of discernment is negated by the pleasure of the flesh.

Yes, it often happens that the contemplative eye is the first to be lost; later the soul is given over to forced labor in this world through the desires of the flesh. Samson is our witness;* when he was captured by the Philistines, he first lost his eyes and then was put to work at the mill. The evil spirits, you see, first gouge out the eye of contemplation inwardly through the stimulation of temptation; then they bind us outside to a continuous round of work. On the other hand, it does happen that we lose sight of doing the right thing externally while we still hold fast the light of reason in the heart. That is what the prophet Jeremiah suggests when he recounts how King Zedekiah was taken prisoner. He actually reports the event as internal captivity, for he says, *The king of Babylon killed the sons of Zedekiah at Riblah before his eyes, and the king of Babylon killed all the nobles of Judah; then he had Zedekiah's eyes put out.**

*see Judg 16:21

*Jer 39:6-7

The king of Babylon is the ancient enemy, the one in possession of internal disorder; first he kills the sons while the father is looking on, because he often destroys good works in such a way that the weeping captive may see what he is losing. The soul, you see, often sighs, being the captive of the desires of his flesh, and loses the good things that are the children of his love; yes, he witnesses these losses he is suffering, but he does not lift up the arms of virtue against the king of Babylon. While still able to see he is struck down by the performance of evil actions, but sometimes he is brought by sinful habits to the point of even losing the light of reason. So after the king of Babylon had first killed his sons, he put out Zedekiah's eyes, because the evil spirit first gets rid of his good works, then later puts out even the light of understanding.

It was right that Zedekiah should suffer at Riblah, because Riblah is interpreted as "all these." The light of

reason is sometimes blinded, you see, in the one who
because of the great number of sins becomes dull from
habitual evildoing. However the sin may appear, or from
whatever kind of circumstances it may show itself, it
remains true that the footsteps of the wicked are always
turned around in the path; they are devoted to evil desires and wish for no good thing, and even if they did,
their wish is halfhearted, and they by no means direct
unshackled steps of their mind to good things. As for
righteous aims, they never begin the journey to them, or
if they do they break it off; they certainly never arrive
there. So it often happens that they wearily return to
their accustomed ways; yes, they wallow in pleasures
of the flesh without attention to the soul, and they think
only of transitory things, caring nothing for those that
may remain with them. So the following words are apt:

XXIX. 38. *Aimless are their steps, and they will perish.** Their steps are indeed aimless, because they take
no fruit of their labor with them. One person sweats it
out trying to obtain honors, another is eager to increase
means, while yet another earnestly wants to deserve
praise, yet here on earth every one of them will die and
lose access to all those things, so they lose their labors
and gain nothing, and they take nothing with them to
meet the Judge. Such conduct is forbidden by the law
that says, *You must not appear before the Lord empty-
handed.** Those who do not provide for themselves the
reward of meriting eternal life by good actions are the
ones who appear before the Lord empty-handed.

That is why the psalmist says about the just, *When
they return they will come with joy, carrying their
sheaves.** Those who have good works to show for themselves, works by which they merit eternal life, are the
ones who come to the Judge's tribunal bearing sheaves.
And so the psalmist also says about each one of the cho-

*Job 6:18

*Deut 16:16

*Ps 125:6

sen, *Their soul is not empty.** That person's soul is empty
who thinks only of the present and cares nothing for
what follows in eternity. The soul of those who neglect
their life and prefer care of the flesh is empty. As for the
just, their souls are not empty; no, their constant intention is to relate all their bodily actions to their souls'
welfare, insofar as while such actions pass, the cause
of the action does not pass, and that cause prepares the
reward of life after life is over. The reprobate sinners,
however, care nothing for these things and neglect them.
Rather, they walk in emptiness; they follow life and flee
from it at the same time, and when they find it they lose
it. Restraint from imitating depraved sinners is best, and
that we do when we remember their end and loss. So
the following exhortation is well put:

XXX. 39. *Consider the paths of Tema and the roads
of Sheba, and wait awhile.** Tema is interpreted *south
wind*, and Sheba *net*. What is meant here by the south
wind blowing heat on our members and relaxing them,
unless it be loose inactivity? What is meant by the net
unless it is fettered activity? Those, you see, who set
their heart on eternity with dissolute minds, lest they approach God with unshackled feet, tie themselves up with
their own disorderly efforts. When they get entangled in
the loose practices of their own conduct, they set their
feet in the meshes of a net, as if they were going to stay
there. As I have said earlier, some people are led back
to faults already overcome through obvious vices not
yet overcome; so others return to conduct they had left
behind through certain acts that cover it up with either
a respectable name or an honorable gesture.

There are a great many people, you see, who even
now have no desire for anyone else's property; having
begun with a liking for a quiet life, they hold themselves
aloof from quarrels in this world, they thirst for the

*Ps 23:4

*Job 6:19

teaching contained in Holy Scripture, and they desire leisure time for the contemplation of heaven. Despite all this they do not abandon their concern for their family with perfect spiritual liberty, and as often as they do care for it duly, they also get involved in banned worldly quarrels. So in their zealous search for the protection of their earthly possessions they abandon quiet of the heart, which they had sought. Fleeting subsistence is protected by constant foresight, while the thought of knowledge of God conceived in the mind is frittered away. This corresponds with the conclusion of Truth that thorns choke the seed fallen by the wayside,* since the insistent solicitude for worldly goods drives God's word out of the mind. They walk with dejected steps in the net, therefore, when they do not abandon the world altogether; they shackle their own feet to keep from walking.

*see Matt 13:7

40. On the other hand, there are a great many people who not only lack desire for someone else's property but even leave behind all their own worldly possessions; they despise themselves, have no need for recognition in this present life, hold themselves aloof from worldly activity, and virtually trample upon any beckoning prosperity. Nevertheless, they are still held fast by the chain of blood relationship. They are careless slaves of the love of kinship, and the consequences of close relationship often cause them to return to those faults that they had already overcome with the contempt due them.

Furthermore, when they love their blood relations inordinately, they are drawn back to the world outside and separated from the heart's parent. Actually we often see certain people who, as far as their own interests are concerned, have no more desires with regard to the present life and have abandoned the world both actively and professionally; yet for the sake of inordinate affection for close relations they burst into the law courts and involve themselves in quarrels over worldly matters, they lose the freedom of interior quiet, and they again get excited about the world, an excitement they had long ago cut themselves off from. Where is it therefore that they are walking if not into a net? They had already begun to live a perfect life away from the present world, but inordinate love for earthly relations again binds them.

41. Those who with earnest zeal and not with faltering steps claim the reward of the eternal encounter leave behind everything they sense as obstacles, just as they despise themselves for the love of God. Also, since it is necessary to serve all those whom they are able to serve for God's sake, they must put aside all private duties, even those toward close relations, for God's sake. That is why a certain man who said, *Let me first go and bury my father,** heard this immediate reply *Matt 8:21 from the mouth of Truth: *Let the dead bury their own dead. You go and proclaim the kingdom of God.** We *Luke 9:60 must notice in this text that since the chosen disciple is deterred from burying his father, no devoted son is free to do this act of carnal affection toward his dead father because of the Lord, although because of the Lord it should be done for strangers. Therefore Truth again says, *If anyone comes to me without hating his father, mother, wife, sons, brothers, sisters, even his own self, he cannot be my disciple.** *Luke 14:26

In this text hatred for oneself is obviously mentioned after hatred for one's close relations, so we are clearly directed to hate ourselves as well as our immediate family, that we may hustle them off to eternal life and esteem their too human attraction less when it becomes an obstacle; thus the controlled skill of discretion will teach us to love them in the right way and to have a salutary hate for them. In this way love will cause hatred to arise, so that we may be able to love our relatives more truly through hate. That is why Moses could say, *He told his father and mother, "I do not know you," and his brothers, "You are strangers." Levi disowned his sons, but he kept your word and your covenant and obeyed your com-* *Deut 33:8-9   mands.* He wants to know God more intimately who for the sake of religion prefers not to know those he knew in a human way.

It is a grievous loss when the knowledge of God is diminished, if it happens with knowledge of the flesh. Anyone who wants more intimacy with the Creator of the world, therefore, ought to become bereft of siblings and relatives; to this end he does well to neglect them for the sake of God, and he loves them more firmly the more he forgets that fragile bond of affection that is based on a closeness that is too human.

42. We ought indeed to do more in a temporal sense for them with whom we are more closely united than for others; when a flame is ignited the fire spreads, but it first burns that place where it started. We must remember the ties of our earthly kindred, but equally we must ignore them when they impede our spiritual journey, inasmuch as even when the faithful soul is set on fire with desire for God it should not despise its lowly ties. Rather, it should give them their proper place in its scale of values and transcend them in its love for heaven. We must exercise wisdom and care and see to it that no merely human charm should secretly arise and turn aside our hearts from the right road or impede the strength of our love for heaven or pull down the rising mind by imposing a burden.

Accordingly, everyone should have compassion for the needs of blood relations in such a way that compassion does not weaken intention; rather, the mind's affection must fill the body, yet it must not turn us away from our spiritual progress. The saints, you see, do not lack love for their relatives when it comes to the supplying of necessary aid, but they are masters of their affection by dint of their love of spiritual things, inasmuch as they moderate that affection by means of the virtue of discretion, which keeps them from turning aside from the right way in the slightest particular.

The saints are symbolized for us by those cows that drew the ark of the Lord up the hill, moving both affectively and sturdily. So is it written, *They took two cows which were nursing calves, yoked them to the cart, and left the calves at home; then they put the ark of the Lord on the cart.** Later it continues, *The cows went straight ahead on the highway leading to Beth-Shemesh, lowing as they went, and they turned neither right nor left.** Now pay attention: the calves were left at home; the cows were tied to the cart holding the ark of the Lord; they moved on lowing, groaning from inside their deepest places, and yet they did not turn their feet from the path. They sensed love through their feelings of compassion, yet they did not turn their necks around. In just the same way those ought to keep going who are yoked to the holy law and who from now on bear the ark of the Lord through internal knowledge, to the point that when they feel sorry for the needy circumstances of their relatives, they do not turn aside from the road of perfection they have begun to follow.

Beth-Shemesh, you know, is interpreted *home of the sun*. Accordingly, when the ark is loaded on the cart and carried to Beth-Shemesh, we are meant to understand from that action that we are approaching the dwelling place of eternal light in the company of the knowledge of heaven. Then only do we drive to Beth-Shemesh when we tread the path of perfection without turning aside to the convenient side road of error, even for love

*1 Sam 6:10-11

*1 Sam 6:12

of family. That love indeed should hold its place in our minds but never hold them back, lest those very minds of ours be untouched by affection and hardened, or touched excessively and turned aside and become lax.

43. We can picture blessed Job, against whose heart's neck the yoke of the fear of God had rubbed; how great is the control of discretion with which he carries the ark of the knowledge of God! The calves are lost, and he lows, because he hears of the death of his sons and falls to the ground with shaven head. Yet he lows and keeps going straight ahead, since his mouth makes a sighing noise when it opens to praise God, as he speaks forthwith: *God gave it, and God took it back; God has done what he pleased; blessed be the name of God.*[*] But untrained minds do not understand how to live this way, and because they desire the ways of God halfheartedly, they foolishly go back to the ways of the world.

*Job 1:21

44. The holy man is right, then, when he mentions the roads of Sheba after the paths of Tema, because those who relax in the reprobate heat of the south wind are certainly caught in the meshes of the net. He describes the actions of wicked men correctly, and he warns us to take a good look, because we like doing perverse things, but when we see others doing them, we judge them harshly. What we think to be less reprehensible in ourselves, we determine in others as disgraceful. So it happens that the mind returns to itself and is ashamed to do what it blames in others. Just as a dirty face seen in a mirror is unpleasant, so the mind is revolted at itself because of similar things in others' lives. So he says, *Consider the paths of Tema and the roads of Sheba, and wait awhile.*[*] He might as well say outright, "See the ill result of another person's lukewarmness, and then you will have a stronger hope in eternity, if you see the unpleasant things in others with the eye of the heart."

*Job 6:19

45. He is right to say, *Wait awhile.** It is often true,   *Job 6:19
you see, that we love this brief present life, as though it
were going to last a long time, but the soul is then deprived of eternal hope. Enjoying the present, it is driven
back by the darkness of its own despair. When the soul
thinks the space of time long that remains to its life, it
suddenly quits this life and finds eternity, which it can
no longer put off. That is what prompted a certain wise
man to say, *Woe to those who have lost their endurance.**   *Sir 2:16 Vulg
They obviously lose endurance who think they are living
in the visible world for a long time and consequently
lose hope in the invisible world. So when the mind that
is anchored in the present life ends, those minds that
are deceived by their own presumption and think it will
happen either never or late are quickly led to unexpected
punishment.

That is what Truth says: *So be on the alert, because
you know neither the day nor the hour.** And somebody   *Matt 25:13
else says, *The day of the Lord will come like a thief at
night.** Since the one drawing near to seize the soul is   *1 Thess 5:2
certainly not to be seen, he is compared to a nocturnal
thief. The day therefore must be feared since it is always
coming, inasmuch as we cannot foresee a coming day.
That is why the saints, who are always aware of the
brevity of life's span, live as though dying every day.
They are all the more fully prepared for that which endures the more they always weigh transitory things as
nothing compared to the end. Accordingly, the psalmist
saw the sinner's life rushing forward at a breakneck
speed and said, *Just a little while, and the sinner will
be gone.** Somewhere else he says, *The life of a man is*   *Ps 36:10
like grass.* Isaiah, for his part, says, *All flesh is grass,*   *Ps 102:15
and its boasting is like the flower of the field.* James   *Isa 40:6
chastens the presumptuous minds: *What is your life? It
is a breath abiding for a moment.** He is right, then, to   *Jas 4:14

say, *Wait awhile*, because that which follows and has no end is great, and whatever ends is small. Obviously nothing should seem long to us that lasts its allotted space and stops being; while it is being led on through moments, its own delaying moments drive it forward. The place it seems to hold escapes its hold.

Accordingly, after blessed Job begins his speech with scorn for the brevity of the present life, he rightly attacks wicked people in the voice of all the elect. He adds,

*Job 6:20   XXXI. 46. *They have been confounded at my hope.** When the evil inflict evil upon the good, if they see their interior hope shaken they are glad that their deception found its mark. They count it the highest gain, you see, when their erring ways find followers, because they rejoice at having companions with them in their downfall. On the other hand, when the hope of good people is fixed internally and never falls back to its lowest ebb because of external trouble, depraved people become confused in mind; why? Because they cannot reach the intimate ground of the afflicted ones, and they are ashamed of their cruelty, which then appears vain. Let the holy man therefore say in his own voice, *They have been confounded at my hope*. Let him say it with the constancy of the entire afflicted and sighing church, which, confronted with the opposition of the wicked, continues to desire the joy of retribution in heaven without any failing of mental fervor, until she reaches life by dying. Job may even say openly, "Because the evil men did not weaken the hold of my rigidity by harsh persecution, they are ashamed beyond any doubt, and their efforts and cruelty are wasted."

Immediately he senses the presence of the good things promised by future recompense, and he awaits the accusation prepared for the reprobate in judgment. He continues:

XXXII. 47. *They came up to me and were covered with shame.** The sinners indeed come up to Holy
Church on Judgment Day, because it is then that they
are led up to see her glory, so that when they are banished to suffer the punishment due for their guilt, that
punishment may be the greater when they perceive their
loss. Yes, then does shame cover the wicked when their
conscience dooms them and bears witness in front of
the Judge. Then the Judge appears externally, but the accusation is felt internally. Then all their guilt is paraded
before their eyes, and their minds are tormented by their
own fire more gravely than that of Gehenna. This reality was spoken of by the prophet: *Lord, let your hand
be raised, that they may not see; let them see and be
ashamed.** The understanding faculty of the reprobate
people, you see, is for the present deservedly blinded,
but later knowledge clarifies their guilt, so that for the
time being they may not see what is to follow, and later
they may perceive it after they have lost it. Now indeed
they disdain the understanding of eternal life, or even if
it is understood, they desire it not. But later on they will
both know and desire what they see beyond any doubt,
yet they will not be able to attain their desire.

48. These words spoken by blessed Job especially fit
his friends, who tried to disturb the holy man's integrity
by reproving him harshly. He said, *They have been confounded at my hope.* He might have said, "While they cannot drive me to despair with their stupid reproaches, they
are confounded by the madness of their own temerity."
The text continues, *They came up to me and were covered
with shame.* He might just as well say, "When they saw
the wounds on my body but did not know of my soul's
integrity, they were bold enough to accuse me of injustice;
yet they still did not come up close to me. Nevertheless
they struck at me with bitter invective while they noticed

* Job 6:20

* Isa 26:11

the steadfastness of my soul in the midst of adversity, so it was as though they came up to me shamefacedly. They came to me, because they know me intimately. They are covered with shame, because no external loss touches me when I stand up bravely." There are some people who do not know how to fear God unless they are afraid of some adversity, whether of their own experience or that of others that they have learned of; prosperity makes them bold, but the contrary weakens and troubles them. And blessed Job accuses his friends of being numbered among them when he immediately adds the following words:

XXXIII. 49. *Now you are here, and you have only seen my trouble, yet you fear.* * He might as well say, "As for me, I feared God before, when I was surrounded by wealth and had been untouched by trouble. It is you who do not fear God out of love but fear him only because of the scourge of adversity."

* Job 6:21

XXXIV. 50. *Did I say, "Bring here some of your wealth, and give it to me," or "Deliver me from the hand of the foe and free me from the hand of strong warriors"?* * If these words are applied to Holy Church, since I have said that blessed Job's friends play the role of heretics, he is right to say he has no need of their wealth. The heretics' wealth, you see, is likely to mean the wisdom of the flesh; surrounded by such wealth unrighteously, their words proclaim them rich, but Holy Church does not seek it, because her spiritual understanding transcends it. Heretics often speak falsely about the faith, yet they do say some things correctly about temptations of the flesh against the ancient enemy. Where they sometimes pretend to have healthy limbs of practice, there their faith is wounded, and their head is held fast by the bite of the serpent.

* Job 6:22-23

Holy Church, however, does not want to hear any of their wisdom with regard to temptations, because although they say some things right about good practices, they end up in falsehood and unbelief. So Job is right to say, *Did I say, "Bring here some of your wealth, and give it to me," or "Deliver me from the hand of the foe and free me from the hand of strong warriors"?* He calls Satan's power the hand of the foe, and the strength of evil spirits he calls the hand of strong warriors. He calls them strong warriors for the reason that they were made without the weakness of the flesh. No such weakness withstands their evil attacks. But here he goes on:

XXXV. 51. *Teach me, and I will be silent; if there is something I do not know, instruct me.** It seems to me   *Job 6:24
unclear how this sentence is to be construed, whether it follows the question earlier put, *Did I say?* Or is it separate from what precedes and spoken by way of provocation? *Teach me, and I will be silent; if there is something I do not know, instruct me.** Actually it fits   *Job 6:24
both constructions, or rather it departs from the path of sound meaning by neither. But since I have already interpreted it allegorically, it remains for me to examine the literal words according to the moral sense.

52. Blessed Job had suffered the loss of his possessions, he had been delivered up to buffeting from the evil spirits, and he felt the pain of their wounds. Nevertheless, he was a lover of God's wise foolishness, he who had trampled upon the foolish wisdom of the world by despising it in his mind. Therefore he is called poor against the rich of the world, an oppressed person against the powerful ones, a fool against the wise. He gave three answers, because neither as a poor man did he seek their wealth, nor as an oppressed person did he seek help against stout warriors, nor as a fool did he seek the teaching of the wisdom of the flesh. The holy man, you see, was mentally raised above himself in such a way that being poor and needy did not distress

him, that he did not suffer from oppression, and that in his voluntary foolishness he was not surprised at the wisdom of the flesh. That is why another oppressed poor man said, *We are perplexed, but not forsaken; we suffer persecution, but we are not abandoned; we are struck down, but not destroyed.**

*2 Cor 4:8-9

Paul further infers the wisdom of holy foolishness and says, *God chose the foolish people of the world in order to shame the wise*, and *If any of you seems to be worldly wise, let him become a fool, that he may be wise.** That is why he elucidates the glory of oppression and the wealth of coveted poverty and says, *We seem to be dying, and yet we live; we seem to be punished, but we are not put to death; we seem to be grieving, yet we are full of joy; we seem to be needy, yet we enrich many; we seem to have nothing, but we possess everything.**

*1 Cor 1:27; 3:18

*2 Cor 6:9-10

53. These considerations allow us to raise the eyes of our mind to the chosen servants of God who are oppressed externally and see the greatness of the interior citadel over which they preside. All that is lofty in the external world definitely lies flat to their hidden gaze and contempt. They are enraptured interiorly above themselves, and their soul is fixed in heaven; they see whatever happens to them in this life as though it were taking place far beneath them. If I may speak thus, while they are trying to be free of the flesh mentally, they virtually do not know the things they undergo. Whatever is conspicuous in time on earth is definitely unimportant in their eyes. They are, as it were, seated on the peak of a high mountain, looking down on the plain of the present life, and they transcend even themselves by that lofty spirituality; whenever the glory of the flesh flouts itself externally, they are internally unmoved.

They do not allow any earthly rulers to go against the truth, but when they notice pride lifting itself up, their spiritual authority casts it down. Therefore, when Moses came up from the desert, he authoritatively confronted the king of Egypt and said, *Thus says the Lord, the God of the Hebrews, "How long will you refuse subjection to me? Dismiss my people, that they may offer sacrifice to me."* * When he was dejected by plagues, Pharaoh said, *Go and offer sacrifice to your God in this land.* * With his authority increased, Moses responded forthwith, *We cannot do it here. Shall we offer to the Lord our God sacrifices that are abominations to the Egyptians?* * In the same way Nathan confronted the sinful King David and first presented him with a similar case to the crime he committed, holding him guilty by the judgment of his own mouth, and spoke up immediately: *You are the man who has done this deed.* * So also the man of God who was sent to Samaria to destroy idolatry while King Jeroboam was offering incense on the altar, without fear of the king, under no constraint or fear of death, fearlessly pronounced the following curse against the altar with the authority of untrammeled voice: *O altar, altar, thus says the Lord: "Behold a son will be born to the house of David, Josiah by name, and he will sacrifice upon you the priests of the high places."* *

There was also proud Ahab, who was sold into the slavery of idols. He was so presumptuous that he taunted Elijah and said, *Aren't you the troubler of Israel?* * Elijah immediately attacked the foolishly proud king with authoritatively free invective and said, *I am not the troubler of Israel, but you and your father's house are. You have forsaken the command of the Lord and followed the Baals.* * Elisha, for his part, was a true follower of the heavenly wisdom of his master; when Joram, Ahab's son, came to him with King Jehoshaphat, he shamed him for his guilt of faithlessness and said, *What are you*

* Exod 10:3

* Exod 8:25

* Exod 8:26

* 2 Sam 12:7

* 1 Kgs 13:2

* 1 Kgs 18:17

* 1 Kgs 18:18

*2 Kgs 3:13

*coming to me for? Go to the prophets of your father and mother.** He also said, *As the Lord of Hosts lives before whom I stand, if it were not for my respect for the presence of King Jehoshaphat of Judah, I would neither*

*2 Kgs 3:14

*look at you nor see you.**

This same Elisha kept Naaman waiting at the door of his house when he came to him with horses and chariots; when he offered money and festal garments, he would not see him or open the door; instead he sent a messenger to tell him to wash in the Jordan seven times. So Naaman went away angrily and said, *I thought he*

*2 Kgs 5:11

*would come out to see me.** In the same line, when the chief priests threatened Peter with flogging and forbade him to speak in the name of Jesus, he answered with great authority unhesitatingly, *It is for you to judge whether it is better in God's sight to obey you instead of God. As for us, we cannot refrain from speaking of*

*Acts 4:19-20

*what we have seen and heard.**

Paul, for his part, when he saw the high priest sitting in judgment against the truth, and when his servant slapped his face, did not angrily curse him but prophesied in the fullness of the Spirit with untrammeled tongue: *God will strike you, you whitewashed wall! Do you sit in judgment over me according to the law and*

*Acts 23:3

*order me to be struck against the law?** Finally, Stephen was not afraid to lift up his voice with authority against the violence of his persecutors, even when about to die. He said, *You stiff-necked people with uncircumcised hearts and ears, you always resist the Holy Spirit. You*

*Acts 7:51

*are just like your fathers.**

54. The saints clearly show that they are not inspired by the vice of pride but by zeal for the truth to speak such lofty words, and they reveal the deep humility that is the source of their strength by other words and deeds, as well as the warmth of their love toward those

whom they reprove. Pride indeed begets hate, whereas humility begets love. The words that love makes bitter certainly rise from the source of humility. How could Stephen have reacted out of pride, when he got down on his knees and prayed for those he accused, who were getting worse and even stoning him? He prayed, *Lord, do not hold this sin against them.** How did Paul speak severely against the high priest of his people out of pride when he cast himself down in servitude at his disciples' feet out of humility? Did he not say, *We do not preach ourselves, but Jesus Christ our Lord; we, however, are your slaves through Christ?**

*Acts 7:60

*2 Cor 4:5

How did Peter resist the leaders out of pride when he sympathized with their mistake and excused their guilt? He said, *I know you acted through ignorance, and so did your leaders. It was God who fulfilled in this way what he had foretold through all the prophets, namely that his Christ would suffer.** Out of mercy he enticed them to life and said, *Repent and be converted, that your sins may be blotted out.** How did Elisha refuse to see Naaman out of pride when he consented to be not only seen but even touched by a woman? It is of that woman we read, *When she came to the man of God on the mountain, she grasped his feet. Ghazi approached in order to extricate her, but the man of God said, "Let her go; her soul is sad."**

*Acts 3:17-18

*Acts 3:19

*2 Kgs 4:27

How did Elijah reprove the proud king out of pride when he humbly ran ahead of his chariot? It is written, *With girt loins he ran ahead of Ahab.** How did the man of God scorn Jeroboam's presence out of pride when he restored his withered hand to its former healthy state out of a caring regard for the man? Here is what we read: *When the king heard the words of the man of God, which he shouted against the altar of Bethel, he stretched out his hand from the altar and said, "Seize him." His hand*

*1 Kgs 18:46

* 1 Kgs 13:4
* 1 Kgs 13:6
* 1 Kgs 1:23
* see Exod 18

*then withered up.** This follows later: *The man of God prayed in the presence of the Lord, and the king's hand was restored to him, just as it had been before.**

Pride clearly cannot produce signs of power, so we are shown the extent of humility that produced the voice of reproof by the signs that accompanied it. How did Nathan address words of reproof to King David through pride, when he threw himself flat on the ground before him at a time when there was no sin for him to reprove? Here is what we read: *They told the king, "Nathan the prophet is here." When he entered the king's presence, Nathan did obeisance to him by prostrating himself on the ground.** How could Moses scorn the king of Egypt when he bravely stood up to him? While he was speaking to God familiarly, Jethro, his father-in-law, came up to him, and he humbly bowed down to him. What is more, he held his advice in such esteem that after his hidden conversation with God, he considered it great profit what he heard from the lips of a man externally.*

55. We learn from the acts of some of the saints how we should interpret the others. The saints, you see, do not speak freely out of pride, nor are they submissive out of fear. When they feel free to raise their voice out of righteousness, they remember their own weakness and retain their humility. They indeed speak out and attack crime and criminals courageously, but at the same time they wisely judge themselves inwardly and put themselves in the place of the lowly. Just because they censure the evil actions of some people, they show themselves all the more severe in correcting themselves; on the other hand, because they by no means excuse themselves from doing better, they are quicker to reprove the deeds of others. What could they find remarkable in what people are capable of externally when they feel contempt for themselves, even when they virtually

draw near to the citadel of internal spirituality? They are right, then, to pass judgment on the external loftiness of worldly majesty, because the weight of swelling pride does not weaken their interior eye.

So when blessed Job encounters worldly wisdom in his friends speaking harsh words, he expresses contempt for their resources and eloquence. He says, *Did I say, "Bring here some of your wealth, and give it to me," or "Deliver me from the hand of the foe and free me from the hand of strong warriors"? Teach me, and I will be silent; if there is something I do not know, instruct me.* [*] He tells us a little later what he thinks of himself: *You attack an orphan.* [*] He gives us a clearer vision of how weak he considers himself to be when he calls himself an orphan.

XXXVI. 56. *Why do you belittle truthful words, when not one of you can gainsay them?"* [*] He who concerns himself with the correction of the faults of other people must be clear of guilt himself; he must not think worldly thoughts, nor may he be subject to low desires. He must be just as astute in seeing what others ought to avoid as he is honest in avoiding those things himself through wisdom and experience. The eye beclouded by dust by no means sees a stain on his arm clearly, and the hand that is full of mud cannot clean the dirt that clings to it. As has been handed on by an ancient tradition, God's voice intimated to David by means of a comparison that he had striven concerning foreign wars. He said, *You shall not build me a temple, because you are a man of blood.* [*] He builds God's temple who is free to correct and instruct the minds of his neighbors. In fact we are God's temple, we who are being built for true life, because he inhabits us. Paul is our witness: *The temple of God is holy, and you are that temple.* [*] A man of blood is not allowed to build God's temple,

*Job 6:22-24

*Job 6:27

*Job 6:25

*1 Chr 22:8

*1 Cor 3:17

because the man who still clings to acts of the flesh must needs blush at the thought of giving spiritual teaching to the minds of his neighbors. So we are rightly told, *Why do you belittle truthful words, when not one of you can gainsay them?** He might as well say, "How boldly you reprove the words you hear! Although you know nothing about the cause of my misfortune, you still utter refutations."

*Job 6:25

XXXVII. 57. *You compose words only to reprove; your speech is against the wind.** Two kinds of speech are insolent and very injurious to the human race. One of them is careful to *praise* everything, even the perverse; the other always tries to *correct* even what is right. The first leads downward with the river; the second tries to block up the streambed against the flowing of truth. The first is checked by fear, the second encouraged by pride. The first hopes to win favor by applause; anger, which aims to start a fight, drives the second. The first lies ready to agree, the second proudly differs. Job declares that his friends belong to the second class when he says, *You compose words only to reprove.* But he immediately takes notice how it happens that people go all the way to brazen words of unjust attack. He adds, *Your speech is against the wind.* Saying what is fruitless amounts to uttering words that turn into wind.

*Job 6:26

What often happens, you see, is that when the tongue can scarcely be restrained from fruitless speech, it runs on to the rash blurting out of foolish verbal attacks. There are, actually, certain definite steps that lead to its downfall, by which the idle mind draws near to the pit and falls into it. When we are too careless to avoid idle words, we soon reach harmful ones. In other words, we freely speak about the concerns of others, and then we go on to detraction and inflict pain on the life of the people about whom we speak; sometimes we even go

so far as to utter direct insults. That is how stakes of
discord are sown, quarrels are started, fires of hate are
lit, and all peace in our hearts is lost. Solomon is right
to say, *A dumping of water is the beginning of a quarrel.** The dumping of water indeed happens when we
let the tongue flow on into speech. On the other hand,
he also asserts with good reason, *Words out of a man's
mouth are deep water.** The dumping of water, therefore, is the starting of a quarrel, because he who does
not control his tongue destroys concord. In a different
sense we find it written, *He who imposes silence on a
fool mitigates wrath.**

58. Anybody who is a slave of loquaciousness cannot be straightforward as regards justice; that is what the
prophet testifies when he says, *The talkative person will
not last on the earth.** Solomon for his part says, *Sin will
not be absent from loquaciousness.** That is why Isaiah
says, *Silence is the cultivation of justice.** He obviously
means by this that justice forsakes the mind when it does
not abstain from immoderate speech. James joins in:
*The man who thinks he is religious without bridling his
tongue deceives his own heart; his religion is worthless.**
He also says, *Let every man be quick to hear and slow
to speak,** and later adds, *The tongue is a restless evil
full of deadly poison.** On his own behalf Truth warns
us, saying, *Every idle word spoken by men must be accounted for on Judgment Day.** An idle word is any word
that lacks suitability or necessity, or is not intended to
supply friendly help. If, then, an account is demanded
for an idle word, we must seriously ask ourselves what
penalty is due that loquaciousness in which there are
also sinful words of pride.

59. It is necessary to realize as well that those
people who slip into harmful words lose the state of
righteousness altogether. The human mind is shut in and

*Prov 17:14

*Prov 18:4

*Prov 26:10

*Ps 139:12
*Prov 10:19
*Isa 32:17

*Jas 1:26

*Jas 1:19
*Jas 3:8

*Matt 12:36

collected like water on high ground. It tries to get back
to the place from which it flowed. When it falls away
it is lost, because it is dispersed among low things and
becomes useless. By as many superfluous words does
it break away from its own silent judgment, as if by
just as many trickles it is enticed away. It is unable to
return within itself for self-knowledge, because it has
been scattered outside through talkativeness, so it has
lost the strength of inner contemplation. It is completely
laid bare to the attacks of the plotting enemy, because
it is not surrounded by any fortification or protection.
So we read, *That man is like an open city without a
wall surrounding it who cannot restrain his mind from
speaking.** Because the city of the mind has no wall of
silence, it is vulnerable to the enemy's spears, and when
it runs outside through words, it openly shows itself
to the adversary, who easily overcomes it to the same
extent that the mind has overcome itself, because it has
fought against itself through talkativeness.

*Prov 25:28

60. We must realize further that when we restrain
our speech because of excessive fear, we are confined
in a prison of silence more than is called for; while we
avoid careless sins of the tongue, we unwittingly get
involved in worse trouble. It often happens, you see,
that when we restrain our speech too much, we endure
accumulated words in our heart, so that thoughts boil
in our minds more, because the impetuous custody of
indiscreet silence locks them up. They frequently range
the more widely the safer they esteem themselves to be
from the eyes of those outside who might reprehend
them. That is how the mind is sometimes given over to
pride, and when it hears anybody speak, it looks down
on them as inferiors. So when we close our physical
mouth, we do not know to how many vices we open
ourselves by pride. We repress our tongue but give our

mind free rein. When we neglect to consider ourselves, we accuse others the more freely, since the accusation is secret, inside ourselves.

We are frequently too silent when we suffer unjustly, and our pain is still greater because we do not speak of what we suffer. If the tongue did speak quietly about the annoyances we are subject to, the pain would leave our awareness. Wounds that are tied up are more painful, because the pus seethes inside the wound, and its ejection soothes the pain and allows the wound to heal. Those who are too quiet when they see other people doing bad things and often force their tongue to be silent are like people who hide the means of healing from the wounds they look upon. They are the cause of death, because they could have gotten rid of the poison by speaking, and they would not. If, therefore, excessive silence were not a vice, the prophet would not say, *Woe is me for my silence.*[*]

*Isa 6:5

61. To what do these considerations lead us but that the tongue must be carefully controlled by a strongly balanced management? It must not be indissolubly chained, in order that it may not freely fall into vice or be so strictly confined as to be also slack and useless. A certain wise man said, *The wise man will be silent until the appropriate time,*[*] obviously in order that he may consider the moment opportune, forget the veto of silence, and speak what fits the situation, thereby making himself useful. So Solomon said, *There is a time to be silent, and there is a time to speak.*[*] Changing times must indeed be carefully weighed, lest the tongue be fruitlessly loosened to speak words at a time when it ought to be restrained, or lest it be sluggishly restrained when it could profitably speak.

*Sir 20:7

*Eccl 3:7

The psalmist rightly thought along these lines and encompassed them with a brief demand: *Set a guard, O*

*Ps 140:3 *Lord, over my mouth, and watch the door of my lips.* A
door is, of course, opened and closed. He, accordingly,
who asks not for a wall to be built over his mouth but
a door placed openly taught that the tongue should be
disciplined and restrained, also that it could be loosed
when the occasion demanded it; so far it is clear that the
discreet mouth allows its voice to be heard at a fitting
time, and that silence closes it at another fitting time.
Now then, either blessed Job's friends or all the heretics whose role they play do not know how to observe
this discipline; that is why blessed Job says their words
are spoken to the wind. Obviously any words that do
not support the weight of discretion hold only light air.

BOOK 8

I. 1. We have already seen in book 7 how blessed Job revealed to us the force of his humility when he said, *You attack an orphan, and you are trying to lay your own friend flat.*[*] In calling himself an orphan, you see, he evaluates the extent of his weakness; yet even his wounded affection cannot renounce love. He wants to know why they are trying to lay him low, yet he still maintains his friendship. But as I have already repeated often, his words are so particularly self-consistent that they also express through the spirit of prophecy the attitude of a faithful people by the voice of the universal church. She endures the opposition of heretics while humbly acknowledging her own weakness, yet she will not abandon the generosity of faithfully maintaining love.

* Job 6:27

The people of Holy Church are indeed children of a deceased father, so they are not without reason called orphans. His risen life, of course, they now live by faith, but they do not yet see it as it really is. The heretics, then, attack an orphan when they injure the lowly people of God with inconsiderate and false accusations. Nevertheless, the one they try to lay low is a friend. Yes, the faithful people of God do not stop calling to truth those whom she lovingly endures when they persecute her. But besides this, it is incumbent on us to know that the saints are not afraid to suffer falsehood through weakness, nor when they are wounded do they ever allow truth to be silenced. So Job continues,

II. 2. *Finish, however, what you have started. Open your ears, and see if I am lying.*[*] He is not afraid to suffer adversity, so he can say, *Finish, however, what you have*

* Job 6:28

149

started. On the other hand, even from his persecutors he does not withhold the proclamation of truth, so he can add, *Open your ears, and see if I am lying.* He could say outright, "Troublemakers give me no anxiety, and even from ungrateful hearers I do not conceal helpful words of correction. My training includes being hard pressed by misfortunes, and I progress in being kindly disposed even toward my persecutors."

For in this battle of temptation the mind of the saints is indeed protected by the shield of patience and armed with the sword of love; they arm themselves with courage to suffer trials; they extend their kindness in order to repay good actions. All this they do inasmuch as they both valiantly accept the darts of hate and resolutely return shafts of love. A man never goes forth armed for war, you see, if he grasps a shield but takes no sword, or if he takes the sword unprotected by a shield. Accordingly, the soldier of God who is overtaken by the war of adversity should carry the shield of patience in front of him, lest he perish; in addition he must be ready to preach by casting the spear of love, so that he may win.

Paul briefly alludes to the gist of this armed preparation when he says, *Love is patient and kind.** When one of these two weapons is missing, there is no love. Obviously, if a person endures evil people without kindness, he does not love them; if, on the other hand, he shows impatience, he neglects to endure those he loves. So in order that we may maintain true love, it is necessary that patience support kindness just as much as kindness supports patience. So we build a tall building in our hearts, where patience supports a citadel of kindness and kindness adorns the well-founded building of patience. So blessed Job with patience in readiness can say, *Finish, however, what you have started.* Endowed with kindness, he can add, *Open your ears and see if I am lying.*

* 1 Cor 13:4

3. Holy Church, you know, is instructed by the guidance of humility, so she speaks the truth to those who stray, not, as it were, teaching with authority, but rationally persuading. So she now says, *See if I am lying.* She might as well say outright, "By no means believe me as though I were an authority when I state these truths; rather, think about them reasonably and see if they are right." And if she ever says anything that reason cannot grasp, she reasonably persuades us that human reason should not be expected in hidden truths. But when they are given an opportunity to use reason, the heretics often drop all restraint and rush into opposition and quarrels. So Job quickly adds the following astute words:

III. 4. *Answer me, I beg you, without contention.*[*]   *Job 6:29
The heretics, you see, make no attempt to find out the truth by their investigation; they only want to seem the winners. Although they desire to appear wise externally, they are inwardly chained by their own stupid pride. So it turns out that they go looking for strife and opposition; they cannot speak peacefully about God our peace, but they make themselves finders of brawls out of a search for peace. Paul speaks the truth about them: *If anyone is disposed to be quarrelsome, we have no such custom, and neither does God's church.*[*]   *1 Cor 11:16

IV. 5. Then he continues, *Speak justice, then, and show it.*[*] When the speaker, you see, waits for the opinion of the hearer of his words, he, as it were, subjects himself to his hearer's judgment. The one accordingly who is afraid of being condemned by his words ought first to examine them himself while he still sits as an impartial and fair judge between the heart and tongue, thinking wisely that if he profitably accepts the true words offered by the heart, the tongue can then subject them to the judgment of the hearers. Therefore let blessed Job proclaim his own words against his friends   *Job 6:29

but at the same time foretell ours against the heretics;
so he can reprove hasty speech, and he can group words
for them to understand. He can say, *Speak justice, then,
and show it.* He could say it plainly: "If you do not wish
reproof for the words that come out of the door of your
mouth, hold the balance of justice within yourselves,
so that your words may be as pleasing externally by
their gravity and truth as is their internal weight on the
scale of discretion." Since those who know how first to
judge their own words assert righteous judgment about
somebody else's words, after he said, *Speak justice,
then, and show it*, he rightly added,

V. 6. *You will find no evil on my tongue, nor will
any foolishness be heard from my mouth.** He could say
openly, "If you weigh your own words more knowingly,
you judge someone else's more truly. When you begin
to tell the truth, you will know justice when you hear
it. By no means will you hear any foolishness from my
tongue, unless it proceeds from your own mind." So
Holy Church is eager first to show hostile assertions to
be false and then be free to preach the truth, since it is
when her enemies think their own position to be correct
that they obstinately attack the correct teaching that they
hear. Accordingly the heretics must realize the error of
their ways before they can stop contradicting the truth
that they hear.

Unless the farmer uproots the briars from the ground
by digging with the plow, the soil will not receive any
seed or produce any crops. Unless the doctor gets rid
of infection by opening the wound, the flesh can hardly
close up and heal in place of the infection. Therefore, if
Job first eliminates the evil, he should say, *Speak justice
and show it.* Then, when he shows righteousness, he
should add, *You will find no evil on my tongue, nor will
any foolishness be heard from my mouth.* The heretics,

*Job 6:30

you know, habitually say some things openly while they
keep other things secret. Open speech indeed is signified by the tongue, whereas a secret treatment is meant
by the mouth.

7. As for Holy Church, neither is anything evil heard
from her tongue nor foolishness from her mouth. No,
the subject of her public preaching is the interior faith
that she holds. She does not teach some things openly
while she keeps other things secret. What she thinks she
speaks outwardly, and what she speaks she lives and
preserves. It is from the banquet of eternal wisdom that
her sermons are preached, and whatever is preached,
she first tastes in the mouth of silent expectation. But
let blessed Job openly say all that he thinks, since he is
a member of the universal church, uniting his own heart
with the hearts of all the elect, that his spoken statement
might give notice of the integrity of his mind:

VI. 8. *The life of men on earth is warfare.* Instead   *Job 7:1
of *warfare* in this passage, in the ancient translation the
life of men is called a *temptation.* But if we attend to the
sense of both words, they will indeed be different when
understood externally, while giving us to understand a
meaning that is basically one and the same. What else
is expressed by the word *temptation* but a battle against
evil spirits? What else but maneuvers against an enemy
is understood by the word for warfare? Accordingly,
temptation itself is warfare, because anyone who keeps
watch against the ambushes of evil spirits undoubtedly
exerts himself in battle uniform. Notice, however, that
the very human life itself is not said to *have* temptations
but is proclaimed to *be* a temptation. It has fallen by
its own accord from the state of its creation and been
subjected to the decay of its own debasement while
it generates trouble from itself; in other words, it has
already become what it endures.

Human life, you see, yielded and deserted its state of mind, so what did it find in itself except movement toward change? Therefore, even when we now rouse ourselves to seek the highest things, we immediately fall back into ourselves, compelled by easy changeability. Humanity wants to stand still and contemplate, but it cannot. We try to fix firmly the step of our thought, but our downward tendency causes us to lose our nerve. This is the burden of our own changeability, which we certainly willingly sought out; that is why we now bear it unwillingly. People could possess their bodies quietly if, after God created them right, they had been content to be possessed by him. But when they plotted to rise up against their Creator, they immediately found in themselves the indignity of the flesh.

Along with our original guilt, punishment is propagated as well, so we are born with our weakness intact, and we, as it were, carry our enemy within us, whom we only overcome with difficulty. So the very life of people is a temptation, because they themselves give birth to that which ruins them. Even if by means of virtue they cut down what their weakness brings forth, they always give birth again by weakness to the offspring that they cut down by virtue.

9. So then, our life is a temptation in the sense that even if we now restrain the actual commission of evil, the doing of good works is darkened, sometimes by the remembrance of evil, sometimes by the mist of self-deception, sometimes by the distraction of our own purposefulness. Suppose now we restrain the body from excess; we still endure the images associated with excess, because we remember the things we have willingly done, and we endure as punishment what we once considered pleasure. Because, however, we fear being led back to a fault we had subdued, we restrain our desire by

the force of extreme abstinence, which causes our face to grow pale. When people notice that our countenance is pale, they praise us for our venerable life.

Soon vainglory arises in the soul of those who abstain, when they hear words of praise. Their mind is alarmed at this praise, and they cannot overcome vainglory, so they try to dissemble the paleness of their countenances, by which vainglory entered. So it happens that their minds are tied up in knots of instability: on the one hand, they want to avoid looking pale, but they are afraid to be again enslaved to excess by good food; on the other hand, if they resist the urge of excess by abstinence, they are afraid that their pale countenances will enlist vainglory. Others overcome the sin of pride and grasp at the status of humility with all their present longing. When they notice some haughty people butt in and seize harmless citizens, their zeal is aroused; accordingly, they are led to postpone slightly what they had decided, and instead they exert the power of righteousness. In fact they oppose the wicked not by meekness but by force.

So it often happens that by eagerness for humility we might abandon zeal for righteousness, or, on the other hand, by our zeal for righteousness we might unsettle that eagerness for humility that we possessed. Since therefore we could not observe both the forceful zeal and the proposed humility at the same time, we become strangers to ourselves by reason of the emotional disturbances; we even seriously doubt whether it is pride that worms itself into our deceived soul instead of forceful zeal or numb fear posing as humility. Others think over what an awful sin deception is, and they decide to guard themselves against it in the citadel of truth, so that no false word may ever again come out of their mouths; thus fortified, they would dissociate themselves from the crime of lying. Yet it often happens that when they speak the truth, they hinder their neighbor's well-being; so when they are afraid of attacking another person, they return to that vice of deception that was formerly suppressed, as though out of an eagerness for loyalty. So it happens that, even if there is no malice in their minds, the cloud of a lie nevertheless hides the sun of truth.

Therefore, because people are often questioned and cannot be silent, they either speak falsely to the pain of their own mind or speak the truth to the hurt of their neighbor. Others are inspired by love for the Creator, and they manage to keep their minds away from thoughts of the world by means of constant prayer; they settle their minds in the quiet security of interior peace, but in the very ascent of their prayer, while they try to rise above trivial matters, they are struck by the images of their weakness. Their eyes reach out for the vision of the light of their mind, but the mind is darkened by the body when images of worldly matters rise up. So it often happens that the seeing soul is done in by personal weakness and either abandons prayer and becomes apathetic and idle or, even if it continues to pray for a very long time, the darkness of rising images grows thick before its eyes.

10. Consequently Job was right to say, *The life of men on earth is a temptation,*[*] so that we even find the punishment of a fall at the very time when we expected to gain advancement and ascent, and our mind is confused precisely when we try to emerge from confusion; in this way we return to ourselves divided by the same path whereby we transcended ourselves with minds already whole and endowed.

Some people might be strangers to the teaching of God's law and hopeless of obtaining salvation because of ignorance. Other people might be endowed with the

*Job 7:1

knowledge of God's law, while they boast in front of others that their understanding of the law is perfect, yet because of their private exultation, the gift of the knowledge they received is wasted. Such people show up worse at the Judgment than others, although temporarily they were more enlightened than others. As for the former, because bestowed virtues do not raise them to a higher level, they turn aside from even the fundamental path of righteousness; thinking themselves cut off from the heavenly gift, as it were, they freely commit sin, because they do not receive the sublime gifts bestowed by heaven.

The spirit of prophecy fills the latter people and lifts them up to knowledge of the future; it shows them coming events as though they were already present. Such people are often lifted up above themselves in many situations, in order that the future may be truly contemplated, but the mind is led astray into self-confidence to the point where it supposes that the spirit of prophecy, which cannot be always possessed, is always present to it. So when it supposes that all its thoughts are prophecy and it attributes prophecy to itself without really having it, it also loses that prophecy it could have had. So it happens that instead of enjoying the esteem of all people, it sadly goes back to common merits. *The life of men on earth is a temptation.* That life is either cut off from virtue and cannot rise to the heavenly reward or, being endowed with spiritual gifts, sometimes runs away from the opportunity of virtue and ends up in a worse state.

11. We said awhile ago, however, that what we called warfare is actually temptation. It is therefore incumbent on us to know precisely that something more than what is conveyed by the word *temptation* is made known to us by the term *warfare*. We grow in our under-

standing of the expression *warfare* when we remember that warfare as a matter of course daily tends to an end; while warfare grows in a particular place, warfare as a whole is at the same time diminishing. *The life of men on earth is warfare*, because, as we have already said, all people move daily toward the end of life through an increase of time by living longer, and so they stop living. They wait for days to come, and when those days do come and make their life longer, they are already subtracted from the length of people's lives; it is the same with the traveler who moves forward step by step and whose journey grows that much shorter. In this way our life is warfare, since, as it grows longer, it ends more quickly and exists no more. So it is well said that *the life of men on earth is warfare*, because while people want to grow older by an increase of time, the same increase of time that they gather only to lose, they go beyond by growing older. Accordingly, this same course of military service is also fitly expressed when Job immediately adds,

VII. 12. *The days of his life are like those of a hired servant.*[*] Hired servants are eager for the rapid passing of their time, that they may receive payment for their labor without delay. The life of a person who thinks true and eternal thoughts is therefore rightly compared to a hired servant's life, because such a person considers the present life to be not the fatherland but the way there, not the bounty but the military service. Such people know that the longer they take to reach the end, the further they are from the prize. We should remember too that hired servants work hard at tasks for someone else but prepare their own reward for their own sake. By the Redeemer's voice is it said, *My kingdom is not of this world.*[*] Accordingly, all those endowed with hope

*Job 7:1

*John 18:36

in heaven, that is, we who are worn out by the labors of the present life, labor in someone else's employment. We are often forced, you see, even to work for the reprobate; we confine ourselves to giving back to the world what belongs to the world. So we indeed wear ourselves out in someone else's service; nevertheless we still receive our own reward. By this means we attain what belongs to us: serving someone else faultlessly. Concerning this state of affairs, Truth told certain persons, *If you are not faithful toward someone else, who will give you what belongs to yourself?** It also behoves us to know that hired servants take great care and see to it that not a day passes without labor, and that the awaited end of time should not come without any wages for them. In their eagerness for work they look for what they can get when the time for payment comes.

*Luke 16:12

When their work grows, you see, trust in payment grows as well; when, however, work slows down, hope for wages grows slack as well. Accordingly, all chosen souls count their life like the days of a hired servant and maintain their hope in the reward all the more truly the more stoutly they now keep adding to their work. They consider carefully where the present course of time leads, they count days along with works, and they worry lest the moments of time should pass without work. They rejoice in adversity, are refreshed after suffering, and survive grief, because they know that the more sincerely they now give themselves to daily death for the sake of the rewards of the next life, the more abundantly they will be repaid with those rewards. That is why the citizens of the heavenly fatherland tell their Creator in the words of the psalmist, *For your sake we are given over to death all day long.** Paul also says, *I die every day for your benefit, brothers.** Somewhere else he says, *Therefore I suffer these things, yet I am*

*Ps 43:22
*1 Cor 15:31

not put to shame. For I know the one I have believed, and I rest assured that he has the power to save what I *2 Tim 1:12 have entrusted to him until that day.* The saints, then, commit to Truth and display as many works now as the pledges of future rewards they already hold locked up inside closets of hope. Yet we feel feverish now in our works so that one day we may be refreshed and tranquil. Therefore Job immediately adds in a fitting manner,

VIII. 13. *As the slave longs for darkness, and as the hired servant waits for his work to end, so I too have had fruitless months, and I have endured nights that *Job 7:2-3 were difficult for me.* For a slave to long for darkness certainly means to seek the repose of eternal refreshment after the heat of temptation and its sweating labor. That is the kind of darkness one slave desired and said, *My soul has thirsted for the living God. When shall I *Ps 41:3 come and present myself before God?* He also said in *Ps 119:5 another place, Woe is me, that my stay is prolonged.* He so to speak runs away from the heat of hard work and looks for a resting place and a house of refreshment; he says once more, *I will enter the place of the wonderful *Ps 41:5 tent and reach the house of God.* Paul too yearned to reach this darkness when he had a desire to die and be *see Phil 1:23 with Christ.* They had reached this darkness when their desire was finally fulfilled, they who said, *It is we who *Matt 20:12 have borne the burden of the day with its heat.*

They are said to desire darkness and are rightly called slaves, because all the chosen ones, insofar as they are confined by their weakened condition and tied to the yoke of corruption that rules them, are in a way detained by the heat of anxiety. The one who has really been stripped of corruption knows freedom and is at peace with himself. Accordingly, Paul for his part rightly says, *The creature will be freed from its slavery to corruption; its freedom will be the glory of the chil-*

dren of God. The pain of corruption grieves the chosen   *Rom 8:21
ones now, but later the undying glory will raise them up.
Just as now no such liberty appears for the children of
God in our present hard constraint, so then for the servants of God no slavery will show itself in the glorious
liberty that follows.

Accordingly, when servitude to corruption has been
cast off, and when the dignity of freedom has been received, the creature is introduced to the glory of the
children of God. When the creature is spiritually united
to God, it is declared to have transcended and put behind
it the very fact that it is a creature. The one who still
wants darkness is a slave, because as long as one bears
the heat of temptation, one bears the yoke of a miserable
condition. Therefore is it fitly added *and as the hired
servant waits for his work to end.*   *Job 7:2

14. As for hired servants, when they see some work
that has to be done, their mind balks at first because of
its duration and difficulty; when, however, they get their
reeling soul to consider the payment due for the work,
their strength of mind returns and they soon exert themselves to do the work. Although they count the work
difficult in itself, they consider it easy because of its
payment. It is exactly the same for each one of the chosen: when they endure adversity in this world—when
they find their character insulted, lose their property,
and suffer bodily torture—they count these experiences
painful. Yet when they direct their gaze to the eternal
fatherland with their mind's eye, they find that their sufferings are light when compared with the reward. What
their pain showed them to be exceedingly unbearable
becomes light by means of the previous consideration
of the payment.

That is why Paul always gets up stronger than before
to overcome adversity, and like a hired laborer awaits

the end of his day's work. Yes, he does count what he endures to be heavy, yet he thinks it light when he considers the reward.* He indeed shows that his sufferings are grave, he whose prison experiences were many, whose beatings were uncountable, and whose deaths he admits were frequent.* From the Jews he received five times forty lashes less one; he was beaten with rods three times; he was stoned once; he was shipwrecked three times, spending a day and a night on the deep ocean; he suffered dangers from flooding, from robbers, from his own nation, from the Gentiles, in the city, in the wilderness, on the sea, and from false brothers. He was afflicted with toil and hardship, much fasting, hunger and thirst, cold and nakedness; he suffered external opposition and internal worry, and he declared that he was oppressed beyond his own strength: *We were stressed beyond limit, beyond our own strength, to the point that even life was too much for us.** Yet he also maintains that he wiped the sweat produced by such grievous trouble with the cloth of reward: *The sufferings of this present life are not worth comparing with the glory that is to come, that will be revealed to us.** Like hired servants we wait for the work to end, and while we weigh the increase in payment, we consider that the fact that we are almost worn out at work is of small moment. But the following verse is apt: *So I too have had fruitless months, and I have endured nights that were difficult for me.**

15. Chosen souls really serve the Creator, and they often suffer want; they cling to God by love, and yet they lack the necessities of the present life. Therefore in their actions they do not seek the present, and they spend their months deprived of the subsidies of the world. They also endure difficult nights, because they bear the darkness of adversity, not only to the point of being in want but

*see
2 Cor 4:17

*see 2 Cor
11:23-27

*2 Cor 1:8

*Rom 8:18

*Job 7:3

often even to the point of bodily torment. It is not hard, you see, for the minds of the saints to undergo contempt and poverty, but when hardship continues to the point of bodily affliction, then beyond any doubt the hardship of pain becomes severe. We may also conveniently understand that all the saints have fruitless months, like hired servants, because although they already notice the labor, they do not yet have the reward. They endure the former and wait for the latter. They endure difficult nights in the sense of accumulating the adversities of the present time by practicing virtues. If they do not want to make spiritual progress, they perhaps experience the adversity of the world less.

16. On the other hand, if this sentence is put in the mouth of the church, its meaning is slightly more clearly searched out. She indeed has empty months, when she puts up with false worldly actions in her sick members without the reward of life. She endures difficult nights, because she bears many kinds of trials in her healthy members. Indeed, in this life some things are difficult, others empty, and still others are difficult and empty at the same time. It is because of the Creator's love, in fact, that it is difficult to undergo the trials of the present life, but such endurance is not empty. On the other hand, it is because of the love of the world that we enjoy pleasures, and such enjoyment is certainly empty, but not difficult. Because of the very same worldly love, we endure certain adversities, and such an experience is both difficult and empty, because the mind is troubled by adversity and yet deprived of the payment due.

Concerning those who already belong to Holy Church and who wallow in pleasures, they are not enriched by the fruit of good works; accordingly, in them she spends empty months, because whole lifetimes are wasted without profit or reward. As for those who are devoted to eternal desires and who bear adversity in this world, in them the church endures difficult nights, because she undergoes the darkness of trials as though she were engulfed in the darkness of the present life. With regard to those who love the passing world and yet are vexed at its contradictions, in them the church bears empty months and difficult nights at the same time, because there is no eternal reward to be paid for their life, and present trials hem them in as well.

Job rightly talks about the church as having empty months, not simply days. The word *month*, of course, signifies a collection and sum of days, and the word *day* could express every single action, but the result of actions is shown by the word *months*. When we do anything in this world and are anxious with the eager expectation of hope, we do not feel that our own action is empty, but after we reach the completion of the action and our desires are not satisfied, we are sad, because we have labored in vain. Accordingly, it is not merely days but months that have passed fruitlessly for us when we realize not at the start but at the completion of our action that we have labored fruitlessly at worldly pursuits. When, you see, adversity follows our labors, it is as though the empty months of our life were brought home to us, because at the completion of action we recognize how useless the sweat of those actions was.

17. Sometimes Holy Scripture uses the word *night* instead of *ignorance*. For example, Paul speaks to his disciples, who have been told about the life to come: *You are all sons of light and sons of the day; we do not belong to the night or to the darkness.** Just before that, he said, *You, my brothers, are not in the dark, to let the day catch up with you like a thief.** Accordingly, in the passage we are considering we may take the words of Holy Church as coming from those of her members

* 1 Thess 5:5

* 1 Thess 5:4

who, after their own dark ignorance, return to the love of righteousness, and when they have been enlightened by the rays of truth, tearfully forsake their erring ways. Everyone, you see, once enlightened, looks back to see how base was the labor for love of this present world.

Accordingly, in them who return to life, Holy Church compares her labors to those of the weary slave and hired servant who desires completion, and she says, *As the slave longs for darkness, and as the hired servant waits for his work to end, so I too have had fruitless months, and I have endured nights that were difficult for me.*[*] In the comparison, you see, he first put two members; then in the expression of fatigue he added two further members. On the one who yearns, indeed, he bestows only empty months, because the more we require eternal rest, the more obvious it is how empty is our labor in this life. To the one waiting for the end he adds difficult nights, because the more we look at the reward we expect from the end of our labor, the more we groan that we have been so long unaware of what we seek.

*Job 7:2-3

Consequently, even the penitents' need is carefully expressed, that they might be said to have spent difficult nights, because the more truly we return to God, the more knowingly and tearfully we reckon up the labors that we have unknowingly undertaken in this world. In proportion as the eternal things that anyone desires become sweeter to that person, the more gravely is that one shown what was endured for the sake of present good things. On the other hand, even if the following words are interpreted according to the literal sense alone, they no doubt express the tearful soul and how it is driven through various desires and emotions, impelled by sadness.

IX. 18. He adds, *If I sleep, I say, "When will I get up?" I will again wait for the evening.*[*] Of course we

*Job 7:4

long for daylight at night, and at midday we long for evening, because, you see, sadness does not allow present reality to be pleasant, since it afflicts the mind through present experience, so it forever makes the mind move toward something else through expectation, as though desire were its consolation. Nevertheless, the afflicted mind is still led by its appetites, and even sadness is endlessly enticed by desires, so he rightly adds, *I will be full of sadness until it is dark.** We are given the reason for this sadness with his next words:

*Job 7:4

X. 19. *My flesh is covered with decay and filthy dust; my skin is dried up and pinched.** But we will discuss this verse in a more appropriate and exact manner if we return to the terms of the former exposition. By sleep is expressed sluggish inactivity, by arising, on the other hand, the performance of an action. The word *evening* again corresponds with sleep, so it also forms the desire for inactivity. Holy Church, therefore, never stops mourning her condemnation to changeability, as long as she leads a life of corruption. For this reason humans had been created, that they might rise inside the citadel of contemplation with their minds alert, and so that no corrupting influence might turn them aside from love for their Creator. But when they moved the foot of their will away from the firm state in which they were born toward sin, they immediately fell away from love for their Creator into themselves. They forsook the love of God, which is obviously the true solid citadel, and they could not stand by themselves, because when they fell inside themselves through corruption, stumbling on slippery changeability, they even opposed themselves. And even now they are not held firm by their creation, but they are always vacillating with the motion of changing desires, so that they want action when they are at rest, and they wish for leisure in the midst of occupation.

*Job 7:5

When their minds could have stayed firm, they refused, so now they cannot stay firm, even when they want to. They forsook contemplation of their Creator, so they lost their protection and safety, and wherever they are put they always weakly seek some other place. So, to express the changeability of the human mind, Job can say, *If I sleep, I say, "When will I get up?" I will again wait for the evening.*[*] He could say it outright: "Nothing the mind receives satisfies it, because it has lost that which could really satisfy it. When asleep I want to get up. When I get up, I wait for the evening. When I am resting, I desire action and motion, and when I am in motion, I want rest and quiet."

    *Job 7:4

20. The verse can be understood in yet another way. Sleep means falling into sin. If, you see, the word *sleep* did not signify guilt, Paul would never tell his disciples, *Arise, you just, and sin no more.*[*] That is why he also counsels his listeners, *Awake, you sleeper; arise from the dead, and Christ will enlighten you.*[*] He says again, *It is time now for us to rise from sleep.*[*] Solomon, too, castigates the sinner and says, *How long will you sleep, lazybones?*[*] All the elect, therefore, when they are beset by the sleep of sin, try to rise to the wakefulness of justice. But when they do rise, they often sense exaltation in the very greatness of their virtues. Accordingly, they desire trials and adversity in this world after virtues, lest they fall into a worse state for their confidence in virtues.

    *1 Cor 15:34

    *Eph 5:14
    *Rom 13:11

    *Prov 6:9

If the psalmist had not known that his salvation would be more assured by temptation, he would never have said, *Prove me, O Lord, and try me.*[*] Job, then, is right to say now, *If I sleep, I say, "When will I get up?" I will again wait for the evening.*[*] Even in the sleep of sin the light of righteousness is sought. When the prosperity of virtues raises up the mind, she desires assistance

    *Ps 25:2

    *Job 7:4

from adversity, so that when the soul exults more than it should in the joy of its virtues, it may forthwith be grounded through the contrary nature of the present life and engage in mourning. Therefore it is emphatically not said "I will *fear* evening," but "I will *wait* for it." We *wait* for prosperity, you see, but we *fear* adversity. So the righteous person waits for the evening, because since he has to be tried by reverses, adversity itself becomes his prosperity.

21. The word *evening* can also signify the temptation to sin, which often assails the mind more fiercely the higher the spirit draws the mind to heavenly realities. Sin, you see, is never abandoned in this life by the practice of justice, so that a person might remain unshaken in that justice, because even if righteous practice should eliminate guilt from the citadel of the heart for a time, that very guilt that is expelled still sits down outside the door of our thought, so that when it knocks, the door may be opened for it. Moses also suggested the same thing spiritually when he described the parts of time being created materially. He said, *Light was made,*[*] and a bit later he added, *Evening came.*[*] The Creator of the world, of course, knew about human guilt beforehand; he then made known in time what now happens in the mind.

*Gen 1:3
*Gen 1:5

Light shines until the evening, to be sure, because the darkness of temptation obviously follows the light of righteousness. But the light of the elect does not go out in time of temptation, and we are absolutely not told that night has fallen, but that evening has come; the obvious reason for this is that temptation often hides the righteous light in the hearts of the just people but does not put it out; it is as though reduced to the paleness of flickering, but not extinguished altogether. The elect accordingly desire to rise after sleep, and after arising they wait for the evening, because they keep vigil for the light of righteousness after sin, and once established in the light of justice, they always hold themselves ready against the enticements of temptation. They do not fear those enticements, naturally, but they expect them, because they know how to profit even from temptation and use it to grow in rectitude.

22. But however great be the virtue wherewith they battle against their own corrupted nature, they cannot be certain of their own salvation until the end of the day of the present life. Therefore Job adds, *I will be full of sadness until it is dark.** For a while adversity bursts in; then for a while prosperity herself beguiles us with cunning cheerfulness. For a while vices awake and wage the war of the flesh; for a while they are defeated and entice the soul to vainglory. So the lives of good people are full of sadness until it is dark, because wherever the life of corruption is led, we are afflicted internally and externally. We have no certainty of salvation until the last day of temptation is over. So it is well that Job immediately adds the reason for this sadness: *My flesh is covered with decay and filthy dust.**

*Job 7:4

*Job 7:5

As we have already said above, humans abandoned the security into which they were born by their own free will, and they sank in the whirlpool of corruption. So now they either slip into impure works or debase themselves by illicit thoughts. They are, so to speak, painfully subjected to their own guilt. Their very nature has now become unnatural. Negligent nature even goes so far as the commission of sinful acts. A strict nature, on the other hand, is sullied by insolent thoughts of sinful acts. Decayed nature infects the flesh by the completion of sinful acts, whereas the eyes are clouded by dust, as it were, because of the levity of impure thoughts. By consenting to vice we are worn away by decay, but by allowing the images of vice in our hearts we are soiled by filthy dust. As he said, *My flesh is covered with decay and filthy dust.* He might just as well say, "Either the corruption of deceitful practices strengthens the life of the flesh that I suffer, or the darkness of thoughts troubled by the memories of vice has pressed down upon me."

23. If on the other hand we take the verse to be spoken by the universal church, at one time we certainly find her troubled by the decay of the flesh, at another by filthy dust. Many of her members are indeed devoted to love of the flesh, and they reek with the decay of promiscuity. There are others who, although they abstain from the desire of the flesh, nevertheless have minds totally devoted to worldly pursuits. The church can therefore say in the voice of one of her members—yes, she can say what she suffers from both these classes of people: *My flesh is covered with decay and filthy dust.* She might as well say it outright: "There are many people who are my members by faith, but they are not healthy and clean members according to their actions. They are either given up to disgraceful desires, collapsing in decay and corruption, or they are devoted to worldly actions and besmeared with dust. In the former class I put up with deceitful people, and I obviously lament their decaying flesh, but in the latter I suffer those who seek earthly things, and what else but filthy dusty flesh do I carry?"

24. Concerning both of these classes at once, Job fitly adds the following words: *My skin is dried up and pinched.** In the body of Holy Church, indeed, those who are devoted only to external concerns are rightly referred to as skin. This skin does of course contract and dry, because the minds of carnal people love the present time and desire what is in a way put next to them, and they refuse to attend to the future by waiting for it. They

*Job 7:5

neglect the richness of interior hope, and they shrivel up and dry. If hopelessness did not dry up their hearts, the heat of pettiness would never make them shrivel up.

The psalmist was afraid of just such a shrinking when in his fear of mental dryness he said, *Let my soul be filled with soft fat.*[*] Soft fat indeed fills the soul when an infusion of heavenly hope refreshes it against the heat of present desires. Accordingly, the skin shrivels up and dries when the heart is devoted to external realities; its dryness is hopelessness, and it does not attend to love for its Creator. Rather, its thought is wrinkled and turns back on itself.

*Ps 62:6

25. We must, however, take into consideration the following fact: if carnal minds are in love with the present time, it is because they never realize how fleeting the life of the flesh is. If they really saw how swiftly it passes, they would certainly not love it, even when it prospered. Holy Church sees in her members every day how rapidly external things pass; therefore she internally holds the foot of anxious attention steady. So Job rightly adds,

XI. 26. *My life has passed more quickly than a weaver's shuttle.*[*] It is certainly an apt metaphor that compares life in the flesh to a weaver's shuttle, because just as a length of cloth grows by adding thread, so mortal life grows by adding days. But the more thread is added, the more surely will it be cut off, because, as we have already said, when we notice that time has passed, the time remaining becomes short, and from the total lifetime the years remaining are fewer, because those that have passed are many. The loom indeed is connected above and below with two wooden beams, so that cloth may be woven, but as quickly as thread is woven at the front, more thread is unwound at the back, so the more the cloth grows and increases in size, the

*Job 7:6

less remains to be done. In just the same way we, as it were, weave our own lifetime in front of us, and it is done, and we unwind what comes behind it, so the more our lifetime passes, the less of its future remains.

Yet even the loom does not express our lifetime well enough, because the momentum assumed by our life exceeds even the swiftness of a loom. So we are rightly told here, *My life has passed more quickly than a weaver's shuttle.* The loom, you see, has a certain slowness of development, but there is no delay in the fading of the present life. The loom's arrival at its end is indeed delayed if its operator's hand stops moving, but as for our lifetime, which is due to end, we never stop using it up. So we arrive at the end of our journey, even if we slow down, and we keep passing onward even when we sleep. Because the chosen ones know very well that the fleeting moments of the present life are rushing away, they never fix the intention of their heart on such a rapidly moving journey. Thereupon Job rightly adds,

*Job 7:6

XII. 27. *and it ends without hope.** So confined are sinners' minds by their love for the present life that they want to live here forever. They would even want their lifetime never to end, if that were possible. They have only contempt for thoughts of the future; rather, they put all their hope in passing things, and their desire is to have nothing except perishable things. And when they think too much about transitory things and hope not at all for things that remain, the eye of their heart is so blinded by dark insensibility that it is not in any way turned toward eternal light. Accordingly, it often happens that distress already shakes the frame and approaching death cuts off the force of life and breath, yet the sinners do not stop caring for worldly things. The punisher is already dragging them away to court, yet they concern themselves with transitory things, anxiously collecting and having no other thought except how they can continue to live in this world.

They dispose of everything that is to be left behind as though they were possessions, because hope of life is not lost even when life is at an end. They are actually being dragged away to court already, and still their only care is to retain control of their possessions. An obdurate mind thinks death is far away, even when it feels its touch. The soul leaves the body in such a way that it still holds on to the present life with improper attachment while it is being led away to eternal punishment, and it does not even know where it is being led. The soul then abandons those things that it refused to stop loving, and it suddenly finds those things that it never expected—without end.

The minds of good people, however, try to attend to eternity, even when the present life is happily associated with it. This association is of great value for the salvation of the body, even if the soul is not detained by trusting it. No suggestion of death as yet appears, but the soul sees its presence every day. Because life never stops weakening, the soul loses any hope of more and more life. So we are rightly told about the days that are passing, *It ends without hope.* He might as well say openly, "My mind has no confidence in the present life, because I trample upon all that passes, and I find it hopeless." Therefore he rightly adds the following words:

XIII. 28. *Remember, my life is as the wind.** Those people, you see, who do not understand the greatness of eternal life that follows love the life of the flesh as though it were permanent; since they do not take into account the permanence of eternity, they mistake exile for fatherland, darkness for light, and the road for its end. For when they do not know the greater reality, they can by no means draw correct conclusions about the smaller.

*Job 7:7

The proper sequence of judgment certainly requires that we be in a higher class than that which we presume to examine. If the soul, you see, is unable to preside over things, it can never see with certitude anything by which it is surpassed. Accordingly, the sinner's mind is not strong enough to evaluate the course of the present life, because love causes it to yield to admiration of it.

The saints, on the other hand, lift up their hearts to eternity, and they consider anything limited by an end to be too brief. Anything that passes becomes worthless in their eyes, because their understanding is enlightened and catches the gleam of that which, once received, never fades. When they see unending eternity, they never again have a great desire for anything limited by an end. The elevated mind is taken up beyond the limits of time even while the body is held fast in time, and the more it knows the unlimited higher truth, the more profoundly it despises whatever is going to end. Yet this very meditation on the brevity of human life is an offering to our Creator of high virtue. So this is also a virtuous offering that is now rightly presented with a prayer, when we are told, *Remember, my life is as the wind.** He could say it more openly: "Look kindly on a man who will quickly pass away, since you ought to look more mercifully on me the more I fix my own eyes on the reality of my own short life." When the present lifetime is cut short, however, there is no going back to the past for the sake of deserving forgiveness, so he is right to add,

XIV. 29. *My eye will not look back to see what is good.** The eye of a dead man will not look back to see what is good. Once the body is dead, the soul does not return to boast of its good works. That is why the rich man whom the flames of hell were burning knew that he could do nothing toward his own reparation. So he did what he could to help his still living brothers, not him-

*Job 7:7

*Job 7:7

self. Here is what he said: *I beg you, father Abraham, to send Lazarus to my father's house to bear witness to the five brothers I have there, lest they too come to this place of torture.* Even a false hope usually revives a dejected soul. But sinners also lose hope of forgiveness, so that they may feel pain all the more keenly. So the one delivered up to the avenging flames wanted to help not himself, as we have said, but his brothers, because with the help of despair he knew that he would never be free of the torture of fire himself. That is why Solomon said, *Whatever your hand finds to do, do without hesitation, because there is neither work, nor reason, nor wisdom, nor knowledge in hell, where you are going.*

*Luke 16:27-28

*Eccl 9:10

Accordingly, his eye will never again see what is good, because his mind has found its recompense, and it will never again recall the exercise of its use. So all that is seen is fleeting, and whatever is to follow will remain. Therefore blessed Job is right to include both realities in the same verse, which runs, *Remember, my life is as the wind, and my eye will not look back to see what is good.* It is while regarding the course of the present life that he says, *Remember, my life is as the wind.* Then he realizes how eternal the things are that follow, and he adds, *and my eye will not look back to see what is good.* Whereupon he rightly speaks in the voice of all mankind, deprived of the gift of redemption, saying,

XV. 30. *No man's eyes will see me.* The eyes of a man are certainly the Redeemer's mercy. When the Redeemer looks in mercy at our harsh impassivity, he softens it. The gospel is our witness, where we read, *Jesus looked at Peter, and Peter remembered what Jesus had said, and he went outside and wept bitterly.* When the soul leaves the body, no one's eyes see it anymore, because the one whom the grace of repentance does not restore before death, it does not free after death. That

*Job 7:8

*Luke 22:61-62

is why Paul says, *Behold now is the acceptable time;*
behold now is the day of salvation.* That is why the
psalmist also says, *Because his mercy is for the present*
age.*¹ Certainly after the present world, justice alone
consigns the one to punishment whom mercy has not
here set free. Thus Solomon says, *In whatever direction*
a tree falls, whether to the north or to the south, there it
will stay.* At the time of a person's death, either a holy
spirit or an evil spirit receives the soul as it leaves the
body's prison, and it holds it by its side forever without
any change. So if it is taken up on high it cannot fall to
the place of punishment, and if it is drowned in eternal
punishment it cannot rise again to escape.

    Let Holy Job, therefore, look at the ruin of the
human race. Let him see that it is leaving the present
world without any knowledge of the Redeemer, only to
be buried in eternal hell without any reprieve. Let him
assume humanity's voice and say, *No man's eyes will*
see me. The one whom the Redeemer's grace does not
now see and correct, that same Redeemer will assuredly
not then look upon and hide from ruin. The Lord is
really coming to judge, and he looks at sinners in order
to strike them; when he sees sinners he does not single
them out for the bestowal of the grace of salvation. He
scrutinizes sin and knows not the life of those who perish. Accordingly, the holy man avows that he cannot be
seen by human eyes after this life is over. Thereupon
he rightly adds,

    XVI. 31. *With your eyes upon me I will not stand*
up.* He might as well say it outright: "You are coming
determined to judge. You do not see anyone to save, but

*2 Cor 6:2

*Ps 117:1

*Eccl 11:3

*Job 7:8

---

¹ Saint Gregory understands this verse differently than do
modern English translators: *saeculum* = "the present age" instead of "forever."

you do see in order to strike, because the person you do not see in the present life with the pity you can bestow, you see with justice in the afterlife and thus annihilate him." Now you see, any sinners who have no fear of God still live; they curse God, and yet they prosper, because the merciful Creator preserves them; God wants correction, so he waits. He does not wish to punish by looking at the sinner. So it is written, *You ignore the sins of men, that they may repent.*[*] But later on when he looks at the sinner, the sinner does not stand. Because the Judge is determined to find out exactly what the sinner deserves, the guilty one does not withstand torture.

[* Wis 11:24]

32. Nevertheless, the words are also appropriate for holy people to say; their minds always anxiously apply themselves to the future judgment. All their actions are a source of apprehension to them, and they carefully regard the greatness of the Judge before whom they are to stand. They contemplate the greatness of his power, and they recall how guilty they are, how that guilt restrains them, and how weak they are. They count up their own evil deeds, and over against them they pile up the good things the Creator has done. They carefully regard the evil that he judges exactly, and they reckon up the good works that he distinguishes, and they already know without any doubt that they will perish if their judgment is handed down without any compassion.

The very fact that we seem to live a good life makes us guilty if when he judges our life the divine mercy does not excuse it in his own eyes. That is why we read in this very book, *Even the stars are not pure in his sight.*[*] When he judges them strictly, he finds that even they, when they shine with holy purity, have dirty spots on them. So Job is right to say, *With your eyes upon me I will not stand up*. It is as if he said outright, impersonating the just man, "If I be grilled under detailed interrogation, when

[* Job 25:5]

judgment is delivered I will not stand up, because there is not enough life for the penalty if that savage but just retribution suppresses it." It is well that both the guilt, albeit briefly, and the penalty of the human race are put forward, when we are immediately told,

XVII. 33. *As a cloud is dissipated and passes away,* *Job 7:9 *so the man who goes down to hell will not reascend.** To be sure a cloud is held up toward the sky, but when it thickens and the wind blows it moves away; then the sun warms it, and it scatters and disappears. The hearts of humans are certainly like that; nature gives us reason, which causes our hearts to leap to the stars, but then the wind of evil spirits pushes us, and our hearts are pulled this way and that by the motion of our evil desires. The searching eye of the heavenly Judge is like the heat of the sun; it dissolves our hearts, which, once delivered to the regions of woe, do not return to their accustomed practices.

Let Holy Job accordingly express the way of pride and the course and fall of the human race when he says, *As a cloud is dissipated and passes away, so the man who goes down to hell will not reascend.* He could say it outright: "By striding on the heights the one falls who by becoming proud aims at ruin. If guilt once drags a person to pay the penalty, no mercy will ever lead him back to forgiveness." Therefore he adds still more:

*Job 7:10 XVIII. 34. *He will never return to his home.** Just as a home is the dwelling place of a person's body, so the home of any mind is that in which the person is accustomed to abide by desire. The person then returns home no more, because everyone who is once delivered to eternal punishment is never again recalled to the object of previous affections. The sinner's hopelessness can also be meant by the word *hell*, and the psalmist *Ps 6:6 speaks of this: *Who will praise you in hell?** Someone else says, *When the evil person reaches the deepest sin, he reaches contempt.** Whoever succumbs to evil immediately leaves behind the life of justice and dies.   *Prov 18:3

But those who after having sinned are also buried in the pit of hopelessness encounter nothing else but the punishment of hell, in which they are buried after death. Accordingly Job is right to say, *As a cloud is dissipated and passes away, so the man who goes down to hell will not reascend.* Hopelessness, you see, often accompanies the doing of evil, and then the way of return is cut off. So the hearts of those without hope are rightly compared to clouds, because they are darkened by error and thickened by repeated sins, but they are broken up and pass away, because when the brightness of the Last Judgment shines upon them, they scatter.

As for home, it can also mean the dwelling place of the heart. That is why a certain man who was cured was told, *Go to your house,** since the proper procedure is surely for sinners to return to their right mind after forgiveness, lest they should again admit that for which they could be righteously struck. But those who go down to hell will not reascend to their home anymore, because those buried in hopelessness have been put outside the dwelling place of their heart and cannot go back inside; they have rushed outside and are driven every day to commit worse crimes. We of course were created to contemplate the Creator, always to seek his beauty, and to live in the temple dedicated to his love. But by disobedience we have been cast outside of ourselves, and we have lost the place of our mind, because having been scattered abroad by dark journeys, we have ended up far away from the dwelling place of the true light. So Job rightly adds the following words,   *Matt 9:6

XIX. 35. *His place will not know him anymore.** The place of humankind is certainly not a local one; rather   *Job 7:10

it is the Creator himself when he appeared and created us so that we might stand by ourselves. This is indeed the place forsaken by humans at that time when they listened to the tempter's words and deviated from the Creator's love. But almighty God showed himself to them even in the form of a body for the sake of redemption; in a manner of speaking he tracked the steps of the one fleeing him, and in order to hold on to the humans he had lost, he came as their place.

If, you see, the Creator could never be called a place, the psalmist in his praise of God would not say, *The sons* *Ps 101:29 *of your servants will dwell there.** We do not say *there* unless we intend to single out a specific place. Yet there are many people who even after they have received the helping hand of redemption sink back into the darkness of despair. The more contempt they show for the remedy offered them by his mercy, the more desperate is their loss. Hence Job is right to say of condemned mankind, *His place will not know him anymore.* The Creator will then be all the more adamant in not knowing them in Judgment the more they are not now recalled to the grace of repentance, even when they shine with holy purity when it is offered. Consequently we must very attentively notice what he did not say, namely, that they would not recognize their place anymore. Rather, he said, *His place will not know him anymore.* When, you see, knowledge is not attributed to a person but to a place, it is obviously the Creator himself who is meant by the word *place*, who comes solemnly to the Final Judgment and says to those who remain obdurately *Luke 13:25 wicked, *I do not know where you are from.** As for all the chosen ones, because they consider how absolute the condemnation of the wicked is, they carefully purify themselves every day from the stains of evil deeds that they have done. And when they see how those who

are going to perish grow cold in their life of love, they
eagerly and passionately give themselves up to tears of
repentance. So Job logically adds,

XX. 36. *Therefore neither will I restrain my mouth.*   *Job 7:11
He who is ashamed to confess the evil he has done cer-
tainly restrains his mouth. Surely the act of using one's
mouth makes it confess the evil one has done. Just people
do not restrain their mouths, because they anticipate the
wrath of the intransigent Judge, so they utter fierce words
of self-confession against themselves. That is why the
psalmist says, *Let us anticipate his presence by confession.* That is also why Solomon says, *He who hides*   *Ps 94:2
*his crimes will not prosper, but he who confesses and
forsakes them will find mercy.* That is also why he says   *Prov 28:13
someplace else, *The just man is his own first adversary.*   *Prov 18:17
But the mouth will never open to confess unless the spirit
is distressed by fearfully remembering the intransigent
Judge. Therefore the following words are apt:

XXI. 37. *I will speak in my spiritual distress.* Spiri-   *Job 7:11
tual distress certainly does loosen the tongue, in order
that the voice of confession may reveal one's guilt in
the case of an evil deed. We must know in addition that
even wicked people often confess their sins, but they
disdain weeping over them. The chosen ones, however,
after they reveal their faults with the voice of confession,
follow up with tears of determined censure. Accordingly
blessed Job was right to follow up his promise not to
restrain his mouth with immediate spiritual distress. It
is as though he openly avowed his intention in words
like these: "The tongue speaks of guilt in such a way, so
that the spirit, by no means destitute of the goad of sadness, may not wander among other thoughts. But when
I speak of faults I disclose a wound; when I think of
faults for the sake of correcting them, I am searching for
a way to heal this wound with the ointment of sadness."

Those, you see, who mention the evil they have done yet refuse to weep over what they have said are like those who uncover and display a wound but like mindless idiots apply no ointment to the wound. All that is necessary is that their voices sadly blurt out their confession, lest the displayed wound remain untreated, though already freely touched and fully known by other men, and become worse and fester. The psalmist, on the other hand, had not only uncovered the wound in his heart but also applied the ointment of sadness to the uncovered wound when he said, *I declare my iniquity, and I will reflect on my sin.** By declaring it he uncovered the hidden wound, and by reflection what else did he do but apply ointment to the wound? As for the afflicted mind that anxiously reflects on its losses, it arouses contention on its own part against itself. When it arouses itself to lamentation and repentance, it tears itself apart by hidden anger. So Job rightly continues,

*Ps 37:19

XXII. 38. *I will hold a conversation with the bitterness of my soul.** When we are despondent at the fearful thought of God's justice and we weep over our evil deeds, the very goad of our bitterness arouses us to shake ourselves up in a more vigilant manner, and we find in ourselves other sins that are still more worthy of tears. That which escapes the languid soul, you see, often reveals itself more acutely to those who weep. The despondent mind is sure to find the evil it has done without realizing it, and its quarrel with itself shows it the extent to which it has deviated from grace and truth. In security it did not recall its guilt, but now it is upset and uncovers that guilt. Bitter repentance lies deep, and it begins to grow strong; to the fearful heart it peremptorily brings up the unlawful deeds it has committed. Repentance confronts the heart with an inflexible judge who threatens punishment, strikes the soul with fear,

*Job 7:11

covers it with shame, scolds it for its improper emotions, and upsets the quietness of its culpable security.

The repentant soul enumerates for the fearful heart all the good things the Creator has done for it and, on the other hand, all the evil ways in which it has responded to these good things: God created humans in a wonderful way and nursed them free of charge; he created them with a rational nature and called them by grace, but even when called they refused to follow, yet the Caller's mercy did not despise their deafness and resistance; the Creator gave them light, yet even after receiving light they were blinded by evil actions that they committed by their own free will; they expiated the errors committed in blindness by the whips wielded by paternal solicitude, and then God led them back from the pains inflicted by whips to the joy of salvation by applying the ointment of mercy; again they were subject to certain faults, even though not serious ones. Still they continued to sin despite the blows of the whip, and even then God's grace neither despised the sinners nor abandoned them. Accordingly, whether by a replay of God's gifts or by shame at one's own actions, the soul's bitterness scolds the afflicted mind so severely that her tongue speaking distinctly in the hearts of the just is there heard internally.

So our text does not say, "I will speak in the bitterness of my soul," but *I will hold a conversation with the bitterness of my soul.** The goad of sadness, you see, reckons up each sin and arouses the languid soul to lamentation, as though it were forming the words of a conversation in which the corrected soul might find itself and awake with anxiety to take over its own guidance at last. So let the just man say with his own voice and with ours, when he plays the role of Holy Church, *I will hold a conversation with the bitterness of my soul.*

*Job 7:11

He might as well openly proclaim, "I hold an interior conversation with the bitterness of my heart in spite of myself, and I hide myself from the external whip of the Judge." But the repentant mind is constrained by pain and bound fast inside itself. She holds herself aloof from all bodily pleasures by means of her courageous intent and desires progress in heavenly things, yet she still senses the contradiction arising from the corrupt state of the body. So Job rightly adds,

XXIV. 39. *Am I a sea or sea monster, that you have* *hemmed me in like a prisoner?** We are hemmed in like prisoners because we often try to ascend the heights by progress in virtues, yet we are at the same time impeded by the corruption of our flesh. The psalmist rightly implores God that he might be stripped of this decadence, saying, *Lead my soul out of prison, that I may praise your name.** But what may we understand by the word *sea* but the hearts of pleasure-seeking people, which are stormy with the excitement of their thoughts? What is meant by the phrase *sea monster* but the ancient enemy? He gets into the minds of worldly people by possession and swims, as it were, in their watery thoughts. The sea monster is taken prisoner, because the evil spirit is thrown down to the lower regions, lest he should gain the upper hand and fly up to heaven; he is forced down by the weight of his punishment, as Peter bears witness: *God did not spare the sinful angels, but he cast them down to the confines of the nether world and delivered them to hell to be kept there for torture at the judgment.**

The sea monster is taken prisoner, because he is forbidden to tempt good people as much as he wants. The sea too is imprisoned, because the swelling and raging desires of self-indulgent minds are confined by the close quarters that make it impossible for them to perpetrate the evil deeds they have at heart. They often want to lord

*Job 7:12

*Ps 141:8

*2 Pet 2:4

it over those who are better than themselves, but God's judgment arranges everything in a wonderful way so that they are laid low by the good people. The proud desire to hurt good people, yet when they are put down by them, they look to them for comfort. They want to live a long life in the present time for the sake of enjoying the pleasures of the flesh; nevertheless they are swiftly snatched away from it. It is of them that the psalmist says, *He held waters as in a bottle.** They are indeed waters bottled up when their acts are not fulfilled, and their watery desires sink down in their pleasure-seeking hearts. The sea and the sea monster, enclosed and surrounded by a prison, are in fact the evil spirit and his followers; he makes their minds his home and therein commands the waters of proud thoughts. They are however subject to God's inflexibility surrounding them and keeping them from fulfilling the evil deeds that they desire.

*Ps 77:13

40. As for the saints, on the other hand, the more they contemplate heavenly mysteries with a pure heart, the more ardently they daily long for them. They already desire full satisfaction from that which they taste with the tongue of contemplation, although as yet too little. They want to have the goad of physical pleasure under complete subjection and to allow no improper thought to arise from its perversity. As the wise man says, *The corruptible body weighs down the soul, and the earthly tent depresses the mind that thinks much.** Yes, the saints are indeed remarkable, with their aspirations already ranging far above themselves, yet they are still subject to unpredictable emotions arising from their weakness, and they deplore the fact that they are shut in the prison of depravity.

*Wis 9:15

It is just as Job said: *Am I a sea or sea monster, that you have hemmed me in like a prisoner?** He could say, more openly, "Sea or sea monster, which obviously

*Job 7:12

means wicked men and their master the evil spirit, desire only the freedom to perform unbridled acts of wickedness, and it is they who deserve to be locked up in a prison as their penalty. But I already desire the freedom of your eternal life, so why am I still confined in the prison of my decay?" On the other hand, this is no insolent complaint on the part of the just, because they are incited by love of truth and they desire completely to break the bonds of their weakness. Nor is it an unjust arrangement on the part of the Master of the just that he delays the granting of their requests and torments them. If he torments them, he purifies them, so that they may be enabled to receive what they desire someday in a better manner, because of the delay. As long as the chosen ones are kept from interior rest, they return to the heart; there they are hidden away from the upheavals of the flesh; there they seek the most pleasant solitude. Yet there they also often experience severe temptations and suffer promptings from the flesh; there they find massive labor where they sought much rest from labor. So when Holy Job hastened to return to the quiet place in his heart from the prison of corruption that had been forced upon him, he found the same struggle there in his interior place from which he fled in the external world. So he immediately adds the following words,

XXIV. 41. *If I say, "My bed will comfort me, and I will find relief by talking to myself on my couch," you will frighten me with dreams and strike me with terror by visions.** In Holy Scripture, bed, bunk, or couch is often understood as the secret place of the heart. That is why the bride in the Song of Songs, who typifies each individual soul when she is moved to holy love by hidden urgings, says, *In my bed at night I sought the one my soul loves.** The beloved is unquestionably sought at night and in bed, because the invisible form of the

*Job 7:13-14

*Song 3:1

Creator, when every image of bodily sight has been put
aside, is surely found on the couch of the heart. That is
why Truth says to these same lovers of his, *The kingdom of God is within you,** and again, *If I do not go, the
Paraclete will not come.** He could say it outright: "If I
do not take my body away from your attentive eyes, I
will not lead you to understand unseen reality through
the Spirit comforter." Hence the psalmist says about
the just, *The saints will be jubilant in glory; they will
rejoice on their beds.**

*Luke 17:21

*John 16:7

*Ps 149:5

Obviously this statement means that when the saints
run away from external troubles, they will rejoice in
their security in the hidden places of the mind. The joy
of their heart will then be perfect, when they have no
external physical battle. As long as the flesh entices us,
you see, it is as though the door of the house shook, and
the internal parlor is also shaken. So the same psalmist again says, *You have shaken his whole house in his
weakness.** This means that when a temptation of the
flesh shakes us up, our bodily weakness in turn trembles
and upsets the den of the mind.

*Ps 40:4 LXX

As for Job 7:14, how do we interpret dreams and
visions unless they be phantasms of that last terrible
Judgment? We certainly visualize the latter through fear,
but we do not see it as it really is. Accordingly, the
saints, as we have said, always go back to the secret
place of the heart when they find unexpected prosperity
in this world or when they suffer adversity beyond their
strength; they are exhausted by external labors, and they
head for the den of the mind, as if it were a bed or couch.
When they see by means of certain thoughts and images how precise God's judgment can be, it is as though
they were resting on their beds and were troubled by
dreams and visions. In their vision they see a stern Judge
approaching; by the power of an immense majesty he

lights up the secret places of the heart, and he displays their faults to the eyes of all beholders. They reflect on the greatness of the disgrace at that time, to be shown up in front of the whole human race, as well as all the angels and archangels. They consider the torture that awaits them after the shame, when guilt consumes the soul that is dying eternally and hell devours the flesh, which keeps failing without entirely giving way.

So when the mind is shaken by such fearful images, what else are they but bad dreams that a person has while asleep? Thus Job can say, *If I say, "My bed will comfort me, and I will find relief by talking to myself on my couch," you will frighten me with dreams and strike me with terror by vision.* He might as well say openly, "Even if I avoid public life and retire within, even if I desire to relax in some way inside the chamber of my heart, even there you force me to contemplate your intransigence, and you terrify me violently through the very images of my foresight." But Job is right to say, *And I will find relief by talking to myself on my couch.* Surely when we return to the silence of our mind in our weariness, it is as though we were conversing on our beds, and we dwell upon secret words in our thoughts within ourselves. But even this conversation of ours is turned into fear, because it releases the sudden awareness in our minds of the fright induced by the threat of impending judgment.

42. Let no one, however, endeavor the close scrutiny of these matters according to the letter. Let us rather give all our attention to the question of how and in what ways the images of dreams affect the soul. Sometimes, you see, dreams are produced by a full or empty stomach, sometimes they arise out of illusion and sometimes out of illusion and thought together, sometimes they come from a revelation and sometimes from thought and reve-

lation together. As for the first two we mentioned, we are all familiar with them by experience, but we find the other four in the pages of Holy Scripture. If dreams in fact were not often started by the hidden enemy through illusions, the wise man would never insinuate as much, saying, *Dreams and idle illusions have caused many people to go wrong,** or, surely, *You shall pay no attention to auguries or dreams.** The use of the word *auguries* shows us how abhorrent such practices are.

*Sir 34:7
*Lev 19:26

Again, if dreams did not sometimes proceed from illusion and thought together, Solomon would hardly have said, *Dreams are the result of many anxieties.** If dreams did not sometimes arise from a mystic revelation, Joseph would not see himself surpassing his brothers by means of a dream,* nor would Truth warn Mary's husband through a dream to take the child and flee into Egypt.* Again, if dreams did not sometimes proceed from revelation together with thought, when the prophet Daniel was explaining Nebuchadnezzar's vision, he would never have begun with the seed of a thought. Here is what he said: *You, O King, were lying on your couch, and you started to think about what would happen in the future; he who reveals mysteries showed you the future,* and later, *You looked and beheld, as it were, a great statue. That large and very high statue stood in front of you, etc.** Accordingly, not only does Daniel respectfully support the fulfillment of the dream, but he also shows the thought from which the dream was born; so it is clear that a dream often arises out of thought and revelation together.

*Eccl 5:2

*see Gen 37:7

*see Matt 2:13-14

*Dan 2:29-31

43. Obviously, if dreams vary so much according to particular qualities, it should be all the more difficult to believe them the less easy it is to discern their source. The evil spirit often promises prosperity to those whom he encounters while they are in watchful love with this

world, even when they are asleep. When he sees those who are afraid of adversity, he threatens them all the more fiercely with adversity in images in their dreams, because he can affect simple minds in various ways and confuse them either by raising hope or by causing fear and depression. In addition, he often tries to weaken the hearts of the saints by dreams, so that they may be turned aside from the effort of serious thought even briefly, for a moment, although they immediately tear themselves away from the images of illusion. But the treacherous enemy, because he never overcomes them when they are alert, attacks them more fiercely in their sleep. God's kind providence, however, allows him to act thus deceitfully, lest sleep itself should be free of the gift of suffering in the hearts of the chosen ones. So it is well said to the Governor of the world, *If I say, "My bed will comfort me, and I will find relief by talking to myself on my couch," you will frighten me with dreams and strike me with terror by visions.** God surely

arranges everything in a wonderful way; he himself does what the evil spirit unjustly desires to do, and he allows it to happen only justly. Since however the life of the just is shaken by temptation in their vigils, since they are worn out by dreams and illusions, since they are troubled externally by their base nature, since they bear up sorely with bad thoughts within themselves, what can they do? How can they pluck out the foot of their heart from so many snares placed to make them stumble? Behold, O blessed man, we know how you are surrounded by turmoil, but let us hear the counsel you devise against it.

XXV. 44. *Therefore my soul chose hanging, and my bones chose death.** What is meant by *soul* here if not presence of mind, what by *bones* if not fortitude of body? Whatever is hung is without any doubt lifted up

*Job 7:15

from the dirt. The soul accordingly chooses hanging so that the bones may die, because while presence of mind is lifted up to the heights, it kills in itself all fortitude for external life. So the saints know most certainly that they can never rest in this life, and on that account they choose hanging, because of course they abandon earthly desires and lift their souls up to heaven. Once hanged, however, they bring death upon their bones, because in their love for the heavenly fatherland they arm themselves to strive after virtue; whatever they had been previously when they were sturdy worldlings they now tie up with the chain of humility.

Let us notice how Paul's soul was hanged when he said, *It is no longer I who live, but Christ who lives in me,*[*] and again, *I want to die and be with Christ,*[*] and *For me to live is Christ and to die is gain.*[*] He who recalled to memory his deeds of earthly fortitude was like a man who counted his own bones, and he said, *I am a Hebrew of the Hebrews, a Pharisee according to the law, and a persecutor of the church according to zeal.*[*] But by hanging his soul he killed those bones of his, so he immediately asserted, *But whatever gain I had, I counted loss for the sake of Christ.*[*]

He suggests further and more emphatically that the bones he still has are dead when he says, *For his sake I counted all things as loss, and I think of them as refuse.*[*] His bones are dead, and he makes clear how lifelessly he hangs when he says in the same place, *That I may gain Christ and be found in him, having no justice of my own from the law, but having the justice that comes from faith in Jesus Christ.*[*] But now, since by his collected testimony we have witnessed Paul suspended on high and dead to the world, let us look at blessed Job and see if he is full of the same spirit and shuns the concupiscence of worldly life.

*Gal 2:20
*Phil 1:23
*Phil 1:21

*Phil 3:5-6

*Phil 3:7

*Phil 3:8

*Phil 3:8-9

XXVI. 45. *I have lost hope, and I will never live again.** There are some just people who love heaven in such a way that they by no means give up hope of earthly goods. They have abundant possessions given them by God for relief of their necessary wants, and they hold great worldly honors that have been granted them. They do not solicit other people's honors, but they accept their own rightful honors. Nevertheless they are strangers to the very things they own, because they are not captivated by desire for their own possessions.

*Job 7:16

There are also some just people who have girded themselves for the attainment of the pinnacle of perfection, since their desire is for the higher internal goods and they have abandoned all the external ones. They have divested themselves of the external goods they had and despoiled themselves of fame and honor. They behave as friends of sadness, because they are enamored of internal goods, and they refuse external comfort. When they mentally draw near to internal joy, they kill the life of carnal delight within them. Such people are told by Paul, *You are dead, and your life is hidden with Christ in God.** The psalmist gave utterance to their voice when he said, *My soul longs and faints for the courts of the Lord.**

*Col 3:3

*Ps 83:3

Those who desire heaven already but are not yet free of earthly delight long for the Lord but do not faint. The one however who desires eternity and does not hold on to his love of worldly things longs for God's courts and faints for them. That is why the psalmist says again, *My soul has fainted for your salvation.** For his own part, Truth warns us, *If anyone wants to come after me, let him deny himself.** He says again, *Unless a man renounces all his possessions, he cannot be my disciple.**

*Ps 118:81

*Luke 9:13

*Luke 14:33

Since the mind of Holy Job is estranged from earthly desires, he counts himself among these disciples and

says, *I have lost hope, and I will never live again.* For
the just person to lose hope means to abandon the goods
of the present life by choosing eternity, to seek the good
things that will remain, and to have no confidence in the
things of time. The one who does these things declares
that he will never live again, obviously because he dies
every day to emotional life by a life-creating death. God
forbid that Holy Job should lose hope in the liberality
of God's mercy, that he should turn back the foot of his
heart from continuing his inward journey, or that he
should abandon the love of his Creator, stop, be forsaken
on the road by his leader, and rush on stabbed, as it were,
by the sword of the robber Despair. But lest we should
seem heedlessly to twist Job's words to the meaning we
want them to have, we should weigh them against the
following words, because he himself explains below
the sense in which he spoke the previous words when
he adds,

XXVII. 46. *Spare me. My days amount to nothing.*[*]   [*]Job 7:16
These words, *spare* and *lost hope*, do not agree. He who
loses hope certainly does not still ask to be spared, nor
does the man who up to now desires to be spared ever
despair. It is from one direction that Holy Job loses hope
and from another direction that he begs to be spared.
Surely while he abandons the good things of the passing
life through loss of hope, he rises up to obtain those that
endure with a stronger hope. He is more effectively led
to hope of pardon through despair who more eagerly
desires the future good and more truly abandons the
present by despair.

Let us notice that Job intimates to us the force of
his heart with an opinion he has already expressed three
times. First he said, *My soul chose hanging.* He repeated
this thought when he added, *I have lost hope.* Finally,
by desiring eternity and letting go of passing things,

he added, *Spare me*. Then to what he had already said, *My bones chose death*, he forcefully added, *I will never live again*. Finally he concluded, *My days amount to nothing*. He is right to evaluate his days as nothing, because as we have often said above, the more truly the saints know the things of heaven, the more loftily they despise the things of earth. Therefore they perceive the days of the present life as nothing, because the eyes of their enlightened minds are fixed on the contemplation of eternity. When they return to themselves from that contemplation, what else do they see in themselves but dust? Aware of their own inconsistency, do they not fear the unswerving judgment? When they confront such forceful energy they dread the scrutiny of themselves. So Job is right to add,

*Job 7:17

XXVIII. 47. *What is man, that you distinguish him or set your heart on him?** God distinguishes humans by enriching them with the choice gift of reason, visiting them with infused grace, and raising them to the dignity of accumulated virtue. While humans are nothing of themselves, God grants them participation in his own knowledge by the free gift of his kindness. Yet he sets his heart on these same ones whom he has distinguished. He passes judgment on them whom he has gifted. He weighs their merits exactly and rigidly examines the weight of their lives; then he exacts punishment as inflexibly as he had generously imparted his gifts to them.

Let Holy Job accordingly survey the immensity of God's majesty, and let him turn the eye of his consideration toward his own inconsistency. Let him see that flesh and blood cannot understand that which Truth himself teaches the spirit. Let him see that even when the human spirit is uplifted, people are not strong enough to bear the trial that God conducts under the scrutiny of unshakable retribution. Let him say, *What is man, that you distinguish him or set your heart on him?* It is as though he were to exclaim, "Man is distinguished by a spiritual gift, yet he is flesh. You, God, examine his life after such a gift without compromise, yet if you pass judgment on him without compassion, not even if the spirit be raised to righteousness can it bear the weight that hangs over him because you distinguished him; even if your gifts magnify him above himself, when he stands for the scrutiny of interrogation his weakness causes him to cringe." So Job is right to add,

XXIX. 48. *You visit him at dawn, and you quickly judge him.** Who is there who does not know that dawn refers to the time when the night is already receding and the brightness of daylight is coming? Consequently the darkness of night hems us in, and evildoing dims our sight. But night turns into light when the knowledge of truth enlightens the darkness of our going astray. Night turns into light when the brightness of justice enlightens our hearts, which the blindness of guilt had darkened. Paul had seen this dawn arise in the minds of his disciples when he said, *Night has faded, and daylight has approached.** Accordingly the Lord visits us at dawn, when he lights up the darkness of our erring ways with the daylight of his knowledge, raises us with the gift of contemplation, and elevates us into a tower of virtue.

* Job 7:18

* Rom 13:12

But we had better notice that as soon as God visits us at dawn he immediately puts us to the test. How? By drawing near he leads our hearts to acts of virtue, and by retiring he allows us to be smitten by temptation. If, you see, after being gifted with virtue the soul were not to be assailed by temptation, we would boast of virtues as if we had gotten them by ourselves. So in order that we may both have the gift of fortitude and humbly know our weakness, we are exalted on high by

an increase of grace, and by its absence we are shown
what we are on our own.

This truth is rightly endorsed by the reading of sacred history, where it is mentioned that Solomon received wisdom from God, and yet after the reception of
that wisdom he was at once challenged by the question
of the two harlots.* As soon as he was given the grace of
so great a revelation, he endured the quarrel of the loose
women. It surely often happens to us, you see, that once
we have been granted virtues, consideration of the interior bounty enlightens our mind, but then loose thoughts
quickly upset us; when our mind is heightened by this
priceless gift and is jubilant, it is struck by temptation,
and we realize what we really are. It was like that with
Elijah, who was visited at dawn and opened the sky
with a word; nevertheless his trial came suddenly, and
he fled through the desert in his frailty because of his
great dread of one woman.* It was like that with Paul,
who was led to the third heaven; when he got there he
contemplated the mystery of Paradise. Nevertheless he
returned to himself and fought hard in the war against
the flesh; he held at bay another law in his members,
and he complained that the spiritual law in him was hard
pressed by the rebellion of that other law. Accordingly,
God visits us at dawn, but he tries us at once upon his
visitation; by bestowing his grace he supports us, and
by withdrawing it slightly he shows us to ourselves. And
this cycle we undeniably endure to the point where the
stains of sin are so completely washed away that we
are substantially remade in the form of the promised
incorruptibility. So Job is again right to add,

XXX. 49. *How long will you not let me alone or dismiss me, that I may swallow my saliva?* * Saliva falls into
the mouth from the head, and from the mouth it glides
to the stomach after it is swallowed. What indeed is our

*see
1 Kgs 3:12, 16

*see
1 Kgs 19:3

*Job 7:19

head but divinity? It is by divinity that we receive the principle of our existence, so that we may be creatures. Paul is our witness when he says, *The head of man is Christ, and the head of Christ is God.** And what is our stomach but the mind? When the mind receives its food, which is obviously heavenly perception, beyond any doubt it is refreshed thereby and rules its members and all their actions. If Holy Scripture, you see, did not sometimes call the mind the stomach, Solomon would certainly not have said, *The spirit of man is the Lord's lamp, and it searches out all the hidden places of the stomach.** The favor of God's notice surely enlightens us, and when it does, it uncovers for us all that is tucked away in our mind.

*1 Cor 11:3

*Prov 20:27

What is meant by the word *saliva* but the taste of interior contemplation? Saliva flows down to the mouth from the head, because it is from the Creator's glory that while we are still living in this world, a bare taste of revelation touches us. So at his coming, the Redeemer mixed saliva with clay and restored the eyes of the man born blind, because the grace of God enlightened our sensual thoughts through the admixture of his contemplation and re-created humans for intelligence out of the blindness they were born with. Once they were exiled from the joy of Paradise, nature brought them forth into this foreign land, so that they grew up, as it were, without eyes. But as Holy Job suggests, this saliva falls indeed to the mouth but is not swallowed, nor does it reach the stomach. Although the contemplation of God touches the perception, it does not fully remake the mind, because the soul is unable to see it perfectly but as yet only fleetingly glimpses it, since the darkness of degenerate nature impedes it.

50. Look now: the minds of the chosen ones already control earthly desire. Already they leave behind all

that they consider to be passing objects; they already cut themselves off from external delights and diligently search for the good things that are invisible. In the course of all these attainments they are often seized by the sweetness of the contemplation of heaven. Already they see something of the internal realities, though, as it were, darkly, and they strive with ardent desire to be among the angels in their spiritual ministries. They feed on the taste of unlimited light, and having been lifted up above themselves, they disdain to fall back into them- selves. *The corruptible body weighs down the soul,** so they cannot stay near the light very long but see it only fleetingly. The very weakness of the flesh pulls the soul down when it is rising above it and, still gasping for breath, forces it to think of base and necessary things.

*Wis 9:15

Accordingly, saliva flows down from the head and touches the mouth, but it never reaches the stomach, because while the liquid of heavenly contemplation indeed flows already in the intellect, the mind is still not satisfied completely. Only the taste is present in the mouth, but satisfaction is in the stomach. So we cannot swallow saliva, because we are not allowed satisfaction from the excellence of heavenly glory but just taste it lightly. It is true that whenever we know heaven in this life it is because God has compassion on us; still we cannot yet know heaven perfectly, and that is a result of the punishment of the ancient curse. So Job is right to say, *How long will you not let me alone or dismiss me, that I may swallow my saliva?** He might as well say outright, "Then will you really spare us, when you admit us to perfect contemplation of yourself, so that we may be inwardly absorbed and see your glory and that our degenerate flesh may not impel us outside? Then will you allow me to swallow my saliva, when the taste of your glory overflows in me abundantly and satisfy-

*Job 7:19

ingly, so that I may never hunger again through desire of that taste? I will then contentedly exist in you, and my mind's stomach will be well watered."

But the man who wishes to deserve the good that he seeks must confess the evil he has done:

XXXI. 51. *I have sinned. What shall I do for you, you guard of men?* * Notice how he confesses the evil he has done, but he does not know what good deed he should offer God in compensation. For the removal of guilt, you see, any power human action can have is pretty weak, unless the mercy of the sparing One should foster it and the justice of the righteous Judge not threaten it. So the psalmist is right to say, *Your mercy is better than life.* * However innocent we may seem to be, in the sight of the intransigent Judge our life does not acquit us if his kind mercy does not mitigate what our guilt deserves. Certainly when Job says, *What shall I do for you?* he clearly points out to us that the very good deeds we are ordered to perform benefit ourselves, not the one who orders them. Once again the psalmist tells us, *You have no need of my good deeds.* *

The lowliness of our insignificance is expressed when God is called the guard of men, because if his protection does not guard us against the ambush of the hidden enemy, our watchful eye sleeps while we are awake. The psalmist is again our witness when he says, *Unless the Lord guards the city, its guards stay awake in vain.* * It is our own fault when we fall, but we cannot get up again by our own efforts. The guilt of our own will lays us low once, but the punishment due our fault daily depresses us more. We try to make the earnest effort to arise and reclaim our lost integrity, but we are held back by the weight of our deserts. So he is right to add,

XXXII. 52. *Why have you made me your opponent? Why have I become a burden for myself?* * Then God has

*Job 7:20

*Ps 62:4

*Ps 15:2

*Ps 126:1

*Job 7:20

made us his opponent when we have forsaken God by
sin. Taken captive by the serpent's arguments, we are
now God's enemy, whose precepts we have despised.
The just Creator has made us his opponent; he has
counted us an enemy because of our pride. This very
opposition of guilt, however, has become a burden of
punishment for us, so that we may falsely become free
slaves of our own depravity, we who enjoyed truly free
slavery to imperishability. We unquestionably deserted
the wholesome refuge of humility and ended up placing
the stiff neck of our heart in the yoke of frailty by becoming proud. We who refused to submit to God's command laid ourselves low because of our own necessities.

I can explain this better if I express what the fallen
one puts up with, first because of the flesh and then
because of the burdens imposed on the mind.

53. To say nothing of the pain we bear and of the
fever that makes us gasp, that state of our body that we
call health is confined by its own illness. We waste away
in idleness and faint at work; we grow weak through
fasting but when fed we revive and survive; when eating we grow lax, but when abstaining we grow light
and vigorous; we pour water over ourselves to prevent
dryness, then we wipe ourselves with towels lest we be
wet from that very bath; we are quickened by labor lest
we grow sluggish through inactivity, then rest restores
us lest we collapse from the exertion of work; worn
out by vigils, we are refreshed by slumber; subdued by
sleep, we are shaken awake lest we be tired out more by
repose; we are covered up by clothing lest the stinging
cold air penetrate our body; wilting under the desired
heat, we are refreshed by the movement of air.

So when we try to avoid trouble we find trouble, so
to speak, infected by ill health because of the very medicine we applied. Safe from fever and free from sickness,

our very health is an illness from which our need for a cure is never absent. The more relief we need to go on living, it seems, the more we attend to the sickness of our own medicine. But the very medicine also turns into a wound. When we use the remedy we sought a little too long, it causes a more serious ailment, although it was only as a restorative that we prudently prepared it. That is of course how presumption has to be attacked and how pride has to be eliminated. Once, you see, we accepted an elevated spirit; behold the decaying clay that we now carry about daily.

54. In fact our mind is itself excluded from the secure joy of the hidden interior place; it is at one time deceived by hope, at another shaken by fear, at another dejected by grief, and at another relieved by false mirth. It obstinately delights in passing things and is continually depressed by the loss of them; it is forever changing, and its course is swift. It is subject to changeable things and is divided from itself. The uneasy mind seeks what it does not have; then having seen and begun to possess a thing, it is tired of seeing what it sought. It often loves what it formerly hated and hates what it formerly loved. It learns with difficulty about eternal realities, but it immediately forgets them when it relaxes the effort. It searches long in order to find the smallest trace of the highest realities, but it quickly relapses to the familiar, nor does it keep there anything of what it had found. It desires learning, but hardly does it cast off its ignorance than, having been taught, it fights more fiercely against its boast of knowledge.

Hardly has it subjected to itself the tyranny of the flesh than it still harbors within itself the images whose external actions it overcame and confined. It arouses itself to seek out its Maker, but this search is beaten back, and the friendly darkness of bodily accompaniments confuses it. It wishes but is unable to see itself in its incorporeal guise ruling the body. It asks in wonder what it cannot answer itself, and, still ignorant, it is at a loss before that which it discreetly asks. Seeing itself both spacious and constricted, it does not know how to evaluate itself truly, because if it were not spacious, it would hardly demand so many things to investigate, and if it were not constricted, it would at least find that very fact that it demands to know.

55. Accordingly Job was right to say, *You have made me your opponent, and I have become a burden for myself.** The rejected human race, you see, bears vexation from the flesh and questions from the mind. Humans surely carry themselves as a heavy burden and are everywhere hemmed in by listlessness; they are everywhere beset by powerlessness. Having forsaken God, they thought they were self-sufficient and could rest, yet they found nothing in themselves but outbreaks of disturbance, and having found themselves, they wanted flight from themselves, but in their contempt of the Creator, they had nowhere else to run. A certain wise man meditated on the burdens of this powerless human race and rightly said, *A heavy burden is borne by the sons of Adam from the day of their leaving their mothers' womb until the day of their burial in the universal mother.**

*Job 7:20

*Sir 40:1

Blessed Job in his consideration of these matters groaned and asked why they had been arranged thus; he did not question justice but pled for mercy, that by humbly inquiring he might stir God's pity to spare humans and change their lot. He might say, in other words, "Why do you despise humans, as though they were your opponents, when I know for certain that you do not wish them to die whom you seem to despise?" So he again rightly confesses his lowliness and adds a word of open inquiry:

XXXIII. 56. *Why don't you take away my sin? Why don't you remove my iniquity?** Surely by these words he means nothing else but desire for the expected Mediator, of whom John said, *Behold the Lamb of God who takes away the world's sin.** Surely the sin of the human race is finally taken away when our depravity is changed through the glory of incorruption. Actually we can never be free of guilt as long as we stay in this mortal body. Those who really hope that their iniquity will be taken away accordingly desire the Redeemer's grace or the security of the resurrection. So Job, who has spoken well up to now of the penalty humans deserved from the beginning, goes on to speak of the judgment he fears for his own actions:

XXXIV. 57. *Behold, now I will sleep in the dust, and if you look for me in the morning, I will not be there.** When the first man sinned he was told, *You are dust, and to dust you shall return.** That exposure of our minds that takes place at the Judge's coming is called *morning*, when our thoughts will be disclosed after the darkness of the night, in a certain sense. The psalmist clearly speaks of that morning when he says, *In the morning I will stand before you, and I will see.** For God to look for man means to question him in close detail and to judge him strictly in accordance with that questioning. Accordingly, let blessed Job consider what was lost to us in the Fall, and see that he is already suffering pain in the present life, besides the still more serious loss he fears for the future; let him say then, *Behold, now I will sleep in the dust, and if you look for me in the morning, I will not be there.** He might as well mourn openly and say, "In the present time indeed I suffer bodily death, yet in addition I am in dire fear of a more serious death at the coming Judgment and of your inflexible sentence; I endure destruction because of my guilt, yet I still have

*Job 7:21

*John 1:29

*Job 7:21

*Gen 3:19

*Ps 5:5 LXX

*Job 7:21

to come to judgment for my guilt to be restored, and after destruction I still am terrified."

So let him consider bodily death and say, *Behold, now I will sleep in the dust*, and let him fear spiritual death and add, *and if you look for me in the morning, I will not be there.* Even the elect, you see, no matter how strong they may be in the virtue of justice, are not self-sufficient as far as integrity is concerned, if their justice is closely examined without compromise. Yet they can be relieved even now at the thought of bodily death by the fact that they humbly realize that they can never be self-sufficient. Therefore they shield themselves from the sword of that terrible censure with the armor of humility, and because they shake with constant fear when they confront themselves with terror at the Judge's coming, they are always more prepared.

XXXV. 58. *Then Bildad the Shuhite answered Job: "How long will you speak in this way? How long will* *Job 8:1-2 *the words of your mouth multiply like the wind?"** The words of righteous people are always too heavy for the unrighteous; when they hear words that are spoken for the purpose of edification, they take them as a burden imposed upon them. Bildad the Shuhite himself openly admits this truth when he says, *How long will you speak in this way?* The man who says, "How long?" shows that he is unable to bear edifying words any longer. When wicked people despise correction, they utter reproaches against good speeches. That is why he immediately adds, *The words of your mouth multiply like the wind.* When a multiplicity of words is blamed, serious understanding is undoubtedly denied as being present in their meaning.

The force and meaning of speeches is distinguished by four characteristics. There are those people, for example, whose dignity of thought and expression brings

them renown; there are those, on the other hand, whose
lack of thought and expression leaves them ignored; others again are effective speakers, but their thought lacks
sharpness; last there are those who are well supplied
with intellectual sharpness, but because of their inepti-
tude of speech, they remain silent. That which we often
see in inanimate creation we also notice in humankind.
Abundant water often finds its way from deep sources,
and by means of many rivulets it bubbles to the surface.
It is just as often scarce underground, hidden, and hard
to get running in trickles, so that the ground just about
sweats for its scarcity. Elsewhere a little water rises in
hidden places and finds openings by which it may flow
out; from a spacious aperture a trickle emanates, and
large rivulets grow, but they have no way to flow out.
Elsewhere again an ample supply rises in hidden places,
but it is confined in narrow openings and flows out only
in weak dribbles.

In the same way some men have an open mouth
to speak, and it is supplied by an abundant fountain
of knowledge. In other men, however, neither does
knowledge increase understanding nor does the tongue
wax eloquent. The mouths of others indeed are open to
speak, but the prepared tongue receives nothing from
the mind to proclaim. Still others have a large overflow-
ing supply of knowledge in their hearts, but their weak
tongues are unequal to the task, like slight dribbles, and
they block up the source.

Of these four different kinds of speaking, only the
third is subject to the reproach that it arrogates to itself
by speaking that which the mind does not manage on
its own. The first kind is praiseworthy, because it ably
manages both. The second is to be pitied, because it
miserably misses out on both. The fourth deserves assistance, because it cannot fulfill what it knows. The

third on the other hand is contemptible and should be suppressed; the speaker's words exalt the person, but their meaning falls flat; the said speaker's words are like limbs swollen with infection, and as such appear overblown and empty to listeners.

That is the reproach that Bildad now turns against blessed Job when he says, *The words of your mouth multiply like the wind.* He who attributes a multiplicity of words to the mouth, you see, certainly reproaches the heart for its emptiness. He might as well say outright, "The words of your mouth bring out an abundance of wind, but you are confined by the limits of your knowledge." Still, depraved people reproach what is right lest they should themselves seem to be ignorant of what is truly right, so they proclaim the good things that everybody knows, having learned them by hearsay, as though they were unknown. So Bildad immediately adds,

*Job 8:3

XXXVI. 59. *Does God hinder judgment? Does the almighty one pervert Justice?* * Blessed Job did not deny these truths in his speech, nor was he unaware of them in his silence. But brazen people, as we have said, beautifully proclaim even things that everybody knows, so that they may appear intelligent in their speeches. They have only contempt for moderation and silence, lest their silence be considered lack of expertise. We should realize, however, that they only praise God's correct judgment when their own safety allows them to exult while others suffer adversity, and when they notice that they are enjoying material prosperity while others are worn out by poverty. While they act wickedly yet consider themselves righteous, they attribute their ready prosperity to their own worth and merits. Then they conclude that God does not judge unjustly from the fact that they, being just, are troubled by no adversity.

But if God should strike at their life forcefully, however briefly, in their misery they at once loudly question
the justice of God's decision, the same justice they not
long before safely proclaimed with admiration; when
that judgment weighs against their own behavior, they
deny that it is just. They argue that God is unfair. They
blurt out words of rebuttal; although they were struck for
their neglect, their neglect increases. So the psalmist was
right when he spoke out against the sinner's confession:
He will praise you as long as it profits him.* Surely the   *Ps 48:19
voice of confession is despicable when it is articulated
by the enjoyment of prosperity. The only confession
that bears the weight of merit is the one undivided from
true righteousness by the pain of sorrow. Adversity, the
heart's witness, sharpens that confession until the voice
makes its judgment. It is no wonder, then, that Bildad
praises God's justice, since he does not yet bear any
adversity from that source.

60. Since as we have said Job's friends play the role
of the heretics, let us say a few words by way of explica-
tion to show how Bildad's words coincide with the heretics' pilfering. Unquestionably, when the heretics see the
church corrected by what they consider to be temporal
visitations, they rear themselves up more brazenly for the
ostentation of their distorted preaching. Then they pretend
to uphold the righteousness of God's judgment, and they
proclaim that their prosperity is due to their own merits,
whereas the church, they testify, is afflicted with the punishment she deserves. But even while she is afflicted, they
seek the opportunity to pilfer, using ingratiating words.
They attack the lives of some after having blamed others
who had died, as if they who refused a faith worthy of
God had deserved to die. So Bildad the Shuhite, having
proclaimed God's justice, continued his discourse:

XXXVII. 61. *Even if your sons have sinned against him, and he has delivered them into the power of their evil ways, if you rise early before God and pray to the almighty one, and if you walk in purity and uprightness, he will quickly rise on your behalf, and he will make the house of your justice peaceful.* It is as though the preachers of error were to tell disheartened Catholics, "Look out for your own lives and realize how twisted the faith is that you hold. Those of you who have died are damned. If your unbelief did not displease the Creator of the world, he would never take away so many of your people by violent ruin." Bildad said, *Even if your sons have sinned against him, and he has delivered them into the power of their evil ways.* He might as well simply say, "They were delivered into the power of their own evil ways, those who refused to imitate our righteous way of life." If, however, you rise early before God and pray to the almighty one . . .

Since the heretics, you see, consider themselves to be the bearers of the light of truth, they are calling Holy Church, whom they consider to be stuck in the night of error, to the morning light of truth. For this she must, as it were, rise early through the knowledge of God and erase the past through the prayer of repentance. *If you walk in purity and uprightness . . . . Purity* refers to thought and *uprightness* to action. *He will quickly rise on your behalf . . . .* He might as well say it simply: "He who does not extend the might of his protection against your present tribulations sleeps and is far from protecting the one going astray." *He will make the house of your justice peaceful.* In other words, he will take away contradiction from the present life, and he will forthwith grant security and tranquility. Bad people, you see, consider worldly happiness to be the good result of God's reward, which they anxiously promote, so they promise it to others as a great good. Accordingly, they often pledge its return to those who have lost it, or they get their audience to expect greater rewards even now in the present life. Bildad obviously expresses this type of expectation when he at once adds,

XXXVIII. 62. *So much so that your beginning was small, but your last days will be far greater.** On the other hand, if by the house of justice he means the mind's own counsel, then the masters of error promise the persecuted Catholics that the house of justice will be peaceful, in that if the heretics draw the Catholics over to their own side, the Catholics will certainly then stop opposing the heretics. The reason is that those who could be enticed to crookedness are now all the more peaceably quiet with worldly tranquility the further they are cut off from eternity. They also promise the burgeoning of the resources of knowledge to their followers. So Bildad adds, *So much so that your beginning was small, but your last days will be far greater.* The words of the heretics, however, are not readily believed, because their life often shows them up as contemptible, so they quote the aphorisms of the ancient fathers, whose righteous ways they bend to serve as a proof of their own erroneous thinking. Therefore he adds,

*Job 8:7

XXXIX. 63. *Question the previous generation and carefully search out the recollection of the fathers.** They inform us, in fact, that the previous generation and the recollection of the fathers is not to be seen but searched out, since they refuse to see in it what is patently clear to everybody. Sometimes, however, they teach moral truths like good people, and they suggest how present truth can be gathered from the past; they also demonstrate from the things that have been withdrawn from our eyes by passing away how those that are now seen amount to nothing. So Bildad adds,

*Job 8:8

XL. 64. *We are from yesterday, and we do not know*
that our days upon earth are like a shadow. We are
advised to question the previous generation in order
that we might be shown that our present lifetime passes
like a shadow. It is obvious that if we remember the life
that was and is now already over, we clearly realize how
quickly that which we are now leading also passes. The
heretics often join us in praising the same fathers whom
we venerate, yet they attack us with those same words
of praise because of their depraved understanding. So
Bildad again adds,

XLI. 65. *They will teach you, and utter words from*
their hearts. Remember what he said above: *The words*
of your mouth multiply like the wind. But now, remembering the fathers, he says, *They will utter words from*
their hearts. It is as though the heretics were cursing the
life of Holy Church by saying, "Your words multiply
like the wind in your mouth, but not in your heart. But
the fathers should be heard as though they were your adversaries who spoke words from their hearts and taught
by righteous living." Deceitful men are often unaware
of the viciousness of their insincerity when they boldly
attack the rectitude of others; in order to obtain support
for their rebuke of good people, they either cite good
sentiments that they have not seen but have heard, or
they falsely impute to others those evil things for which
they are themselves responsible. When, however, they
mention the good conduct they decline to practice, we
should realize that truth often sounds from the mouths of
adversaries, as though it moved their tongue and struck
a blow at their life at the same time. Accordingly they
speak of the summit of righteousness, of which they
have no knowledge, so that they become their own
judges by their words and their accusers by their acts.

*Job 8:9

*Job 8:10
*Job 8:2

Bildad certainly speaks admirable words against the hypocrites, but he turns the sword of the word against himself, since unless he were an imitator of justice in some small way, he would never presume to teach just men so rashly. The words he speaks are admittedly strong words, but he ought to say them to fools, not to a wise man, to deceitful people, not to a righteous man; the one who passes withering gardens to pour water into a stream declares himself to be a fool. But let us for the moment pass over the one to whom he speaks and consider attentively what he says, so that his words may instruct us even if they impugn the behavior of the speaker. *Can a rush live without moisture, or sedge grow without water?*[*] To what does Bildad compare a rush or sedge? He at once tells us himself when he adds,

                                       [*]Job 8:11

XLII. 66. *While still in flower, before the hand picks it, before all other plants it withers; such are the ways of all those who forget God. The hope of the hypocrite will perish.*[*] By the word *rush* or *sedge* he means to

                                       [*]Job 8:12-13

signify the hypocrite's way of life, which indeed has the appearance of greenery but has no fruit or usefulness for any human purpose; rather it remains dry and useless and has only the sterile color of green. But neither the rush without moisture nor the sedge without water grows up, because the hypocrite's way of life, to be sure, receives an infusion of God's grace for good works, yet in all that the hypocrite does he desires explicit praise, so remaining fruitless as regards the infusion received.

Hypocrites often do wonderful and significant work, you see; they expel spirits from haunted bodies, and through the gift of prophecy they forestall the future by knowledge. Nevertheless, their intended aim sets them apart from the Giver of such great gifts, because it is not his glory that they seek with these gifts but their own approbation. So when they exalt themselves by the good things they have received and praise themselves, they fight the Giver with his own gifts. By behaving this way they surely grow proud against the Giver, when they should rather humble themselves before him. Later on a more severe sentence will strike them down, because now God's goodness generously enriches these ungrateful ones. These rich gifts become for them an increase of damnation, because, though watered, they bear no fruit but grow high and empty under a green appearance of color. Truth spoke fairly of them in the gospel, saying, *Many will tell me on that day, "Lord, Lord, did we not prophesy in your name? Did we not cast out demons in your name? Did we not work many miracles in your name?" And then I will assure them, "I never knew you. Get away from me, you evildoers."* *Rush and sedge accordingly do not live without water, because hypocrites do not receive the green color of good works without God's gift. But because they claim the good works as their own for the sake of their self-praise, they are assuredly green with water, but their growth is vain growth.

*Matt 7:22-23

67. So he is right to add, *While still in flower, before the hand picks it, before all other plants it withers.* *The flower of the rush is the praise of the hypocrite. The sedge, however, grows with sharp thorns, and no hand picks it, because when the senses have been irritated by haughtiness, the hypocrite disdains correction of his wickedness. The flower of the sedge cuts the hand of the picker, because poised for praise, lest anyone dare correct him, the hypocrite immediately wounds the corrector's life with his sharp tongue. He does not want to be holy but to be called such. When by chance he is corrected he is, as it were, cut down in the full bloom of his reputation. He is angry because his depravity has been found out; he forbids his accuser to speak to him,

*Job 8:12

because he is pained like a man whose hidden wound has been touched. He wants to be esteemed by everyone in the same way that strangers see him. He is more ready for death than correction, and he is rendered worse by contradiction, because he considers pure words as darts of evil omen.

So when he is irritated he straightway breaks out with insults that magnify the evil, and he plots against the life of his corrector. He longs to show how the guilt of his reprover is beyond comparison so that he may prove his own innocence, not by his own acts but by someone else's misdeeds. A person may often regret having spoken anything by way of refutation, just as grief, so to speak, might run from the life of the one who corrects, as though it were blood from the hand of the sedge picker. So Solomon was right to say, *Do not censure a mocker, lest he hate you.** The just person need not fear the mocker's insulting reply but fear lest, being moved to hate, the mocker become worse.

*Prov 9:8

68. While we are on the subject, we must know that the good deeds of just people grow more abundant until the end of their lives, because they start from the heart. The acts of hypocrites, however, are never rooted in the hidden place, so they often run short before their lives are over. They often enter upon the study of sacred learning. Yet their interest in these studies does not have the purpose of earning merit but of acquiring human praise and by that means to reap the favor of temporary advancement; they then devote their whole attention to the service of worldly cares and quietly leave sacred learning unattended. Their subsequent actions show how great is the love for material things among those who formerly preached eternal ones. They often project the appearance of a maturity they have assumed, and they adorn themselves with calm taciturnity, long-suffering

patience, and the virtuousness of continence. But when these adornments have gained for them the longed-for dignity at the very top, and when they finally receive universal homage, they throw themselves into wanton licentiousness without delay, and they themselves witness that their good behavior was not meant from the heart, since they departed from it so soon.

There are others who sometimes give away their possessions and distribute them all to the poor; nevertheless, before the end of their life they feel the itch of avarice, and they who seemed to be giving their own away grasp at someone else's property; with tightfisted cruelty they go around collecting what they previously gave up with feigned kindness. So we are now rightly told, *While still in flower, before the hand picks it, before all other plants it withers.**

*Job 8:12

Even the just are plants according to the flesh, as the prophet tells us, *All flesh is grass.** But we are told that the rush withers ahead of every plant, because while the just remain good, the lives of hypocrites dry up and lose the green color of their pretended righteousness. Other plants dry up too, because the good works of just people disappear along with their physical lives. But the rush is the first of the plants to wither, because before hypocrites leave the flesh behind, they first abandon the virtuous acts that had adorned them. Of these the psalmist also spoke pointedly, *Let them become like grass on the house, which dries up before it is uprooted.** The grass on the house indeed grows on the roof, but it is by no means firmly rooted, because hypocrites' acts are indeed perceived as significant, but they are not strengthened by those acts, because they are not performed with purity of heart. Grass indeed dries up quicker, even when it has not been rooted up, because hypocrites while still living this present life obviously

*Isa 40:6

*Ps 128:6

flourish, yet they already lose their virtuous acts, like the appearance of greenery. Because, you see, their striving was to do good without the intention of uprightness in thought, they lost their good works, and this loss shows that they grew without roots.

69. Now Bildad, as we have already said, in the same passage makes it clear what he compares the rush and the sedge to. He says, *Such are the ways of all those who forget God. The hope of the hypocrite will perish.** For what do hypocrites hope from all their works except respect for dignity, fame, praise, and reverence from the higher nobility, and for all to call them virtuous. But the hope of hypocrites cannot last, because they do not want eternity, and they flee from what they have. By no means, you may be sure, is the intention of their mind fixed on that glory that is an endless possession; rather they pant after passing favor, and so doing they lose the fruit of their labor in the reception. Truth testifies, *Amen, I tell you, they have received their reward.**

This hope of receiving a reward, however, cannot be held very long, since honor is given for works that are displayed, but life presses on to its end. Praise resounds, but time rushes on to its termination along with praise. Since the mind is by no means rooted in love of eternity, it falls immediately along with the objects of its love. No one can love changing things while remaining unchanged. One who embraces passing things is, by the very fact of being involved with moving objects, drawn along on their course. Let Bildad then say, *The hope of the hypocrite will perish*, because human praise, which the hypocrite desires and labors for, runs its headlong course moment by moment. So he is right to add,

XLIII. 70. *His folly will not satisfy him.** Surely it takes great folly to labor and covet windy praise, or to be devoted to heavenly precepts with all one's strength

* Job 8:13

* Matt 6:2

* Job 8:14

while seeking a reward such as worldly salary. Those who desire human favor in return for the exercise of virtue, so to speak, consider a priceless object on the market worth a paltry sum. When they could earn the kingdom of heaven, they take instead the penny of transitory speech. They sell their work for a paltry sum, because they offer great things and receive little. Who are the hypocrites like if not flourishing vines that are neglected? They bear abundant fruit, but they are never carefully raised from the ground. Whatever the green sprouts bud forth is trampled underfoot by wild beasts, and when they see that the vine thrown upon the ground bears more abundant fruit, they consume it all the more avidly.

The works of hypocrites show up clearly, of course, and like fruitful plants they flourish, but because they desire human praise, they are, as it were, abandoned on the ground. So the wild beasts of the earth, obviously evil spirits, eat them up, since they twist them away for the sake of perdition, and they tear them all the more fiercely the more clearly they perceive them to be great works. So the prophet was right to say, *The standing grain has no heads, and it will yield no meal; even if it were to yield, strangers would eat it.** Of course the grain has no heads when the life is without merit or virtue. The grain yields no meal when the one who prospers in this world understands nothing with discrimination and bears no fruit of good works.

*Hos 8:7

71. Even should the grain yield some meal, strangers often eat it up, because even when the hypocrites show off their good works, only the desires of evil spirits are satisfied therewith. Those people, you see, who do not wish to please God by their good works do not in any sense feed the owner of the field, but strangers. Accordingly, hypocrites are like a budding vine sprout that is

neglected; it cannot hold its fruit because the cluster of good works lies on the ground. Yet they are fed by their own foolishness, because all honor them for their good work. They take precedence over others, they hold the minds of other people in subjection, they are honored in high places, and they enjoy high favor.

This foolishness of theirs pleases them for the time being, but a time will come, the time of retribution, when it will not please them; rather, in punishment, their former foolishness will displease them. Then they will understand how stupid their actions were, when from God's displeasure they receive the sentence for taking pleasure in praise. Then they will consider that they have been foolish, when everlasting torture punishes them for the temporary honor that they received. Then punishment opens up true knowledge, because they clearly gather from it that all passing things were nothing.

XLIV. 72. So Bildad is right to add, *His confidence is like a spider's web.** Rightly is the hypocrite's confidence said to be like a spider's web, because hypocrites labor at everything in order to attain honor, and the wind of mortal life blows it all away. Because they do not seek eternal reality, they lose the good things of time when time passes. It is also worth consideration that the threads of a spider are woven in an orderly way, since hypocrites also arrange their work with discretion. Spiders weave their webs carefully, but they are undone in a moment by the wind, because whatever the hypocrite laboriously manages, the breeze of human favoritism takes away. Since the work fails in longing for human praise, it is as though the wind blew it away.

*Job 8:14

The deeds of hypocrites, you see, often last even to the end of their life on earth, but they do not seek the praise of the Creator by them, so they were never good works in God's eyes. As we have already said,

these hypocrites often back themselves up by studying the holy law, they speak the words of doctrine, and
they support all their opinions with written testimony.
Nevertheless they do not use all these things to further the daily lives of their hearers, but only their own
careers; they could not offer anything else but words
that would move their audience's hearts to chant their
praises, hardly words to move them to tears. Of course
the mind that is occupied with superficial desires does
not ignite the fire of God's love; consequently the words
spoken out of a cold heart cannot ignite those who hear
them to heavenly desires. Obviously nothing can ignite
another thing unless it is on fire itself. So it often happens that hypocrites' words do not teach others and even
make themselves worse, filling them with pride from
self-praise. Paul is our witness: *Knowledge inflates, but*
*1 Cor 8:1   love builds.** So if love by building does not lift up,
knowledge overthrows by inflating. Hypocrites often
afflict themselves with astonishing degrees of fasting, to
the extent that they wear out their bodily health and, as
it were, while living in the body utterly kill the body's
life. They are so close to death through fasting that they
live well nigh dying every day.

   Yet they want people's eyes to see their fasting, and
they seek recognition and admiration, as Truth testifies: *They disfigure their faces, that they may seem to*
*Matt 6:16   men to be fasting.** Their faces become pallid, their bodies shake with decrepitude, and groans break out from
their chests. Meanwhile they wait to hear ejaculations
of wonder from the mouths of their neighbors; nothing
but human esteem is intended by such intense labor.
Simon certainly epitomized these people, that Simon
who was compelled to bear the Lord's cross during the
passion; of him we read, *They found a man from Cyrene*
coming toward them, whose name was Simon; him they

pressed into service to carry Jesus' cross.* Anything we do by compulsion we do not do by intent of love. Bearing Jesus' cross by compulsion, accordingly, means to support the trials of fasting with some intention other than the one we should have. Does the one not bear the cross of Jesus by compulsion who, presumably obeying the Lord's command, masters the flesh but still has no love for the spiritual fatherland? So then this Simon bears the cross but by no means dies, because all the hypocrites indeed afflict their bodies through fasting yet still live for the world through their love of honor. *Matt 27:32

73. Against such as these, Paul rightly says of the elect, *Those who belong to Christ have crucified their flesh with its sins and concupiscence.** Yes, we do crucify the flesh with its sins and concupiscence, if we restrain the stomach in such a way that we no longer seek any worldly dignity. Those who abuse the body, you see, yet pant after honors, put their flesh on the cross indeed while living more sadly for the world through concupiscence. Base people, you see, often reach a place in the government by projecting an image of holiness when, unless they were able to appear virtuous in some way, no amount of effort could earn it for them. Yet what they desired passes away, and the punishment that follows remains. Now the proof of holiness is offered by a person's face, but when the internal Judge scrutinizes the secrets of the heart, he does not call for external witnesses to that person's life. So Bildad was right to say, *His confidence is like a spider's web.* When the witness of the heart is in evidence, all a person's external confidence in human approval is lost. So Bildad adds another well-chosen phrase: *Gal 5:24

XLV. 74. *He will lean upon his house, but it will fall.** Just as the home of one's usual external habitation is the house where the body abides, so the home of our reflection is anywhere the soul abides by love. *Job 8:15

Yes, whatever we love, we dwell in that thing and come to rest therein. Paul accordingly had set his heart on heaven although positioned on earth, albeit a stranger to earth; he said, *Our commonwealth is in heaven.** As for the hypocrites' minds, they reflect on nothing else in all that they do but the fame of their own reputation, and they care nothing for the goal where their deserts lead them, but only for what they are called at the moment. Therefore their home is their joy in popularity, where they live and are apparently at rest. Their whole soul reclines in popularity through their works, but this house cannot stand, because praise dies along with the breath of life and human popularity does not withstand judgment.

So the foolish virgins who did not take along flasks of oil took pride in strangers' voices, not in their own self-knowledge; they were taken by surprise at the bridegroom's arrival and said, *Give us some of your oil, because our lamps are going out.** To ask for oil from one's neighbor surely means to beg from a stranger's mouth a testimony of approval for a good deed. The empty mind, you see, with all its labor would find that internally it had kept nothing. So it seeks external testimony. It is as though the foolish virgins said outright, "When you see that we are cast out without any reward, speak out whatever you see concerning our works."

75. But it is in vain that hypocrites lean on this house, because no human testimony supports them in the judgment. Why? Because they already earlier received as a gift the very human praise that they now require as a testimony. Certainly hypocrites lean on their house when they are deceived by false approval and lifted up as though by belief in their holiness. Hypocrites surely do many bad things secretly even while they do some public good. Accordingly, while they receive praise for obvi-

*Phil 3:20

*Matt 25:8

ous good works, they turn away the eyes of their careful regard from their secret sins, and they believe themselves to be precisely what they hear externally instead of what they know they are internally. So it often happens that they even come confidently to the heavenly Judge, because they believe themselves in front of the internal tribunal as what humans hold them to be externally.

But the hypocrites' house cannot stand, because all rehearsed confidence in holiness falls flat for dread of the inflexible tribunal. When they realize that for them there is no testimony available from a stranger's mouth, they apply themselves to the listing of their own works, adding these words as well: *If he supports it, it will not rise.*[*] Seeing that the house cannot stand by itself, they support it so that it might stand. Because hypocrites know that their life must fail at the Judgment, they try to help it stand by listing their deeds. Do they not on every hand support the dwelling place of their popularity at the Judgment, those who, as we have already said, list the things they have done, saying, *Lord, Lord, did we not prophesy in your name? Did we not cast out demons in your name? Did we not work many miracles in your name?*[*] But the house of popularity shored up with so many protestations will never stand, because the Judge replies unhesitatingly, *I never knew you. Get away from me, you evildoers.*[*]

*Job 8:15

*Matt 7:22

*Matt 7:23

Remember that when something rises from below, it is lifted up to the higher level. Hypocrites' houses therefore cannot rise, because through anything that they could do according to the heavenly precepts, they have never lifted up their soul from the earth. Rightfully, then, they will never be lifted up to receive a reward in heaven, because the work they display here and now is tied to the desire for temporary honor.

Now, since the life of hypocrites has been characterized by being called a rush, and we have heard how it will be reproved at the Judgment, let us hear how people are impressed by it before the appearance of the exacting Judge:

*Job 8:16
XLVI. 76. *He appears wet before the sun rises.** Holy Scripture often portrays the Lord by the word *sun.* For example, the prophet says, *For you who fear the* *Mal 4:2 *name of the Lord, the Sun of justice shall rise.** Again, the wicked are described in the book of Wisdom as cast down in the Judgment and saying, *We have gone astray from the road of truth, and the light of justice did* *Wis 5:6 *not shine upon us, nor did the sun rise for us.** Accordingly the rush looks wet before the sun rises, because before God's intransigence shines out in judgment, all hypocrites display themselves as covered with the radiance of holiness. They look vigorous, because they are reckoned as just, and they attain honorable seats, with power rising from the brilliance of holiness, at which all men and women render them veneration, repute, and popularity. This rush is therefore wet at night, but it dries when the sun rises, because of course hypocrites are believed holy by everybody in the darkness of this life, but when the intransigent Judge comes, it will be obvious how wicked they are. Let Bildad then say, *He appears wet before the sun rises.* The hypocrite exhibits himself now to human eyes as a vigorous plant but will later dry up in the heat of God's judgment.

*Job 8:16
XLVII. 77. *At his birth his seed arises.** On germinating, most plants sprout first from the ground; they are touched by air and warmth, nourished by sun and rain, and only then does their flower open up to bring forth the kernel of their seed. The rush, however, germinates together with its flower, and as soon as it sprouts from the ground, it brings along the kernel of its seed. Any

of the saints is therefore rightly designated by any of
the other plants, but the hypocrite by the rush. Why
is that? It is because before the just bud forth through
acts of holiness, they endure the winter of this life, and
they are tested in the fire of grievous persecution. When
they do righteous acts, they never expect a reward for
their righteousness here below, and when they leave the
troubles of this world behind them and reach the eternal
fatherland, they enjoy the long-awaited reward. Hypocrites, on the other hand, try to earn honor in the present
world as soon as they sprout a good work. Like a rush,
they are born with seed, and because they began to live
rightly, they expect everybody to honor them without
delay. Accordingly, the presence of seed at birth means
a reward for beginning.

Some people, you see, abandon the ways of open
lawlessness and often adopt the appearance of holiness;
as soon as they enter the place of righteousness, they
forget what they were and refuse the way of repentance
for their past misdeeds. They expect recognition for
having begun a righteous life, and they want precedence
over others, including those better than themselves. It
often happens, moreover, that prosperity in the present
life accompanies them according to their aspiration,
and they become even worse than they had been before,
assuming the appearance of holiness. Occupied with
many affairs and confused by their preoccupation, not
only do they not bewail what they have done but they
even do worse things that they should bewail.

78. Those who abandon the world, you see, ought
not to be attracted to external service, unless they grow
stronger in contempt of the same world through humility. Goods that people notice too early disappear too
fast, because trees that are planted and grow together
before the roots are established dry up if some violent

hand pulls on them. If on the other hand the root is inserted deeply and takes hold, being moistened by the wet earth, someone's hand might pull it but not disturb it. Even if the wind should blow strongly against it and bend it, that root will not be moved. Accordingly, lest the work that has begun lose its life, the heart must root itself long and firmly in the deep soil of humility, so that when the wind of detraction or favoritism blows from some human mouth, even if it should bend some emotion in one direction or another, it will not uproot the deeply planted soul. Rather the soul will immediately return to its upright position after bending if its root remains strong.

What is stronger among growing things than a rising wall? If, however, someone pushes against it while it is still under construction, it immediately falls in ruins without effort. On the other hand, if the mortar is allowed to dry over time, it cannot be knocked over even by a battering ram. In just the same way, when our good works are immediately revealed, they fail, but when they are long hidden they acquire solidity; when someone's hand touches and seizes the life of our conversion that has only begun, it knocks it down as though it were a recently built wall. It is easily ruined, because it has not yet lost the moisture of its fragility. But when the soul holds itself fast in a quiet humble state for an extended period, it hardens itself against any blows, like a wall that has dried, and any solid substance that strikes it immediately falls back shattered.

That is why Moses would not allow the lives of firstlings to be used in human activities, saying, *You must not make a firstborn ox work, nor may you shear a firstborn sheep.** Making a firstborn ox work certainly means publicly displaying acts that are the firstfruit of a conversion to a good life. The shearing of the first-

*Deut 15:19

born sheep also means to uncover for human eyes our first efforts of good works, removing the cover under which they are hidden. We are therefore forbidden to drive the firstborn ox, and we are not allowed to shear the firstborn sheep. Even if we begin some particularly hard task, we must not be too quick to work at it openly, and if in our life we undertake something simple and harmless, it is proper for us not to abandon the veil of secrecy, lest we display it naked to human eyes like a sheep without its fleece.

79. The firstborn bulls and sheep should avail only as sacrifices offered to God, so that we may immolate on the altar of our heart in honor of the internal Judge whatever strong and harmless work we begin. This offering will no doubt be accepted by him all the more readily the more hidden it is from human sight and unblemished by any desire for popularity. The beginning of a fresh conversion, however, is often still accompanied by some elements of self-indulgence. That is why we should not be too quick to notice what has begun, lest when we praise the good deeds that please us, the soul be flattered by the praise it receives and should fail to detect the evil that lies hidden in those deeds.

So Moses again spoke rightly when he said, *When you enter the land that I am going to give you and you plant fruit-bearing trees there, you will set aside their first fruits. The fruit they bear will be unclean for you, and you will not eat them.*[*] The fruit-bearing trees are surely works bearing the fruit of virtue. We set aside the firstfruits of the trees when we are suspicious of the shortcomings of beginners and when we withhold approval from the first results of our works. We hold the fruit they bring forth to be unclean, and we do not use them in our diet, because when the first results of a good work are praised, it is proper that it should not feed

*Lev 19:23

the worker's soul lest he delightedly pluck the praise so
received and the fruit of the work be devoured prematurely. Accordingly, the one who receives praise from
human lips for beginner's virtue is like the one who eats
the fruit of the planted tree before it is ripe.

80. For this reason Truth tells us through the psalmist, *It is useless for you to get up before daybreak. Get
up after you sit down.** Getting up before daybreak
surely means to rejoice in the darkness of the present
life, before the clear day of eternal judgment is visible.
Sitting down therefore comes first, that we may really
get up, because those who do not voluntarily humiliate
themselves now will never be lifted up by the glory that
is to come. Therefore the act of rising before daybreak
in the psalm verse just quoted means that hypocrites
mentioned by Eliphaz bring forth the bud at their birth,
because the one who desires human praise upon origi-
nating a good work immediately desires as well to obtain the glorious reward.

Had not those of whom Truth spoke brought forth
the bud in their beginning? *They love*, he said, *places
of honor at banquets and first seats in synagogues and
greetings at the marketplace and being called Rabbi by
men.** So because they begin to do good works but try to
be honored by men, they are like rushes that germinate
and grow along with their seed. Of course when they
want to do good, they first with careful minds look for
witnesses of their acts. They carefully calculate whether
there are people around to see what they are going to
do and whether the witnesses can speak nobly about
what they have seen. If, however, no one happens to
be present to see their deeds, they judge that they have
undeniably lost their fruit, and they assume that the eyes
of the internal Judge were virtually absent, because they
refuse to accept any future recompense from him for

*Ps 126:2

*Matt 23:6-7

their deeds. And since whenever hypocrites do anything good they want it to be seen by many people, it is again well said of this rush as follows:

XLVIII. 81. *On a heap of stones his roots will spread, and he will dwell among rocks.*[*] What do we understand by the word *root*, if not hidden thoughts that arise secretly and then openly manifest themselves by the display of works? The prophet also spoke of the seed of the word: *Whatever is saved from the house of Judah, whatever is left, will take deep root and bear fruit above.*[*] To take deep root surely means secretly to multiply good thoughts, while to bear fruit above means to display the righteous efficacy of works that are the result of thoughts. By the word *stones* Holy Scripture means to symbolize people, as Holy Church is told through Isaiah: *I will make your rampart out of jasper and your gates out of cut stones.*[*] He then made it clear what he meant by these stones when he added, *All your sons will be taught by God.*[*] Peter for his part taught the church, saying, *You are like living stones in a building made into a spiritual house.*[*]

 In this passage of Job, however, the word *stones* is used without the modifier *living*, so it is possible that both the reprobate and the elect are included in the unqualified epithet *stones*. The rush accordingly dwells among stones, and its roots spread out on a pile of rocks, because all hypocrites think furiously of ways to obtain human admiration. Because in their secret thoughts they need the praise of humans, all that they do serves only to spread their roots on a heap of stones like rushes. Those who are on the point of acting surely think of their own praise, while those who have been praised mull over their praise alone and silently in their thoughts. They boast that they have been distinguished and that they have shone in the esteem of the world.

*Job 8:17

*Isa 37:31

*Isa 54:12

*Isa 54:13

*1 Pet 2:5

When they are elated by the favor shown them, they get proud and often wonder at themselves, speechless at their own importance. They want to be seen every day as more and more powerful, and their works grow by their admirable inventions, because just as virtues weaken every vice, so arrogance strengthens vices. Arrogance causes the mind's desires to awaken and to prevail over its own faculties, since the love of praise orders that which one's normal condition of vitality denies. So the hypocrites, as we have said, seek judges of what they have done. But if no witnesses of their deeds are present, they proclaim their actions on their own. When they begin to be elated by the praise they receive, they often add lies to the story they have told themselves about what they have done. If on the other hand they speak the truth, in so doing they make the deeds unrecognizable, and when they are awarded the popularity they seek, they lose the reward of their own interior recognition.

82. When they publish their own good deeds, the hypocrites display the prey they have gotten to the evil spirits, who are, as it were, the enemy in ambush. The hypocrites' way of life is surely prefigured by Hezekiah's error, which is well known to all people. After a single prayer, and in the course of a single night, an angel struck down and killed 180,000 enemy soldiers; when the sun was near its setting, God led it back to a higher place in the sky. Hezekiah's life was already shortened and near its end, but God extended it and gave him more time. After all this, he received the envoys of the kings of Babylon and showed them all the treasure he possessed.* But immediately afterward he heard this message from the prophet: *Behold, the days are coming when all that is found in your house will be taken away to Babylon; nothing will be left, says the Lord.**

*2 Kgs 19:15-19, 35; 20:11, 6-7, 12-13

*2 Kgs 20:17

Surely in just the same way the hypocrites, since they disdain caution against the hidden ambush of the evil spirits and will not remain hidden by the very virtues that allowed them to become great, profit the enemy by displaying their good works; they quickly lose all that they struggled so long to achieve. For this cause the psalmist says, *He surrendered their powers to captivity and gave up their wealth into the hands of the enemy.** Yes indeed, the power and wealth of these haughty ones is given up into the enemy's hands, because every good deed that is displayed through love of praise is surrendered to the jurisdiction of the hidden adversary. Those who display their wealth to the notice of their enemies, you see, invite them to plunder. As long as we are separated from the security of the eternal homeland, we walk on a road subject to ambush by robbers. Therefore those who fear robbery on the road must hide any wealth they are carrying.

*Ps 77:61

O wretched people, those who desire human praise themselves throw away the fruit of their labor. They want to display themselves to the eyes of strangers, but they condemn their own work! They are the ones whom the evil spirits provoke to brag, and in so doing they steal their works and strip them naked, as we have said. That is why Truth has spoken through the prophet, using the image of a particular people to symbolize the malice of the ancient enemy. *He has made*, he said, *my vineyard a wasteland, he has killed my fig trees, he has despoiled them and left them empty, and their limbs have been whitened.** God's vineyard is surely made a desert by the spirits in ambush, when the soul full of good fruit is dissipated by its longing for human praise. A certain nation has killed God's fig tree; after seducing the mind into desire for approval, it seized it and drew it

*Joel 1:7

on to ostentation and ripped the cover of humility off it. Stripping it naked it despoiled it, because as long as it was hidden in its good deeds, it was clothed in the bark of its own garment.

When the mind longs for its actions to be seen by others, like a despoiled fig tree, it has lost the bark that covered it. So the prophet correctly added, *Its limbs have been whitened*. Its works are displayed and are shining for human eyes. A name for holiness is obtained when righteous actions are published. The branches of the fig tree wither because the bark has been peeled off, so also we must wisely notice that when arrogant deeds are displayed for human eyes, they aim to win favor, but instead they are dried up. Accordingly the mind that puts itself forward by boasting is rightly called a dead fig tree, because it is both shining white because of its display and withered, because naked and uncovered.

We must therefore keep within us what we have done if we expect to receive from the internal Judge payment for our work. That is why Truth said in the gospel, *Do not let your left hand know what your right hand is doing, that your almsgiving may be secret, and* * Matt 6:3-4   *your Father who sees what is secret will reward you.** That is also why the psalmist says about the church of the chosen people, *All the glory of this daughter of kings* * Ps 44:14   *is within her.** For this reason Paul also says, *Our glory* * 2 Cor 1:12   *is this: the witness of our self-awareness.** The daughter of kings is surely the church, who has been conceived by the preaching of spiritual princes in good works; she has her glory within her, because what she does, she does not possess by boasting or ostentation. Paul calls his glory the witness of self-awareness, because he has no desire for approval from someone else's mouth, and he does not know how to place the joy of his life outside himself.

83. We must therefore hide our works, lest while we carelessly carry them with us on the journey of this life we lose them in an attack by robbing spirits. It is true that Truth has said, *Let them see your good works and glorify your Father who is in heaven.** But it is one thing to seek the glory of the Giver by a manifestation of the work and surely something different to desire personal praise for the gift of the Giver. Accordingly, Truth also said these words in the same gospel: *Be careful not to act piously in front of men in such a way as to be seen by them.** Therefore, when our work is displayed to humans, we must consider first, searching in our heart through scrutiny of that very display, what it is we are seeking. If we are seeking the glory of the Giver even when our works are made known, we should keep them secret in his sight. If on the other hand we desire our own praise for these works, they are already cast out from his presence, even if they are still unknown by the crowd.

84. Now it belongs to high perfection to seek the Creator's glory by displaying our works in such a way as to be unable to rejoice in our own exaltation when we are praised. A praiseworthy work is displayed without harm to the doers only when their mind loftily disdains and truly treads upon the praise that is offered. But since most people are weak and do not master self-praise by perfect contempt, it remains necessary that they hide the good that they do. It often happens that at the very beginning of their display they seek their own praise. On the other hand, they often want to reveal the Creator's glory by displaying their work, but when they receive exceptional favor they are seized with longing for self-praise. When they neglect to judge themselves internally, in their external dissipation they do not know what they are doing. Their work ministers to their own

*Matt 5:16

*Matt 6:1

pride, and by this very fact they think they are serving the Giver.

The rush therefore stays between the rocks, because the hypocrite stands in the place where he fixes the intention of his mind. When he goes around soliciting statements of approval from many people, you see, it is as though he stood in the middle of a group of rocks. Such hypocrites are designated by the title of *rush*: when they master their body by self-denial, when they labor with pious zeal to distribute their possessions, when they are instructed in the knowledge of the law of God, when they perform the duty of preaching the word: if anyone saw them full of such generosity, would one think they were outside the grace of the Giver? Yet the divine plan grants them the gift of works and denies them the inheritance. God generously endows them with works but disowns the lives of the workers. Because they turn the office they receive to their own popularity, they are darkened by the shadow of pride in the sight of the deepest light. So Bildad rightly goes on,

XLIX. 85. *If he is moved out of his place, God will*
*Job 8:18   *deny him and say, "I know you not."* Hypocrites are moved from their place when death intervenes, and they lose the popularity of this life. When they are moved, the internal Judge denies them and declares that he does not know them. Yes, Truth does not know the counterfeit life and rightly reproves it, nor does he recognize the good the hypocrites have done, because good though it is, it did not proceed from a right intention. That is why when the hypocrites come for judgment, Truth tells the
*Matt 25:12   *foolish virgins, *"Amen," I tell you, "I know you not."* When Truth sees their corrupted minds, he condemns their uncorrupted bodies.

If only the hypocrites were satisfied with their own damnation alone and never with their perverse zeal incited others so ardently to live a double life! This action, unfortunately, seems to be a common trait: that people want to make others like themselves, to join them; they avoid any different way of life and impose the imitation of that which they prefer. Therefore from the hypocrites' point of view, all simplicity is an object of reproach. They pass judgment on those minds that are uncommitted, and they call purity of heart sluggishness. All those whom they want as followers they turn away from the path of simplicity, and as though they had banished foolishness, they esteem themselves as teachers of those in whom they conquer simplicity of mind, which is the citadel of wisdom. Since, however, it is not only for their own perversity that hypocrites are reproved, but also for the connected ruin of their followers, after we are told that the Judge does not know them, it is immediately added advisedly,

L. 86. *His joy in life consists in this: that others are again born from the earth.** He might as well say it openly: "When the Judge comes he certainly does not acknowledge him but punishes him severely, because his happiness in his evil ways was all the greater the more he spread the evil to other people." The one, you see, for whom his own evil life was not enough should necessarily be tortured at the end and rightly for the guilt of others. Now therefore let the counterfeiters rejoice and boast that they have won human judgment; let the simplicity of the just be despised and be called foolishness by the cunning wiles of double-minded people. The contempt held for simple people will pass quickly, and also the boasting of those of double mind will quickly run its course. So Bildad rightly adds,

LI. 87. *God will not reject the blameless man, nor will he extend his hand to the wicked.** When he appears as the righteous Judge, God will certainly lift up

*Job 8:19

*Job 8:20

the lowered countenance of the blameless people and glorify them, while he condemns the boasting evil ones and casts them down. The evil are termed hypocrites, who do good deeds badly, and what they do right is done in hope of praise. When we stretch out our hand to someone, we obviously lift that person from a low position. Accordingly, God does not extend his hand to the wicked; no, he leaves in their lowliness those who are in search of worldly prestige; moreover, however righteous their deeds may seem to be, he does not raise them to the enjoyment of heaven.

At least the evil are called hypocrites, because while they show kindness to their neighbors, they cover up the malice of their evildoing. In everything that they do or say they display uprightness externally, but internally they calculate the fine texture of their duplicity. They imitate transparency on the surface, but under the appearance of transparency they continually hide malice. Moses rightly spoke against such practices: *You must not wear clothes that are woven of wool and flax*. Wool signifies simplicity and flax cleverness. Consequently the garment woven from wool and flax hides the flax behind the surface presented by the wool. Therefore anyone who in speech or action hides the cleverness of malice inside and presents upright simplicity outside wears a garment woven of wool and flax. Since cunning cannot be detected under an appearance of wholeness, it is like flax that hides behind thick strands of wool.

On the other hand, after reproving the double-minded, Bildad presents the reward of the just people and immediately adds,

LII. 88. *Until your mouth is full of laughter and your lips with jubilation.** The mouths of all the just will then be full of laughter, when their hearts, with the tears of their wandering wiped away, are full of exultation at

*Job 8:21

eternal joy. Truth spoke of this laughter to his disciples when he said, *The world will rejoice; you will be sad, but your sadness will turn into joy.** He also said, *I will*   *John 16:20
see you again, and your hearts will rejoice, and nobody will take that joy from you.* Solomon, too spoke of this   *John 16:22
laughter of Holy Church: *She will laugh on the last day.**   *Prov 31:25
He also said elsewhere, *It will be well with the man who fears the Lord at the end.** His laughter at that time will   *Sir 1:13
not be a physical one, but a laughter of the heart.

When we laugh our physical laugh now, it arises from weak licentiousness, but the laughter of the heart at that time will arise from the joy of salvation. Accordingly, when all the chosen ones are filled with the joy of palpable contemplation, they leap, as it were, for the mirth of laughter in the mouth of their minds. On the other hand, we call it jubilation when we conceive a joy of the heart so great that we cannot express it satisfactorily in words. Nevertheless, the exultation of the mind is heard in the voice, even when words do not explain it. Rightly is the mouth said to be full of laughter and the lips of jubilation, because in that eternal homeland, when the minds of the just are seized with jubilation, their tongues are uplifted in songs of praise. Because they see so much that they cannot speak, they are jubilant and laugh, since they cannot explain by sound what it is they love.

89. He says *until*, not because almighty God does not raise up evil persons before he raises his chosen ones to the enjoyment of jubilation, as though he would deliver from punishment those whom he previously abandoned in their guilt and condemned. It is rather that he never does it even before judgment, as long as it can seem doubtful to humans whether he does it. After the jubilation of his chosen ones it is clear from the very irreversibility of the Last Judgment that he does not

extend his hand to the wicked. That is why the psalmist says, *The Lord said to my lord, "Sit at my right hand,* *Ps 109:1 *until I make your enemies your footstool."** It is not that the Lord does not sit at the Lord's right hand after he strikes down his enemies and subjects them to his power; rather it means that he presides in eternal blessedness over everyone, even before he tramples upon the hearts of those who rebel against him.

And obviously in that state of blessedness, with his enemies cast down, he also reigns afterward as well, and endlessly. So we read in the gospel concerning Mary's husband, *And he did not know her until she brought* *Matt 1:25 *forth her firstborn son.** It does not mean that he knew her after the birth of God, but that he never touched her, even when he did not know that she was the Creator's mother. Because he could never touch her after he knew that the mystery of our redemption was being enacted from her womb, from that very time it was necessary for the evangelists to bear witness to the fact that might be doubted because of Joseph's ignorance. The present case is similar: *God will not reject the blameless man, nor will he extend his hand to the wicked, until your* *Job 8:20-21 *mouth is full of laughter and your lips with jubilation.** He might say in other words, "Not even before judgment does God abandon the life of the blameless ones, nor even before he appears does he forbear from smiting the minds of the evildoers by abandoning them." There is certainly no doubt that he tortures the guilty ones endlessly, or that the chosen ones reign forever after his appearance.

LIII. 90. *Those who hate you will put on confu-* *Job 8:22 *sion.** The enemies of the righteous people will wear confusion at the Last Judgment, because they will see the evil they have done spread out before the eyes of their mind, and consequently their guilt will cover them completely like a garment and weigh them down. They will then bear the memory of what they have done as punishment, because they are now strangers to the use of reason, and they gleefully sin. There they will see how they ought to have fled the object of their love; there they will see how sad was the blame on which they congratulated themselves. Then guilt will overshadow their soul, and their own conscience will attack them with the darts of their memories. Who therefore could accurately suppose the greatness of the confusion that will then belong to the wicked, when the eternal Judge will appear externally and before their internal eyes their guilt will hover? They finally came to this because here below they loved only passing things. Therefore Bildad immediately adds with justice,

LIV. 91. *The tent of the wicked will not last.** Obviously a tent is constructed in order to protect the body from heat and cold. What therefore in this verse is meant by the word *tent*? It can be nothing else but the building of earthly prosperity through which the wicked provide many things that are bound to fall, so that they may protect themselves from the necessities of the present life, as if from heat and rain. They contend for more and more honors lest they seem contemptible. They increase their worldly possessions and add still more, lest they waste away with cold and want. They scorn providing for the future, and they do all they can to see to it that they lack nothing in their present circumstances. They eagerly spread their own name lest it be unknown, and if everything be supplied as they desire, they consider themselves ready for anything and content.

Accordingly, the place where they build their mind's dwelling is beyond doubt the place where they pitch their tent. They bear adversity impatiently, and they enjoy prosperity without restraint. They think only of

*Job 8:22

the present, and they do not sigh with affection at any reminder of the heavenly homeland. They are glad when the good things they want are supplied to them. When they rest in the bodily sense, they kill and bury the mind; in fact they have already been struck down by the spear of worldly concerns, and they carry about with them internally through their thoughts the heap of earthly possessions that they have sought and multiplied externally.

92. Upright people, on the other hand, do not accept a great deal of the good things that are offered them here below, nor do they greatly fear any evils that confront them. Rather, even when they make use of any present goods, they worry about approaching evils, and when they complain of present evils, they are comforted by the love of the good things that follow. They are revived by temporal succor in a way comparable to a wayfarer's making use of a pallet in a stable. He rests and hurries to be on his way; his body grows quiet while his mind heads off to another place. Sometimes the upright even desire to suffer adversity and run away from the temporary enjoyment of prosperity, lest the enjoyment of the journey should delay their arrival at the homeland and lest the footstep of their heart be arrested on the road of their journey and should arrive someday within sight of the heavenly fatherland without recompense. They rejoice when they are despised, nor do they grieve when they suffer need.

Accordingly, those who do not protect themselves against present adversity are like those who refuse the protection of tents against wind and rain. That is why Peter was rightly reproved when he wanted to pitch a tent on the ground, because he was not yet fortified by purity of mind when he had realized the glory of Truth.* The upright therefore do not bother with housing here below, where they realize that they are guests and pil-

*see Luke 9:29-33

grims. Because they wish to enjoy their own home, they will not be happy in someone else's. As for the wicked, the further they find themselves separated from their inheritance in the heavenly homeland, the deeper into the earth they sink the foundations of their thoughts.

Therefore Enoch was the seventh born of the chosen race from the first creation of man.[2] Therefore Cain called his firstborn son Enoch, and he also named the city that he built after his son Enoch.* The name Enoch in fact means "dedication." The wicked therefore dedicate themselves in the beginning, because in this life that comes first they plant and root their hearts, so that here they may flourish as their hearts desire and, being planted away from the heavenly homeland, which comes next, they may then entirely wither. Enoch, however, is born seventh for the upright, because the festal dedication of their life is reserved for the end. As Paul bears witness, Abraham dwelt in tents, because he was waiting for the city with foundations, which the supreme Architect builds.* So also Jacob humbly follows his flock of sheep and Esau goes out to meet him as a lord accompanied by a numerous throng, because, of course, the chosen people here below are not lifted up, but the evildoers are proud and happy with their possessions according to the flesh.[3]*

So the Lord tells Israel, *If you choose someone from the people of the land and make him your king, he must*

*Gen 4:17

*Heb 11:9

*Gen 32:6; 33:1, 14

---

[2] Gregory obviously counts Cain's wife, whose birth is not recorded, and Seth, who was born in place of Abel, whom Cain slew.*

[3] Gregory no doubt paraphrases from memory. *Tumultu multiplicis*￼ refers to Esau's retinue of four hundred men. Gregory assumes that Esau is on horseback so refers to him as *elevatus*, whereas Jacob proceeds *humiliter*, that is, on foot or in a lowly manner.

*Gen 4:25

*a numerous throng

*Deut 17:16
*not have his own horses and cavalry.** Nevertheless, the first king chosen from the same people acquired for himself three thousand horsemen as soon as he had reached the position of power, and he immediately ad-

*1 Sam 13:2
vanced in pride;* he quickly built on the height he had attained. He could not restrain externally by equality the pride above other men with which his soul had internally swelled up. The rich man had built himself a fortified tent when he said, *Soul, you have many possessions stored up for many years. Take it easy. Eat, drink, and*

*Luke 12:19
*enjoy yourself.** His tent, however, was not built upon the foundation of truth. So he heard forthwith, *Fool, this very night your soul will be taken from you. These*

*Luke 12:20
*Job 8:22
*goods you have prepared: whose will they be?** So it is well said that *The tent of the wicked will not last.** The reason is that those who love this fleeting life and so eagerly set themselves up in present circumstances will be rapidly carried off into eternity.

BOOK 9

I. 1. Once perverse people exert themselves against resolute opposition, it does not matter whether they hear their opponents utter what is correct or what is false; they will take the opposite position, because the opponents displease them merely for their opposition, and even when the opponents speak the truth, they will not accept it. As for good people, on the other hand, hatred of any person does not enter their hearts, only hatred of sin; accordingly they evaluate perversity in such a way that they accept the truth that is spoken. They are then the fairest judges of the intentions of adversaries, and their method of denying false charges allows them to accept whatever truth they recognize. Along with hundreds of thorns, for example, we usually find the heads of fruitful grain growing. Farmers, then, must work with a careful hand to throw away the thorns and cultivate the grain, inasmuch as they zealously get rid of the plants that hurt and knowingly save those that nourish. Therefore blessed Job knew that Bildad the Shuhite spoke well when he asked, *Does God hinder judgment? Does the Almighty One pervert justice?* * He had indeed produced true and solid arguments against hypocrites, and understanding their application to extend to all other evildoers as well, he leaves himself no concern for defense. So Job approves what he has heard and at once answers,

II. 2. *Yes, I know that is how it is: no one is justified in God's sight.* * People unquestionably receive justice when they are subject to God, but when equaled with God they lose it; any who compare themselves with the

*Job 8:3

*Job 9:2

241

Creator of goodness deprive themselves of the good they have received. Those who claim for themselves the good things they have received fight against God with God's own gifts; so when contemptible people lift themselves up, it is only right that the one lifted up be cast down. Because holy people, on the other hand, know very well that all our powers and worth are defective when judged strictly by the internal tribunal, Job is quick to add,

III. 3. *If anyone wanted to debate with him, he could* *Job 9:3* *not answer him one word for a thousand.** Holy Scripture ordinarily applies the number one thousand to the meaning of totality. For example, the psalmist says, *Ps 104:8* *The word he commanded for a thousand generations.** The evangelist, you know, only counts seventy-seven generations from the creation of the world to the com-*see Luke 3:38* ing of the Redeemer.* What else, then, does the number one thousand express but the perfect totality of the race known beforehand, in order that a new people might be revealed? John, for his part, says, *They will reign with* *Rev 20:6* *him a thousand years,** obviously because the kingdom of Holy Church is firmly established in perfect totality. Our single number, you see, is multiplied to make ten, and the ten is then multiplied by itself to make one hundred; that hundred is finally multiplied by ten and makes one thousand. We began with one and reached a thousand.

What is signified in this passage of Job by naming *one* except the beginning of righteous living? What is signified by the greatness of the number one thousand but the perfection of that good life? To debate with God means not to attribute to him the renown of one's virtue but rather to arrogate it to oneself. But let the holy man recognize that those who have already received the highest gifts and boast of what they have received lose all that they have received. Let him say, *If anyone*

The side notes read:
*Job 9:3
*Ps 104:8
*see Luke 3:38
*Rev 20:6

wanted to debate with him, he could not answer him one word for a thousand. The person who argues with the Creator cannot answer one word for a thousand, because when we grow proud over perfection, we show that we have not even begun to live rightly. We ourselves cannot answer one word for a thousand, because we flaunt ourselves for the perfection of a good life, and in so doing we prove that we have not even begun. We are then more truly alarmed at our shortcomings, however, if we carefully think over the infinite power of the Judge. So Job continues,

IV. 4. *His heart is wise and his power great.** It is no wonder that we call the Creator wise, since he is the Creator of wisdom, and we know that he is Wisdom himself. It is no wonder either that Job calls him powerful, since everybody knows that he is Power personified. Yet having used these two words to praise the Creator, the holy man suggests something to us in order to frighten us to self-knowledge. God is rightly called wise, because he knows our secrets thoroughly; he is additionally called powerful, because with power he strikes at our thoughts. We cannot deceive him who is wisdom, nor can we escape his power. Now God as wisdom invisibly sees everything; then as power those he condemns he irresistibly punishes. It is he who ordains this law here with power and wisdom, so that when the human mind rises up against the Creator the human mind may also be confounded by its pride. So Job continues,

V. 5. *Who has withstood him and remained at peace?** It is he who creates everything in a wonderful way and arranges creation so that it may be self-consistent. Thus anything created that withstands the Creator loses the consistency of peace, because nothing can be arranged that loses its agreement with the heavenly

*Job 9:4

*Job 9:4

Governor. Those things that would remain subject to
God in tranquility are confounded apart from him. They
find no peace in themselves, because they contradict
the peace that comes from above in the Creator. So that
highest angelic spirit, who could have remained subject
to God in the highest place, was cast down and now suffers himself, because he wanders outside through the
restlessness of his own nature. So also the first father of
the human race rebelled against the Creator's command
and immediately experienced the resistance of the flesh;
he who refused obedience and subjection to the Creator
was debased beneath his status and lost physical peace.

So Job says well, *Who has withstood him and remained at peace?* The devious mind, you see, is confounded by the very means by which it reared itself up
against the Creator. We are said to resist God when we
try to undo his arrangements. Our frailty, of course, does
not oppose his unchangeable purpose, yet we make the
attempt at what we cannot finish. Human frailty often
secretly knows the power of his arrangements, even when
we desire the ability to change them. If people do all they
can to go against him, they break themselves on the very
sword of their opposition. If they oppose the internal order
of creation, their own efforts defeat and chain them. The
resister can have no peace, because confusion follows
pride, and what is foolishly attained by sin is in a wonderful way turned against sinners for their pains. The
holy man, however, is filled with the power of the spirit
of prophecy and sees the confusion of human pride in a
general sense, while he immediately turns his mind's eye
to the special problem of the people of Israel. He demonstrates from the ruin of one people the punishment in store
for all the proud ones, quickly adding the following words:

VI. 6. *It is he who removed the mountains, and they
did not know it; he overturned them in his wrath.** In

* Job 9:5

Holy Scripture the word *mountains* often signifies the loftiness of preachers. The psalmist for example says of them, *Let the mountains receive peace for his people.* *Ps 71:3 The chosen preachers of the eternal homeland are surely not undeservedly called mountains, since they have left the earth behind because of the lofty life they lead, and they have become neighbors of heaven. But Truth removed the mountains when he took these holy preachers away from the stubborn Jews. That is what the psalmist rightly says: *The mountains will be moved to the heart of the sea.* * The mountains were moved to the heart of the *Ps 45:3 sea when the unbelieving Jews repulsed the preaching apostles, who then came to the understanding Gentiles. That is what they say in Acts: *We were bound to speak the word of God to you* first, but since you reject it and *Jews have judged yourselves unworthy of eternal life, we now turn to the Gentiles.* * *Acts 13:46

Those very persons, however, who by God's wrath were overturned knew nothing of this removal of the mountains, because when the Hebrews exiled the apostles from their territory, they considered it a gain for themselves that they had lost the light of their preaching. They deserved to be struck by a righteous censure, so blinded were they by an error of judgment, to the point that when they lost the light, they considered it happiness. But once the apostles were expelled, Judaea was at once destroyed by the Roman general Titus, and the Jewish nation was lost and scattered among all the Gentile peoples. Accordingly, with the mountains moved away, Job adds,

VII. 7. *He shakes the earth from its place, and its pillars tremble.* * The earth was indeed shaken from its *Job 9:6 place when the people of Israel were expelled from her borders and even bent her neck to the Gentiles because she refused subjection to the Creator. The earth to be

sure had columns as well, because in the priests and in
the princes, as well as in the teachers of the law and in
the Pharisees, structures of her obduracy rose, structures
that would collapse. In their persons, you see, she fash-
ioned the letter of the law, and in the time of peace she
bore the burden of animal sacrifice as though it were a
superstructure. The mountains, however, were moved
away and the pillars trembled, because the apostles
withdrew from Judaea, and even the Jews were not allowed to stay there, since they expelled the preachers
of life. Yes, they deserved to be brought into subjection
and to lose their earthly homeland, for whose love they
were not afraid to fight the soldiers of the heavenly
homeland. But after the saintly teachers were expelled,
Judaea became paralyzed from within, and by the sentence of the just Judge she closed her mind's eye on the
darkness of her error. So Job again adds,

VIII. 8. *He commands the sun, and it does not rise;*
*he shuts up the stars with a seal.** Sometimes Holy
Scripture uses the word *sun* to designate renowned
preachers. For example John says, *The sun became*
*as black as sackcloth.** On the last day, then, the sun
will look like sackcloth, because the shining life of the
preachers will assume a severe and contemptible aspect
before the eyes of reprobate sinners. These preachers are
also symbolized by the brightness of the stars, because
while they preach righteousness to sinners, they light
up the darkness of our nights. That is why the prophet
says of the preachers' absence: *The stars and the rain*
*have been withheld.**

Now the sunshine lasts all day, but the stars light up
the night, and Holy Scripture often uses the word *day* to
mean the eternal homeland, whereas she uses the word
night to mean the present life. The holy preachers shine
like the sun for our eyes when they open up for us the

*Job 9:7

*Rev 6:12

*Jer 3:3

contemplation of true light, but they shine in the darkness like the stars when they propose the disposition
of worldly affairs to profit our earthly needs through
an active life. They shine like the sun during the day,
when they sharpen our mind's eye for the contemplation
of our homeland with internal clarity; they shine like
stars at night, when they do earthly chores and again
and again keep the feet of our activity from stumbling
by the example of their own rectitude.

But when the preachers were exiled, there was nobody left to show the Jewish people the glory of contemplation in the night of their unbelief or reveal to them
the light of the active life. Truth indeed was spurned,
and he deserted that people by withdrawing the light
of preaching; he blinded them for their own perversity.
It was truly spoken, *He commands the sun, and it does
not rise; he shuts up the stars with a seal*. He forbade
the sun to rise on the one from whom he sent away the
eloquent preachers. He shut up the stars with a seal,
because he held the preachers within themselves by
silence, and in so doing he hid the heavenly light from
the unresponsive senses of the wicked.

9. We should consider this: when we seal anything
it is for the purpose of putting it out in plain sight when
the time is ripe. In addition we have learned from the
testimony of Holy Scripture that Judaea, which is now
deserted, will be gathered into the bosom of the faithful
at the end. That is why Isaiah says, *Even if the number of
the sons of Israel is like the sand on the seashore, only
a remnant will be saved.* Paul for his part says, *Until
the full number of Gentiles enters in; then all Israel will
be saved.* Therefore he now takes away his preachers
from the sight of Judaea, but later he displays them; he
seals up the stars, as it were, so that the spiritual stars
that were at first hidden might later burst forth and light

*Isa
10:22 LXX

*Rom
11:25-26

up the night of Israel's unbelief. Now she is repulsed and sees nothing, but then, enlightened, she will see.

Remember that those two exceptional preachers whose death was undone were taken away so that they might be called back at the end for the purpose of preaching. Of them John writes, *These are two olive trees, two candlesticks who stand in front of the Lord of all the earth.* Truth himself foretells one of them in the gospel where he says, *Elijah is going to come and restore everything.* The stars are then, as it were, sealed, and those two are now also hidden and kept from appearing; later they will appear so that they may prevail. The people of Israel will be completely gathered at the end, whereas in Holy Church's beginning she was unmoved and stubborn. She refused the preachers of Truth and spurned their helpful words. This happened through the Creator's wonderful providence, because if the glorious preaching had been received by that people alone, it could have lain hidden, but when it was rejected, it spread to all the Gentiles. So Job aptly added the following words:

IX. 10. *He alone spread out the heavens.* What does he mean by the word *heavens* if not this heavenly life of the preachers? The psalmist says of them, *The heavens declare the glory of God.* These preachers are called the heavens; they are also called the sun. They are called the heavens, because they intercede and offer protection; they are called the sun, because when they preach they demonstrate the power of light. The earth was shaken and the heavens spread out when Judaea threatened violent persecution; the Lord then extended the lives of the preachers in their acquaintance with all the Gentiles. Judaea herself was captured and scattered into the world by God's judgment, but the preachers were honored by grace, and they spread out everywhere.

*Rev 11:4

*Matt 17:11

*Job 9:8

*Ps 18:2

The heavens were confined when there was only one people to hold so many illustrious preachers. Which of the Gentiles would know Peter if he had stayed to preach to the people of Israel alone? Which of them would know Paul's excellence if Judaea had not introduced him to our knowledge by persecution? Yes, those who were driven out by the people of Israel with stripes and insults are now honored all over the world. The Lord alone then spread out the heavens; it was by a wonderful dispensation of his secret plan that he allowed his preachers to be oppressed by that people, the purpose being to make them spread out to the ends of the earth. But not even those Gentiles who were devoted to the present world freely accepted the words of life when the apostles tongue-lashed them for their shortcomings. Rather, they at once swelled up with pride and opposition, and they became stirred up to the point of cruel persecution. But when they tried to contradict the preachers' words, they were subdued immediately by wonder at the signs they worked. So the following words of praise are fittingly addressed to the Creator:

X. 11. *And he walks upon the waves of the sea.** What else is meant by the word *sea* but the hostility of this world which kills good people in its wrath? The psalmist spoke of this: *He gathers the waters of the sea as though in a bottle.** The Lord gathers the water of the sea as though in a bottle when he exercises wonderful management in the universe and disarms the threats of carnal people by confining them inside their own hearts. So the Lord walks upon the waves of the sea, because when the storms of persecution are stirred up, they are dissipated by astonishment at his miracles. God, you see, calms the excitement of human madness and, as it were, tramples down the waters when they accumulate and are heaped up.

*Job 9:8

*Ps 32:7

When the Gentiles notice that their customs are being set aside because of the preaching of a new way of life, when the rich people in this world see that the actions of the poor contradict their pride, when the wise people in the world think that the words of uninstructed people oppose them, all these people immediately become infuriated, and storms of persecution are raised. Yet those who are angered at the opposing words and start the storm of persecution are calmed, as we have said, by wonder at the signs. In this flood the Lord walks, inasmuch as he works miracles for the proud persecutors. Therefore the psalmist wisely says once more, *Wonderful is the surging of the sea, and the Lord is wonderful on high.**

*Ps 92:4

The world has indeed surged in a wonderful way and moved the water of persecution against the lives of the chosen, but the Creator on high has still more wonderfully subdued the water by exalting the power of the preachers. Yes, he has displayed the power of his ministers and their miracles, and he has shown it to exceed the pride and wrath of earthly power. The Lord proclaimed through Jeremiah, who while recounting external events intimated internal realities, *I have made the sand the boundary for the sea; it is an eternal law that will not pass away. Its waves will toss but not prevail; they will billow but not pass their boundary.**

*Jer 5:22

Yes, the Lord made the sand a barrier for the sea, because he chose outcasts and poor people to destroy the boasting of the world. The waves of that sea indeed lift themselves up when the worldly powers rush to start a persecution, but they cannot cross the boundary of the sand; rather, they are subdued by the humble miracles of the outcasts. But while the sea threatens, while it is lifted up by the waves of its madness, the display of interior virtue treads the beach. As time passes, Holy

Church then progresses and rises to the status planned for her. So Job is right to continue at once,

XI. 12. *It is he who made Arcturus and Orion, the Pleiades and the chambers of the south.** The words of Truth certainly do not follow the ridiculous fables of Hesiod, Aratos, and Kallimachos. We should imagine a bear's tail of seven stars on hearing the name Arcturus! Orion should make us think of a mad lover holding a sword! These names for the stars were unquestionably invented by the practitioners of self-indulgent wisdom. Holy Scripture, on the other hand, had a reason for using the same words: to express the realities that the customary language was intended to convey. If on the other hand it had spoken of the stars in question by using words unknown to us, those for whom Holy Scripture was written would undoubtedly not understand what they were hearing. Accordingly, those who were wise in the ways of God used the same words in Holy Scripture as did those who were wise in the ways of the world; in the same way God, the Creator of humankind, also used a word in Holy Scripture for the edification of humankind, a word that denoted a human emotion: he said, *I am sorry that I created man on earth.**

**Job 9:9

**Gen 6:6-7

Now he who sees all things that happen before they come to pass would never regret anything that he made after it was done. Why then should we wonder if spiritual people use the words of sensuous-minded people, when he who is both ineffable Spirit and Creator of the universe himself utters a word of flesh so that he might entice a person of flesh to understand him? Accordingly, when we hear from Holy Scripture these well-known names for stars, we know which stars are being talked about. When we consider the stars that are mentioned, it remains for us to arise from their movements to the mysteries of spiritual understanding. Nor is there anything hard to believe when we are told that God created Arcturus, Orion, and the Pleiades, since it is obvious that there is nothing on earth that he did not create. Yet the holy man says that the Lord created these stars through which he knew that spiritual events were fittingly symbolized.

13. Arcturus is found in the northern sky, and the rays of seven stars shine from it;[1] what does its name imply to us but the universal church, which is symbolized in John's Apocalypse by seven churches and seven candlesticks? She holds in herself the seven gifts of the Spirit, and she shines with the radiance of God's power; her light is from the region of truth. We should also remember that Arcturus continues to hover aloft and never sets, because Holy Church unceasingly endures persecution from evil people, yet she remains without fail until the end of the world. Reprobate sinners have often persecuted her to the bitter end, so that they believed her completely destroyed; but she carried on from there and returned to her former state just as often as she labored to the point of death at the hand of her persecutors. Arcturus then hovers and rises, because the more fervently Holy Church spends herself in speaking the truth, the more powerfully she is restored in truth.

14. So Orion follows immediately after Arcturus, and that too is fitting. Orion of course rises in the same dreadful season of winter, and at his rising storms gather and ravage both earth and sea. What is meant by Orion's

---

[1] It appears that Saint Gregory has confused *Arcturus*, *Boötes*, and *Ursa Major*. *Arcturus* is not a constellation, but the brightest star in *Boötes*, and it is *Ursa Major* (The Great Bear, or the Big Dipper, as it is more commonly known) that has seven stars (*Boötes* has only five). Admittedly, the confusion serves Gregory's theological symbolism very well.

being mentioned after Arcturus unless it is the martyrs? While Holy Church is rising for her commission to preach, the martyrs are exposed to the elements as in winter, for they are to suffer the dreadful violence of persecution. Accordingly, at Orion's rising, sea and earth are in turmoil, because the Gentiles are pained by the dissolution of their customs when the martyrs' courage is publicly displayed; in consequence they have aroused not only the wrathful and disorderly people but also the quiet ones, to kill them. Winter therefore turns dreadful at Orion's rising, because at the public constancy of the saints the cold minds of unbelieving pagans were aroused to storms of persecution. The sky then presented Orion when Holy Church sent out the martyrs. And when they dared to speak the truth to the mob, they bore the whole brunt of cold opposition.

15. He is right to add Pleiades immediately, because when the youth of spring is brightening, Pleiades rises in the face of the sky, and when the sun is already growing strong and hot, Pleiades shows himself. Pleiades, you see, is attached to that sign that the worldly wise call Taurus.* After his rising, the sun also rises and grows warm, extending and lengthening the day. Who but the teachers of Holy Church are signified by Pleiades, mentioned after Orion? Soon after the death of the martyrs, these teachers were made known to the world because faith was shining more brightly, the winter of unbelief was over, and the true Sun was growing hot in the hearts of the faithful. Forgotten were the times of persecution, and the long nights of unbelief were over when the teachers of Holy Church arose; then for the church a brighter year began with the springtime of faith.

*the Bull

Nor is it incongruous that the holy teachers should be given the name *Pleiades*. In Greek, you know, υετός* means "rain," and the word *Pleiades* takes its root from

*hyados

υετός, because the rain starts as soon as Pleiades rises.[2] So the preachers can indeed be called *Pleiades*, because they have received their status in the universal church, just as the Pleiades have their place in the sky, and the rain of holy preaching falls on the arid ground of the human breast. If the words of preaching were not rain, Moses would hardly have said, *My word will be awaited like rain.** Nor would Truth speak these words through Isaiah—*I will order the clouds not to send down rain upon her**—nor these words I have already quoted earlier: *So the stars and the rain have been withheld.**

*Deut 32:2

*Isa 5:6
*Jer 3:3

Accordingly the Pleiades bring rain, and the sun moves to the higher regions of the sky, because when the teaching of the doctors is made known, and when our mind is inundated with the rain of their preaching, the heat of faith increases. The earth is inundated and brings forth fruit when daylight lights up the sky, because we bring forth the fruit of good works more abundantly when our hearts burn more ardently, set on fire by the flame of holy teaching. More and more every day these preachers teach the knowledge of heaven, and a springtime of internal light begins for us, so that a new sun may shine brightly in our minds, known to us by their words, and that its light may increase daily.

The end of the world is upon us, and the knowledge of heaven increases and continues to increase with the passing of time. This is what Daniel foretold: *Many people will come and go, and knowledge will grow.** That is what the angel told John in the beginning of his revelation: *Seal up what was spoken by the seven*

*Dan 12:4

[2] There are two Greek forms: *Hyadas* and *Pleiades*. I've used *Pleiades* as being more familiar, but Gregory uses the Latin *Hyadas*, and obviously the root υετός belongs rather to *Hyadas* or, to use the Greek letters, Υαδας.

thunders.* But at the end of the same revelation he or-   *Rev 10:4
dered him, *Do not seal up the words of the prophecy of*
this book.* Yes, the first part of the revelation is ordered   *Rev 22:10
sealed, but the end is not allowed to be sealed, because
whatever was hidden in the beginning of Holy Church
is unveiled daily at the end.

There are some who think that the Greek letter upsi-
lon (Y, υ) signifies Pleiades. Even if they are correct, it
does not negate the explanation we have offered. Teachers are not wrongly expressed by these stars, if they
take their names from Greek letters. But although the
Pleiades do not contradict the image derived from the
letter in question, what is certain is that υετόσ means
"rain" and that in arising the Pleiades bring rain.

16. Let the holy man therefore wonderingly contemplate the order of our redemption and in his wonder
exclaim, *He alone spread out the heavens, and he walks*
upon the waves of the sea. It is he who made Arcturus
and Orion and Pleiades. Accordingly, after he had
stretched out the sky, the Lord made Arcturus, because
when the apostles were introduced and honored, he
founded the church in heavenly communication. After
Arcturus was created he made Orion as well, because
when the faith of the worldwide church was confirmed
he sent out the martyrs against the storms of the world.
After Orion was created, he brought forth the Pleiades,
because when the martyrs grew strong against adversity,
in order to inundate the deserts of human hearts he made
the teaching *magisterium.* These, then, are the hierarchy
of the spiritual stars, whose virtues are conspicuous and
who shine forever from heaven.

17. But what is left after all that except for Holy
Church to receive the reward of her labor and come
forward to see the internal places of the heavenly homeland? Therefore it is only right that after he had said, *It*

is he who made Arcturus and Orion and Pleiades, he should add, *and the chambers of the south*. What does the word *south* in this passage mean if not the excitement of the Holy Spirit? When anyone is filled with that, he is on fire with love of the spiritual homeland. Therefore the bridegroom in the Song of Songs cries out, *Arise, North wind, and come forth, South wind; let your breath fill my garden, and may its scents be carried abroad.** Obviously when the south wind rides out, the north wind up and flies away, and at the coming of the Holy Spirit the ancient enemy is expelled, he who had confined and numbed the mind, and abandons it.

*Song 4:16

The south wind blows upon the Bridegroom's garden so that its scents may be carried abroad, because when the Spirit of Truth fills Holy Church with the power of his gifts, he distributes the aroma of her good works far and wide. As for the chambers of the south, they are those secret ranks of angels and the most hidden bosom of the heavenly country, which is full of the warmth of the Holy Spirit. There the souls of the saints, now deprived of their bodies but later to have their bodies restored to them, are stars hidden, as it were, in secret places. There the sun's fire burns bright all day as at noon, because the Creator's glory, here dimmed by the shadow of our mortality, is seen more and more clearly. As the glow of the fiery sphere reaches out to include more and more space, so truth itself enlightens us more and more thoroughly. There the light of interior contemplation is beheld without any shadow of changeability to dim it. There the heat of the highest luminary is felt without any dark body. There the invisible choirs of angels shine like hidden stars; here people cannot see them, because the flame of true light makes them shine too brightly.

It is indeed wonderful how the Lord stretched out the heavens when the apostles were sent, how he walked

upon the waves of the sea when the storms of persecution broke and repressed them, how he created Arcturus
when the church was established, how he made Orion
when the martyrs were strengthened against adversity,
and how he made Pleiades when the places of the teachers were filled in peace. But after all that it is still more
wonderful that he prepared the bosom of our eternal
homeland for us as the chambers of the south.

18. All these things we see on the face of the sky by
the help of God's providence, and they are beautiful. But
their invisible counterpart is incomparably far lovelier.
Accordingly the Bridegroom again praises his Bride in
these fine words: *How lovely you are, my sweetheart,
how lovely! Your eyes are doves. But that is nothing
compared to the hidden beauty inside.**Song 4:1 He says she is
lovely and then repeats it, because the loveliness of her
present behavior as it is witnessed is one thing, and the
loveliness of her reward that will be given later, when
she is raised up through the Creator's presence, is quite
another. Her members are all the elect who walk in
simplicity, and her eyes are called dove's eyes, which
glow with abundant light because they are crowned with
signs and miracles. But how great is this immense miracle that can be seen!

But that internal miracle that cannot now be seen is
still more wonderful. That is what is aptly described by
the words, *But that is nothing compared to the hidden
beauty inside.* Great indeed is the glory of her obvious
works, but far greater is the glory of her reward, and in-
comparable. That which blessed Job calls stars Solomon
alludes to by the word *eyes.* Solomon says, *That is nothing compared to the hidden beauty inside,* and blessed
Job intimates the same thing when he commends the
chambers of the south. But look now, the holy man
wonders at external manifestations, he contemplates

internal matters, he announces obvious facts, and he even enters into hidden places; in short, he attempts to tell us all that happens internally and externally. But when will the tongue of flesh explain the works of highest greatness? That is why he includes these very same works immediately, though by indirection, when he says,

XII. 19. *God does great, inscrutable, and wonderful things that cannot be counted.* * We only really explain the actions of God's power when we realize that we cannot explain them. We speak more eloquently when we are stumped by his actions and hold our peace. In order to announce the works of God adequately, our defective ability has a way to use its tongue correctly, so that when it cannot understand properly, it may fittingly praise by remaining silent. So also the psalmist is right to say, *Praise him for his powerful deeds; praise him for his surpassing greatness.* * Those who know that they are insufficient to praise God adequately certainly praise him for his surpassing greatness. Let Job therefore say, *God does great, inscrutable, and wonderful things that cannot be counted.* Obviously they are great in power, inscrutable by reason, and uncountable by their very multitude. He cannot explain God's works by speaking, so he has defined them more eloquently by indirection. But why are we led so far afield in external considerations when we are still ignorant of that very deed that is also done for us? So he is right to add,

XIII. 20. *If he comes to me, I will not see him, and if he goes, I will not know it.* * The human race is shut off from internal joy, as its sin requires, and it has lost its mind's eye, so that it does not know where its steps deservedly lead as it walks on. What it considers wrath is often a gift of grace, and what it accounts as grace is often wrath and a judgment of God. Humans often rate grace as a reward for virtue, you see; yet they are puffed

*Job 9:10

*Ps 150:2

*Job 9:11

up with pride because of such rewards and lose ground.
They often fear the strife against temptations like the
wrath of God, yet after the struggle with these temptations they begin to guard their virtue more cautiously.
Would they not think they were drawing near to God if
they realized that the gifts of God were causing them
to grow, if they sensed in themselves either the gift of
prophecy or the ability to teach sacred doctrine, and if
their skill to cure diseases grew strong?

Yet the mind often relaxes and loses its sure virtue,
the adversary lays traps for it, and a spear of unsus-
pected guilt wounds it. Thus humans become estranged
from God in eternity after having drawn near to him in
time without vigilance or caution. Do people not think
they are already abandoned by God's grace after they
have experienced a state of purity and subsequently
been buffeted by temptations of the flesh, with the soul
embarrassed by disgrace? When shameful and perverse
images parade before the mind's eye, do they not vex
the soul? Yet they do not overcome it, nor do they defile
the soul with impurity. Rather they assist it to attain
humility, so that it realizes how weak it is when tempted
and surrenders itself entirely to God's assistance, totally abandoning self-confidence. So it happens that
the mind clings to God more truly precisely in those
areas where it moaned that it had fallen away from God
more grievously.

Our mind accordingly knows very little about its
own nearness to God or distance from him as long as
the end of changing circumstances is unknown. For example, regarding temptations it is unclear whether they
try us or ruin us, and regarding gifts of grace we never
discover whether they reward abandoned souls in this
life or help them along on the road in order to lead them
to heaven. Humans were therefore once exiled from

internal joy so that they might see the doors of the spiritual hideout closed against them; cast out by themselves to the external world, let them cry out in the flesh when they look upon their ruined state of blindness and say, *If he comes to me, I will not see him, and if he goes, I will not know it.* It is as if they openly deplored their misery and said, "Once I lost my eyes by my own volition, and now I suffer the blindness of a night I wanted, and I know neither when the sun rises nor when it sets." Yet those who are depressed by the punishment of their weakened state and handicapped by the darkness of their blindness hurry on to the judgment of heavenly light, so that they may give an accounting for their actions. So the text continues:

XIV. 21. *If he suddenly questions anyone, who will answer?** God's sudden interrogation happens when he calls us unprepared to his strict judgment. But to give an answer in that interrogation, everyone falls short. If judged without mercy in that questioning, even the life of the just fails them. Well, he surely questions us when he afflicts us with grievous trials, as happens when our mind prides itself in its long tranquility and then discovers itself as it really is in disturbance. We often groan at our chastisement, but a reply is unsatisfactory, because while chastisement is distasteful, when we look at ourselves we hold our peace; we are afraid to appeal against God's judgment, since we know we are only dust. That is why Paul says, *Who are you, a man, to answer back to God?** He who is called man is warned that he cannot answer back to God. Because he was taken from the ground, he is unworthy to appeal against God's judgment. So the following words are not unsuitable:

XV. 22. *Or who can ask him, "Why do you act this way?"** The Creator's acts are always awesome and unappealed, because they can never be unjust. To demand

*Job 9:12

*Rom 9:20

*Job 9:12

a reason for his secret counsel is certainly nothing else but rebellion against his counsel. Accordingly, if no reason is found for things that happen, there is nothing left for us to do but humbly hold our peace concerning his works, because the carnal mind is never able to penetrate the secret counsel of God's majesty. Those therefore who see no reason in God's acts but know their own shortcomings know why they do not see. Thus Paul again adds after the foregoing notice, *Does the clay ask the potter, "Why did you make me this way?"** Because he knows he is the work of the divine artisan, he convinces himself not to spring back against the hand of his Maker; he who kindly made something that did not exist would not unjustly forsake what does exist. Let the mind therefore return to itself in time of adversity and not demand what it cannot grasp, lest if it appeal the case of God's wrath, it should arouse still more serious wrath. The wrath one could have placated by humility, one arouses insatiably by pride. So concerning this very wrath Job at once adds,

XVI. 23. *It is God whose wrath no man can withstand, beneath whom they bow who hold up the world.** Isn't it strange that we are here told that no man can withstand God's wrath, when Holy Scripture testifies that a number of people have withstood manifestations of heavenly anger? Or did Moses not stand up against God's wrath, upright in front of the falling people? By offering his own death he held off the attack of the heavenly blow and said, *Either forgive their sin or blot out my name from the book you have written.** Or did Aaron not withstand God's wrath when he stood between the living and the dead, took up his censer, and cooled the fire of the divine presence with the smoke of incense?* Or did Phineas not withstand God's wrath when he killed Israelites in mid-fornication with foreign

*Rom 9:20

*Job 9:13

*Exod
32:30-32

*see Num
16:47-48

*see
Num 25:11

*see
2 Sam 24:25

*see
1 Kgs 18:44

women and appeased the divine jealousy with his own zeal, turning away wrath by using his sword?* Or did David not withstand God's wrath when he offered himself to the striking angel and thus demanded the grace of forgiveness before the time stipulated?* Or did Elijah not withstand God's wrath when the earth was already long without rain and he restored wetness from the sky by uttering a word?* How then is it that we are told that no man can withstand God's wrath, when we have learned from many examples that men have often withstood it?

But if we skillfully weigh blessed Job's words in the present instance, as well as the anecdotes cited, we will understand the truth that no one withstands God's wrath, as well as the truth that many have in fact withstood it. All the saints, you see, who oppose God's wrath receive from him the ability to stand against the blow of his might; if I may speak so, they rise against him aided by him. Divine power opposes itself and takes their side. Because they hold this ground externally against the fury of the one besetting them, the grace of the wrathful one encourages them internally; he internally supports his servants whom he externally holds off as attackers. He bears the opposition of those who plead, and he favors that opposition. That which he himself commands to be done is imposed upon him as though against his will.

Here is what he told Moses: *Let me alone; let my wrath blaze up against them; let me destroy them. Then I will make you a great nation.** What does it mean to tell the servant, *Let me alone*, but to give him the boldness to plead? He might as well say openly, "Measure the amount of what you can do before me, and know that you can obtain from me whatever you ask for the people." Since that is the intention to be carried out, forgiveness immediately follows and is borne witness to. But when the divine indignation, if I may so express

*Exod 32:10

it, is aroused from the very marrow, human opposition does not hold it back, nor does any human intercession successfully oppose God when he makes any decision from his internal wrath. That explains Moses' fate: it is true that his prayers wiped away the people's sin in the Lord's sight, and he appeased the force of the Lord's wrath when he offered himself as a hindrance,* yet when he came to the rock of Horeb and doubted the outpouring of water, the Lord became angry, and he could not enter the promised land. Moses often suffers because of this weakness of his, and he is upset when the desire grasps him. Nor could he who withdrew God's anger from the people when the Lord wished it turn it away from himself when God determined punishment.*

*see Exod 32

*see
Num 20:12

Such was David's fate after the plague among the people when he restrained the angel's sword; he wailed and lamented before he fled from his son with bare feet, and he never managed to placate God's wrath in his own case until he had received full punishment for the sin he had committed.* It was also Elijah's fate as a man to get too little for himself from God's nod; he who opened the sky by a word was terrified by a woman's indignation and fled across the desert, and he who appeased God's wrath toward others by his intervention was fearfully weak in his own case.* Accordingly, God's wrath may be withstood when he who is angry lends his aid; it may absolutely not be withstood in the following case: being aroused to vengeance, God discourages intercessory prayer. So Jeremiah is told, *You are not to pray for this people, nor are you to adopt praise or intercession for them, because I will not listen, if they ever cry out to me.* He is again told, *Even if Moses and Samuel stood before me, my ears are closed to this people.*

*see 1 Sam
24:17; 15:30

*1 Kgs 17:1;
19:2-4

*Jer 11:14
*Jer 15:1

24. Concerning this point, we might profitably question why with so many of the ancient patriarchs passed

over, Moses and Samuel alone should be singled out for
the intercession of prayer as being more excellent and
efficacious. The answer, though, is easily grasped, once
we evaluate that grace by which we are commanded to
love even our enemies. That prayer that even attempts
intercession for enemies is especially welcome to the
Creator's ears. Truth for his own part says, *Pray for*

*Matt 5:44   *those who persecute you and speak falsely against you.*
Elsewhere he says, *When you stand up to pray, forgive*

*Mark 11:25   *anything you may have against anyone.* Now when
we reflect upon the actions of the ancient patriarchs as
we read them in Holy Scripture, we do find that Moses
and Samuel prayed for their adversaries. One of them
indeed fled from pursuit by his people, who were angry
with him, yet he interceded for the life of his pursuers.
The other was deposed from leadership of the people,
yet he told those who rose against him, *God forbid that
I should sin against the Lord by ceasing my prayers on*

*1 Sam 12:23   *your behalf.*

What accordingly is so hard about introducing the
intercession of Moses and Samuel if the purpose is
to make it abundantly clear that not even they could
stand up against God's anger, they who could intercede for their friends more quickly precisely because
their custom was to pray to God even for their enemies?
Therefore this same Jewish people is told, *I struck you*

*Jer 30:14   *with an enemy's blow, a cruel punishment,* and again,
*Jer 30:15   *Why complain about your ruin? Your pain is incurable.*
The holy man can therefore consider that when God's
wrath is implacably aroused, no one's intervention can
restrain it. He can say, *It is God whose wrath no man
can withstand.* We rightly understand this sentence in
a special sense when we evaluate the loss of the people
Israel, whom the Redeemer, made manifest through his
mysterious dispensation, abandoned to their own pride

while calling the Gentiles to the grace of the knowledge of him. So he fittingly adds, *Beneath whom they bow who hold up the world.*

25. Yes, those who support the burdens of the present life hold up the world. Everyone is indeed compelled to support as many burdens as he is responsible for in this world. So the earthly ruler is rightly called βασιλευς in the Greek language. Λαος means people, so βασιλευς can be parsed as βασ ις λαου, which becomes *basis populi* in Latin.* The one who holds fast the burden of power and rules the actions of the people obviously supports the people. Because of bearing the burdens of the subjects, such a one is like a foundation bearing the pillar placed upon it. So blessed Job, being full of the spirit of prophecy, can consider by its power how Judaea is abandoned and how the kings of the nations bow down in worship before the divine nature, and he can say, *It is God whose wrath no man can withstand, beneath whom they bow who hold up the world.* He could even avow it openly in words like these: "You both uncompromisingly abandon your former subjects and mercifully bend the upright powers of the nations."

*support of the people

26. On the other hand, the words *beneath whom they bow who hold up the world* could also be understood as the angelic powers. It is they indeed who hold up the world and who attend to the management of governing the world, as Paul testifies: *Are they not all ministering spirits sent out to be ministers for those who are to inherit salvation?** Job says, as you know, *It is God whose wrath no man can withstand, beneath whom they bow who hold up the world.* It is as though he beheld the lowliness of all creation and in a tremulous voice spoke words like these: "What man among the wretched race of mortals could resist your will, to the fear of whom even the angelic powers bend low?" Or at least,

*Heb 1:14

since when we bow we do not see what is above us, he might say, "Those clever spirits would be straight and tall, if they were really able to reach the full power of his majesty."

But those who hold up the world bow down before God, because however high they can see, not even the angel hosts can fully take in the high essence of his divinity. The just man does not go that far on account of his lowly nature, but he estimates it as well as he can from the subject ministries of the highest spirits, and he collects himself for his own meditation, carefully humbling himself and casting himself down before the power of overruling majesty. He says,

*Job 9:14

XVII. 27. *What, then, do I amount to, that I should answer him or speak to him in my own words?** He could say it openly: "If those creatures that are not burdened with the weight of flesh are unable to look upon him, how do I dare dispute his justice, limited as I am by the weight of corruption?" Just as God's word to us is often judgment that tells us his decision concerning our actions, so our words to him are the works we perform. But humans cannot speak to God with words, because in the presence of God's exact judgment, human actions hold no confidence. So Job rightly adds,

XVIII. 28. *Even if I did have a certain justice, I would not answer: rather will I implore my Judge.** As we have often said, all human justice if judged strictly proves to be injustice. People therefore need prayer as well as justice, because justice may prove false and fail; only from the Judge's kindness is rehabilitation possible. Even when justice is had fully by those who are the most perfect, one can only say that some justice is had, because the human mind hardly ever practices what it learns, and what it does understand is extremely limited. Let Job say it then: *Even if I did have a certain* *justice, I would not answer: rather will I implore my Judge.* He might as well confess it more openly: "Even if I should grow so far as to practice works of virtue, not my merits but his kindness will strengthen me for life." We must accordingly make an effort to pray when we do what is right, so that we may humbly preserve all our just living. But even our prayers are often shaken by so many temptations that they almost seem to be cast out from the Judge's sight. Yet the merciful Creator sees them. Our prayer indeed is not strong enough to prevail undiminished, as we wish it to, and so we fear the judgment of the reprobate.

XIX. 29. So Job continues, *And when he would have heard my cry, I do not believe that he would have listened to my voice.** The mind is often set afire with the force of divine love and raised up to behold heavenly and hidden realities; it is quickly swept away to the heights, wounded by perfect desire, and estranged from the earth. Then a sudden temptation attacks it just when its firm intention is inclined straight to God; transfixed, it bends over with thoughts unfulfilled, in such a way that it cannot discern itself, and finding itself between vice and virtue, it knows not which side is stronger. The mind, you see, is often led precisely to this point so that it may wonder how it has reached so high a place when evil thoughts have defiled it. On the other hand, the wonder is how it has dallied with evil thoughts when strong spiritual fervor had swept it above itself. The psalmist saw these changing waves of thoughts in the soul when he said so aptly, *They rose all the way to heaven, and they fell all the way to the pit.**

We actually rise all the way to heaven when we touch high contemplation; we fall all the way to the pit when we are suddenly flung down from the high place of contemplation through disgraceful temptations. The

*Job 9:16

*Ps 106:2

soul's emotions alternate between prayer and imperfection; accordingly, they becloud the soul's assurance of a hearing. So it is rightly said, *And when he would have heard my cry, I do not believe that he would have listened to my voice.* The mind itself shakes inwardly because of its own propensity to change, and because it suffers unwillingly it supposes that it is spurned and despised.

30. Let us notice the great discrimination with which Holy Job judges himself, lest there should be found in him anything for which God's judgment might reprove him. Considering his own frailty he says, *What, then, do I amount to that I should answer him or speak to him in my own words?* Having no confidence in the value of his own justice but trusting only in the hope of pleading, he adds, *Even if I did have a certain justice, I would not answer: rather will I implore my Judge.* Yet fearful even about his own plea, he adds, *And when he would have heard my cry, I do not believe that he would have listened to my voice.* Why this anxiety and caution? Why this uneasiness and dread? He must be eyeing the Judge with alarm at the Last Judgment; he would not withstand that fierce trial, so he considers all that he does to be insufficient to save himself, and he at once adds,

*Job 9:17

XX. 31. *He would wrack me with a whirlwind.** Every sinner who seemed secure and tranquil is wracked in the whirlwind, because while God's patience suffers him for a long time, the extreme severity of judgment kills him. It is rightly called a whirlwind, since it appears as the violent upheaval of the elements, as the psalmist testifies, *God will visibly come; our God will not be silent. Fires will burn in His sight. There will be*

*Ps 49:3

a raging storm all around Him.* That is why another prophet says, *The path of the Lord is through storm and*

*Nah 1:3

whirlwind.* And in that whirlwind, take note, the just

man is certainly not wracked, precisely for the reason that his constant preoccupation here below was that he not be wracked. While still living the exile of the present life, he knows how the Accountant of the fruits of human acts comes as Judge and how he condemns some of those caught with the guilt of original sin on that day, even without its works. So the holy man immediately adds in the voice of the human race,

XXI. 32. *He will increase my wounds even without cause.*[*Job 9:17] Some people, you see, are withdrawn from the present world before they manage to acquire merits of active life, whether good or evil. Because the sacraments of salvation did not free them from the guilt of original sin and they did nothing in this life on their own account, they at last suffer torture in the next life. They are born with one corruptible wound, and the other is bodily death. But after death follows eternal death as well, so it is by hidden and just judgment that wounds also increase without cause. They indeed receive everlasting torture, even when they have not sinned by their own will. Therefore it is written, *No one is pure in his sight, not even an infant a day old upon the earth.*[*Job 15:14] That is why Truth himself has said, *Unless a person be born again of water and the Holy Spirit, that one will not have eternal life.*[*John 3:5] Paul says for his part, *We were natural sons of wrath like the others.*[*Eph 2:3]

In that case those who add nothing of their own but are only troubled by the guilt of original sin, what else do they suffer at that Last Judgment, as far as the human mind can judge, but a wound without cause? On the other hand, this is justice according to God's judgment: that the human race, like an unfruitful tree, should keep the bitterness in its branches that it received from the root. That is why Job says, *He would wrack me with a whirlwind, and he will increase my wounds even without cause*. It is as though he looked upon the ruin of the human race and said openly, "By what act of censure does the strict Judge cut down those whom the guilt of their own actions condemns, if he even sends to eternal punishment those whom no personal guilt sets apart?"

33. We know that these words are not inconsistent with the special case of blessed Job when we investigate how truly they were spoken. He evaluates himself acutely, you see, and judges his every action, so he implies how anxiously fearful he is of the power of God's judgment. He says, *He would wrack me with a whirlwind*. He could say it outright: "I fear him always, even in times of tranquility, precisely because I know very well that he may come in the whirlwind by the trials he sends." By his fear of those trials he foresaw them, and by foreseeing them he endured them. So he adds, *And he will increase my wounds even without cause*. We have already repeatedly said that blessed Job was not struck down so that the blow should wipe away sin but so that it should increase his merit. So when he asserts that he has been wounded without cause, he says externally what Truth says about him secretly: *You incited me against him, to cause him affliction for no reason at all.** Accordingly the holy man does not speak out of pride, but he speaks the truth. Nor does he shake off his rectitude by these words, which are in accordance with those of the Judge. Besides that, he declares that these same wounds continue to hurt, adding,

*Job 2:3

XXII. 34. *He does not allow my spirit to rest, but he fills me with bitterness.** The practice of virtue on the part of the just often involves bearing only external adversities. But in order that they be taught to exercise their prowess in a battle that involves a full trial, at times both external torments trouble them and internal temptations try them. Accordingly the holy man as-

*Job 9:18

serts that he is filled with bitterness, because when he is
buffeted externally, what he suffers internally from the
adversary's temptations is worse. Yet the extreme pain
is somewhat mitigated when he considers the fairness
and power of the one who strikes. So he adds,

XXIII. 35. *If I want courage, he is the strongest; if
I want fairness in judgment, no man will dare speak up
for me as a witness.** The one who does not depend on
someone else's testimony for knowledge of the condi-
tions of life certainly considers them critically himself;
the one who is one day to be revealed as a determined
exactor of punishment has often been a silent witness
of guilt. The prophet says in his name, *I am both Judge
and Witness.** Another prophet says, *I was forever silent,
I held my peace, and I was patient; now I will speak
as a woman giving birth.** When a woman gives birth,
you see, she painfully releases the burden she has borne
so long in her womb. The Lord, then, is like a woman
giving birth, keeping silence for a long time and then
speaking. He is now silent and bears something within
himself, but at the retribution on Judgment Day he will
finally and painfully reveal it. But we must ask ourselves
now whether the just man will live, whether anyone will
be courageous enough to render testimony on his behalf,
whether someone will free him from guilt. And if no
one does bear witness on his behalf, will he himself be
strong enough to bear witness for himself?

XXIV. 36. *If I want self-justification, my mouth will
condemn me; if I prove my innocence, it will make me
guilty.** It is as if he freely said, "What could I say about
other people when I cannot even be a witness on my own
behalf?" But if you are unable to testify to your own
innocence, how do you even know if you are innocent?
He continues:

*Job 9:19

*Jer 29:23

*Isa 42:14

*Job 9:20

XXV. 37. *Even if I were blameless, that also would my soul be unaware of.** If we often know the good that we do, we are led to pride; if we do not know, we certainly do not preserve it. Are we not proud, ever so slightly, of knowing our virtue? Do we, on the other hand, preserve the good that is in us when we do not know it? But against both extremes what is left for us to do except to be knowingly ignorant of our good deeds, so that we both evaluate them correctly and esteem them as too little? We must do so to the extent that the knowledge of proper conduct alerts the soul and puts it on its guard so that its low self-esteem keeps it from growing proud.

Nevertheless, there are certain things that we cannot easily know, even when they happen. For example, the study of right conduct often gets us incensed against the failings and weaknesses of other people so that we are moved to anger beyond the bounds of justice, yet we esteem this excess of ours as righteous zeal. We often take up the duty of preaching so that we might be helpful to our brothers, but if we do not please those to whom we speak, they hardly freely accept the message we preach. And when the mind eagerly strives to please and be helpful, it shamefully falls away into the enjoyment of self-praise. Whereas the mind's intention was to free other people from the servitude of vice, it ends up being itself a captive to the favor of others. The desire for human praise is indeed like petty thieves who latch on to those who are walking a straight path; out of the bush they spring with drawn sword to take the lives of wayfarers. So when the intention of helpfulness strays into eagerness, it is frightful the way we sinfully finish the act that we began virtuously. Often from the very beginning one thing is intended by thought and another is shown by action.

38. Often enough even thought shows itself untrue to itself, because it holds one object before the eyes of the mind while the intention hurries out to meet another far-off object. For example, some people often desire earthly rewards; they maintain justice, esteem themselves as people without any guilt, and triumphantly proclaim themselves defenders of rectitude. But if their hope of monetary gain is disappointed, their defense of justice immediately ends. Nevertheless, they still think themselves champions of justice, and they assert that they are upright people, although it is by no means rectitude but money that they are after. Moses rightly speaks against them saying, *Maintain justice rightly.**   *Deut 16:20

But the one who rather than striving for virtue pretends to defend justice while desiring an earthly reward certainly maintains justice unrighteously. And those who do not even fear the act of selling the very justice that they pretend to uphold certainly maintain justice unrighteously. To maintain justice rightly means to seek that very justice that we assert. We often act righteously and by no means expect rewards or human praise. But the mind still lifts itself up and trusts itself. It disdains the art of pleasing those from whom it asks nothing, and it spurns their judgment; it drives its falsely free self along the precipices of pride. There it falls into more vicious sin, where it boasts of being subject to no desires, as though all viciousness were overcome.

39. We often question ourselves more than is prudent, and consequently we go astray even more indiscreetly from the zeal for discretion; our mind's eye grows darker the more it tries to see, just as the man who foolishly observes the sun's rays directly grows blind: where he wanted to see more, he is forced to see nothing. Therefore, if we are too slow in our examination, we know nothing whatever of ourselves, or if we

search ourselves with exact scrutiny, we are often in
the dark about our virtues or vices. So it is well said:
*Even if I were blameless, that also would my soul be
unaware of.* He might as well say, "How rash it is for me
to question the Creator's judgment against me, when I
do not even know myself in my feeblemindedness and
ignorance!" So the prophet is right to say, *The abyss
uttered its voice from its deep imagination.*

*Hab 3:10
LXX

The abyss indeed has a deep imagination when the
human soul, dark as it is with boundless thoughts, does
not sound itself even by its own searching. Yet it can
still utter a voice from this deep place, because while it
cannot uncover itself, it is forced to rise in admiration,
and it dares not scrutinize that which is above it, because
knowing its own incomprehensibility, it cannot find out
what it is. But the hearts of just people cannot perfectly
examine themselves; that is why they bear the exile of
their blind existence so poorly.

*Job 9:21

So he adds, *Then my life will bore me.* The just
man finds life tedious, because he continues working
and seeking livelihood, yet he cannot find out what his
life is worth. True, he draws the standard for evaluating
himself from his interior sense of justice, but he falls
short as regards effective discovery there because he is
taken out of himself, and his power to search grows. But
the just and incomprehensible power of the Creator is a
consolation in our darkness when it returns to the soul.
It does not leave the wicked without taking vengeance,
but it envelops the justice of righteous people with his
vast incomprehensibility. Therefore Job is right to add,
XXVI. 40. *What I have said is all one thing: he consumes both the blameless and the wicked.* The Creator

*Job 9:22

consumes the blameless man, because, you see, however
complete may be his simplicity, the simplicity of God's
greatness obliterates him. However zealously we pre-

serve our simplicity, when we take interior purity into consideration, we realize that the very simplicity we cultivate is not simplicity at all. The Creator consumes the wicked as well, because God arranges everything in a wonderful way, so that the wicked are tied up by their own wiles. Where they boast of their smart actions, there they unknowingly trip themselves up in due punishment. Accordingly, almighty God both encompasses the blameless life of good people by his simplicity and condemns the wicked by seeing through their wiles, so Job is right to say, *What I have said is all one thing: he consumes both the blameless and the wicked.* He could say it openly: "I advisedly spoke those words, because if my innocence is strictly questioned, I will not come out innocent, nor if I try to hide my wickedness will I escape the scrutiny of the heavenly questioner."

No, the uncompromising Judge knows all, and he sees through the hidden malice in a wonderful way. He arranges all things well and condemns the wicked by their own devices. Either that, or he is said to consume both the blameless and the wicked in the sense that even if their mind's way of being is different, they are equally subject to bodily death by the guilt of original sin. That is why Solomon says, *The learned and the ignorant die together,*[*] and again, *Everything is subject to vanity; all things go to the same place. They were made from earth, and to the earth they also return.*[*]

[*] Eccl 2:16

[*] Eccl 3:19-20

XXVII. 41. *If he strikes, let him kill at once and not make fun of the sufferings of blameless people.*[*] Who would not think that these words were uttered in pride without hearing the decision of the Judge, who said, *You have not spoken the truth before Me like My servant Job?*[*] Let no one then dare question the author's words, which we know that the Judge praises. Rather, the more harsh they sound externally, all the more carefully and

[*] Job 9:23

[*] Job 42:7

intelligently we must search them in the depths of our heart. So the holy man is looking at the losses of the human race and their causes; he is considering how the man and the woman wanted to have the knowledge of good and evil that the adversary promised and in the act lost themselves as well. So he can truly say, *Even if I were blameless, that also would my soul be unaware of.* But after the sentence of exile, we also suffer the scourge of corruption, and even after this torture, we expect bodily death or even the death of the soul, so that Job can really say, *He consumes both the blameless and the wicked.*

Against these scourges he beseeches the grace of the Redeemer and says, *If he strikes, let him kill at once.* Because we have abandoned God in our minds and our flesh returns to dust, we are cursed by a double death. But he came to us who would die for us only the death of the body; he would unite his single death to our double death and free us from both our deaths. That is what Paul means when he says, *The death he died he died to sin only once.** So let the holy man look upon that which we lost by corruption and plead for that one death that would destroy both of ours: the death the Mediator died. Let him desire that death and say, *If he strikes, let him kill at once.*

*Rom 6:10

42. But now see how humility is opposed when he immediately adds, *and not make fun of the suffering of innocent people.* If, however, we evaluate this line with a humble mind, we will easily understand that it is exceedingly humble. The fact that any desire whose attainment is put off becomes a pain makes everything clear. Solomon bears us witness when he says, *Unfulfilled hope afflicts the soul.** The laughter of God means his refusal to pity human suffering. That is why Solomon again says in the voice of God to the wicked who continue to sin, *I too will laugh at your ruin.** In other

*Prov 13:12

*Prov 1:26

words, "I will have no kindness or compassion for your suffering." Before the Redeemer's coming, accordingly, all the elect had their own pain to suffer, because their desire burned hot to see the mystery of his incarnation, as the Redeemer himself bears witness: *I tell you, many prophets and just men desired to see what you are seeing, and they did not see it.*[*]   *Matt 13:17

The hardship of blameless people is the desire of the just. As long, therefore, as the Lord puts off the pleading of the elect without compassion, what else does he do but laugh at the hardship of the blameless? Then let the holy man consider the gifts of the Redeemer who is to come and gravely accept the putting off of his own pleas; let him say, *If he strikes, let him kill at once and not make fun of the sufferings of blameless people.* It is as if he prayed aloud, "Our everyday life is buffeted by the whip of vengeance for our guilt; let him now come who is guiltless but dies once for us, that God may no longer laugh at the sufferings of the blameless when he appears himself in flesh that can suffer; desire for him causes our mind to suffer agony."

43. On the other hand, Job certainly calls joy God's laughter and says that God laughs at the suffering of blameless people in the sense that we seek him more ardently and make his joy in us sweeter. We make him happy in a way by our suffering when we chastise ourselves for the sake of love through our holy desires. That is what makes the psalmist say, *Let the whole community join the solemn procession up to the horns of the altar.*[*]   *Ps 117:27
Whoever persistently afflicts himself in his desire joins the community in the solemn celebration for the Lord. Of course he is commanded to attend the solemn celebration up to the horns of the altar, because everyone must be involved as far as the height of the heavenly sacrifice, that is, he must reach eternal joy.

The righteous man therefore wants his desires satisfied, not delayed, so he humbly says, *Let him not make fun of the sufferings of blameless people.* It is as if he said, "Let him freely accept our devotion and delay no longer but openly display him who tries us in our expectation of him." Blessed Job especially petitioned him to be killed at once, the one who suffered bodily death alone for us at the end of the world, as he now makes clear when he adds the very passion story, saying,

XXVIII. 44. *The earth is given into the hands of the wicked one, and he covers the face of his judges.** What is expressed by the word *earth* if not flesh, and who but the devil is meant by naming the wicked one? Those who brought about our Redeemer's death were the hands of this wicked one. The earth is accordingly given into the hands of the wicked one, because when the ancient enemy was unable himself to infect the Redeemer's mind by temptation, he was allowed through his accomplices to do away with his body for a period of three days. Unaware of God's loving plan, he abetted it by reason of this permission. He attacked our Redeemer with three temptations, but he was unable to darken the heart of God. He did, however, move Judas's mind toward his bodily death, and he brought the cohort and the servants of the priests and Pharisees to him, so that wicked one certainly stretched out his hands to the earth.

The judges of this earth were the chief priests, Pilate, and the soldiers who mocked him. This wicked one accordingly covered the faces of the judges, because he cast a veil, a cloud of malice, over the hearts of the persecutors, lest they recognize their Creator. That is why Paul says, *Even until the present day, when Moses is read, a veil covers their hearts.** He also said, *If they had known, they would never have crucified the Lord of Glory.** The judges' faces were then covered because the

*Job 9:24

*2 Cor 3:15

*1 Cor 2:8

minds of those who persecuted him, whose body they could restrain, could never know him as God, even by a miracle. The ancient enemy, however, forms but one person together with all the wicked people, so Holy Scripture often speaks of the head of the wicked people, in other words of the devil, in such a way that it can be straightway extended to his body, or rather his followers. The persecuting people, therefore, may be intended by the name of the faithless wicked one, and the following verse certainly corresponds with that assumption:

XXIX. 45. *But if it is not he, then who is it?** Who is ever supposed to be wicked if that people who persecuted kindness personified is not wicked? Yet having considered the faithlessness of the Jewish people, the holy man turns the eye of his mind toward himself. He is sad because he cannot see the one he loves; sorrow grips him because he is taken out of the present world before the salvation of the world is revealed. So he adds, *Job 9:24

XXX. 46. *My days have been swifter than a runner; they have fled away and seen no good.** A runner's job indeed is the reporting of what is to follow. All the elect, then, who were born before the Redeemer's coming, heralded him either by their lives alone or also by their speeches; they were then, as it were, his couriers in the world. Yet they foresaw their own departure before the expected time of redemption, and they wept because their own passage was so swift. They groaned because their own life was short, and they did not live long enough to see the Redeemer's light. So Job is right to say, *They have fled away and seen no good.* *Job 9:25

All created things are good. Moses is our witness: *God saw all that he had made, and behold it was very good.** But this one good thing is the original good thing, through which all things are good, and those existing good things are not original. Of that good Truth himself spoke in the *Gen 1:31

*Luke 18:19 gospel: *No one except God alone is good.* So the days of the ancient fathers were over before God revealed himself to the world in human flesh. Accordingly Job rightly says of those days, *They have fled away and seen no good.* He could say it outright, "They elapsed before the awaited time arrived, so they could not reach the Redeemer's presence." So he again adds,

*Job 9:26 XXXI. 47. *They have passed like ships carrying fruit.* Those who bring fruit and cross the sea enjoy the odor of the fruit indeed, but they bring the fruit for others to eat. For what purpose then did the ancient fathers exist but to be ships carrying fruit? They prophesied the mystery of God's incarnation. They indeed held the odor of hope, but they brought us the fruit of that realized hope. The scent they were carrying in expectation is what we touch and sense in fullness. As the Redeemer told his own disciples,

*John 4:38 *Other men have labored, and you have joined their labor.* Their days are obviously compared to ships, because they sail; they are rightly compared to fruit-bearing ships, because they were able to revive by expectation through the spirit of prophecy all the chosen ones whom they carried before the Redeemer became present. But they were unable to refresh them by his full revelation.

At least when ships carry fruit, the fruit is mixed with straw, so that it may be carried safely to port. In that case the days of the ancient fathers are rightly described as fruit-bearing ships, because the words of the fathers foretold the mystery of the spiritual life, so these words are preserved like fruit packed with the straw of history, and the covered fruit of the spirit is brought to us in the context of words of the flesh. When particular stories are told, you see, they are often elevated to the plane of God's own secrets. Those who look upon that divine plane are often unexpectedly plunged into the mystery of his incarnation as well. So he rightly adds once more,

XXXII. 48. *Like an eagle hovering over its prey.**Job 9:26
It is the eagle's usual practice to eye the sun with unwavering stare, but when the need of food becomes insistent, he bends the stare of his eyes, with which he
had glared at the rays of the sun, toward the focus of
carrion; although he flies in heaven, yet for the sake of
eating flesh he seeks the earth. In exactly the same way
the ancient fathers, as far as human weakness permitted
them, contemplated the light of the Creator with minds
awake. Yet they foreknew that he would take flesh at
the end of the world, so they bent their gaze to the earth
as though turning away from the rays of the sun. As
though they came from the highest to the lowest, they
knew him as God above all things and as man within all
things. From afar they saw him who would suffer and
die for the human race, by which death they knew that
they themselves would be refreshed and re-created for
life. Just like the eagle, after contemplating the rays of
the sun, they sought food in a dead body.

We can watch the eagle contemplate the sun's rays,
that eagle who said, *Strong God, Father of the world
to come, Prince of peace.**Isa 9:6 From on high may he come
to earth in lofty flight; let him search out his food in
lowly carrion. A little further on, you see, he added, *He
bore the chastisement of our peace, and we were healed
by his sores.**Isa 53:5 Another prophet says, *Such is man; who
will know him?**Jer 17:9 LXX The mind of the just man, accordingly,
supported by godhead, contemplates the grace of God's
plan in his flesh and, like an eagle, suddenly swoops
down upon his meal.

But look now at this people Israel, so long filled with
the tremendous spirit of prophecy. They lost the gift of
prophecy, and they did not remain faithful to the truth
they had foreseen and proclaimed; rather they denied
the Redeemer's presence and rejected him, that presence

that they had foretold and announced to all their followers. Therefore Job immediately turns his compassionate
attention to their hardness of heart, showing how the
grace of prophecy abandoned them. He adds,

XXXIII. 49. *If I say, "I will not speak in this way,"*
the expression on my face changes, and I am distorted by
Job 9:27   sadness. The Jewish people, of course, refused to speak
as they formerly did; rather they denied him whom they
had foretold. The expression on their faces changed, and
they were distorted by sadness. Falsehood made them
hideous, and it spoiled the appearance of the inner man,
which the Creator would have recognized, so they stood
condemned by the eternal decree of punishment merited
by their present conduct. They were not recognized by
their Creator because of their transformed facial expression, and they were become reprobate, having lost the
integrity of a good conscience. It is no wonder, then, that
the sadness of punishment should distort the countenance
of the one whom the Creator neither recognizes nor owns.

We have now read the text, interpreting it with the
sense of redemption; let us repeat it according to the
moral sense.

50. *My days have been swifter than a runner; they*
Job 9:25   have fled away and seen no good. As I have often said
already, humans were first created in such a way that
they could live their life through time in a straightforward manner without change. But because they willfully
fell into sin and touched the forbidden object, they have
steered a course that people in the present life, enslaved
by desire as they are, both bear and choose unceasingly. They plead to go on living without end, yet as
days are added to their life, they keep aiming toward its
end. They never grasp the fact that the passing of time
amounts to practically nothing, except when events that
seemed far away are suddenly over.

Let the holy man accordingly look upon his status as creature, speak with the voice of the human race, and groan because of what he has lost through his present course of life. Let him say, *My days have been swifter than a runner; they have fled away and seen no good.* He might as well say, "Men and women were created for the purpose of being able to see the good that God is. But those who refused to stand in the light lost their eyes by fleeing, because by sinning they started to run to the depths and hence accepted blindness, lest they see the interior light."

About these days he also adds the following words: *They have passed like ships carrying fruit.** These ships that carry fruit, you must notice, are taking that which the earth produces and bearing it over the waves. The earth was once a human paradise, which could hold them still unhurt if they had wished to stand in their innocence. But they fell into the water of changeability by sin, so they entered the sea of this life after leaving the earth. The fruit of this earth was also the spoken commandment, the possibility of work that was permitted, the understanding of the Creator inherent in nature. That is the fruit we refuse to eat on earth; we carry it over the sea, because in Paradise we refused to keep the good effects of so many gifts intact, and we try to hold them now in our trials. We set our course for the destination, and we are driven by the wind of the present life, tired out as we are from battling the waves of our changeability. Nevertheless, we are bound up closely with the good things implanted in nature through the mystery of the cross, so we do, as it were, carry fruit in wood.

*Job 9:26

Yet we may understand it in yet another way. Ships that carry fruit, you see, give off a sweet odor, and they do not bear a heavy burden. The human race was exiled from the delightful Paradise; it lost the power of contemplation as well as that firm courage in which it was created. When therefore it lifts itself up to seek heaven again, it has indeed the fragrance of memory, but it does not hold any weight worthy of life. The ship of our mind is therefore full of fragrant fruit, but it is driven here and there easily, because we remember the odors of the heavenly Paradise, and we put up with the insistent waves of temptation in our bodies.

So he rightly adds, *Like an eagle hovering over its prey*. The eagle, you know, flies exceedingly high, hovers in midair, and then with a sudden rush is carried up into the upper air; then its body grows hungry, and it again swoops down to the earth, suddenly leaving the heights for the depths. In exactly the same way did the human race's first parents fall to the depths from the highest, where the dignity of creation had kept them poised in the lofty reaches of reason, as though in the free air. They touched the forbidden fruit contrary to the commandment, so they reached the earth because of their desire for food. They fed, as it were, on flesh after their flight, since they lost the free inspiration of contemplation, and here below they enjoy the body's prey. Like the eagle swooping down to its prey, our days pass quickly, because when we seek the lowest things, we are forbidden to let our life last.

51. When our mind's eye ruminates upon these thoughts in our everyday meditation, however, we are silently oppressed by hard questions: Why did almighty God create humans whom he already knew would perish? Why did he who is the mightiest and best of beings not after all wish to make humans in such a way that they would be unable to perish? But when the mind silently asks these questions, it is afraid to ask them outright lest it fall into pride; it therefore restrains itself humbly and restricts its thoughts. Yet it suffers more

intensely, because among its burdens it now also counts the hidden and painful awareness of its creation. So it adds the following words as well: *If I say, "I will not speak in this way," the expression on my face changes, and I am distorted by sadness.*

We tell ourselves that we should not speak when, transgressing the limits of our weakness for the sake of our inquiries, we fearfully reproach ourselves and curb ourselves with the thought of supreme reverence. That reverence indeed causes a change in the face of our mind. Previously it did not reach the highest reality that it rashly sought, so after a time it realized its weakness and began to venerate the reality it did not understand. There is pain in that shift, because the mind suffers intensely from the awareness of original sin and is too blind to understand even what is within itself. Yet it considers its sufferings merited and is afraid lest its sadness cause excessively free speech. It imposes silence on its lips, but pain is aroused and increases precisely because it is restrained.

Let Job therefore say, *If I say, "I will not speak in this way," the expression on my face changes, and I am distorted by sadness.* It is often when we try to mitigate our sorrow, you see, that we are more grievously afflicted, as if by trying to comfort ourselves. But any time we attentively study the fall of the human race, brought about by the sin of our first parents, we must still be afraid of adding our own sins. So the holy man, after having mentioned what is common to all humanity, quickly adds the particulars:

XXXIV. 52. *I was afraid of all my own works, because I knew you would not spare the sinner.** The text of this sacred history has shown the works that blessed Job performed. He tried to please the Creator by offering a great number of sacrifices. He arose early in the

*Job 9:28

morning, we are told, and offered holocausts for each one of his sons. Moreover, he purified them not only from evil actions but also from unclean thoughts. And on this Holy Scripture bears us witness: *For he said, "Perhaps my sons have sinned and cursed God in their hearts."** He felt compassion, because when pressed by the questions of his friends, he spoke of himself: *I even wept at times for the afflicted man.** He freely offered his services: *I was an eye to the blind and a foot to the cripple.** He had purity of chastity at heart, since he openly bore witness to himself, saying, *If my heart has been led astray to a woman.** From his inmost heart he held the peak of humility, saying, *If I disdained undergoing judgment with my male or female slave, when they complained against me.** He extended kindness and generosity, saying, *If I ate my meals alone, and did not have the orphan eat them with me,** and again, *If his loins did not bless me, or if he was not warmed by the fleece of my sheep.** He exercised the ministry of hospitality who said, *The pilgrim did not remain outside my door, but my gate lay open for the traveler.**

Besides all this he crowned his virtues by a more excellent way of life and loved his enemies. He said, *If I rejoiced at the downfall of the one who hated me,** and again, *I have not given my throat to a sin, that I should seek his life with a curse.** Why did the holy man fear his own works when he always performed those works by which God is ordinarily appeased concerning injustice? How is it that when his works were admirable, he was still afraid of them, shuddered, and said, *I was afraid of all my own works*? Perhaps what we get from the holy man's words and actions is this: if we really want to please God after our perverse actions, we must even be afraid of those things we have done well.

53. To be sure, there are two points we must zealously fear in our good works, namely, deceit and laziness.

Margin notes:
*Job 1:5
*Job 30:25
*Job 29:15
*Job 31:9
*Job 31:13
*Job 31:17
*Job 31:20
*Job 31:32
*Job 31:29
*Job 31:30

That is why the prophet says according to the primitive translation, *Cursed be everyone who does God's work deceitfully and slothfully.* But it is important to realize that the source of sloth is boredom, whereas deceit arises from self-love. Weak love for God allows sloth to grow, but inordinate self-love that possesses the mind causes deceit. Whoever loves oneself too much while doing the right thing certainly perpetrates deceit in God's work, because of being in a hurry to obtain the good reward that passes.

*Jer 48:10 LXX

We should also realize that there are three ways in which deceit as such is perpetrated, since by means of deceit, beyond any doubt, one desires either the silent esteem of a human heart or the wind of favor or external advantage. On this point by contrast the prophet rightly says of the just person, *Blessed is the one who closes his hand against any bribe.* Since deceit is not only found in the reception of money, there is undoubtedly more than one type of bribe. There are three ways of taking a bribe, and deceit hastens toward all of them. The bribe is taken by the heart once the thought permits it. The bribe is taken by the mouth led astray by applause and boasting. The bribe is taken by the hand as a reward for what is given. But the hands of the just are closed to bribes, and their righteous actions receive from the human heart no dubious encouragement or any applause from human lips, nor do they seek any gift from human hands. They alone do not do God's work deceitfully who apply themselves eagerly to good works in which they yearn for neither any concrete reward nor any words of praise nor any human applause.

*Isa 33:15

Accordingly, our true good, because it cannot avoid the sword of lurking sin unless we are daily on our guard with solicitous fear, is subject to the wise words of the holy man, who says at this point, *I was afraid of all my own works.* It is as if he humbly confessed and said, "I see what I have openly done, but I do not know what I have secretly perpetrated through it." Our good works, you see, are often lost because of the robbery of deceit, when worldly concupiscence attaches itself to our good works. They often fail by the intervention of laziness, because when love grows cold, the enthusiasm with which we began is lost. Because sin creeps up on us and even in the very act of virtue is difficult to overcome, what security is left for us except that we should always carefully fear even virtue?

54. But the verse that follows shows itself to the heart as exceedingly grim: *I knew you would not spare the sinner.* If the sinner is not spared, you see, who will be safe from eternal death, when no one is found free of sin? Does God spare the penitent and not spare the sinner? When we mourn our sins, are we then no longer sinners? What about the denying Peter, who is looked at and reduced to tears by the denied Redeemer? What about Paul, who tried to destroy the Redeemer's name on earth but was privileged to hear his voice from heaven? The sins of both men were punished. As for Peter, the gospel bears us witness: *Then Peter remem-bered Jesus' words . . . , and he went out and wept*

*Matt 26:75   *bitterly.** As for Paul, Truth both called him and said about him, *I will show him how much he must suffer for*

*Acts 9:16   *my name.** Accordingly, God never spares the sinner, because he does not leave the sin without its punish-ment. Either people punish themselves by repentance, or God along with those people punishes the sin. So the sin is never spared, because in no sense is it left alone unpunished.

David was also allowed to hear the words, *The Lord*

*2 Sam 12:15   *has taken your sin away.** Nevertheless he was gravely afflicted later in his flight, and in this way he suffered the punishment for the sin he had committed. So also we ourselves are cleared from the sin of our first parents by the water of salvation, but even when we are purified of the guilt of that sin, even though cleansed, we still suffer bodily death. So it is well said, *I knew you would not spare the sinner*. In fact either through us or through his own intervention God cuts off our sins, even when he goes easy. He zealously purges the marks of sin from his chosen ones by means of temporary afflictions, because he does not want to see those marks on them in eternity. But the mind is often more afraid than it should be: it shakes with fear and is beset by sinister suspicions, so that we are weary of this life and we doubt that we will reach eternity, even laboriously. Therefore Job again adds,

XXXV. 55. *If I am such a wicked man, why have I labored in vain?** If in other words we are struck down without mercy, our work deserves punishment, work that we expected to be rewarded by a prize. Therefore the holy man in his fear of hidden judgment says, *If I am such a wicked man, why have I labored in vain?* He is not sorry for his labor; rather he regrets even while laboring that his repayment is in doubt. We must understand, however, that holy people doubt in such a way that they trust, and they trust in such a way that their security does not make them inactive. It often happens that the mind is intent upon doing things right and worries about that, so after a good work is accomplished, tearful entreaties are required to the end that the humble entreaty might gain the merit of a good work for the purpose of eternal rewards. Nevertheless we must understand as well that life and tears are unable to render us perfectly clean as long as the mortality of our corruptible state holds us bound. Therefore Job rightly adds,

XXXVI. 56. *Even if I washed myself with snow and my hands shone like the purest white, you would still*

*Job 9:29

*Job 9:30-31 *find me dirty, and my clothes would make me ashamed.**
The water of snow is likened to the tears of humility.
Humility is the highest of all the virtues in the eyes of the
supreme Judge, and therefore it shines with the whiteness
of high merit. Some people, you know, can weep, but they
have no humility; they weep out of their affliction, but
even through their tears they rise up against their neighbors' lives or against the fixed order established by the
Creator. Yes, their tears are wet, but that water is not from
snow; they cannot be pure, because they are certainly not
washed with the tears of humility. On the other hand, he
had washed away his sins with snow who confidently
*Ps 50:19
LXX said, *God does not spurn a humble and contrite heart.**
Those however who afflict themselves with tears but who
at the same time murmur and act rebelliously scourge
their minds, but they have no use for humility.

The water from snow can be interpreted in another
way, though. Spring or river water, you see, rises from
the earth, whereas the water from snow has its source in
the sky; many people torment themselves with prayers
and lamentation but wear themselves out with all this
labor and tears for only one purpose: the satisfying of
worldly desires. Their prayer arises from compunction,
but they seek the enjoyment of earthly happiness. So
snow water does not wash them clean, because their
tears come from below. It is as though they were drip-
ping with earthly water when they pray with compunction for earthly goods. Those, however, who mourn
because they desire the reward of heaven are the ones
who are washed with snow water, who are filled with
heavenly compunction. When they desire the eternal
fatherland with tears, when they are aflame with desire
for that fatherland and wail for it, they receive from
above the ability to be purified. As for the hands, what
else do they signify but works? That is why the prophet

told certain people, *Your hands are full of blood,** in other words, of the works of violence.   *Isa 1:15

57. Let us notice that the holy man did not say, "if my most pure hands shone," but *if my hands shone with the purest white.* The reason is that as long as we are held by the penalty of corruption, whatever good works we do, we in no wise attain real purity, but we imitate it. That is why he rightly adds, *you would still find me dirty.* He says that God finds us dirty in order to show that we are covered with dirt, because the closer we approach him by good works, the more clearly we realize how dirty our life is and how detestable compared to his purity. So he says, *Even if I washed myself with snow and my hands shone like the purest white, you would still find me dirty.* He might as well say openly, "I might drip with the tears of heavenly compunction, and I might keep working zealously performing good works, but I see your purity, and I see that I am still not pure." His corruptible flesh, you see, still distracts his soul, intent upon God as it is, and soils his beautiful love with dirty emotions and impermissible thoughts.

58. So he adds, *my clothes would make me ashamed.**   *Job 9:31
What is meant by the word *clothes* but this earthly body, which covers the soul that puts it on lest she should seem naked in her natural simplicity? It was for this reason that Solomon said, *Let your clothes always be white.** In other words, "Let the members of your body   *Eccl 9:8
be pure from sinful actions." Isaiah also says, *The garment mixed with blood will be burnt up.** The mixing   *Isa 9:5
of a garment with blood obviously means the pollution of the body with sensual desires. The psalmist had naturally feared pollution by such desires when he said, *Deliver me from bloodguilt, O God my Savior.**   *Ps 50:16

That is why John heard the angel's voice saying, *You have a few people in Sardis who have not dirtied their*

*Rev 3:4
*robes.** It is customary in Holy Scripture to say, *Our clothes make us ashamed* when we are in fact ashamed. Peter for his part says of Judas, *He owned a field that
*Acts 1:18
was the reward of iniquity,** but Judas could hardly own the potter's field bought with the price of blood, because when the thirty pieces of silver were paid, he punished himself for the sin of that transaction by his own more sinful death, which took place immediately afterward. Still, the verb *to own* does make him the owner. However that may be, we read here in Job, *my clothes would make me ashamed*, so the man is ashamed when the members of his body rise up against his mind and when they interrupt his intense holy desires with their feverish temptations.

Consequently the soul that finds itself in the midst of such a battle realizes that God must still find it despicable. It wants to undergo its final correction, but it cannot, because it is still covered with the dust of impure thoughts. Paul had felt this shame of his clothes when he said, *I see another law in my body, resisting the law of my mind, and making me a captive of the law of sin
*Rom 7:23
residing in my body.** He could not be perfectly acceptable in those clothes that he would one day put on again in a better form, but for now he wanted to take them off, as he said, *Unhappy man that I am, who will deliver
*Rom 7:24
me from this mortal body?** So let the just man say, *Even if I washed myself with snow and my hands shone like the purest white, you would still find me dirty, and my clothes would make me ashamed*. However high he rises, you see, out of the compunction of contemplation, and however prepared he may be for action through the exerting of effort, from the mortal body he still senses something unfit, and he considers himself detestable in much of the baggage he carries in his state of corruption. And to him this point is still more grievous, that

he often does not even understand how he has sinned. He accepts his punishment, but what in him displeases the supreme Judge, whether great or small, he does not know. So he adds,

XXXVII. 59. *It is not the man who is my neighbor whom I will answer, nor can he be heard equally with me at the judgment.** When we contend with anyone in judgment on an equal footing, and we know what is spoken against us, and our own words are heard, then because we easily understand the charge, we boldly reply to it. On the other hand, the invisible Judge sees our acts as though he were listening to our words, but we by no means fully understand what it is that displeases him, so it is as though we do not know what he says. The holy man accordingly sees his dirty clothes, and he worries all the more, because he cannot be heard at the Judgment on an equal footing. To the extent that he is burdened by his state of corruption, in his punishment he bears the still heavier burden that he knows not his accuser's mind. He might as well say it openly: "I do not get an equal hearing, because all my actions are clearly seen; nevertheless I myself do not know all the charges against me."

*Job 9:32

XXXVIII. 60. The next verse: *There is no one who is able to argue both sides of the case, or put his hand on both claims.** It sounds brazen for anyone to ask someone to argue with God, but it will not sound brazen if we remember what God says through a prophet. Here is what he preaches through Isaiah: *Stop your evildoing and learn to do what is good. Seek justice. Help the man who is oppressed. Give judgment for the orphan. Defend the widow. Then come and argue with me, says the Lord.** Him whom we accuse we confront with the authority of reason. How is it that when God warns us to act in a holy manner, he adds, *come and argue with me,*

*Job 9:33

*Isa 1:16-18

unless he is openly pointing out how much confidence
he places in good works? It is as though he clearly said,
"Do what is right, and you will meet the expressions of
my displeasure no longer with sighs and pleadings, but
with the confidence of authority."

That is why John says, *If our heart does not reproach*
1 John 3:21   us, we have confidence toward God. That is why Moses,
the acceptable servant, was heard though silent, and in
*Exod 14:15   his silence was asked, *Why are you calling me?* That is
why he restrained God in his wrath when he heard him
say, *Let me alone; let my wrath blaze up against the*
Exod 32:10   people. That is why the Lord complained that he did not
have anyone to argue with him when he said through the
prophet, *I looked for a man who might set up a wall in*
front of me and withstand me, lest I should destroy the
Ezek 22:30   earth, but I found none. That is why Isaiah mourned
deeply and said, *We have all fallen like leaves, and our*
sins have blown us away like the wind. There is no one
Isa 64:7   to call upon your name or to stand up and clutch you.

61. Any of the righteous people may, however,
sometimes avoid the movement of censure in the present
time through the merit they have gained of an innocent life; they cannot by their own virtue, on the other
hand, remove the punishment of coming death from the
human race. Let the holy man accordingly consider the
human race and how it has fallen. Let him look steadily
at the loss incurred by eternal death. It is immediately
obvious that no human righteousness contradicts that.
Let him see how obstinately humans sin, and how ir-
reversible is the Creator's anger against them. Let him
plead for the Mediator of God and humanity, him who
is both God and humanity. He sees him coming a long
time afterward. Let him say in desperation, *There is no*
one who is able to argue both sides of the case, or put
his hand on both claims.

It is absolutely the Redeemer of the human race who became the Mediator of God and humanity through his flesh; he is the only one who was found just among humans. Even though he was without sin, he at length paid the penalty for sin. He both pleaded with humans not to sin and withstood God lest he strike. He exemplified innocence and paid the penalty of wickedness. In his suffering he preached to both sides. He took away human sin by obtaining justice, and he mitigated the Judge's wrath by his death. He put his hand on both claims, because he both gave humans an example to imitate and showed God those deeds in himself by which God might be reconciled to humans. Before him there was never a person who could intercede for the sins of others in such a way as not to have any of his own. No more could anyone prevent eternal death in the case of others and be personally free of guilt. The new man accordingly came to men and women as the adversary of their guilt and the friend of their sentence; he performed wonders and suffered cruelty. So he put his hand on both claims, because on the one hand he taught the guilty one what is right, and on the other he appeased the angry Judge. And in this he also worked more wonderful miracles, in that he reformed the hearts of sinners rather by gentleness than by alarm. The next verse:

XXXIX. 62. *Let him take away his rod from me, and let not his fear terrify me.** God had certainly held the rod through the law, since he said, "If anyone should do this or that, he will die the death." When he took flesh, however, he took away the rod, because he showed us the way of life through gentleness. That is why the psalmist tells him, *Set out, prosper, proceed, and reign, for the sake of truth, gentleness, and justice.** He did not wish to be feared as God; rather, his aspiration was that he should be loved as a father. That is clearly what

*Job 9:34

*Ps 44:5

Paul says: *You have not received a spirit of slavery, that you should be again in fear, but you have received the spirit of adoption as sons by which we cry out, "Abba,*
*Rom 8:11
*Job 9:35
*Father."** Then he rightly adds,

XL. 63. *I will speak, and I will not fear him.** The holy man, you see, sees the Redeemer of the human race coming as a meek person, and he does not assume fear as toward the Lord, but affection as toward a father. He even feels contempt for fear, because the grace of adoption inspires him with love. Therefore John says,
*1 John 4:18
*There is no fear in love, but perfect love casts out fear.** So Zechariah says, *That we might be delivered from the*
*Luke 1:74
*hands of our foes to serve him without fear.** Accordingly fear was unable to free us from the death of sin, but the infused grace of gentleness raised us up to a living status. This reality is nicely symbolized by Elisha in the raising up of the Shunammite's son. He by no means succeeded in resuscitating the dead child by sending his staff ahead with his servant. Instead he came himself and stretched himself out on top of the dead boy, placing his own body parts on top of his; after walking to and fro, he breathed in the mouth of the corpse seven times. In this way he at once returned the boy to the light of
*see 2 Kgs 4:30-34
new life through the ministry of compassion.*

God the Creator of the human race unquestionably mourned over what was in a way a dead child when he in pity looked down upon us who had died from the sting of iniquity. Because he sent fear of the law ahead through Moses, it was as though he sent a servant with his staff. The servant could not, however, raise the dead with the staff, since Paul bears us witness, *The law made*
*Heb 7:19
*nothing perfect.** But God came himself and humbly stretched himself out on top of the corpse, so that he might reduce himself to the size of the members of the dead body. *While he was in the form of God, he did not*

consider it robbery that he should be equal to God;
yet he emptied himself and took the form of a slave; he
became like men, and in outward appearance he seemed
to be a man.* He walked to and fro, because he called
both the Jews close at hand and the Gentiles far off.
He breathed seven times on the dead boy, because by
the opening granted by God, the Spirit of the sevenfold
grace breathed upon those who lay in the death of sin.
He lived and was quickly raised, because the boy whom
the rod of fear could not raise returned to life through
the Spirit of love. Let Job then say with his own voice
and with that of the human race, *Let him take away his*
rod from me, and let his fear not terrify me. I will speak,
and I will not fear him. After that he rightly adds,

*Phil 2:6-7

    XLI. 64. *Because if I am terrified, I cannot answer.**
We are said to answer anyone when the works we do are
of the same quality as that person's. Accordingly, when
we answer God, we render fitting praise for the gifts
we have received from him. So also certain psalms, in
which holy works are reported in order to be imitated,
are prefaced as written for response. God therefore made
men and women right, and when they went wrong he
suffered it patiently. He looks on sin every day, and yet
he is not quick to cut off one's living space. He is kind
and lavish with his gifts and associates with evil people.
Men and women should respond to so much kindness,
yet in their fear they cannot respond, because they are
still slavishly afraid of the Creator of the human race,
and they clearly do not love him.

*Job 9:35

    We only render true worship to God when because
of the confidence of love we do not fear him, when affection, not fear, drives us to good works, and when evil
no longer pleases us, even if it were allowed. Those who
are restrained by fear from acting perversely, you see,
would act perversely if they were allowed to. They are

not really righteous at all, then, who are still not free
of the desire to do wrong. So it is well said, *Because if
I am terrified I cannot answer.* We do not render true
worship to God if we obey his commandments out of
fear rather than out of love. Yet when our mind is inflamed by love of his sweetness, every desire for the
present life grows weaker and affection goes flat; the
mind sadly puts up with this life, whereas formerly she
was captivated by it and served it with base desire. So
Job logically continues,

*Job 10:1   XLII. 65. *My life is burdensome to my soul.* But
when the present life begins to cheapen, and when
love of the Creator begins to sweeten, the soul rises
up against itself, saying it should accuse itself of sin,
whereas when it was previously unaware of higher
things, it defended its sins. So he again rightly adds,

*Job 10:1   XLIII. 66. *I will turn my eloquence against myself.*
It is as though he had used his eloquence in his own favor
when he tried to excuse the wicked things he had done.
But he turns his eloquence against himself when he begins to accuse himself for his sinful ways. Even when
we sin, however, we often pass judgment on our actions.
The mind accuses itself for what it is doing. Yet it by no
means abandons its desire, so it is ashamed to confess
what it has done. But since it now presses hard against
the concupiscence of the flesh with all its judgment, it
lifts itself up with a courageous voice in confession and
self-accusation. So he now rightly says, *I will turn my
eloquence against myself.* The mind is now strong and
begins to let out against itself the damning words that it
previously weakly and shamefacedly retained inside itself.

There are those, however, who admit their faults
with open voice but cannot groan in confession; instead
they say cheerfully what should be said mournfully. So
he again rightly adds,

XLIV. 67. *I will speak in the bitterness of my soul.*   *Job 10:1
Those who speak of their guilt with aversion must nec-
essarily speak of it in bitterness of soul in such a way
that that bitterness would punish whatever the tongue
should condemn through the mind's judgment. We must
realize, however, that when the mind imposes the penalty of repentance upon itself, it sometimes senses security because of that fact; hence it rises more confidently
to be interrogated by the heavenly Judge, so that it finds
itself more prepared for whatever may be decided in
whatever way in its case. So Job immediately adds,

XLV. 68. *I will tell God, "Do not condemn me. Show
me why you judge me in this way."* The one who ac-   *Job 10:2
knowledges himself a sinner in bitterness of soul—what
else does he say to God but that he should not condemn
him? The bitterness of the presence of repentance can-
cels the punishment of the wrath pursuing him. God
judges people in this life in two ways: either he begins
already to inflict future torments through present misfortune, or he does away with future torments by means of
present adversity. If the just Judge did not punish some
people both now and later, you see, those whose sins
demanded punishment, Jude would certainly not have
said, *Later he condemned those who did not believe.*   *Jude 5
Furthermore, the psalmist would not say, *Let them be
covered with their own shame as with a cloak.*   *Ps 108:29;
                                                Latin *diplois*
We call it a cloak because it wraps double.[3] They are
accordingly covered with shame as with a cloak, because
they are smitten with both present and eternal punishment

---

[3] Obviously the idea of *double* does not enter into the English *cloak*. Saint Gregory is here interpreting the Greek διπλοις,
which means a double garment. It is not clear at this stage how
it was put together. The meaning, however, neatly falls in with
Gregory's theological interpretation.

as the penalty for their guilt. The penalty frees from punishment only those whom it changes. Those whom present misfortune does not correct, it leads to future ruin. On the other hand, if present misfortune did not protect some people from eternal punishment, Paul would never have said, *When we are judged by the Lord, we are corrected,* *1 Cor 11:32 *that we might not be condemned with this world.** So the *Rev 3:19 angel tells John, *Those I love I rebuke and chastise.** Elsewhere it is also written, *Him whom God loves he chastises,* *Heb 12:6 *and he beats every son he receives.**

69. Accordingly, the minds of the just are often deeply anxious about making sure of their greater safety; when they are surrounded by trials, they are troubled by uncertainty with regard to heavenly judgment. They are afraid that all their sufferings might constitute only the beginning of their coming condemnation. They question the Judge in their thoughts, because their sufferings cause them to doubt the innocence of their lives. When the virtues of their lives pass before their mind's eyes, they provide some comfort with which to answer the Judge, who by no means strikes in order to ruin those whose conduct he maintains in innocence by striking.

So it is well said here, *Show me why you judge me in this way.* He might as well say outright, "Because you judge me with trials, show me that you are rendering me safe from judgment through trials." There is another way to understand it. The just, you see, often experience trials in order to be proven just; with the greatest precision they take their life apart, and although they both know and confess themselves sinners, they do not know for which particular sin they are struck. Therefore in time of trial their fear is all the greater because of their ignorance of the reasons for their trial. They ask the Judge to show them to themselves, so that what he strikes in judgment they themselves may chastise and weep over.

They know, of course, that the Avenger is most fair and afflicts no one unjustly in any way, but they strike their breast in great fear, because they suffer trials painfully and yet cannot find perfectly in themselves the sin they deplore. So Job adds yet again,

XLVI. 70. *Does it seem right to you that you should calumniate and oppress the poor man, the work of your hands, and that you should abet the counsel of the wicked?** This statement is certainly put in the form of a question, so that it might be denied. It is as though he plainly said, "You who are the highest good, I know that you do not think it good that you should oppress the poor man by calumny. Therefore I know my sufferings are not unjust. I am all the sadder, because I do not know the charges justice brings against me." Notice, however, that he did not say oppress "the blameless man," but *the poor man*. He who questions the inflexibility of the Judge does not stand on his blameless status, but on his poverty; no longer does he appropriate temerity, but rather he obviously shows himself weak. So he fittingly adds, *the work of your hands*. It is as though he said outright, "You cannot unfeelingly oppress the one whom you remember having freely made."

*Job 10:3

71. So he rightly adds, *that you should abet the counsel of the wicked*. Whom does he here label wicked if not evil spirits? These spirits cannot themselves return to life, so they ruthlessly look for companionship in death. It was unquestionably their counsel that God's judgment should strike blessed Job and that he who had appeared just in his prosperity might at least sin in adversity. But God did not abet their impure counsel, because whereas he allowed them to try Job's body, he denied them his life. The evil spirits never stop offering such counsel against good people, so that those whom they see serving God willingly in prosperity may be

shaken by adversity and driven off into a pit of guilt.
But the sting of their counsel is plucked out, because
the kind Creator modifies adversity according to our
strength, lest the pain be greater than we can bear and
human weakness give in through the cunning of power.

For this reason Paul says, *God is faithful, and he will
not let you be tempted beyond your strength, but he will
send along with the temptation a way for you to resist.*
Unless the merciful God, you see, suited the temptation
to our strength, there would certainly be not a single
person who would resist the deception of the evil spirits
without falling; if the Judge does not impose a limit on
temptations, by the very fact that people bear burdens
beyond their strength, they who stand fall. Blessed Job
asked those questions in the denying mode, just as he
now denies the following statements in the asking mode:

XLVII. 72. *Do you have eyes of flesh, or do you see
as man sees? Are your days like the days of a man? Are
your years equal to human time, that you should seek
out my iniquity or scrutinize my sin? Can you know
that I have done nothing evil?* Eyes of flesh do not see
the objects of time unless they are also in time. These
eyes of flesh grow with time in order to see, and with
time they also close. The human sense of sight does
not anticipate any work that follows, because it only
sees what exists and in no way knows the future. The
days and years of humans are also not parallel with the
days and years of eternity. Our life begins in time and
ends in time. While time is forming us in the folds of its
bosom, eternity is swallowing us up. The immensity of
eternity assuredly stretches out near and far and above;
it neither begins nor ends, and its eternal being goes
on and on. It loses neither what has already happened
nor what is future; those beings that do not appear are
not missing. He who has eternal being sees all things

*1 Cor 10:13

*Job 10:4-7

simultaneously; he does not look in front and behind, but his vision suffers no change.

Let Job say it then: *Do you have eyes of flesh, or do you see as man sees? Are your days like the days of a man? Are your years equal to human time, that you should seek out my iniquity or scrutinize my sin? Can you know that I have done nothing evil?* It is as if he humbly inquired as follows: "Why do you interrogate me in time with the whip, me whom you knew perfectly before time in your presence? Why do you question me about my sins with blows, me to whom you were no stranger before my creation through your eternal power?" The burden of his power soon finds expression when he adds,

XLVIII. 73. *Is there anyone who can force open your hand?** He might as well ask openly, "What alternative do you have except forbearance? Can anyone resist your power? Since there is no one who can restrain your censure by virtue of personal goodness, your affection should the more easily exact from you the favor of forbearance." But since we were conceived in sin and brought forth in iniquity, we have either done evil to our hurt or carelessly done even that which is good and sinned in that way. Accordingly we have nothing whereby the strict Judge might be favorable to us. But although we cannot show any of our works to his gaze as worth consideration, our only alternative is to offer him his own work, that we may become acceptable to him. So Job adds,

* Job 10:7

XLIX. 74. *Your hands formed me and completed me all about, and now you suddenly cast me down.** He might humbly say, "My works are unworthy of your favor in a just judgment, but weigh them with the scale of mercy, so that your work might not perish." Job's words also condemn the perverse doctrine of Mani, the

* Job 10:8

inventor of two principles, who tried to assert that spirit is from God and created flesh is from Satan. The holy man is full of the spirit of prophecy and of grace, and he contemplates the distant future; he foresees the false reasoning giving birth to error, which he tramples underfoot and says, *Your hands formed me and completed me all about.* He asserts that he is both formed and completed all about by God, leaving nothing either in the flesh or in the spirit for the people of darkness. He reports that he was formed for the sake of the internal image, and he mentions that he was completed all about, since he stands forth covered with the garment of flesh.

75. We should notice, however, that when he asserted that he was formed by God's hands he confronted the Judge's mercy with the dignity of his own creation. Although everything was created by the Word, who is coeternal with the Father, in the very relation of creation we are shown how far humanity surpasses all the animals and even the heavenly objects (those without sensation, of course). Regarding all things, indeed, *He spoke and they were created.** When, however, God decided to make humankind, he prefaced the creation with words we should reverently ponder, saying, *Let us make man according to our image and likeness.** That action was not the same as what was written concerning the others: *Let it be done . . . and it was done.** Nor did the earth bring forth humankind, as the water brought forth flying creatures; rather, before it was done, he said, *Let us make*, so that it might be obvious that the rational creature was created, as it were, after a council had been held. Humankind was formed from earth intentionally, as it were; they were vivified by the Creator's breath and the power of living spirit so that they might stand forth, not through the voice of command but through the dignity of creation, since they were made according to the Creator's image.

*Ps 148:5

*Gen 1:26

*Gen 1:3

What therefore humans received preeminently on earth at their creation above the other creatures, Job in the midst of his trial pleads before his Maker's kindness, as he says, *Your hands formed me and completed me all about, and now you suddenly cast me down.* He might as well say, "Why do you despise as worthless him whom you created with such dignity? Why do you sadly put aside him whom you favor with the gift of reason over all other beings?" Nevertheless, this very dignity of ours shines out through the image, and it is far above the perfect happiness of the flesh, because when spirit associates with dust, in a way it joins weakness. This weakness is what blessed Job pleads before the Judge's kindness when he adds,

L. 76. *Remember, I beseech you, that you made me like clay.*[*] The angelic spirits sinned without possibility of return, because they could remain so much more steadfast, untrammeled as they were with the baggage of flesh. Humans, however, were able to receive forgiveness after their sin, precisely because through a body of flesh they had received something less than themselves. Accordingly, in the Judge's sight the argument of kindness is this very weakness that is in flesh. After all, the psalmist says, *He was merciful, and he forgave their sin; he did not let them be lost. He often turned away his wrath from them. He did not let his anger blaze against them freely; rather he remembered that they were flesh.*[*] Humans were therefore made like clay, because they were taken from the mud to be created. Yes, indeed they are mud, because water was sprinkled on the earth. Humans were therefore created like mud, because just as water flows upon dust, so the soul irrigates the body. And this is what the holy man correctly pleads before the Judge's kindness when in his petition he says, *Remember, I beseech you, that you made me like clay.* It

[*] Job 10:9

[*] Ps 77:38-39

is as though he said plainly, "Look at the weakness of flesh, and loosen the guilt of sin." The death of this same flesh is also clearly added when he at once continues,

*Job 10:9

LI. 77. *and you grind me to dust.** It is as if he openly made the request: "I beseech you to remember that I came from the earth through flesh, and by the loss of flesh I return to earth. Look, then, upon the matter of my origin and upon the penalty of my end and spare the guilt of him who is quickly passing away." But because he has declared the quality of the created human, he now joins to it the order of his birth, saying,

LII. 78. *Did you not pour me out like milk and curdle me like cheese? With skin and flesh you clothed me, and*

*Job 10:10-11

*with bones and sinews you constructed me.** In creation humans were formed like clay, but in their propagation they were like milk poured out with seed, and their flesh was like curdled cheese. They were clothed with flesh and skin, and their bones and sinews hardened. Clay, accordingly, expresses the quality of our first condition, and milk the means of the later conception of humans, for they grow through curdling, and little by little their bones harden. But this description of the created body is stingy praise of God unless it is followed by the expression of the wonderful inspiration of life. So Job adds,

*Job 10:12

LIII. 79. *You have granted me life and mercy.** But it would be in vain that the Creator granted us good things if he did not himself also guard all that he granted. So

*Job 10:12

Job adds, *And your visitation guards my spirit.** We have said these things about the external person, but they can also be understood of the internal person, as I shall show by briefly repeating the text.

80. *Remember, I beseech you, that you made me like*

*Job 10:9

*clay.** Yes, our interior person appears like clay, because the grace of the Holy Spirit is poured forth into the earthly mind so that it may be attentive to the knowledge of its Creator. Human thought dried up because of the sterility of its sin, but the power of the Holy Spirit caused it to grow green again, like irrigated land. It often happens, however, that while we enjoy the uninterrupted excellence of the heavenly gift that we receive, we have easy self-reliance because of our enjoyment of unbroken prosperity. So it often happens that the Spirit who had supported us leaves us alone little by little, until he shows us what we are like. This is what the holy man describes for us when he adds, *and you grind me to dust.*

The mind is left alone for a while in temptation through the absence of the Spirit, and it is as if the earth grew dry and lost its former moistness so that in its abandonment it might feel its weakness and might realize how dry we have become without the flow of heavenly grace. We are fittingly said to be ground to dust, because left to ourselves we are taken away by the wind of any temptation. Left alone we are visibly shaken, but meanwhile we more wisely think of the gifts we knew in the Spirit. So Job adds, *Did you not pour me out like milk and curdle me like cheese?*[*] Accordingly our mind is estranged from its former way of life through the grace of the Holy Spirit, and in this way it is poured out like milk; in other words, it is formed in a kind of fine tenderness of a new beginning. It is curdled like cheese, because it is pressed in a mold of consolidating thought, so that it may no longer flow away through desires but be collected in one love and rise in a solid new form.

The flesh, however, often rumbles from below, comfortable in its old habits, against these very beginnings of spiritual life, and the mind endures a war waged by the external person that it bears. So he adds, *With skin and flesh you clothed me.*[*] The internal person is indeed clothed with skin and flesh, because whenever we are

[*] Job 10:10

[*] Job 10:11

intent upon heaven, we are besieged by emotions of the flesh. But the Creator never abandons those who strive for justice when they are tempted; he even forestalls the sinner by outpouring his grace. He girds the ready mind for war externally, and he strengthens the internal person. Therefore Job again rightly adds, *With bones and sinews you constructed me.*

We are clothed with skin and flesh, but we are constructed with bones and sinews, because although we are visibly shaken by the temptations that rise externally, the Creator's hand strengthens us internally to keep us from giving in. He humiliates us through emotions of the flesh for the sake of his gifts, but through the bones of virtues he strengthens us against temptation. So Job says, *With skin and flesh you clothed me, and with bones and sinews you constructed me.* He might as well say in other words, "You leave me alone in my external trial, but you keep me internally from ruin by binding me with virtues." God grants us the uprightness of living a good life, because he kindly forgives us our past sins. Hence Job again rightly adds, *You have granted me life and mercy.*

81. Life is unquestionably granted when goodness is infused into evil minds. Life can never, however, be received without mercy, since God does not help anybody to receive the good things that justice provides unless he first mercifully absolves the evil deeds that we have already committed. Well, at least he grants us life and mercy in that the mercy that goes before us helping us to live good lives also guides us later. Unless, you see, mercy accompanies life, the life that is granted cannot be kept. This very human life that we live every day surely grows old; with the quickness of thought the impulse of the external person causes us to leave the internal. Unless a heavenly visitation either animates our

love by some twinge or restores our fear by some trial, the mind is totally ruined by a sudden fall, just when it seems to be renewed by long-standing effort for virtue.

So Job adds, *and your visitation guards my spirit.* *Job 10:12 The heavenly visitation unquestionably guards the human spirit when it unceasingly either strikes it with trials or prompts it with love just when it is rich in virtue. If, you see, God grants his gifts but does not aid the human spirit by means of his continual restorative action, the good gift is quickly lost, because the Giver does not guard it. But notice that when the holy man humbly knows himself, he finds that the secrets of divine mercy are to be bestowed on all people: when he frankly admits his weakness, he is suddenly lifted up high to learn of the vocation of the Gentiles. Then he at once adds,

LIV. 82. *Even if you hide the knowledge in your heart, nevertheless I know that you remember all things.* *Job 10:13 He might as well say, "Why am I anxious about myself, when I know that it is you who gather all the nations? You hide in your heart what you do not yet reveal by outward speech. You who remember all things undoubtedly reassure me of forgiveness." What we must know is this: in certain acts we are reassured of forgiveness, and after we have committed sins, we are strengthened by the certitude of absolution, with amendment and repentance to follow. Nevertheless we still retain the sins we have committed in our memory, and we are unwillingly and shamefacedly buffeted by sinful thoughts. So he rightly adds,

LV. 83. *If I have sinned, and you forgave me at the time, why do you now refuse me purity from my sin?* *Job 10:14 God forgives the sin at the time when he washes away the guilt of sin, as soon as we have given in to tears. He refuses us purity from our sin, however, because we really committed sin willingly, and we sometimes put up with the memory of it with unwilling pleasure. That which is now blotted out from the Judge's sight, you see, because of intervenient tears, often returns to the soul, and the fault that has been overcome tries to worm itself back into delightful thoughts; it then reappears in the ancient battle with its attack renewed. So that fault that the body formerly committed, the mind now repeatedly broods over with unquiet thoughts. That spiritual champion who knew how to understand carefully said this: *My scars are rotten and decayed because of my folly.**

*Ps 37:6

What are scars but healing wounds? Accordingly, he who wept over his scars had seen his pardoned sins return to delight his memory. For the scars to grow rotten is unquestionably for the wounds of sins already healed to worm their way again into temptation, and from their prompting us to feel again the decay and pain of guilt after the skin of repentance has closed. Notice carefully that this action really takes place, not externally but only internally, in sinful thought. The mind is held fast by inflexible guilt unless it is washed by anxious weeping.

84. Therefore Moses was right to say, *If any man among you should be defiled by a dream at night, he must leave the camp, and he is not to return until evening, when he washes himself with water; then at sundown let him return to camp.** The nocturnal dream is a secret temptation, through which something shameful is conceived in the heart by a shadowy thought, but the thought is not carried out by a physical act. Nevertheless the man is ordered to leave the camp after being defiled by a dream at night, because it is obviously fitting that one who is defiled by impure thoughts should consider himself unfit to associate with the faithful community; rather let him place before his eyes what his guilt deserves and blame himself for his lack of esteem from good people.

*Deut 23:10-11

For the defiled man to leave the camp, accordingly,
is for the one battling an attack of shameful thoughts
to despise himself in comparison to chaste people. He
who washes himself with water in the evening, when
he looks upon his shortcomings, turns to the sorrow of
repentance so that he may blot out with tears everything
that the secret dirt of the soul confesses. But he returns
to the camp at sundown, because when the violent temptation cools, it is necessary that he should again assume
his place in the community of the faithful. Of course
he washes himself at sundown and returns to camp, he
who after the sorrow of repentance, when the flames of
unacceptable thoughts have subsided, is restored to his
allotted place among the faithful. He should no longer
consider himself an outcast when he rejoices at the loss
of his internal fire and his consequent purity.

Nevertheless we must realize that the reason we are
sometimes attacked by impure thoughts is that certain
actions of everyday life, even if normally acceptable,
continue to occupy our minds. Whenever a worldly action, even the smallest, is touched by desire, the ancient
enemy's power against us grows and our mind is defiled
by the imposition of temptation, and not the smallest.
That is why the law prescribes that the priest cut the sacrifice into pieces and burn the head and the fat with fire,
but that he first wash the legs and entrails with water.*
We certainly offer God a sacrifice ourselves when we
consecrate our lives to his worship. We cut the sacrifice
up into pieces and place it on the fire when we immolate
the works of our life distinguished by virtues. We burn
the head and the fat when we burn with the flame of
divine love in our mind, which rules the whole body,
and in our secret desires.

*see Lev 1:6-13

On the other hand, the law demands that the feet and
entrails of the sacrifice be washed. The feet, you know,

touch the ground, and the entrails carry excrement. It often happens that we are at one time inflamed by a desire for heaven, and at another time with all our heart's devotion we yearn to have the appetite of mortification satisfied. Yet because we still to a certain extent act in a worldly manner because of our weakness, some of our actions are also unacceptable ones that we have already given up but still retain in our hearts. So when impure temptations defile our thoughts, what else do they amount to but the entrails of a sacrifice, which carry excrement? But just as the entrails should be washed so that they may be fit to be burned, so also it is absolutely necessary that tears begotten by fear should wash the impure thoughts that heavenly love burns in acceptance of the sacrifice. So whatever the mind suffers from unfought battles or memories of the previous life, let it be washed, so that it may burn more sweetly in the sight of its Beholder, so long as it places nothing worldly or deceitful on the altar of its prayer when it begins to stand before him.

So let the holy man contemplate the loss of the human mind; let him see that the mind is often defiled by impure thoughts. After the Judge's remission of the guilt of our works, while Job laments his own case let him show us what we should lament. Let him say, *If I have sinned, and you forgave me at the time, why do* *Job 10:14 *you now refuse me purity from my sin?** He might as well say, "If in forgiveness you took away my guilt, why did that forgiveness not wipe away guilt from my memory?" The mind is often so shaken by the memory of guilt that it is driven more urgently to commit the same sin than it was formerly led to do. Detected in sin, it is anxious, and driven by various emotions, it troubles itself further. It is indeed fearful lest it be overcome by temptation, yet even while resisting it begins to tremble

at being afflicted by its lasting weariness of battle. So
he rightly adds,

LVI. 85. *If I am wicked, woe is me; if I am righteous,
I will not lift up my head. I am full of affliction and misery.** The wicked person, you see, expects woe, and the
just person misery, since eternal damnation pursues the
bad one, whereas all the elect are purified by suffering
temporary adversity. The wicked lift up their heads, but
in their pride they cannot escape the woe that follows.
The just are dejected at the toil of the battle they wage,
and they are not allowed to lift up their heads, but even
though hard pressed, they are freed from eternal torture.
The former are lifted up with pleasures but sink in the
following penalty. The latter are dejected in sorrow but
hidden from the weight of eternal scrutiny.

Let the holy man then reflect that a person either
resists vice and is rewarded by present hardship or yields
and is delivered for eternal torture; let him say, *If I am
wicked, woe is me; if I am righteous, I will not lift up
my head. I am full of affliction and misery.* It is as if
he openly deplored his lot and said, "Either I give myself up to desires of the flesh and am subject to eternal
damnation, or I resist unacceptable emotions and am
tortured by present pain. All this means that I am not
exempt from the press of battle." God wills that we
serve the heavenly dispensation with all our hearts, and
he allows us to be tried by the resistance of our flesh,
lest our minds should presume by trusting in their own
steadfastness to be lifted up to pride. Instead, when we
fear tottering, we put the foot of hope firmly down in the
Creator's assistance alone. So Job again astutely adds,

LVII. 86. *For my pride you will capture me like a
lioness.** When she goes in search of food for her cubs,
the lioness willingly falls into the trap set for her. As
the custom is in certain countries, a pit in which a heifer

*Job 10:15

*Job 10:16

is tied is dug in her path, so that the lioness may be instigated by her appetite to spring upon it. The pit is so constructed that it is narrow as well as deep, so that she may fall into it as she stalks but be quite unable to leap out of it. A second pit is also dug and connected to the first; in fact, it partly opens on to it at one end. In the first pit the heifer is tied. The second pit holds a cage, because when the lioness falls in she is beset by dread of the outside, and so she wishes to hide herself in the more inaccessible part of the pit and willingly enters the cage. Her ferocity is then no longer a concern, because she is locked in the cage and can be carried. She sprang into the pit, you see, by her own volition, and now surrounded by bars she returns to the upper world.

In precisely the same way the human mind has been captured; it was created with a free will, but like a lioness going in search of food for her cubs, it wanted to feed the desires of the flesh. It fell into the pit of her own deception when at the enemy's instigation it stretched out its hand for the forbidden fruit. But it immediately found a cage in the pit, because it willingly came to death and soon reached the prison of its own decay. Finally it is led back to the free air by the intervention of grace. But when it tries to do many things and is unable, it is its own corrupt nature that hinders it, like the bars of a cage. In fact it has already escaped from that trap of condemnation into which it had fallen, because it has overcome the penalty of death that was to follow, by the helping hand of redemption returning to forgiveness. Nevertheless it endures its confinement in a cage, because it is also hemmed in by the bonds of heavenly teaching, lest it go astray through the desires of the flesh.

Accordingly the mind fell into the pit by its own volition, and it returns to the free air imprisoned, because it both fell into sin through freedom of the will and still restrains its free emotions, unwillingly constrained by the Creator's grace. So after the pit it tolerates the cage, because it escaped the eternal penalty only to have the emotions of depraved liberty curtailed by the dispensation of the heavenly Architect. Therefore Job is right to say, *For my pride you will capture me like a lioness.* First, you see, humans were free, but they brought death upon themselves through food; subsequently they returned to be forgiven and lived as prisoners under a better discipline. Humans were consequently captured for their pride like a lioness, because the discipline of their corruption depresses them now, precisely because they had no fear of transgressing the commandment but boldly leaped into the pit.

87. But if we briefly avert our mind's eye from the sin of our first parents, even today we find ourselves captured like a lioness through the vice of pride. Men and women, you see, after gaining virtues are lifted up to arrogance and insolence, but a wonderful arrangement of God's kindness causes something to happen before their very eyes and trips them up. So when they desire something sinfully, what else do they do but hunger for the bait in the trap? By their own volition they stand agape and fall, but they cannot get up under their own power. Those who know that they are nothing by themselves learn beyond any doubt whose help they stand in need of. God's mercy pulls them out when they are, as it were, caught in a trap; it restores them to pardon when they realize their frailty.

Like a lioness, they return to the upper world in a cage because of their pride; since they were renowned for their virtue and fell into desires, they were tied with the bonds of humility. Formerly they had perished by means of their own presumption, but by the wonder of God's love something happened to make them realize their frailty, and now they live as though imprisoned. The holy man knows that such things often happen to us, so he makes himself the voice of our plight. He does so in order that we might recognize ourselves in his tears and learn about those things in ourselves that are worth crying about. Whenever our mind is lifted up by pride, the pinprick of love for the highest leaves us. But whenever God's grace visits us, he immediately incites our desire for him through tears. So Job is right to add,

*Job 10:16   LVIII. 88. *When you turn around again, you torment me wonderfully.** When the Creator leaves us alone, we do not feel to any extent the tragedy of our abandonment. As long as the Creator forsakes us our heart grows progressively harder, loves none of the things God wills, and by no means desires heaven. Because we have no warm interior love, we lie in the cold dust, and we are to be pitied for getting daily worse the more unconcerned we are. The heart forgets how far it has fallen, nor does it fear the coming judgment, and it knows not how forlorn it is. But if the heart is touched by the breath of the Holy Spirit, it wakes up forthwith and considers its wretched state; it shakes off its lethargy and seeks heaven; it grows warm with the love of God and considers the losses that threaten it. Its progress reaches the point where it weeps over its ruin, which formerly gladdened it.

It is well that the Creator is told, *When you turn around again you torment me wonderfully*. Almighty God, you see, visits our heart and awakens it to love him and thereby afflicts it grievously to the point of tears. It is as though Job said, "When you leave me alone, you hardly benefit me, because you render me without feelings, but when you return you torment me, because when you enter my heart, you show me how forlorn I am." Job then by no means calls his torment a penalty, but rather a marvel, because the mind through tears is raised up on high, and then it rejoices in admiration at the penalty of its compunction. It suffers freely, because by means of its suffering it knows that it is raised up on high. God's kindness often takes notice when we grow tired of the effort required for holy desires, and he places before our eyes the example of his followers. In this way the lazy negligent mind is brought to consider the extent of other people's watchfulness and hence to be ashamed of its own indolence and negligence. So Job rightly adds,

LIX. 89. *You call your witnesses against me, and your wrath is redoubled; penalties are loosed against me.* God's witnesses are those who through holy works testify to the faithful rewards that will follow his chosen ones. Therefore we recognize those also who have suffered for Truth in the Greek word μαρτυρ, which we translate as *witness*. According to John, the Lord says in the angel's voice, *In the days of Antipas, my faithful witness, who was killed among you.* The Lord calls his witnesses against us when he redoubles his chosen ones and in order to teach us makes their lives adversaries to our crimes. Accordingly he calls his witnesses against us, because all their works are adversaries against our eagerness in crime. That is why truthful speech is called an adversary, when the Mediator's voice is heard in the gospel: *Be quick to agree with your adversary while you are still with him on the road.* Evil persecutors of this same Redeemer said of him, *He is an adversary of our doings,* and a little later, *And his life is not like that of other men.*

The Lord then calls his witnesses against us when in order to correct us he shows us how other people do the good works we neglect to do ourselves, in order that we who are unmoved by commandments might at

*Job 10:17

*martyr

*Rev 2:13

*Matt 5:15

*Wis 2:12
*Wis 2:15

least be aroused by examples and that our mind might not consider any action too difficult in its desire for righteousness when it sees other people perform it perfectly. Furthermore, it often happens that when we see the good others do in their lives, we fear loss in our own all the more keenly, and it is clear how heavy a scrutiny threatens us later when our present lives and behavior are so far out of tune with those of good people.

90. So then, having mentioned the calling of witnesses, Job immediately adds with propriety, *Your wrath is redoubled.* God's wrath against us is said to be redoubled because we now know a great deal about the life and labor of good people, and we also know that if we refuse to amend our lives while there is still time, the accumulated judgment will smite us. We unquestionably see that God's chosen ones do holy deeds and put up with a large amount of harsh treatment. From this fact it is clear with what intransigence the intransigent Judge there strikes those he finds guilty, when here he torments those he loves. Peter is our witness when he says, *The time has come for judgment to begin with God's house, but if we are first, what will be the end for those who do* *1 Pet 4:17 *not believe the Gospel of God?* *

Accordingly almighty God calls witnesses against us and redoubles his wrath; when he forces us to see the lives of good people, he reveals the intransigent judgment with which he will punish our stubbornness in carrying out evil purposes. For those who follow him alone, you see, he stores up gifts, while he shows that he has already abandoned those who continue slothful. When therefore we see goodness in other people, it is absolutely necessary that we unite exultation with dread and dread with exultation on our own account, inasmuch as charity rejoices at the advancement of other people, while conscience trembles at its own weakness. But when our neighbor's advancement revives us and we feel the intransigent internal judge threaten us for our own sluggishness, what is left for the soul to do but to return to compunction and to punish whatever evil or crime it finds in itself? So Job rightly adds, *Penalties are loosed against me.*

Without a doubt God's witnesses have been heard and weighed, and penalties are loosed against us, because we see their wonderful works; consequently we are dissatisfied with our own lives compared to theirs, and we torment and scold ourselves. We do so in order that anything inside ourselves that spoils our good works may be washed away by our tears, and if anything still defiles us by guilty pleasure, the pain of sadness may wipe it away. Because blessed Job, therefore, looks upon the lives of the ancient fathers, he acutely knows in himself that which should cause him to groan. In the school of intense suffering, he mourns over himself and meanwhile teaches us tears, so that when we see virtuous people, we may anxiously fear our own sins in the sight of the intransigent Judge.

LX. 91. He continues, *Why did you bring me forth out of the womb? Would that I had died before any eye could see me.** Job had already spoken these words in his first speech: *Why did I not die in the womb?** In the present passage he adds, *It would have been as though I were not, as though carried from the womb to the tomb.** In that earlier passage he said the same thing in different words: *I would be like one prematurely born and hidden away, who would not live, like those conceived who did not see the sun.** Since we have already explained these words at length, in order to avoid wearying the reader we will not repeat that exposition. He continues,

LXI. 92. *Will not my few days be quickly over?** He obviously lives in a cautious and careful manner,

*Job 10:18
*Job 3:11

*Job 10:19

*Job 3:16

*Job 10:20

because he considers the present life short, and his eyes are not on life itself but on its end. So he can gather from the end that life's transitory pleasures amount to nothing. That is why Solomon says, *Even if a man should live many years and be happy in all of them, he ought to remember dark times and the many days that will* *Eccl 11:8* *come and inflict vanity.* So he wrote earlier, *In all your* *Eccl 7:40* *works remember your last end, and you will never sin.* Accordingly, when sin tempts the soul, the mind must be aware of the short duration of its pleasure lest evil snatch it away to a living death, since the fact remains that mortal life rushes on quickly to its climax. On the other hand, our contemplative eye is often troubled when sadness continues to increase because of our many misfortunes. The exile of the present life freely lets us groan, but concerning its actual affliction the mind cannot calculate the loss entailed by its blindness. So Job immediately adds,

LXII. 93. *Let me alone, then, for a little while, to* *Job 10:20* *bewail my grief.* Just as a moderate affliction makes us shed tears, so immoderate affliction inhibits them, because sorrow itself becomes, as it were, without sorrow; it consumes the mind of the afflicted person and takes away the feeling of sadness. Consequently the holy man is afraid he will be struck by more blows than are sufficient, and he says, *Let me alone, then, for a little while, to bewail my grief.* He could say it openly: "Strike your blows slowly, that I may deal with moderate affliction and may be enabled to measure sorrow with tears."

Nevertheless it can be understood another way. Sinners, you see, are often so confined by the chains of their evil practices that they indeed bear the weight of sin but do not know that they bear it. Even if they know how much guilt hems them in, they try to break out but cannot, nor can they hunt it down with their mind free and completely converted. So they are unable to weep for their sad plight, because they consider the guilt of their evil life, but because of their burden of worldly business, they are in no way free to groan over it. They cannot weep for their sorrow; they indeed attempt to go against their evil inclinations, but increasing desires of the flesh still weigh them down. The presence of this sadness tormented the prophet's mind when he said, *My grief is always before me, because I declare my iniquity, and I will reflect on my sin.** On the other hand, the man who knew he was freed from the chains of iniquity said exultantly, *You have broken my chains, and I will offer you a sacrifice of praise.**

*Ps 37:18-19 LXX

*Ps 115:16-17

94. Accordingly, when the Lord lets us alone to bewail our grief it is time for him to show us the evil we have done and help us weep for what we know. He displays our faults in front of our eyes, and with the loving hand of grace he loosens the chains from our hearts so that our minds may be lifted up and free to repent; released from the chains of flesh, the mind can simply turn the steps of love toward its Creator. We often, you see, blame ourselves for the way we live, yet we let ourselves do what we correctly blame ourselves for doing. Our spirits urge us to act rightly while our flesh forces us to follow our habits. The mind resists self-love but is immediately captivated by pleasure. It is well said, *Let me alone, then, for a little while, to bewail my grief.* Unless we are mercifully let alone, you see, from the guilt of sin by which we have bound ourselves, we cannot perfectly weep over that in ourselves over which we grieve against ourselves. Only then is the sorrow of our guilt really mourned when that dark retribution of hell is foreseen with intense fear. So Job fittingly adds,

LXIII. 95. *Before I go to that place from which I will not return, the dark land covered with the shadow*

*Job 10:21 *of death.** What is meant by the words *dark land* but the hideous prison of hell? The darkness of everlasting death covers it, because all the damned souls are forever cut off from the light of life. Nor is it wrong for hell to be called a land, because all those who have been captured by it are held fast. It is indeed written, *A generation passes, and a generation arises, but the* *Eccl 1:4 *earth remains forever.** Rightly therefore are the prisons of hell called a dark land, because when they receive those subject to punishment, they do not torment them with a transitory pain or with a fanciful apparition, but they hold them for enduring punishment and lasting damnation. This dark land is, however, sometimes called a lake, as the prophet bears witness saying, *They have borne their own disgrace, along with those who go down* *Ezek 32:24 *to the lake.**

Accordingly hell is called a land, because those it receives it holds firmly; it is also called a lake, because those it has once caught it keeps pulling down, thrashing and tossing in winding eddies. The holy man therefore, whether speaking in his own voice or in that of the human race, pleads to be let alone before he goes away. He does not say he is going to walk to the dark land because he would bewail his sins; rather, he says that he who neglects weeping is surely going there. He is just like the creditor who tells his debtor to pay up before he goes to the debtor's prison, who on the other hand would not be imprisoned if he did not delay the paying of his debt. So Job correctly adds, *I will not return,* because never again does sparing mercy free those whom the just Judge once condemns to the place of punishment. This place is still more lucidly described when he says,

*Job 10:22   LXIV. 96. *It is the land of misery and gloom.** Misery goes with pain, gloom with blindness. That land, accordingly, that holds those who have been driven away from the unwavering Judge's presence is declared to be a land of misery and gloom, because pain torments them externally while blindness darkens them internally, since they are cut off from the true Light. The land of misery and gloom can, however, be understood in another way. This very earth, on which we were born, you see, is a land of misery, but not of gloom, because we suffer much on it from our own decay; nevertheless we still return to the light through the grace of conversion here on earth. Truth convinces us when he says, *Walk while you have light, lest the darkness catch up with you.** *John 12:35 That, however, is the real land of misery and gloom combined, where no one who goes down to suffer its torment ever returns to the light again. Job follows up this description, as follows:

LXV. 97. *It is where the shadow of death and disorder reigns.** Just as material death separates the flesh *Job 10:22 from the soul, so spiritual death separates the soul from God. The shadow of death is then the darkness of separation, because when each condemned soul is set on fire with the eternal flame, it is darkened as far as spiritual light is concerned. The nature of fire, you see, includes both its light and its power to burn, but that flame that avenges sinful lives burns only and sheds no light. That is why Truth tells reprobate sinners, *Depart from me, you accursed, into the eternal fire prepared for the devil and his angels.** In another place he addresses the whole *Matt 25:41 gang of sinners in the person of one and says, *Tie up his hands and feet and throw him out into the darkness outside.** *Matt 22:13

For that reason, if the fire that burns reprobate sinners could have had light, he who is thrown out would hardly be said to be cast into the darkness. Therefore the psalmist also says, *Fire fell upon them, and they did*

*Ps 57:9 LXX   *not see the sun.**[4] Fire then falls upon the wicked, but the sun is unseen while the fire is falling, because those whom the flame of hell is burning up it also blinds as far as the sight of the true Light is concerned. Thus the pain of fire torments them externally, while the penalty of blindness covers them internally. Those who abandoned their Creator body and soul are also punished body and soul. They should be penalized body and soul, because during their lives they served their evil desires body and soul. So the prophet was right to say, *They went down*

*Ezek 32:27   *to hell along with their weapons.**

The weapons of sinners are unquestionably their bodily organs, with which they fulfill the sinful desires that they have devised. That is why Paul wisely said, *Do not present your bodies as weapons for sin and wicked-*

*Rom 6:13   *ness.** Accordingly, going down to hell along with one's weapons means to suffer the torture of eternal punishment, along with the very bodily organs with which they fulfilled their desires for pleasure. Pain would then completely engulf those who, now being subject to their own enjoyment, fight a total war against the judgment of the one who judges justly.

98. But there is a riddle where we read *disorder*. Almighty God, you see, rightly punishes wrongdoing and never allows disorder or struggle; no, even the very punishment decreed by the scale of justice can never be inflicted in a disorderly way. How will there be disorder in punishment when due retribution pursues all persons condemned according to the rank of their crime? That

---

[4] The LXX here differs markedly from the Hebrew. According to the RSV, the Hebrew has, *Let them be . . . like the untimely birth that never sees the sun.* Since Gregory follows the LXX, so must we. Interestingly, Gregory inserts *eos* between *super* and *cecidit.* The Vulgate has a compound verb: *supercecidit.*

is precisely why we find it written, *Mighty men will be mightily tortured, and more powerful than those who hold power will be the scourge that strikes them.** That is also why Babylon's condemnation is described thus: *As great as was her exultation and the pleasure she felt, so great make her torture and her grief.**

           *Wis 6:6, 8
               LXX

           *Rev 18:7

Therefore, since the punishment is meted out according to the seriousness of the crime, we must conclude that an order is followed in the administration of punishment. Unless sinful acts corresponded to the resultant punishment, the coming Judge would never promise that he was going to tell the harvesters, *Gather the chaff and wrap it up in bundles for burning.** If there were disorder in the administration of punishment, why is the chaff wrapped up in bundles for burning? Undoubtedly the wrapping up of bundles for burning means that those who are destined for eternal fire are associated like with like; those defiled by similar guilt should also be liable to a similar penalty. Those who are not unsoiled by the same wickedness should not be tortured by a different scourge. By the same token, a like condemnation should consume those whom a similar pride exalted. All those driven by similar ambition should be covered by similar distress. A like flame of punishment should torture those whom a like flame of sin sets on fire with debauchery. Just as *In the Father's house there are many mansions** for the different virtues, so the different sins require that those condemned be subjected to different penalties in the fire of hell.

           *Matt 13:30

           *John 14:2

Although there is obviously one hell for all the sinners, it does not burn them all with the same kind of fire. Similarly we are all reached by one sun, but we are not all warmed by it in the same degree, because different types of bodies feel its intense heat differently. In like manner all the damned souls feel the same hell, but it does not burn them all in the same degree; rather, here below the healthy state of our bodies makes us different from one another, and these differences show up at the Judgment according to different levels of merit. How, then, can we say there is disorder in punishment, when all the sinners suffer punishment exactly according to the degree of their guilt?

99. But after the holy man introduced the shadow of death, he added the degree of confusion to be found in the minds of the condemned, because the very punishment ordained by God's justice to come upon them is beyond a doubt not ordained in their hearts as they are dying. I said earlier that each condemned soul is burned externally by a flame, and at the same time it is burned internally by blindness; while in pain it is confounded internally and externally, and its confusion aggravates its torture. In this way there will be disorder for the damned souls in their punishment, because that terrible mental confusion ravages them in their death. The just Judge ordains this disorder with wonderful power, so that the penalty might confuse the souls as if they were disordered. Otherwise there is said to be disorder in punishment, because the various factors that arise in punishment cause the souls to lose their own identity. So Job immediately adds,

*Job 10:22   LXVI. 100. *Everlasting terror dwells there.** In this life's torments there is pain in fear but no fear in pain, because fear does not trouble the mind that has already begun to suffer what it feared. On the other hand, the shadow of death darkens hell, and everlasting terror abides there, because those who are delivered to its fires feel pain in its punishment and, even as they shake in the distress of pain, are being continually struck with fear. So they both endure what they fear and in return fear continually what they endure. It is written about them,

*Their worm will not die, nor will their fire be put out.** *Isa 66:24
Here the burning fire gives light, but there, as I have
shown above with the psalmist's words, the fire that
inflicts pain darkens. Here fear is lost when we already
begin to endure what we feared. There they are both
wracked with pain and cornered by fear. In a terrible
way, accordingly, the reprobate sinners will then feel
pain along with fear and fire with darkness.

This is precisely the way in which the full weight of
final justice ought to be felt by condemned sinners. They
had absolutely no fear of acting against the Creator's
will while they were alive, so whenever they meet their
death, their very torment will act against their nature,
inasmuch as where they are at strife with themselves
their torture increases, and when their variety appears,
they feel it in many ways. Those punishments torture
the souls who are plunged into themselves beyond their
strength and, while ending their life resources, preserve
them; this is so in order that the end may punish their
life. Torture lives on forever without an end, because
while life rushes on to an end through torment, it unend-
ingly fails and endures. For these miserable souls there
is death without death, unending end, and unfailing
failure, because death lives on, the end always begins,
and failing knows no failure. So then death kills without
ending, pain tortures but in no way banishes fear, and
the fire burns but absolutely does not scatter the darkness. As far as the knowledge of the present life lets us
know, there is disorder in punishment, because through
all its modalities it does not retain its own quality as
punishment.

101. Although that fire has no light for comfort, it
does have some light for greater torment. The reprobate
sinners, you see, are one day going to be looking at their
own followers, who will then be with them in torment

with the flames giving them light. For love of those followers they sinned; indeed they had loved their life in
a carnal manner against the express commands of the
Creator, and therefore the ruin of those people should
afflict them as well, so as to intensify their own condemnation. We find that the gospel is unquestionably our
witness to this truth. There Truth himself proclaims* that
the rich man finally went down to the torture chamber of
eternal fire, where he is said to have remembered his five
brothers. So he petitioned Abraham to send someone to
teach them lest they should one day come to that place
for their sins and suffer torment. He who in this way
remembers the absence of relatives to add to his own
pain could undoubtedly see them present a little later, to
heighten his own suffering. Why should we wonder if he
should see those reprobate sinners also burning beside
him when he could see Lazarus, whom he had despised,
resting on Abraham's bosom, to intensify his own pain?

*see Luke
16:23, 28

Regarding him to whom one of the elect appeared
in order to heighten his pain, why should we not believe that he could also see in his punishment those
whom he had loved contrary to God's will? We gather
from all this that those whom reprobate sinners now
love inordinately, they will see beside them later in torments by a wonderful dispensation of justice, so that
the carnal relationship that they preferred to the Creator
should contribute weight to the penalty for their own
sin, since the others were condemned before their eyes
by a similar vengeance. We must therefore suppose that
the fire that tortures sinners in the darkness does give
light for the purpose of torment. But if we cannot prove
this fact from direct testimony, we must have recourse
to an indirect witness.

102. Three young men of the Hebrew nation were
thrown into the flames of a red-hot furnace with hands

and feet bound at the command of the king of Babylon. But the same king, when he looked at them in pity inside the fiery furnace, found them walking about with clothes unburnt.* From the story we obviously gather that by a miraculous dispensation of the Creator the nature of fire was changed and its power diversified, with the result that the young men's clothing was unburned but their bonds were loosed, so that the flames grew cold for the saints without bringing them torment, burning only to help free them. Accordingly, just as the fire could burn for the chosen ones' comfort but not for their torment, so on the other hand for the reprobate sinners the fire of hell does not give light for the sake of comfort, but it does give light for punishment. This fact is so in order that the fire of punishment might not burn with brightness for the eyes of damned souls yet might show them how their loved ones were tormented in order to add to their own pain.

*see Dan 3:19-25

What wonder is it if we believe that the fire of hell holds punishment in darkness and light at the same time when experience shows us that a pine torch burns with smoke? Later the consuming flame burns those whom now pleasures of the flesh pollute; later the yawning pit of hell eternally devours those whom now vain pride puffs up. Furthermore, he who has here done the bidding of a crafty prompter in any sinful act will later reach that place of torment along with his accomplice as a reprobate sinner.

103. Although the natures of angels and of men are altogether different, the same penalty nevertheless involves both, because the same guilty sin binds them. The prophet suggests this truth wisely and briefly where he says, *There will Assyria be found and its entire horde; all around him will be tombs.** Who is meant by Assyria, the name of a proud king, if not the one who fell through

*Ezek 32:22

pride, the ancient enemy who, because he dragged many with him into sin, went down into hell's prison with his entire host? Tombs hold those who are dead. Who has suffered a more bitter death than the one who spurned his Creator and abandoned life? He indeed is the dead one, whom human hearts receive and become his tombs. But these tombs are all around him, because in whatever minds he is now buried through desires, he is later associated with them in torment. And because reprobate sinners now receive evil spirits into themselves by committing crimes, they will later burn like tombs, with the spirits' dead bodies inside.

104. We are left with these facts: we know that souls are damned by a penalty, and Holy Scripture teaches us how hot the fire of damnation is, how thick the darkness of that fire, and how intense the fear felt in that darkness. There is no room for doubt. But what good is it to know all these things beforehand if we take no steps to avoid them? We must devote our whole attention, when we have free time, to make sure that we exercise a proper zeal for living in a holy manner, in order that we may escape the avenging torture for wrongdoing. That is certainly why Solomon said, *Whatever your hand finds to do, do without hesitation, because there is neither work nor reason nor wisdom nor knowledge in hell, where you are going.** That is also why Isaiah said, *Seek the Lord while he may be found; call on him while he is near.** Paul says, for his part, *Behold, now is the acceptable time; behold, now is the day of salvation.** He also says, *While there is still time, let us do good to all people.**

105. It often happens that the soul braces itself for the path of integrity and throws off laziness; it is so completely enraptured by heavenly desires that nothing from below seems to have remained in it. Yet it is led back to

*Eccl 9:10

*Isa 55:6

*2 Cor 6:2
*Gal 6:10

earthly concerns, without which the present life can in
no way be led. But this fact makes the soul so depressed
that it feels as though nothing spiritual had occurred.
Then the soul hears the words of a heavenly oracle, and
it is lifted up to love of the heavenly homeland; then a
concern for the present life again arises, and the soul is
buried in the tomb of some earthly worry. The seed of
heavenly hope does not grow in the soil of the heart,
because there the thorn of lowly thought thickens. Truth
himself pulls out that thorn by the root with the hand of
holy exhortation, saying, *Do not worry about tomorrow.** *Matt 6:34
Paul for his part speaks out against that thorn and says,
*Do not be concerned about the flesh in your desires.** In *Rom 13:14
these words of our Captain and of his soldier, we undoubtedly know that the soul is dealt a mortal wound by
the flesh when it does not observe a judicious measure.

106. For us you see who still live in this mortal flesh,
concern for the flesh is never totally abrogated; it is
only limited, so that we may care for the soul discreetly.
Truth, you know, forbids us to worry about tomorrow,* *see
but he does not deny us any care for the present life; Matt 6:34
rather, he vetoes the extension of that care to the time
that follows the present. Paul too does not allow care
for the flesh in concupiscence, but he certainly concedes
necessary care of the body. That care therefore must be
restrained by the discretion of a great ruler, so that the
body may be a handmaid and by no means a princess;
she must not win over the soul or be its mistress, but she
must do the bidding of the soul and serve it as a slave.
When called she should be present, and when dismissed
by a nod from the heart she should retire. Hardly should
she appear behind a holy thought, and never stand facing
the one who thinks correctly.

All this is nicely pictured for us in the Bible's sacred history, when we are told that Abraham met three

*see
Gen 18:2

angels.* He immediately left the tent and greeted those who were arriving, but Sara stayed inside the tent. Obviously the man is master of the spiritual house, and so our intellect ought to leave the house of flesh to think about the Trinity, to go outside the door, as it were, of a lowly dwelling place. Care of the body, accordingly, like a woman, should not appear externally. She should blush to be seen acting blatantly; rather, her place is behind the man with spiritual discretion, intent only on what is essential. By no means should she know how to unveil impudently but should show modest restraint.

Care for the flesh is often told that it should by no means take anything for itself but give itself over completely to trust and hope in God. But it spurns such a project; it has no confidence that its vital resources can still be available for it if it abandons its solicitude. That is why this same Sara laughs when she hears God's promises, but when she laughs she is corrected, and being corrected, she is at once made fruitful. She who in vibrant youth could not conceive conceives in a feeble womb when bent with old age. In the same way care for the flesh loses its self-confidence but then receives a promise from God against its hope that it will have what human reason led it to doubt. The one conceived is accordingly called Isaac, that is "laughter," because when she conceives confidence and hope in God, what else does our mind give birth to but joy?

We must then be careful lest care for the flesh should go beyond the limit of necessity, or in that which we do moderately we let the flesh act for itself. The soul is often deceived, and what it desires for pleasure's sake it considers a necessity, inasmuch as anything that is allowed, it supposes to be owed as useful for life. Because the effect follows forethought, the mind is often lifted up in self-confidence. When we see that we have what others lack, we rejoice in our secret thoughts at the extent of our foreknowledge. But so far are we from real foreknowledge that we do not know that very pride from which we suffer. Therefore we must with skillful intention estimate the guardianship over our works and the thoughts of our heart that we should exercise, lest external earthly worries should multiply and impede the operation of our mind or some inner thought should gradually lift itself up against the mind's dominance. When we fear divine judgment with worldly circum- spection, we avoid the punishment of everlasting terror.

BOOK 10

I. 1 Whenever a powerful wrestler goes down to the pit of the amphitheater, his less capable competitors advance to contend with him one by one. When he beats one, another immediately steps up against him. When he puts that one down, another takes his place. They hope eventually to find his fighting force somewhat less inflexible, since his frequent wins sap his strength. Inasmuch as a new contestant keeps coming forward, the one who cannot be overcome by resourceful strength might at least be bested by relays of persons.

In precisely the same way blessed Job, that robust champion, has excelled in this contest of angels and men. The more he wins over the changing opponents, the more his unflagging stamina shines. Eliphaz was the first to oppose him, and Bildad came next; finally Zophar joined in to refute him. They all withstood him and rained blows upon him with all their strength, but these blows did not reach far enough to hurt his noble breast. Their very words, of course, clearly suggest that their blows are cast against empty air, since they falsely accuse a holy man, and as these words are spoken in vain, they lose their force. This fact is plain to see, when Zophar the Na'amathite answers Job with insults, as follows:

II. 2. *Will not the long-winded speaker also listen?* *Will the talkative man be justified?* * Some people have the disconcerting habit of answering back and contradicting words that have been truly spoken. They do this for fear of seeming inferior if they agree to what was said. To them the words of righteous people, even if few

*Job 11:2

334

of them were spoken, are too many, since they attack
their vices and annoy their sense of hearing. So that is
construed as a crime that was righteously proclaimed
against crime. Assuredly Zophar contradicts him who
spoke strong words of truth. He calls him talkative,
when wisdom from the just man's mouth rebukes faults,
and that wisdom sounds like useless prolixity to the
ears of fools.

Depraved people consider nothing good except what
they themselves approve of. They rate the conversation
of righteous people vain, because they find it to be at
odds with their own interests. Zophar's statement is
certainly not false when he says that a talkative person
cannot be justified; anyone who allows his conversation
to run on loses the gravity of silence and cannot guard
the mind. That is why Scripture says, *Silence is the cultivation of justice.** Solomon says, for his part, *That man*   *Isa 32:17
is like an open city without a wall surrounding it who
cannot restrain his mind from speaking.* He also says,   *Prov 25:28
In much speaking there is no lack of sin.* The psalmist   *Prov 10:19
adds, *The talkative person will not last on the earth.**   *Ps 139:12

The value of a true statement is lost, however, when
that statement is made without the guidance of discretion. Of course it is true that a talkative person cannot
be justified. But the good word is not well said, because
Zophar in speaking does not consider the listener. It is
surely a true statement against offenders, but when it
attacks the integrity of good people, it loses its own and
falls back diminished because of the solidity of the breast
it struck. Zophar openly implies that depraved people
cannot patiently listen to good words and that while they
neglect the amendment of their lives, they are getting
ready to answer charges. So he adds the following,

III. 3. *Will men shut their mouths for you alone?*
When you ridicule others, will no one put you down?*   *Job 11:3

The ignorant mind, as we have said, reluctantly bears a truthful statement; such a mind deems silence a penalty, and it esteems as its own shame and derision whatever is said to be correct. When a truthful word, you see, reaches the ears of depraved people, guilt stings their memory and prompts them to deny their crimes when their minds are internally reached by the thought of them, and they externally hasten to contradict their guilt. The mind cannot bear the word, because it feels pain in the wound caused by guilt, and we feel the word spoken in general terms against wickedness as a personal attack. The mind remembers internally what it has done and is ashamed to hear it externally. Therefore it prepares itself for defense so that it may hide its shameful guilt by words of lying refutation.

Whereas righteous people evaluate words of reproof concerning their past misdeeds as a service rendered out of love, unrighteous people consider such words as insulting and derisory. The former immediately prostrate themselves in compliance, but the latter are aroused to the frenzy of their own defense. The former value helpful correction as the support of their lives, through which errors committed during the present life are rectified and the wrath of future judgment is mitigated. The latter, when they realize that they are confronted with a reproof, take it as an attack with a sword, because their sins are uncovered by a word of correction, and thereby their reputation and present dignity are tarnished. That is why Truth speaks in praise of the just man through Solomon in this fashion: *Teach the just man and he hurriedly complies.** Therefore he scorns the stubborn behavior of depraved people in these words: *Anyone who teaches a mocker does himself an injury.**

*Prov 9:9

*Prov 9:7

Now it often happens that when people cannot deny the wrongs they have been accused of, shame makes them worse. So haughty do they become in their own defense that they start scrutinizing the lives of their accusers for crimes. If they can point the finger at someone else's sins, they think their own sins will not be counted. But when they cannot find anything really wrong, they pretend to find it, so that they may have something themselves that they may seem to reproach with a confident justice. So Zophar, who complained of being reproached and mocked, at once falsely adds,

IV. 4. *You said, "My words are above reproach, and I am innocent in your sight."* * Anyone who remembers what blessed Job said knows how false it is to put these words in his mouth. How indeed can he be calling himself innocent when he says, *If I want self-justification, my mouth will condemn me?* * This is the custom of depraved malice, when it will not weep over its own true crimes but fabricates the crimes of others. Such is the consolation of sin that the one who enjoys it can slander and befoul the life of the accuser. We should remember, however, that bad people often nominally desire good things so that they may prove that the things that presently prevail are bad, and as though supportively praying for prosperity, they may seem to be kindly disposed. So Zophar continues without a break:

V. 5. *If only God would speak to you and open his mouth before you!* * People indeed talk to themselves when through their thoughts God's Spirit does not withdraw them from the knowledge of carnal wisdom. The flesh makes itself felt and arouses the mind, provoking it to understanding, as it were. In such a case Truth tells Peter, who is still thinking worldly thoughts, *You do not understand the things of God, but those of men.* * When he was declaring truth, however, he was told, *Flesh and blood did not reveal this to you, but my heavenly Father.* * What do we take God's mouth to be if not

*Job 11:4

*Job 9:20

*Job 11:5

*Mark 8:33

*Matt 16:17

his judgment? When the lips are closed, speech is cut off, and the thoughts of the silent person are unknown; when they are open and talk is resumed, the mind of the speaker declares itself.

God then opens his mouth when he shows humans his will through open judgments. It is as though he speaks with an open mouth when the darkness of his internal design is cleared, and he refuses the further hiding of anything he wills. As though speaking with closed lips, he does not reveal his meaning to us when through hidden judgments he conceals the reason for his actions. Zophar, then, so that he could contradict blessed Job on his carnal wisdom and at the same time show how benevolent he is himself, wishes good things for Job, though even when Job has them, Zophar is apparently unaware of them. He says, *If only God would speak to you and open his mouth before you!* He could have come right out and said, "I pity your ignorance more than your punishment, because I know you are endowed only with carnal wisdom and without any trace of the spirit of truth. If you really knew the hidden judgments of God, you would not intone such shameless statements about him." When almighty God raises us up to the consideration of his judgments, he immediately puts to flight the blindness of our ignorance. So Zophar immediately adds a demonstration of the teaching with which God, opening his lips, would profit us. He says,

VI. 6. *Would that he might show you his secret wisdom and the complexity of his law!* * The works of heavenly wisdom are well known, since almighty God rules creation, perfects the good things that he begins, and helps with his inspiration those whom he enlightens with the dawn of his visitation. It is plain to all that those whom he freely created he kindly disposes. When he lavishly grants spiritual gifts, he himself perfects

*Job 11:6

that which he began himself by the favor of his kindness. The secrets of heavenly wisdom are, however, the works that God created and abandoned; they are the good things that God began and set afoot but did not follow up and bring to completion. He enlightens us with the glorious light of his brightness, yet when he allows temptations of the flesh, he strikes us with blindness and darkness. He does not stand guard over the gifts he confers. He entices our minds with desire for him, yet by a hidden judgment he confines us in a difficult situation compounded by our own weakness.

7. Now then, concerning God's secret wisdom, there are certainly very few who can search it out, and none who can find it; as for the things that eternal Wisdom not unjustly arranges for our good, it is absolutely just that we mortal creatures should be still ignorant of them. Nevertheless, to contemplate these mysteries of his wisdom is even now to see in some way his incomprehensible power. Even when we fail to search out his plan, in that failure we learn more truly from him whom we should fear. Paul had himself striven to know this secret wisdom when he said, *O the deep riches of God's wisdom and knowledge! How mysterious are his judgments and unsearchable his ways! Who has known the mind of the Lord? Who has counseled him?* * Paul grew tired of this constant search, yet he profited from his weariness and gained knowledge of his own weakness; then he made this challenge: *Who are you, a man, to answer back to God? Does the clay ask the potter, "Why did you make me this way?"* *

*Rom
11:33-34

*Rom 9:20

He therefore who is unable to reach God's secret plan has returned to knowledge of his own weakness, and his failure has called him back to teach himself. If I may speak in this way, he finds this secret wisdom by not finding it. When he wore himself out in his search

for the heavenly plan, he learned to fear God more humbly. Paul's weakness shrank from intimate knowledge
of God, but humility joined him more truly to him. Accordingly Zophar, instructed as he was by the pursuit of
knowledge, was ignorant enough to flaunt his bombastic
speech. Since he had no personal dignity, he wished
for the better man* what that man already had, saying,

*i.e., Job

*If only God would speak to you and open his mouth
before you, that he might show you his secret wisdom!*
In fact Zophar thought he himself towered far above his
friend in wisdom, and by wishing wisdom on Job, he
displayed Job's wisdom immediately by adding, *and
the complexity of his law.*

What should we take God's law to mean in this context but charity, since it is through charity that we always
keep the commandments of life in mind, in the sense
that they are followed by action? The voice of Truth
speaks of this law as follows: *This is my commandment,
that you love one another.** Paul chimes in: *Love is the
fullness of the law.** Elsewhere he says, *Bear one another's burdens, and in this way you will fulfill Christ's
law.** And what can be more fittingly understood by
Christ's law than love, which we perfectly fulfill when
we carry a neighbor's load out of love?

*John 15:12
*Rom 13:10

*Gal 6:2

8. This law is called complex, because charity reaches
out eagerly and anxiously for all virtuous acts. Charity
takes its cue, certainly, from two commandments, but
it reaches out to perform innumerable actions. Love of
God, you see, and love of neighbor are the beginning of
this law. The love of God has three divisions, because the
Creator demands that we love him *with all our heart, all
our soul, and all our strength.** On this subject we must
take note that when the Word of God commands us to
love God, it proclaims both the organ and the amount,
since it includes the word *all.* So those who wish to please

*Deut 6:5; see
Luke 10:27;
Matt 22:37

God perfectly obviously leave nothing of themselves for themselves. Love of neighbor is derived from two commandments: a certain just man said, *What you would not want done to yourself, do not do to another.** For his own part, Truth says, *As you wish men to act toward you, do you act toward them likewise.**

*Tob 4:16

*Matt 7:12

By these two commandments of both testaments, be it noted, one of which restrains malice, the other that inculcates benevolence, we are to stop hurting one another, since the evil we do not want to suffer, each one of us is to stop doing. On the other hand, we offer to our neighbor the good we want done to ourselves and out of kindness exert ourselves on our neighbor's behalf. When we reflect on these two commandments with careful attention, our hearts unquestionably reach out to innumerable helpful acts of virtue, lest our anxious minds be so stirred up by desires as to admit improper thoughts or be weakened by inactivity and too indolent to perform their proper functions. When, you see, we avoid doing such things to a neighbor as we by no means want to suffer from a neighbor ourselves, we turn our attention anxiously toward ourselves: we do not want to give our pride full rein, lest it should lift us up and dishonor our soul, to the point of contempt for the neighbor. We do not want avarice to shred our thoughts or to enlarge itself to the point of desiring someone else's possessions, thus confining our spirit. We do not want lust to dishonor our hearts, bind them to concupiscence, and corrupt them through illicit acts. We do not want anger to irritate us and inflame us to the point of insulting the neighbor. We do not want envy to sting us with jealousy over someone else's happiness and burn us with its torch. We do not want extreme talkativeness to captivate the tongue and force it into wanton detraction. We do not want cunning to kindle hatred and urge the mouth to shout curses.

On the other hand, we should behave toward others as we expect them to behave toward us. When we consider this counsel, we decide that we should render good for evil and better things for good. For example, we should show gentleness and patience to those who impose themselves, we should show favor and kindness to those who suffer from the plague of malice, we should unite in peace those who disagree and encourage those who agree to desire true peace, we should bestow the necessities of life on the needy, we should guide those who go astray to the way of righteousness, we should soothe the despondent with words of compassion, we should calm those who are excited by worldly desires with words of reproach, we should reasonably soften the threats of the powerful, we should relieve the distress of the oppressed by aiding them as much as we can, we should oppose by patience those who resist us externally, we should patiently teach discipline to those who are full of interior pride, we should moderate zeal with meekness toward the sins of those who are subject to us as long as we do not weaken devotion to justice, we should burn with zeal for punishment as long as we do not transgress the boundary of duty, we should stir the ungrateful to love by benefits, we should preserve the love of all the grateful by serving them, we should be silent when we cannot correct the evil deeds of our neighbors so that we might avoid the silence of consent when they can be corrected by speaking, we should endure those things that we do not speak about in such a way that the poison of annoyance does not fester, we should show the insolent the favor of kindness in such a way that that such favor does not exceed the limit of righteousness, we should extend to our neighbors all that is in our power, but while acting thus we should avoid arrogance, we should fear the precipice of arrogance in our benevolence in such a way that we are not ashamed to do good works, we should bestow our possessions in such a way that we expect in return the full amount of the Rewarder's abundance, and while we bestow our worldly goods we should not think about our own poverty too much, lest in offering our gift some sadness should cloud our cheerful face.

9. The law of God is certainly well named as complex, because although charity is one and the same, if it completely fills the mind, it incites the mind to innumerable works of many kinds. We briefly express this diversity if we count and touch upon the works of charity in each one of the elect. Charity through Abel offered chosen sacrifices to God and endured the sword of his brother without resistance. Charity taught Enoch to live a spiritual life among people and took him away from people to live in heaven even in his body. Charity, having looked down on all humans, found only Noah to be pleasing to God, and she made him work for a long time building the ark; she also preserved him in the world as a survivor to continue doing good works. Charity through Shem and Japheth humbly blushed at the respected nakedness of their father and covered it with a cloth held behind them, so not seeing it.

Charity made Abraham the father of nations with uncountable progeny, because in obedience he raised his right hand against the life of his son. Charity broadened Isaac's mind because he always clung to purity, so that in the blindness of old age he saw far into the future. Charity drove Jacob to grieve internally for his favored son, whom he lost, and to endure the society of the less favored ones with composure. Charity taught Joseph, when he was sold by his brothers, to suffer slavery with his liberty of spirit unbroken, and later to assume leadership over these same brothers without a proud spirit.

Charity caused Moses to prostrate himself in prayer to the point of asking for death when the people sinned; she also forced him to rise and instigated him to kill the people because of his earnest zeal, in order that he might both offer his death for the people who were perishing and at once act harshly and wrathfully against the people in God's place. Charity strengthened Phineas's arm to avenge the sinners, so that with drawn sword he might stab them in the assembly and in his anger appease God's wrath. Charity taught Joshua among the spies, first to defend the truth by speaking against the people who spoke falsely and later to proclaim it with the sword against the enemy.

Charity showed Samuel how to be a humble man as judge, and she kept him uncorrupted in retirement, since he loved the people who deposed him, and he bore witness to himself that he had no love for the honorable place from which he was deposed. Charity prompted David to flee an unjust king out of humility and filled him with respect so that he might forgive; in fear he fled his persecutor as his master, yet when he found he had power to strike him, he did not take him as an enemy. Charity upheld Nathan in his authority to speak freely against a sinful king, and when the king was innocent, she made him prostrate himself humbly as a petitioner.

Charity was not ashamed of bodily nakedness in the preaching of Isaiah, but by the removal of clothes she revealed heavenly mysteries. Charity taught Elijah the spiritual life through his fervent zeal, and then she removed his bodily life to heaven. Charity taught Elisha to love his master simply, and then she filled him with a double share of his spirit. It was through charity that Jeremiah forbade the people to go down to Egypt, and then in his love for the disobedient he also went down to the place he had forbidden them to go. Charity first raised

Ezekiel from the level of worldly desires, and then she held him up in the air by the hair of his head. Charity had Daniel restrain his appetite from the delights of the king's table, and for him she later closed the mouths of hungry lions. Charity first subdued the attacks of vice for the three young men when they found themselves in peaceful circumstances, and then in time of trial she controlled the flames for them in the furnace.

Charity bravely resisted the threats of terrorizing princes for Peter and had him humbly listen to the words of his subordinates in the question of the restriction of circumcision. Charity humbly endured the hands of persecutors in Paul's case, but in the matter of circumcision he boldly spoke out against the position of one far more highly placed. This law of God is accordingly complex while unchanged, corresponding to so many individual traits and without variation joining so many and various causes.

10. Without question Paul described the great variety of this law when he said, *Charity is patient and kind; she is not envious or boastful; she is not depraved or scheming, nor is she self-seeking; she is not irritable; she thinks no evil; she does not rejoice over wickedness but rejoices with the truth.*[*] Of course charity is patient, because she endures the bad things that are done to her with equanimity. She is kind, because she freely bestows good for evil. She is not envious, because she has no desire for the things of this world, and so she cannot envy any worldly success. She is not boastful, because when she anxiously desires the reward of interior recompense, she does not exult over exterior possessions. She is not depraved, because only love of God and neighbor excites her, and she has nothing to do with any departure from rectitude. She is not a schemer, because she ardently pursues her own interior

[*] 1 Cor 13:4-6

interests, so she by no means desires another's exterior possessions. She is not self-seeking, because whatever transitory possessions she has here below she neglects, as though they belonged to someone else; she recognizes nothing as belonging to herself except that which remains close to her.

She is not irritable, because even when she receives an injury, she is not provoked or moved to self-defense, and she hopes for a greater reward hereafter for her grave troubles here. She thinks no evil, because she secures her mind with the love of purity, and she roots out all hatred from herself, so she cannot allow anything impure in her soul. She does not rejoice over wickedness, because she desires to have only love toward all, so she does not even exult at the discomfiture of an adversary. She rejoices with the truth, because when she loves other people as herself, seeing their rectitude, she becomes happy as though it were by the advancement of her own interests.

Accordingly this law of God is complex, affording defense with the shield of her instruction against every dart of sin loosed against the mind to destroy it. The ancient enemy, you see, attacks us on various fronts, so charity also fights him for us in many ways. And if we consider this law carefully, it lets us know how grievously we sin against our Creator day after day. If we evaluate our faults, then surely we willingly bear afflictions. Those whose conscience judges and condemns them do not angrily give way to impatience through pain. Zophar, then, knew very well what he said, but he did not know the person to whom he said it. So after he said, *Would that he might show you his secret wisdom and the complexity of his law,* he straightway added,

VII. 11. *That you might understand that God exacts of you much less than your sins deserve.** As we

*Job 11:6

have said, the pain of trials is mitigated once we realize our sins, because the more we see how decayed is the member that is cut off, the more patiently we endure the surgeon's knife. Those who finally understand the complexity of the law evaluate all their sufferings as being relatively minor, because they realize the heavy weight of sin, and so the pain of trials seems light in comparison.

12. Nevertheless we must remember that Zophar himself is not without grave error in accusing a just man and making him a subject of reproach for crime. That is why Truth justly contradicted the friends' boldness, although he kindly received them back into his favor, because before the merciful Judge guilt is never released without forgiveness when through an excess of zeal sin is committed out of love. It often happens to intelligent and wonderful teachers that when they are inspired by great love, they exceed the limit of correction, and say what should not be said by the tongue, because love inflames the mind to its capacity. But the word of intended insult is more speedily spared when we evaluate the source from which it arises.

Therefore through Moses the Lord rightly gave this command: *If a man goes into the forest with his friend openly to cut wood, but his axe flies off its handle and the steel falls into his friend, striking and killing him, he is to flee to one of the cities of refuge. He will live there, lest the avenger of bloodshed should pursue him at the pain of grief, overtake him, and take his life.** We enter the forest with a friend every time we turn aside with any neighbor in order to scrutinize our sins, and we cut wood openly when we hack off the sins of offenders with a pure intention. But the axe flies off the handle when the scolding is protracted into severity beyond due measure; the steel axe head flies through

*Deut 19:5-6

the air when harsh words exceed the requirement of correction. It strikes the friend and kills him, because the insulting words kill the hearer as far as the spirit of love is concerned. The mind of the corrected person, you see, straightway proceeds to hatred, if an immoderate scolding inculcates more guilt than it should. But the one who carelessly cuts wood and kills the neighbor must run away to three cities, in order safely to live in one of them, because if that one is converted to penitential tears and is hidden away by faith, hope, and charity in sacramental unity, he is not held guilty of the crime of manslaughter. If the blood relative finds him, he will not kill him, because when the unwavering Judge comes, he who joined himself to us by association with our nature, he will undoubtedly not avenge the guilt of sin on the one whom he hides with his pardon in faith, hope, and charity. That sin, accordingly, is more readily forgiven that is committed by no intentional malice. Zophar calls Job an evildoer, him whom God's sentence had praised, yet Zophar is neither rejected nor excluded from forgiveness, because he was provoked to insulting words by his zeal for love of God. Because he knows nothing about blessed Job's merits, he again adds with ignorant derision,

VIII. 13. *Perhaps you will recognize God's footsteps and discover the Almighty One completely.** What does he call God's footsteps if not his kind visitation? By his footsteps we are summoned to advance to a higher level; we are touched by the breath of his spirit, raised up beyond the limitations of the body, and through love we recognize the form of our Creator, which is presented for contemplation and for our attention. When love for the spiritual homeland, you see, incites our mind, it, as it were, points out the road for us to follow; it makes an imprint on the ground of the heart of the outline of

*Job 11:7

God's footstep, so that the heart might hold the course
of life with correct steps of thoughts. Him whom we
do not yet see we are necessarily reduced to tracking
by means of the footsteps of his love, inasmuch as the
mind sometimes in contemplation finds even the form
of him whom now we follow, as it were, from the rear,
groping through holy desires.

The psalmist knew very well how to follow these
footsteps of our Creator when he said, *My soul cleaves
to you.** He had his work cut out for him, though, to re-
discover him finally in the vision of his heavenly being,
as he said elsewhere, *My soul has thirsted for the living God. When shall I come and present myself before
God?** Then assuredly almighty God is discovered and
knowledge of him revealed when our mortal corruptible body is completely destroyed and we are raised up
in the glory of his divinity, and we shall see him. Now,
however, the infused grace of the Spirit lifts the soul out
of the thought of the flesh and exalts it in the contempt
of passing things. The mind now despises all its former
desires as being low and is on fire with heavenly desire;
by the power of its contemplation it is lifted up above
the flesh while it still remains in the flesh through the
weight of corruption. The mind tries to see the radiance
of unlimited light, but it cannot; that light is what the
soul encumbered by weakness by no means reaches yet
loves, even though repulsed.

In the present time the Creator presents that of himself that can be loved, yet he hides the actual vision of
himself from his lovers. So we see only his footsteps as
we walk, and through the signs of his gifts we follow
him whom we do not yet see. Even his footsteps can
by no means be grasped, because whence, where, or by
what means the gifts of his Spirit appear is unknown.
Truth is our witness, who said, *The Spirit breathes as*

*Ps 62:9 LXX

*Ps 41:3

*John 3:8

he wills, and you hear his voice, but you do not know where it comes from or where it goes.* It is true that almighty God can be found at the summit of retribution through the form of contemplation, but this cannot be experienced perfectly, because even if we sometimes see his glory, we do not see his full essence. When, you see, an angelic or human mind stands agape before the uncreated Light, it is limited by the very fact that it is a creature; it is indeed drawn upward by attraction, yet it is neither equipped nor assisted to grasp its brightness, since it transcends and bears all things, and by filling them it completes them. So Zophar again adds,

IX. 14. *He is higher than the sky, and what can you do? He is deeper than the nether world, and how can you know? He is longer than the earth and wider than the sea.** God is higher than the sky, deeper than the abyss, longer than the earth, and broader than the sea: so is he described, and the fact should be interpreted spiritually precisely for the reason that it would be sinful to think anything about him in terms of material reality. Rather, he is higher than the sky because by the boundlessness of his Spirit he transcends all things; he is deeper than the abyss, because in his transcendence he supports it from below; he is longer than the earth, because he exceeds the limits of creation by the endlessness of his eternity; he is broader than the sea, because he rules and possesses the waves of the events of time in such a way that he surrounds and controls them with every way in which his power is present.

*Job 11:8-9

On the other hand, the word *heaven* could designate angels, the word *abyss* devils, the word *earth* the just, and the word *sea* sinners. Then he is higher than heaven, because even the chosen spirits do not perfectly discern that deep heavenly vision; he is deeper than the abyss, because he judges and condemns the cunning tricks that the evil spirits devise far more subtly than they would have guessed. He is longer than the earth, because the patience of God's endurance is greater than our forbearance; he tolerates our sins and waits for our conversion and the opportunity to reward us. He is broader than the sea, because he fills sinful activity everywhere with the presence of his retribution, so that even when he is not actually present, his judgment is felt as though it were present.

15. All these places, however, might be understood in terms of humans alone: they could be heaven when they already cling to the heights through desire; they could be the abyss when, troubled by the darkness of their own temptations, they lie prostrate in the depths; they could be the earth when they bear fruit in good works by the fruitfulness inherent in the object of their firm hope; they could be the sea when they shake with fear at certain events and are troubled by the movement of their own changeability.

But God is higher than heaven, because we are surrounded by his great power even when we are raised above ourselves; he is deeper than the abyss, because he judges more than our soul discovers in itself when tempted; he is longer than the earth, because not even by hope do we in this life grasp the fruits of life that he awards to us at the end; he is broader than the sea, because the human mind like waves guesses at many things still in the future, but when it begins to see the things it had guessed at, it realizes how far short the guesses were.

Accordingly he is higher than heaven, because even our contemplation of him is deficient. That is why when the psalmist set his heart on the heights, he knew he had not yet found him and said, *Your knowledge is too wonderful for me; it is masterful, beyond my reach.** Paul

*Ps 38:6

knew that God was deeper than the abyss, because he
scrutinized himself yet was in mortal fear of God's more
exacting justice and said, *I am unaware of anything
against myself, but that does not clear me of wrong;*
*1 Cor 4:4   *my judge is the Lord.** He clearly saw that God was
longer than the earth, since he evaluated the wishes of
the human mind as less than God when he said, *He is*
*Eph 3:20   *able to do all things better than we ask or imagine.**
He perceived that God is broader than the sea, he who
fearfully judged that the human mind may never measure the immensity of unrelenting justice, no matter
how it is tossed about in its inquiry. So he said, *Who
knows the power of your wrath, or how to estimate your*
*Ps 89:11-12   *anger fearfully?**

        Our excellent teacher implies God's power to us
briefly when he tells us, *I want you to be able to understand with all the saints the length, the breadth, the*
*Eph 3:18   *height, and the depth.** God is unquestionably broad,
because he extends his love even to the point of gathering in his persecutors. He is long, because of his long-
suffering patience in leading us to the homeland of life.
He is high, because he even transcends the understanding
of those who have been received into the congregation
of heaven. He is deep, because he incomprehensibly
exerts strict justice toward those condemned to hell. It
is noteworthy that he exercises these four powers toward
all of us living on this earth, since he shows breadth in
his love, length in his tolerance, and height by surpassing not only our intelligence but also our wishes; by
strictly judging our hidden and inadmissible emotions
and thoughts, he also shows his depth. No one, however,
knows how unsearchable are his height and depth except
the one who is drawn to the heights by contemplation or
who resists hidden emotions and begins to be troubled
by importune temptations. So blessed Job is told, *He is*

higher than the sky, and what can you do? He is deeper than the nether world, and how can you know? It is as though Zophar despised him and asked him, *When could you confidently know his depth and excellence? You can neither be drawn up to heaven by virtues nor reprove yourself in time of temptation.*

The next verse:

X. 16. *If he should destroy all creation or force everything into one mold, who could contradict him?*[*] Who can ask God, "Why are you doing this?"[1] The Lord destroys heaven when he brings down our elevated contemplation by his fearful hidden plan. He undermines hell when he allows anyone's fearful mind to suffer temptation and to fall into worse evils. He undermines earth when he allows the fruit of good works to be lost by the intervention of adversity. He subverts the sea when he defeats the hesitation of our indecisiveness by the sudden jolt of fear. It is absolutely because of its doubting that the anxious heart by its very faltering is in dread, and it is as if the sea were overturned when our quaking fear of God at the consideration of his fearful judgment unsettles our hearts. Therefore, since heaven is shaken, like hell, earth, and sea, as we have briefly explained, it remains for us now to speak a bit more industriously, so that we may show how all these elements may be forced into one mold.

17. It often happens that when the spirit is already raising the mind to the heights, the flesh attacks the mind with troublesome temptations. When the soul is led to heavenly contemplation, it is beaten back by attacks of images related to prohibited actions. The sting of the flesh suddenly wounds it just when holy contemplation

[*]Job 11:10

---

[1] The Vulgate differs slightly from the LXX here, a difference reflected in Gregory's text.

was pulling it away from the flesh. Accordingly, heaven and hell are forced together when one and the same mind is raised up to the light of contemplation and darkened by troublesome temptations. This compression occurs in order that the mind might both intentionally see what it desires and, by falling back in thought, endure its shame. Obviously light dawns in the heavens, but darkness governs the abyss. Therefore, heaven and hell are reduced to one when the mind considers the light of the heavenly homeland yet at the same time bears the darkness of secret temptation from its war with the flesh.

Certainly Paul had already climbed the summit of the third heaven and already learned the secrets of Paradise, yet he still groaned and endured the war with the flesh. He said, *I see another law in my body, resisting the law of my mind, and making me a captive of the law of sin residing in my body.*[*] What is it in the breast of this great preacher, if not heaven and hell forcefully united by God? Paul had already received the light of interior vision, and yet he still endured the darkness of the flesh. Above himself he had seen what he should joyfully desire; inside himself he saw what he should sadly fear. The light of the heavenly homeland had already shone upon him, but the darkness of temptation still caused his soul to stumble. Along with heaven, accordingly, he endured hell, because security raised him to a state of illumination, and groans prostrated him in temptation.

18. It also happens that faith already grows vigorously in the mind, but in some small part doubt causes it to waste away, inasmuch as faith rises above the visible world in certitude yet is troubled and uncertain about some things. The mind, you see, often lifts itself up to desire eternity, yet it is agitated by stimulating thoughts that arise, and so it contradicts itself. Earth and sea are

*Rom 7:23

forced together in unity when one and the same mind is strengthened by the certitude of robust faith and yet wavers in doubt because of some changeable movement of disbelief. Did not the person who felt earth and sea moving together in his breast hope through faith and waver through unbelief, saying, *I believe, Lord. Help my unbelief?* * How is it that he both asserts his faith and pleads for help in his unbelief, unless the fact is that he had discovered earth pressing against the sea in his thoughts? He was already secure enough in faith to begin to pray, but he was still so insecure that he endured the waters of faithlessness and refusal to believe.

    19. This contradiction is allowed by a hidden decree of providence, because when the mind has once begun to lift itself up to righteousness, it has to fight against what is left of its depravity, inasmuch as this resistance either strengthens the fighter or breaks the will of the one enticed by pleasure. So it is rightly said, *If he should destroy all creation or force everything into one mold, who could contradict him?* * (Or *Who can ask him, "Why are you doing this?"* *) God's judgment, you see, can neither be weakened by adversity nor known by inquiry, since it takes away the virtues it had bestowed, or if it does not take them away altogether, it allows them to be buffeted by attacks from vices. The heart is often lifted up by pride when it is strengthened in virtue by joyful success, but when the Creator sees hidden emotions of boldness in the thoughts, he abandons us by showing our self to ourselves, in order that the abandoned mind may discover what it is that in its false security rejoices in itself. So then, after we were told that all creation was destroyed or forced into one mold, Zophar immediately adds,

    XI. 20. *He knows the vanity of mankind; do you think he does not see wickedness and keep it in mind?* * It is as if he said, "Because he tolerated vices and saw them

*Mark 9:23

*Job 11:10
*Job 9:12
LXX

*Job 11:11

grow, in his judgment he overthrew his gifts" to clarify his earlier words. Correct order, however, has been observed in the description, since he asserts that vanity is recognized first, and later wickedness is considered. Surely all wickedness is vain, but not all vanity is wicked. We act in a vain manner, of course, as often as we think of transitory matters. So we say that something disappears when it is suddenly removed from before the eyes of its beholders. That is why the psalmist says, *Every man alive is completely vain.** Because insofar as we are alive we are subject to death, we are correctly called vain, but by no means are we also called wicked. Even if, you see, our mortality is the penalty of sin, nevertheless the fact itself that our life ends is not sin. Therefore, vanity refers to transitory things, as in the words of Solomon: *All things are vanity.**

*Ps 38:6

*Eccl 1:2

21. It is fitting, however, that after vanity wickedness should at once be mentioned, because whenever we encounter transitory things, we are detained by certain things that are bad for us. When the mind does not hold on to the state of incorruptibility, it falls away from itself and runs headlong into vices. By means of vanity, therefore, it falls into wickedness when it becomes accustomed to changeable things, being always driven from one thing to another, and it becomes soiled by faults that rise up from below. Vanity, on the other hand, can be understood as a fault, and by the word *wickedness* we may speak of graver guilt. If, you see, vanity were not sometimes a fault, the psalmist would not say, *Although man walks in the image of God, nevertheless he is vainly anxious; he stores up, but he knows not for whom he gathers.**[2]

*Ps 38:7

[2] The Vulgate lacks *Dei*, which Gregory probably supplied. There are other minor differences in Gregory's text: *quamquam*

Although we keep the image of the Trinity in our nature, we are excited by emotions of pleasure, and we sin in our way of life. Our behavior is forever changing while avarice excites us, fear disarms us, joy caresses us, and sorrow discourages us. From vanity, accordingly, as we said above, we are led on to acts of wickedness after we have first slipped into trivial faults, and, habitually slighting all things, we no longer have any fear of committing even more serious crimes. For example, the lazy tongue neglects restraint and allows a habit of remissness to grow, so that we boldly utter words of slander; when we give ourselves up to gluttony, we forthwith betray the madness of inconstancy; when the mind refuses to subdue the pleasure of the flesh, it often rushes over the brink of the pit of faithlessness. That is why when Paul looked upon the loss of the people of Israel, in order to avert the evils that threatened his listeners he carefully recited the events that occurred, saying, *You should not become idolaters, as some of them did, as it is written: "The people sat down to eat and drink and got up to play."* * Eating and drinking impels one to play, and play in turn leads to idolatry, because if the fault of vanity is not cautiously restrained, the unguarded mind is forthwith seized by wickedness.

    *1 Cor 10:7

Solomon is our witness: *He who despises small things fails little by little.* * If we are careless and neglect

    *Sir 19:1

---

instead of *verumtamen*, *ambulet* instead of *pertransit*, *tamen vane* instead of *sed et frustra*, *congreget* instead of *congregabit*. Although these changes do not significantly alter the sense, *imagine Dei** does. By Saint Gregory's time the image of God plays a major part in Western theology influenced by Saint Augustine, so any occurrence of a form of *imago* in the Biblical text would instantly cause a reminiscence of Gen 1:27. The sense of the Hebrew, however, is "shadow" or "shade," rather than "image" as concrete representation.

    **imago*

little things, we are unknowingly led on boldly to commit even graver crimes. It is also noteworthy that wickedness is not said to be seen but to be kept in mind, and when we keep something in mind, we view it more diligently. God therefore knows our vanity and keeps our wickedness in mind, because he does not even let our little faults go unpunished, and he is ready to strike at our greater sins still more severely. Accordingly we begin with lighter faults and go on to graver sins, because vanity beclouds the mind, and wickedness blinds it. The mind certainly soon loses the light, and the more it lifts itself up by pride, the more helpless it becomes in the trap of wickedness, so that it drifts even farther from truth. So he rightly also exposes how vanity along with wickedness leads us astray when he immediately adds,

*Job 11:12   XII. 22. *The vain man lifts himself up in pride.** Vanity ends up in wounding the mind with sin and then making it bold because of its guilt inasmuch as, forgetting its crime, it is not sorry for having lost its innocence; since it has been rendered blind by a just judgment, it loses humility at the same time. It often happens that when the mind is enslaved to sinful desires, it unties itself from the yoke of the fear of God, and as if it were now free to do evil, it goes ahead to do all that pleasure leads it to do. So after the vain man is said to lift himself up in pride, in the same place we are told,

*Job 11:12   XIII. 23. *Like the colt of a wild ass, he thinks himself born free.** By *the colt of a wild ass* is unquestionably implied all wild animals that are allowed to follow the motion of nature and are not controlled by the harness of masters. The beasts of the field, as you know, enjoy the freedom to go where they please and to lie down when tired. Humans are certainly of more value than beasts without understanding, but what the brute animals can freely do, humans are often not allowed to do.

Concerning those creatures that are not kept for a special purpose, you see, their motion is undoubtedly not confined by control or training. Humans, however, are led to another life, and so it is absolutely necessary that they should be harnessed to a way of life and training in all their activities; like domesticated animals harnessed by reins, they should be under obedience and live subject to the eternal plan. Accordingly, what else do those who want to fulfill all their desires in unbridled liberty crave but to be like the colts of a wild ass, so that the harness of an orderly life should not hold them and that they might run boldly wild in the forest of their desires?

24. God's pity, however, often sees people exceed their bounds in unbridled and disallowed freedom and tames them by the intervention of adversity in their lives; in this way they are struck down and learn how they have swelled with pride in their own boastful sinfulness. Consequently they are now subdued because of the trial they have undergone; like domesticated cattle they bend the necks of their minds under the harness of precepts, and they follow the path of the present life under the direction of a leader. He knew very well by whose harness he was tied who said, *I became like a beast before you, and I am always with you.** So also   *Ps 72:23
that fierce persecutor who was led from the garden of treacherous delight to the house of faith received a blow from the spurs of his Creator and heard the words, *It is hard for you to kick against the goad.**   *Acts 26:14

So it remains true that if we do not want to be like the colt of the wild ass anymore, in all our desires we must first seek the nod of the interior dispensation, so that our mind in all its initiatives may be guided by the reins of God's government and may there fulfill its desires for life where it tramples upon the striving of its own life and against its own will. Zophar has said much that is good, but he is unaware that he is speaking to a better man than himself. So he again adds these insulting words:

XIV. 25. *You, however, have toughened your heart and stretched out your hands to God.** The word *toughened* does not here indicate strength but the lack of feeling. Any soul, you see, that subjects itself to the scrutiny of internal judgment soon cowers for fear of that scrutiny, and the arrow of the fear of God pierces that soul while it humbly covers its quaking entrails. On the other hand, whoever harden themselves by obstinate immovability toughen their hearts, as it were, to keep the arrows of the fear of God from penetrating them. That is why God mercifully told some people through the prophet, *I will remove your stony hearts and give you a heart of flesh.** Beyond question he takes stony hearts from us when he removes from us the hardness of pride, and he gives us hearts of flesh when he at once changes our hardness to the power of feeling.

As for the hands, however, we have already taught you often enough that they signify works. Accordingly, we stretch out our hands to God sinfully when we become proud about the value of our works against the grace of the Giver. Those therefore who speak in the sight of the eternal Judge and attribute to themselves the good that they do stretch out their hands to God in pride. In this way unrepentant sinners act against the just, and in this way heretics certainly always give free rein to their reproaches against Catholics, so that when they cannot blame their works they may try to reprove good people for pride in their works; inasmuch as they cannot blame good people for any flaw in their actions, they accuse them of the sin of pride. So the good deeds done externally are evaluated as not being good at all, because they are presented as virtual products of haughty conceit.

*Job 11:13

*Ezek 36:26

These are the proud ones who always criticize lowly actions and do not realize that by their words they aim their blows at themselves. But up to now Zophar has been correcting the just man with reproach. So now, as though to teach him, he adds,

XV. 26. *If you put aside the wickedness you have in your hand, and if there remains in your tent no injustice, then you will be able to lift up your face unsoiled, and you will be secure without fear.** Every sin is either committed only in thought or is the work of thought and deed. Wickedness in the hand is accordingly a guilty deed, whereas injustice in the tent is the wickedness that is in the mind. The mind is certainly not improperly called a tent, because we hide ourselves there when we do not show ourselves outwardly in some deed. Remember, Zophar is a just man's friend, and he knows what he should say; yet he plays the role of the heretics and upbraids the just man, so he does not know how to discourse correctly on what he knows. But let us erase his proud words and weigh the words that are true if they were spoken properly. First, then, he teaches that wickedness must be removed from the hand, and afterward he cautions us to cast out injustice from the tent. Obviously any who have already rid themselves of evil deeds externally must return to themselves and examine themselves carefully as regards their mind's focus, lest the guilt no longer found in their actions still persist in their thoughts.

*Job 11:14-15

That is why Solomon rightly says for his part, *Prepare your external work and accurately plow your field, that you may later build your house.** What does he mean by preparing the external work and accurately plowing the field unless that we should uproot the briars of wickedness and cultivate our actions in order to bear the fruit of retribution? What does he mean by building

*Prov 24:27

the house after plowing the field if not that we often learn from good works how to build purity of life in our thoughts? Almost all good works, you see, proceed from the thoughts, but some starting points of thoughts arise out of actions; just as the deed begins with the mind, so on the other hand the soul is instructed by the deed. The mind unquestionably receives the first sparks of God's love and in turn orders good works to be done, but after the orders begin to be carried out, the mind is enlightened by its own actions and learns how little it knew when it started to order good works. The field is plowed externally then so that the house may later be built, because we often gather from external works the extent of the deep sense of equity we should have at heart. Zophar was eager to preserve this order when he said that wickedness must first be snatched away from the hands and later injustice from the tent. The soul, you see, never fully rises up in thought while it is still externally at fault in deed.

27. If we purify ourselves completely of these two vices, we straightway lift up our faces to God without blemish. The mind is certainly our internal face, by which we are unquestionably recognized and loved by our Creator. When we lift up this face to God, we raise our soul to him by eager prayer. A blemish stains that lifted face, however, if an awareness of guilt accuses the attentive mind, because its trust and hope are immediately broken when the memory of some fault not yet overcome strikes it as it attempts to pray. The mind does not really believe it can receive what it desires, because it right away remembers that it does not yet want to do what it hears from God. That is why John says, *If our heart does not reproach us, we have confidence toward God, and we will receive from him whatever we ask.** That is why Solomon says, *The man who closes his ears*

*1 John
3:21-22

to keep from hearing the law: his prayer is accursed.*   *Prov 28:9
Our heart does indeed reproach us in our petitions when
we remember that we resist the precepts of him whom
we petition. That prayer is accursed that turns away
from the law, and it is certainly fitting that anyone who
does not want to be subject to God's commands should
be excluded from God's benefits.

28. In such a case the healing remedy is this: when
the mind reproaches itself for the sin it remembers, it
must first weep in its prayer for having strayed. Insofar as the blemish of its straying is wiped off by tears,
the face of the heart will appear clean to the Creator
when the mind makes its petition. We cannot be careful
enough, however, to keep from falling back into that sin
from which we rejoice that we have been cleansed by
tears. Otherwise the lamented sin is again committed,
and in the just Judge's sight even the lament is lightly
regarded. We must wisely remember the Scripture, *Do
not repeat words in your prayer.** In saying this the   *Sir 7:15 Vulg
wise man certainly does not forbid us to ask forgive-
ness often, but he forbids us to repeat sins. He could say
it more clearly, "When you weep for your evil deeds,
never again do that which you would again bewail in
your prayers."

29. Accordingly, if we want to lift up a spotless face
in prayer, we must always consider carefully before
the time of prayer anything that might be an object of
reproof at prayer. When we stop praying, we should let
the mind hasten to display itself in the guise in which
we would want the Judge to see us at the very moment
of prayer. We often in fact have impure or bad thoughts
in our minds when we stop praying, but when the mind
rises to undertake the activity of prayer, it falls back and
suffers from the images of those things whereby it was
previously encumbered when idle. It is as though the

soul can no longer find the strength to raise its face to God because she is ashamed of her corrupted mind and the blemishes of defiled thoughts. We are often freely preoccupied by the cares of the world. When we leave them to turn our minds to zeal for prayer, the mind will not raise itself to heavenly concerns because the weight of earthly cares presses it down to the deepest pit; it does not present a clean face in prayer because it is defiled by the dirt of impure thoughts.

30. Sometimes, on the other hand, we shake all this out of the heart, and even when we are not at prayer we avoid improper emotions. Nevertheless, just because we commit sins extremely rarely ourselves, we are all the more reluctant to forgive them in others. The more anxiously our soul fears sin, the more intransigently we shrink back from others who sin against us. Therefore it happens that whoever carefully avoids guilt is slow to forgive. When we are ourselves afraid to transgress against someone else, we are all the more obdurate in demanding the punishment of any transgression against ourselves. But what could you find that is worse than this sad blemish, which in the sight of the Judge does not darken charity but kills it?

Any sin indeed defiles the life of the soul, but resentment cherished against the neighbor kills it. Like a sword it sticks in the mind, and its point bores into the hidden entrails. Unless this sword is first pulled out of the heart into which it has been thrust, prayers will obtain nothing from the divine storehouse, because the ointment of salvation cannot be applied to the wounded members until the steel is removed from the wound. That is why Truth himself has said, *Unless you forgive men their sins, your heavenly Father will not forgive you your sins.** So he warns us, *When you stand up to pray, forgive anything you may have against anyone.**

*Matt 6:15

*Mark 11:25

Again he says, *Give and more will be given you; forgive,* *Luke 6:37-38
*and you will be forgiven.** Thus he made reciprocity a
condition for the granting of pardon and said, *Forgive*
*us our debts, as we forgive our debtors.** Certainly the   *Matt 6:12
good thing we ask of God in compunction we should
first do for our neighbor by a change of heart.

It is only when we neither commit any lawless acts
ourselves nor hold a grudge out of self-love concerning
what has been done against us that we lift up a spotless
face to God. At the time of prayer our mind is depressed
and seriously confused if either its own actions still
defile it or persisting pain at someone else's malice de-
tains it. When we clean both of these from our face, we
forthwith rise free for that which follows: *You will be*
*secure without fear.** Unquestionably, you see, he fears   *Job 11:15
the Judge less insofar as he stands secure in good works.
Yes indeed, he overcomes fear who retains stability, because on the one hand while he more anxiously strives
to complete the task the Creator mildly orders, he also
securely thinks out what he frightfully threatens.

31. We must realize also that there are some good
pursuits in which we persevere indefatigably, and then
again there are others from which we keep falling and
slipping away and yet to which, from time to time, by
strenuous efforts we return. The mind, you see, is unceasingly fixed in the active life, but from the contemplative life she grows weary and is defeated by the weight
of her own weakness. The former indeed lasts the more
robustly the more it exerts itself in the neighborhood for
the profit of those close by. The latter, however, fails the
more quickly the more often it transcends the limits of
the flesh in its attempt to go beyond itself. The former
moves about on a level plain, and therefore it plants its
feet more robustly in works. The latter, because it desires
the heights above itself, more quickly falls down beaten.

All this is astutely and briefly told by Ezekiel when he describes the movements of the animals he has seen. He says, *They did not turn when they went.* A little later he adds, *The animals went forward and returned.*

*Ezek 1:9
*Ezek 1:14

The holy animals indeed sometimes go and do not turn; at other times they go and immediately turn back because the minds of the chosen few, when they abandon the way of error through the grace of active life allotted to them, cannot return to the evil ways of the world that they have left behind. When, on the other hand, through the gaze of contemplation, they also hover above that same active life, they go and return. They have not the strength, you see, to persevere long in contemplation, so they again occupy themselves in works so that they may restore their strength by involving themselves with those things that are near at hand. Then they can again arise above themselves in contemplation. While this same act of contemplation is repeated from time to time in the way proper to it, we certainly remain steadfast and persevere, but when the weight of weakness gains the upper hand, the mind fails; still its repeated efforts strengthen the mind and lift it up again. We should not say, however, that the mind's contemplation became unstable; rather, even when it falls back and loses touch, the mind always seeks contemplation again.

XVI. 32. *You will also forget misery, and like water that has run away, you will not remember it.* The soul finds the evils of the present life more troublesome the more it neglects the value of the good that follows it. When it does not wish to consider the reward that is still to come, it evaluates its sufferings as grievous. Its blind thoughts complain loudly against the blows of the whip. Misfortune seems to have no end, although as the days pass in their course they do end, and their misfortunes with them. If, however, we only lift ourselves up to

*Job 11:16

eternal realities and fix the eye of our heart on those things that remain unchanging, we see that anything that rushes to its climax is virtually nothing. We put up with adversity in the present life, but we evaluate all that fails as almost nothing. Because we heartily celebrate interior joy, we feel external suffering less intensely.

So Zophar is not at all afraid but boldly and heedlessly dares to teach a better man than himself, exhorting him to act with justice and showing how the eyes of the just man see no penalty. It is as though he said openly, "If you taste the joy that abides internally, all that you suffer externally at once becomes light." He is right, however, to compare the misery of the present life to running water, because a transient calamity never overwhelms the mind of a chosen soul with a shattering blow but rather touches it with sadness. The soul indeed drips with the blood of the wound, but it does not lose the certitude of its own salvation. It often happens, however, that not only do trials afflict the soul, but all the saints also experience the temptation of evil spirits, so that they suffer external buffetings, and internally they become to a certain extent numb because of temptations. But grace never deserts us, for the more grievous its providential blows, the more loving is its guidance. When we begin to experience internal darkness through temptation, internal light again dawns for us.

XVII. 33. *Like the noonday light he will shine for you at evening.** New strength in temptation is indeed like noonday brightness in the evening, so that the mind becomes vigorous with the unexpected fervor of love when it had again and again feared that the light of grace had gone out for it. Zophar clarifies this truth for us still more cleverly when he adds,

XVIII. 34. *When you think you are done for, you will rise like a morning star.** So many temptations

*Job 11:17

*Job 11:17

often beset us, you see, that their very number almost drives us to fall into despair. We often become weary and hardly even consider our loss of virtue; we suffer everything, and yet we are already strangers to the feeling of pain. We are broken, and we cannot count the disconnected thoughts by which our minds are overrun. We see ourselves about to collapse moment by moment, and our own grief contradicts us more fiercely when we take up arms to fight it. Darkness besets us as our eyes dart about, and blindness keeps on impeding our vision, while the dejected mind sees nothing but blackness.

Often, however, the mind's own distress, which keeps increasing its striving prayer, effectively obtains mercy for us from the Judge. Then the Creator sees the darkness of our grief, and he renews the rays of the light that had been withdrawn. Thereupon the mind rises up refreshed by this gift, which shortly before the contending vices had kept down under the heel of pride. Soon the burden of numbness falls away, and the light of contemplation bursts forth after the darkness of confusion. The mind proceeds further and soon is lifted up in joy, though, beset by temptations, it had been driven by desperation to fall into a worse state. Untroubled by thoughts, it feels contempt for the present, and, unhindered by doubt, it has confidence in future retribution.

The just man accordingly, when he thought he was done for, rises like the morning star, because as soon as he begins to darken with the shadow of temptations, he is refreshed by the light of grace. The day of justice dawns in him who a short time previously feared the night of sin. The life of the just man is rightly compared to the morning star. The morning star rises before the sun and announces it. What does the innocence of the saints cry out to us except the glory of the Judge who follows? In this wonder we see what we should value

concerning the majesty of the true light. We do not yet
see the power of our Redeemer; nevertheless we marvel
at his strength in the conduct of his chosen ones. That
is why the lives of good people point out the power of
truth for us to see when we consider them. They are a
bright morning star, which rises before the sun.

35. We must know, however, that these elements
we have discoursed upon concerning the opposition of
spiritual temptations can also be understood to apply to
external reverses. The saints, you see, love heaven with
all their hearts, yet they suffer harshly here below; at the
end they find the light of happiness that they give up in
this brief space of the present life. That is why Zophar
now says, *Like the noonday light he will shine for you at
evening.** The daylight of sinners is darkened at evening,   *Job 11:17
because they are transported by happiness in the present
life, but at the end they are destroyed by the darkness
of adversity. The midday brightness, on the other hand,
rises for the just man in the evening, because he knows
how much glory remains for him when the sun already
begins to set. Thus it is written, *It will be well with the
man who fears the Lord at the end.** The psalmist also   *Sir 1:13
says, *When he gives sleep to those he loves, this is the
inheritance of the Lord.**   *Ps 126:2-3

When those who are still posted in the battle of this
life think they are done for, they rise like the morning
star, because although they fall externally, they are renewed internally. The more they suffer adversity externally, the more generously are they crowned internally
with the light of virtue. Paul is our witness when he
says, *Although our outer man gets worn out, still our
inner man is renewed every day. Our light, temporary
affliction in the present time brings about in us beyond
measure an eternal weight of glory in heaven.** It is   *2 Cor
noteworthy that Zophar does not say, "When you are   4:16-17

done for," but *When you think you are done for*, both because what we see is doubtful and because what we hope for is certain. That is why Paul also did not know but thought he was destroyed, he who both worn out by trouble and adversity and shining like the morning star said, *We seem to be dying, and yet we live; we seem to be grieving, yet we are full of joy; we seem to be needy, yet we enrich many.** We must also realize that because the minds of good people bear with misfortune for the sake of truth, they all the more surely hope for the reward of eternal life. So he rightly adds,

*2 Cor 6:9-10

XIX. 36. *You will have confidence for the hope that has been promised you.** Hope in God, you see, rises more firmly to the extent that anyone suffers more grievously for its sake, because the joyful reward of eternal life is never collected unless it has first been prepared here by suffering out of love. That is why the psalmist says, *Those who left went out weeping and sowing their seeds; when they return they will come with joy, carrying their sheaves.** Paul for his part adds, *If we die with him, we will also live with him; if we suffer, we will also reign with him.** He also teaches his disciples, *It is through many trials that we must enter God's kingdom.** So also the angel shows John the glory of the saints and says, *These are the ones who have come out of the great tribulation and washed their robes, making them white with the blood of the Lamb.** Now we sow our seed through trials precisely in order that we may later harvest the fruits of joy; therefore the more desperately our afflictions have confined our expectations here for the sake of truth, the greater is our confidence, which strengthens our souls. So he rightly adds at once,

*Job 11:18
*Ps 125:6
*2 Tim 2:11-12
*Acts 14:21
*Rev 7:14

XX. 37. *You will be buried and sleep in safety.** Just as the wicked who are safe in the present time reap labor, so the good who labor in the present time reap

*Job 11:18

eternal security. He already knew himself to be buried
and safely sleeping who said, *I am already being poured
out, and the time of my departure is at hand. I have
fought a good fight. I have finished the race. I have kept
the faith. There remains for me a crown of justice, which
the Lord, just judge that he is, will bestow upon me on
that day.** Because he had fought against passing evils
without fail, he unquestionably anticipated joys that
would remain without wavering.

*2 Tim 4:6-8

38. The word *buried*, though, can be understood in
another way. You see, when we are preoccupied with
transitory business, we often neglect to consider how
great our sins are, but if we refocus our critical eye and
eliminate from our heart the heap of worldly thoughts,
we discover whatever was hidden in the mind. That is
why the saints do not cease their scrutiny of the hidden
places in their souls but investigate themselves thoroughly and cast out their solicitude for earthly objects.
Then with their thoughts effectively buried, when they
find that no guilt or sin vexes them, they rest secure, as
it were, on the bed of their hearts in their own presence.
They even desire a hiding place from the actions that
take place in this world and wish always to consider
only their own affairs. When they are restrained by no
harness or regime, they refuse to pass judgment on any
matters strange to themselves. They are buried, and they
sleep in safety, and while they vigilantly look into their
own interior lives, they hide themselves away and rest
quietly, safe from the heavy burdens of this world. So
he again adds,

XXI. 39. *You will rest, and there will be no one
to frighten you.** Anyone who seeks present honor unquestionably fears scorn. Any who long for gain are
obviously forever afraid of loss. When they are relieved
by the reception of anything, they are undoubtedly

*Job 11:19

wounded by the loss of that possession. When they are obliged to cling to passing and perishable possessions, they lie in the lowest depths, far away from the citadel of security. On the other hand, any who fix their desire on the ground of eternity are neither stirred by prosperity nor downcast by adversity. Nothing in the world attracts them, nor does anything in the world frighten them. That is why Solomon says, *Nothing that happens to the just* *Prov 12:21 *man frightens him.** He also says, *The just man is like* *Prov 28:1 *a fearless lion.**

So Zophar is right to say here, *You will rest, and there will be no one to frighten you.* The more effectively, you see, people eliminate that fear in themselves that is worldly, the more truly do they overcome in themselves the concupiscence of the world. Did not Paul remain with a fearless heart when he said, *I am assured on that account that neither death, nor life, nor angels, nor principalities, nor the present, nor the future, nor powers, nor height, nor depth, nor anything created can separate us from the love of God, which* *Rom 8:38-39 *is in Christ Jesus Our Lord?** The strength of his love is praised by the true voice of Holy Church, which we *Song 8:6 *find in the Song of Songs: *Love is as strong as death.** Love is compared to the power of death because it effectively kills the mind that it has once seized, as far as the pleasures of the world are concerned. Furthermore, the stronger it makes that mind's power, the more invulnerable it is to fear. Nevertheless we must realize that when the lawless preach what is right, it is extremely difficult for them not to blurt out what they secretly want to obtain. So Zophar at once adds,

*Job 11:19 XXII. 40. *Many people will entreat your favor.** Actually not even the just watch their step and follow the path of innocence with this end in view, that they might be entreated by others. Heretics, on the other hand, or any other perverse people, insofar as they live quasi-innocent lives among men and women, want to look like intercessors for men and women. Their speech is holy, and they worm themselves in while they promise others as though what they want for themselves were important. They preach about heaven, yet in quick promises they show what it is they want. Lest they make it clear what they are by continuing to promise earthly gain, they soon return to words of righteousness. So Zophar continues,

XXIII. 41. *The eyes of wicked men will grow weak, and there will be no escape for them.* That the word *eyes* expresses the power of attention, the gospel of Truth bears witness, saying, *If your eye is simple, your body will be full of light.* Obviously, if a pure intention precedes our actions, whatever else may be seen by people, in the eyes of the internal Judge the pure form of the action that follows will show up. Accordingly the eyes of the wicked are their attention to the desires of the flesh. If these eyes therefore grow weak, it is because they neglect eternity and always look out for transitory things alone. Undoubtedly they think about worldly honor as a thing to be obtained, and they eagerly desire to increase their worldly possessions. They daily steer their course of passing gains toward death, but they cannot think about mortality in a mortal way. The life of the flesh fails moment by moment, yet desire of the flesh continues to grow. The wealth one has wears away, and the end draws near, yet the anxiety of having does not end.

Nevertheless, when death removes the wicked, their desire is forthwith terminated along with life. Their eyes, be it noted, then grow weak because of heavenly retribution, because here below by their own judgment they refused to let worldly pleasure grow weak.

*Job 11:20

*Matt 6:22

The psalmist had seen their eyes close to their wonted pleasure when he said, *On that day all their thoughts will perish.*[*] They both find eternal evil that they never thought of and quickly lose the passing goods that they had long pursued. There is no escape for them, because their malice finds no place where it might hide from the gaze of the intransigent Judge. At present, you see, when the wicked encounter some sadness or adversity, they do find hiding places of escape, because they have instant recourse to the pleasures of carnal desires. Lest poverty distress them, they caress their soul with riches. Lest the scorn of their neighbors depress them, they lift their spirits with honors. If the body is tired of common food, it is nourished by a variety of exotic delights that are placed before it. If the soul is dejected by some impulse of sadness, it is soon relieved by the introduction of light jokes. In fact they have in this world as many escapes as pleasures that they arrange for themselves.

*Ps 145:4

Sooner or later, however, their escape fails them, because when they lose everything, their minds see only themselves and their Judge. Then their pleasure is taken away, the guilt of pleasure remains, and the miserable ones suddenly learn by perishing that they were holding on to perishable objects. Nonetheless, as long as they live in the body, they go on seeking what will harm them. So Zophar again adds,

XXIV. 42. *The object of their hope is the horror of the soul.*[*] Sinners hope for nothing else in all their deliberations but the following: that their power should prevail over all others, that the multitude of their possessions should exceed what all others have, that they should subjugate their adversaries under their dominion, that the wonder of their presence should become known to all their admirers, that their wrath might be satisfied according to their wishes, that they might show them-

*Job 11:20

selves kindly disposed when they are praised, that they might offer their stomach whatever pleases it, that they might satisfy their desires in whatever they demand by gaining all that they require.

The object of their hope, then, is rightly called the horror of the soul, because those things that carnal-minded people solicit, spiritual-minded people and those who are guided by the judgment of rectitude turn away from. What sinners regard as pleasure, the just beyond any doubt know as penalty. The hope of the sinful is therefore the horror of the soul, because the spirit positively fails when the flesh is at rest. Just as the flesh is nourished by soft food, so the soul is nourished by harsh treatment. Blandishments encourage the former, whereas severity trains the latter: the former is fed by pleasure, the latter enlivened by bitterness. Just as harsh treatment wounds the flesh, so also caresses kill the spirit; just as hardship stops the former, so also pleasure extinguishes the latter. Accordingly the hope of carnal-minded people is called the horror of the soul, because whenever the flesh lives agreeably in the present time, the spirit dies to eternity.

43. Zophar would have a right to say these things if blessed Job had not preached more bountifully, especially by his way of life. After Zophar tries to instruct a holier man on how to live, however, and attempts to teach someone smarter than himself as a master of wisdom, he weakens the importance of his words by his indiscretion and insolence; he negates all that he says by pouring the liquid of knowledge into a vessel that is already full. Precisely in this way indiscreet people possess the resources of knowledge, just as fools often possess those of material wealth. There are those, you see, who are supported by an abundance of worldly goods, and sometimes they give away property to those

who already possess it, so that they may seem to all people to be still richer.

In the same way, when dishonest people understand truth, they speak of rectitude even to the righteous, not in order to teach any of their listeners but so that they may themselves become famous for the vast extent of their teaching. They think that their wisdom unquestionably surpasses that of everybody else, and on that account they consider that nothing they tell anyone exceeds the measure of their own greatness. In this way dishonest people, in company with all the heretics, fearlessly teach their betters, lifting up their voices, since they consider everyone else their inferiors. Holy Church, however, recalls all the proud ones from the pinnacle of their own self-esteem, and with the hand of discretion she remakes them into a new building of equality. Accordingly blessed Job, who is himself a member of this Holy Church, sees that the mind of his friend is swollen with pride through the words of erudition that he has spoken. So he immediately answers, saying,

XXV. 44. *Well then, you are the only man, and with you wisdom will die.*[*] Anyone who assumes that his faculty of reason is better than everyone else's does nothing other but exult at the fact that he is the only man. It often happens in fact, that when the mind is lifted up on high through pride, people become haughty in self-admiration and scornful of everyone else. Self-praise springs up in their thoughts, and their folly congratulates them on their unique wisdom. They think over what they hear and the words they speak, and they admire themselves while laughing at others. So those who esteem themselves as the only wise ones, what else do they do but assume that this wisdom dies with them? That which they deny that others have and bestow on themselves alone they certainly limit to the time of their brief life.

[*] Job 12:2

Let us notice, then, how discreetly the holy man acts,
in order that the haughtiness of his proud friends might
be brought low, when he at once adds,

XXVI. 45. *I too have a heart, just as you have, and
I am not inferior to you.** Who is there who does not
know how far blessed Job's life and knowledge exceed
the knowledge of his friends? He denies that he is their
inferior in order that he might cure their pride, but lest
he should go beyond the limit imposed by his own humility, he does not say he is superior to them. Not out-
running them but accompanying them, he demonstrates
what they who of themselves are far from being his
equals might learn about themselves. Thus whereas an
eminent wisdom readily bends itself down, a low-lying
knowledge can never stretch beyond its own powers.
He soon recalls them to a feeling for equality, since
he judges that their pride in their special greatness has
exceeded itself. Accordingly he adds,

XXVII. 46. *Who does not know this truth that you
know?** He might as well ask outright, "Since everybody
knows what you are saying, why are you so singularly
proud of the knowledge you speak of?" Accordingly,
since he recalls these proud and arrogant people to the
community of equality and lectures them with perfect
correction, he forthwith holds forth with decisive teachings, so that his humbled friends may learn the weight
of truth before reverently listening to it. He goes on:

XXVIII. 47. *A man derided by his friend, as I am,
will invoke God, and God will answer him.** When weak-
minded people are acclaimed and praised by men and
women for their good works, their mind is often diverted
to external enjoyment so that they may delay the satisfaction of their internal desires and lie idle, resolutely
and freely listening to external attractions. They end up
boasting of being called blessed, rather than of becoming

*Job 12:3

*Job 12:3

*Job 12:4

so. They stand agape listening to voices of praise directed to them, so they abandon what they began to be.

When the mind therefore seemed praiseworthy because of God, then it is separated from God. Sometimes the soul supports itself by persevering at honest labor, and yet it is beset by human derision; people work wonders and are reproached, and those who could have been renowned and praised are spurned with insults and return to themselves. They root themselves all the more firmly in God because of not being able to find a resting place outside. All their hope is then fixed on the Creator, and among the clamor of derision they beseech only the interior Witness. Dejected souls approach God all the more closely the more they become strangers to the esteem and favor of people. Their prayers are immediately poured out; externally depressed, they are refined to a purer form so that they may reach their internal regions.

So Job well says at this point, *A man derided by his friend as I am will invoke God, and God will answer him.* When depraved people denounce the intelligence of good people, they show them whom they should seek as a witness of their own actions. While their soul in compunction girds itself for prayer, it is united to the Most High, who hears internally, precisely there where it is separated from external human praise. We should notice, however, how prudently the phrase *as I am* is inserted, because there are those who are depressed by human derision and yet who do not gain a hearing by the divine ear. When derision, you see, is initiated against a sin, obviously there is no merit or virtue generated because of that derision. For example, the priests of Baal cried to Baal at the top of their voices when they were derided by Elijah, who said, *Cry out louder, for he is a god, and perhaps he is conversing or at an inn.** This derision had no purpose of merit but was instigated by

*1 Kgs 18:27

sin. He is prudent then in saying, *A man derided by his friend as I am will invoke God, and God will answer him.* Derision brings those whose innocent life keeps them away from human depravity close to God. So Job goes on,

XXIX. 48. *The honesty of a just man is derided.* The wisdom of this world causes people to hide the true feelings of their hearts by cunning devices and to conceal their insight by words; they display falsehood instead of truth, and they make the truth seem deceptive. Such prudence is practiced by young people, and children learn it for prizes. Those who know this prudence despise others in their pride; those who do not know it are timid subjects who admire others, because they love this evil duplicity while changing the name, since the mind's perversity is styled refinement. This wisdom teaches such behavior to the followers of these people: to seek the highest honors, to celebrate the attainment of the vanity of worldly glory, to return many times over the evils inflicted upon them by others, to give in to no adversaries when they have the power and, when they do not, to pretend peaceful kindness toward adversaries for whatever they cannot maliciously avenge.

*Job 12:4

On the other hand, the wisdom practiced by the just has nothing to do with pretense or display; it opens up perception with words, loves truth as it is, avoids falsehood, extends kindness without stint, is more ready to tolerate evil than to do it, seeks no revenge for insult, and considers insults a gain for the sake of truth. Still, this simplicity of upright people is derided, because the wise people in this world consider the virtue of purity to be foolish. Actually, they judge any harmless action to be stupid, and whatever good work is approved by truth sounds foolish to worldly wisdom. What seems to the worldly wise more stupid than to speak one's mind using words, or to make no pretensions by cunning devices, or never to repay injuries with insults, or to pray for those who curse us, or to seek poverty, or to give up one's possessions, or not to resist robbery, or to turn the other cheek to the one who strikes us?

That is why a certain famous wise man of God told the lovers of this world, *We shall offer to the Lord our God sacrifices that are abominations to the Egyptians.* Egyptians unquestionably disdain the eating of the meat of sheep, but what Egyptians abhor Israelites offer to God, because righteous people make as a virtuous sacrifice an upright conscience, which all unrighteous people scorn as the lowest and most abject pose. Righteous servants offer up their purity and meekness to God, an offering that reprobates abhor and consider madness. This simplicity of righteous people is surely briefly but adequately expressed when Job at once adds,

*Exod 8:26

XXX. 49. *The lamp is despised among the thoughts of the rich.* What does the word *rich* mean in this passage unless it be the haughtiness of the proud, who have no respect for the Judge who is coming, and who became pompous with their proud thoughts? There are those whose property does not cause them to become proud but rather exalts them through works of mercy. There are others who when they notice that they have an abundance of material possessions do not go in search of God's true riches; they have no love for the eternal homeland, because they think it is enough for them that they are well supplied with worldly goods. Property is therefore no sin, but pleasure in it is. All that God has created is good, but those who use good things badly undoubtedly act in such a way that by that bread on which they should live they die through gluttony.

*Job 12:5

Lazarus the poor man had reached his resting place, but the pompous rich man suffered torture. On the other hand, Abraham himself, who held Lazarus in his bosom, had been rich, but when he spoke to his Creator he said, *I who am dust and ashes speak to my Lord.** How ac- *Gen 18:27*cordingly can this same man evaluate his own riches when he thought of himself as dust and ashes? Will his possessions ever extol him who himself, their very possessor, considers himself so abject?

50. Then again there are some for whom even earthly possessions are not available, and yet their arrogance and pride are aroused. They have no property, of course, so they are not led to a display of power, but their insolent manner places them among the reprobate rich. Everyone accordingly whom love for the future life does not humiliate is called rich by the word of God in this passage, because it makes no difference in the Final Judgment whether pride results from one's experience or from one's behavior. When people see the upright live in this world in a lowly and abject manner, they forthwith ridicule them, looking down on them in their pride. To be sure, such people know that the upright are totally lacking externally in those things after which they themselves yearn internally with all their hearts. As fools, therefore, they despise those who obviously have none of those things that they themselves are dying for, either by having them or only by wanting them; they count the upright dead and by no means think them to be neighbors according to the flesh.

Those who are dead as far as desire for this world is concerned are of course also considered utterly dead to the attitude of the earthly minded. This truth is rightly signified by a miracle worked by our Redeemer by which he freed a man from an unclean spirit. Concerning this event it is written, *Crying out and causing him to writhe violently he** left him, and he became as if*   *the unclean* *dead; many of them said, "he is dead." Jesus, however,*   *spirit*

* Mark 9:26 *took his hand and lifted him up, so he got up.** He who is freed from the power of an evil spirit is unquestionably shown to be virtually dead, because any who have already subjected earthly desires have extinguished in themselves the life of pleasant relationships. They seem to be dead to the world because they are without that evil possessor whose activity expressed itself through unclean desires. Many people say such people are dead, because those who have no spiritual life consider those whom bodily pleasure does not accompany to be completely lifeless.

51. Because even those who deride simpleminded people are nominally counted as Christians, they are subdued by reverence for the sacred, and they are ashamed to display publicly the bad image of derision. So it happens that the pride in them has them silently deriding those whom they consider seriously abject and lowest of the low because of their simplicity. So it is well said, *The lamp is despised among the thoughts of the rich.* No proud person, as I have already said, can esteem the good things that follow; therefore the proud also have no esteem for those whom they do not see possessing the good things that they like. It often happens, you see, that some of the elect who are being led on to eternal happiness are saddened here by continuing adversity; they are supported by no abundance of material possessions, their honor is not displayed by any show of dignity, no concourse of flatterers welcomes them, and no spread of awnings is arranged to honor them in the eyes of men and women. All people find them worthy of contempt and consider them unworthy of the favor of this world.

In the eyes of the hidden Judge, however, such people shine with virtues and sparkle because of their meritorious life: they fear honors, do not avoid contempt, cultivate bodily continence, grow fat on love alone in their soul, are always ready to be patient of mind and set on justice, rejoice at the insults they receive, feel compassion in their hearts for those who are afflicted, are glad for the prosperity of good people as if it were their own, carefully masticate the food of the Word in their mind, and under questioning do not know how to speak eloquently with a double meaning.

The internal lamp shines, but the external lamp is despised and does not shine. The flame of charity burns internally, but no pride in beauty shines externally. Those whose virtues glow and cause them to be accounted abject therefore shine while they are held in contempt. Pleasure-seeking minds can unquestionably not deal with goodness, except that goodness that they see as pleasant. That is why Holy David's own father despised him, refusing to present him before the eyes of the prophet Samuel. When David's father had led seven sons forward for the grace of anointing, the prophet asked him whether the number of his sons was complete, and he replied in serious desperation, *There is one little boy guarding the sheep.*[*] When David was produced and chosen, his father heard these words, *Man sees the face, but God sees into the heart.*[*]

[*] 1 Sam 16:10-11

[*] 1 Sam 16:7

David's lamp was his innocence, but he was held up to contempt because his lamp did not shine on those who saw the external appearances. We must realize, however, that nobody who is righteous has worldly honor; if anybody does have worldly honor he throws it away, so that he may emerge free from that honor, lest he be overcome by it and give in to pleasure. That is why that illustrious preacher had humbled the honor of his apostolate before the eyes of the world when he said, *We have not made use of that power, even though we could have been burdensome to you as Christ's apostle, but*

*1 Thess 2:6-7 *we became like children among you.*[3]* Unfortunately the arrogance of the rich had remained in the hearts of his hearers, who said, *His letters are harsh and stern, but* *2 Cor 10:10 *his bodily presence is weak and his speech despicable.** They assumed that if the person they had known could say such things, he could not live among them in their community. When they both saw him living in a humble fashion and considered his diction of high quality, their pride forced them to despise the words and physical presence of him whose written letters had given them cause to fear.

What, accordingly, was Paul but a lamp of contempt among the thoughts of the rich, he who when he displayed the teaching of humility got in return from his crude disciples insults flung by pride? In a horrid fashion, then, the growing disease of pride, instead of shrinking as it ought to have done, increased in size; the proud pleasure-seeking mind rejected as contemptible that which the teacher presented as worthy of imitation. Was he not a despised lamp who shone with all the virtues and put up with so much adversity from his persecutors? He was an ambassador in chains, and his chains were on display all over the palace; he was beaten with rods, and he was beset with many dangers from his own race and from the Gentiles. At Lystra he was stoned and dragged by the feet outside the city,

---

[3] The alert reader will doubtless notice that this is not an exact quotation. Gregory adds some words not in the original, perhaps quoting from memory. Vulgate: *nec quaerentes ab hominibus gloriam . . . cum possimus oneri esse ut Christi apostoli sed facti sumus lenes in medio vestrum*; Gregory's Latin: *non usi sumus hac potestate cum possimus oneri esse ut Christi apostoli sed facti sumus parvuli in medio vestrum*. Actually the words: *non usi sumus hac potestate* are found in the Vulgate text of 1 Corinthians 9:12.

because they thought he was dead. How long does this
lamp suffer contempt? How long is he held in derision?
Will he never reveal his brightness? Will he never show
the world how clearly he shines? He does show it fully.
After the lamp is said to be despised among the thoughts
of the rich, we are told the following:

XXXI. 52. *It is ready at the prescribed time.*[*] The   *Job 12:5
prescribed time of the despised lamp is undoubtedly the
predestined day of the Last Judgment, when all the righteous people who are now despised are presented with
the fullness of their shining light. Then indeed they who
are now judged unjustly for God's sake come as judges
along with God. Then their light shines as brightly
as now the persecutors' hand lies heavily upon them.
Then the eyes of the wicked will see clearly how they
are supported by heavenly power, those who willingly
renounced all earthly possessions. That is why Truth
told his chosen ones, *You who have followed me, in the
new world, when the Son of Man sits on His majestic
throne, will also sit on twelve thrones and judge the
twelve tribes of Israel.*[*] It is not that the internal meet-   *Matt 19:28
inghouse will not seat more than twelve judges, but the
number twelve obviously signifies a universal quantity.

Those you see who have been inspired by God's
nudge to abandon their possessions here below will
there beyond any doubt obtain the fullness of judicial
power, so that then together with the Judge they may
become judges who now by considering judgment discipline themselves by a poverty that is freely chosen.
That is why Solomon says of the Bridegroom of Holy
Church, *Her husband is honored at the gate, where he
sits with the princes of the land.*[*] That is why Isaiah   *Prov 31:23
says, *The Lord will come for judgment with the elders of
his people.*[*] That is why Truth called those same elders   *Isa 3:14
no longer servants but friends, saying, *I no longer call*

you servants but my friends. The psalmist certainly foresaw them and said, *To me your friends are exceedingly honorable, O God.* When he saw how elevated their hearts were and how they trod earthly honors underfoot, he added, *Their leadership is exceedingly strengthened.* Lest we should consider the number small of those whom we know to rise even to the highest level of extreme perfection, he again added, *If I count them, they are more than the sand.*

    Accordingly, as many now freely humble themselves for love of truth as their lamps will then shine in judgment. Let it then be clearly said, *The lamp is despised among the thoughts of the rich; it is ready at the prescribed time.* The soul of any one of the just is despised and abject while passing time here below and having no honor, but that soul seems admirable when it shines from above.

    53. It is a pleasure at this point to lift up the eyes of our minds to the Redeemer's paths and little by little to come away from the members to the Head. He indeed appeared as a lamp for us by dying on the cross for our redemption and flooding the darkness of our minds with light through the cross. John had seen this lamp enlightening us when he said, *He was the true light that enlightens every man who comes into this world.* This lamp, however, he saw despised among the thoughts of the rich when he added a little later, *He came to his own people, and his own did not accept him.*

    Herod wanted to feel the flames of this lamp when he desired to see his miracles, as we find it written: *He had been longing for a good while to see him, because he had heard many reports about him, and he hoped to see some sign worked by him.* This lamp, however, emitted no ray of light before Herod's eyes, because he showed him no miracle, since Herod's intent was not

*John 15:15

*Ps 138:17

*Ps 138:17

*Ps 138:18

*Job 12:5

*John 1:9

*John 1:11

*Luke 23:8

holy but curious. When questioned, the Redeemer was silent; expected to display a miracle, he showed contempt, maintaining his reserve. Those whom he found seeking superficial things he left outside unrewarded. He chose rather to be openly despised by the proud than to be praised with empty voices by those who did not believe in him. So this lamp was forthwith despised, as Luke adds, *Herod treated him with contempt, as did his soldiers; he mocked him and clothed him in a white robe.**   *Luke 23:11

54. The despised lamp put up with derision on earth, but from heaven as judgment he shines forth. So Job was right to add, *It is ready at the prescribed time.* The psalmist spoke of this time as follows: *When I know the time, I will judge with justice.** Truth himself announces in the gospel, *My time has not yet come.** Peter for his part says, *Heaven must receive him until the time of restoration.** Accordingly, the lamp that is now the subject of contempt is coming prepared at the prescribed time, because he who now bears with the derision of sinners judges sin on the last day. His judgment at that time will be the harsher in proportion as he now continues to endure mildly for the sake of recalling sinners.   *Ps 74:3   *John 7:6   *Acts 3:21

He who waits long for conversion, you see, torments those who do not convert without reconsideration. This truth is briefly alluded to by the prophet, who says, *I was forever silent, I held my peace, and I was patient; now I will speak as a woman giving birth.** As I have already said, a woman gives birth with pain, and what she held for a long time in her inward parts she ejects. He who was always quiet, accordingly, speaks like a woman giving birth. The coming Judge long bore with the deeds of men and women without avenging them, but sooner or later, with the burning heat of an ordeal like mental pain, he reveals the verdict of accumulated   *Isa 42:14

punishment he had held within. Let no one therefore despise this lamp while it is hidden, lest when the Judge appears from heaven, he should burn up those who hold him in contempt. Those whom he now does not burn for forgiveness, he will later without a doubt burn for punishment. Therefore, because we have received the time of our call through heavenly grace, while it is still possible, let us escape the wrath of him who is everywhere present by changing our ways for the better. That punishment fails to reach only the one whom correction has hidden.

55. It should be enough that we have now produced these two parts with the Lord's help. Since we cannot master the extended sequence of the Holy Book with the mystical interpretation by means of a brief exposition, we must reserve it for a future volume, so that readers may return more ardently to the study of the book inasmuch as they have rested during the interruption of the reading.

Book 10 and the second part are complete. Thanks be to God. Amen.*

*a colophon present in one manuscript

BOOK 2.LII.84–LV.92 *See Job 1:11

The final portion of book 2 of Gregory's Moral Commentary *on Job was accidentally omitted in the translation of the first volume of the work published in 2014. With our apologies, it appears below; the index to these passages follows the index to books 6 through 10.*

[LII]. 84. Whenever our minds are lifted up in pride, we break out in rebellion, as it were. Like all tyrants, we have cronies or thoughts that support our boasts, but when an enemy attacks the tyrant, the support of his cronies disappears. Whenever there is opposition, the cronies run away, and in their fright they desert the one whom they crassly flattered as long as they were not threatened. When his cronies are put to flight, the terrified soul is left alone to face the enemy; thoughts of pride have scattered, and he sees only himself and the temptation. Accordingly, the head is shaved at the news of adversity, and when we are fiercely beset by temptations, the mind is freed from its presumptuous thoughts. Why do Nazirites let their hair grow, unless it be because their lives of strict continence give rise to an increase of presumptuous thoughts? And why is it that the Nazirite is told to shave his head and put his hair in the sacrificial fire once his act of devotion is complete, unless it be because we finally reach the summit of perfection when we overcome our external vices to such an extent that we even erase inconsequential thoughts from our minds?

Burning them in the sacrificial fire surely means setting them on fire with the spark of divine love, in such a way that our whole heart is on fire with God's love,

which burns up the inconsequential thoughts as though
they were a Nazirite's hair consumed with perfect devotion. We must notice also that he fell on the ground in
adoration. Those who humbly realize that they are dust
attribute no virtue to themselves. Rather, they acknowledge that their good deeds come from the mercy of the
Creator and show God true adoration.

LIII. 85. It is therefore fitting that he should add,
*Naked I came out of my mother's womb, and naked will
I return.*[*] It is as though the tempted soul were made
aware of its weakness and powerlessness and said, "I
was naked when grace first brought me forth in faith,
and I will still be naked when grace again saves me
and lifts me up." This is a great consolation for the soul
sorely tried; it sees itself almost devoid of virtues and
attacked by vices, and its only recourse is its hope in
God's mercy. Just because it is humbly aware that it is
lacking in virtue, it is dissatisfied with this nakedness.
Suppose it has no virtue to cover it in time of temptation: it knows its own weakness very well, but it is
better for it to be covered with this humility. It is much
stronger as it lies there than if it were standing upright,
because it no longer attributes to itself without God's
help whatever it has.

LIV. 86. Job soon humbly recognizes the hand of his
generous Judge and says, *God gave it, and God took it
back.*[*] You see how he learns from his temptations and
grows through them; by the virtue he has he knows the
generous Giver, and by the discomfiture of his courage
he knows God's power to take it away. His courage,
however, is not taken away; he is only taken aback and
disheartened. His mind is appalled and he is afraid, seeing himself about to lose his courage at any moment, but
as long as he is still humble he never loses it.

LV. 87. *God has done what he pleased; blessed be the name of God.** Whenever we are buffeted by our internal conflicts, we do well to have recourse to our Creator's judgment, so that our hearts may render greater glory to God our Helper for the fact that when we are cast down, we are more acutely aware of our weakness and powerlessness.

*Job 1:21

LVI. 88. *Through all this Job committed no sin, nor did he say anything foolish against God.** Therefore, when the sorrowful soul is beset by internal temptation it must guard itself constantly against letting out the words of forbidden speech, against murmuring about being tried. If it does murmur, the fire that burns the soul like gold will turn it into chaff because of the exaggerated words that should not be uttered.

*Job 1:22

89. It would not be wrong for us to understand what we have said about virtues in relation to the gifts of the Holy Spirit given as proof of virtue. Some virtues that are given thus have to do with prophecies, some have to do with different tongues, some have to do with healing; these gifts, however, are not always present in the mind in the same way, and they obviously can be taken away at times to keep the mind free from pride and presumption. If the Spirit of prophecy were always present to prophets, the prophet Elisha would certainly not have said, *Let her go; her soul is sad, and the Lord has not revealed the reason to me.** If the Spirit of prophecy were always present to prophets, Amos the prophet would not have said when challenged, *I am no prophet*, or added, *or son of a prophet; I am a herdsman, a dresser of sycamore trees.**

*2 Kgs 4:27

*Amos 7:14

How was he not a prophet, when he predicted future events so accurately? How was he a prophet, if he denied the truth about himself in the present? No, at the very moment when he was answering, he sensed that the Spirit of prophecy had left him, and he testified to the truth about himself when he said, *I am no prophet.* But he immediately added, *Now hear the word of God. The Lord says this: your wife will be a harlot in this city, your sons and daughters will fall by the sword, your land will be measured with a line, you yourself*

*Amos 7:16-17

*will die in an impure land.** By these words the prophet clearly shows that even as he was speaking, he was filled with the Spirit; because he humbly admitted he was no prophet, he deserved the gift of immediately receiving the Spirit of prophecy. If the Spirit of prophecy were always present to the prophets, when King David was taking counsel on the building of the temple, the prophet Nathan would never have granted what he was to refuse

*see 2 Sam 7:2-17

a short while later.*

90. Therefore the gospel rightly tells us, *The person upon whom you shall see the Spirit descending and*

*John 1:33

*remaining is the one who baptizes.** The Spirit indeed comes down on all the faithful, but it is only the Mediator on whom he remains in a special way; in fact, the Spirit has never left the human nature of the Mediator, and it was from his divine nature that he proceeded. Therefore he remains in him who alone can do all things at all times. The faithful who receive him, on the other hand, cannot always have his gifts or work his signs in the way that they wish, and they bear witness that they have received him, as it were, in a passing way, for a manifestation.

Yet when he spoke to his disciples in person about this Spirit of Truth, Jesus said, *He will remain with you, and he will be in you.** How is it that this remaining of the Holy Spirit is declared by God's voice to be the sign of the Mediator, as we have already said, *The person upon whom you shall see the Spirit descending and re-*

*John 14:17

maining? If the Master's voice has told us that he also remains in the disciples, how is it already a sign of the Mediator that he remains on him? We will find it easier to understand this if we look a little closer at the gifts of the Holy Spirit.

91. Some of his gifts are necessary for eternal life; others make holiness of life possible for the good of the faithful. Meekness, humility, patience, faith, hope, and charity make up the list of his gifts without which people cannot attain eternal life. Prophecy, the gift of healing, different kinds of tongues, and interpretation of tongues are, however, those of his gifts that make his power present for the edification of the witnesses. The Holy Spirit is present in those gifts that are necessary for the attainment of eternal life, and he always remains in his preachers and in all the elect. He does not, however, always remain in his preachers in the other gifts, which do not minister to our own eternal life but seek by revealing him to give life to others; over his preachers' hearts, indeed, he always hovers, that they may live rightly, but he does not always perform signs that manifest his power through them. Sometimes, indeed, he withdraws himself from this manifestation of power so that his power may be more humbly shown when it is not subject to their control.

92. The Mediator between God and men, the man Christ Jesus, always, in everything, and continuously keeps the presence of the Holy Spirit; it is from him, indeed, that that same Holy Spirit proceeds substantially. While he remains in his holy preachers, therefore, he is rightly shown to remain in the Mediator in a special way; it is by grace indeed that he remains in the former, for a purpose; in the Mediator, however, he remains substantially and forever. Just as our body sometimes perceives through the sense of touch, but

394 Gregory the Great

our head together with our body perceives through all
five senses at once—that is, it sees, hears, tastes, smells,
and touches—so also the members of the Head who is
in heaven are foremost in certain virtues, but the Head
himself shines out with all the virtues.

The Spirit, then, abides in him in a different way;
being of the same nature, he never leaves him. His gifts,
by which we journey toward eternal life, cannot be lost
without danger; the gifts by which holiness of life is
displayed are often, as we have said, removed without
danger. The former are needed for our edification; the
latter are sought for the purpose of inviting others. We
are in fear and trembling lest we should lose the former; the latter are sometimes taken away for a time
to humble us, lest they should cause our minds to be
lifted up in pride. When therefore the powers that have
been given us are taken away, we do well to say, "God
gave it, and God took it back; God has done what he
pleased; blessed be the name of God." We demonstrate
the fact that we have used these gifts in the right way
when we peacefully accept their being suddenly taken
away for a time.

Scriptural Index

BOOKS 6–10, JOB 5:3–12:5

Scriptural references are cited by book and Maurist (Arabic) paragraph. For example 8.21 refers to Book Eight, paragraph 21.

Gen 1:3	8.21, 9.75	Exod 8:25	7.53	Judg 16:21	7.37
Gen 1:5	8.21	Exod 8:26	7.53, 10.48	1 Sam 2:5	6.5
Gen 1:12	6.54	Exod 10:3	7.53	1 Sam 2:9	6.39
Gen 1:26	9.75	Exod 14:15	9.60	1 Sam 6:10-11	7.42
Gen 1:31	9.46	Exod 18	7.54	1 Sam 6:12	7.42
Gen 2:2	6.43	Exod 19:12-13	6.58	1 Sam 12:23	9.24
Gen 3:19	8.57	Exod 19:18	6.58	1 Sam 13:2	8.92
Gen 4:17	6.7, 8.92	Exod 32	9.23	1 Sam 15:30	9.23
Gen 4:25	8.92n2	Exod 32:10	9.23, 9.60	1 Sam 16:7	10.51
Gen 6:6-7	9.12	Exod 32:30-32	9.23	1 Sam 16:10-11	10.51
Gen 18:2	9.106	Lev 1:6-13	9.84	1 Sam 18:20-27	6.30
Gen 18:27	10.49	Lev 19:18	7.28	1 Sam 18:25	6.30
Gen 19:9-11	6.38	Lev 19:23	8.79	1 Sam 24:17	9.23
Gen 23:19	6.56	Lev 19:26	8.42	2 Sam 12:7	7.53
Gen 29:26	6.61	Num 16:47-48	9.23	2 Sam 12:15	9.54
Gen 32:6	8.92	Num 19:6	6.56	2 Sam 24:25	9.23
Gen 33:1	8.92	Num 20:12	9.23	1 Kgs 1:23	7.54
Gen 33:14	8.92	Num 25:11	9.23	1 Kgs 3:12	8.48
Gen 37:7	8.42	Deut 6:5	7.28, 10.8	1 Kgs 3:16	8.48
Gen 37:7-9	6.29	Deut 15:19	8.78	1 Kgs 13:2	7.53
Gen 37:19-20	6.29	Deut 16:16	7.38	1 Kgs 13:4	7.54
Gen 37:24-25	6.29	Deut 16:20	9.38	1 Kgs 13:6	7.54
Gen 37:28	6.29	Deut 17:16	8.92	1 Kgs 17:1	9.23
Gen 39:1	6.29	Deut 19:5-6	10.12	1 Kgs 18:17	7.53
Gen 39:17	6.29	Deut 22:11	8.87	1 Kgs 18:18	7.53
Gen 41:41	6.29	Deut 23:10-11	9.84	1 Kgs 18:27	10.47
Gen 41:48	6.29	Deut 32:2	9.15	1 Kgs 18:44	9.23
Gen 42:1-2	6.29	Deut 32:39	6.42	1 Kgs 18:46	7.54
Gen 42:6	6.29	Deut 33:8-9	7.41	1 Kgs 19:2-4	9.23

Matt 6:12	10.30	Matt 26:75	9.54	Luke 23:8	10.53
Matt 6:15	10.30	Matt 27:32	8.72	Luke 23:11	10.53
Matt 6:16	8.72	Mark 8:33	10.5	Luke 23:21	6.35
Matt 6:22	10.41	Mark 9:23	10.18	John 1:9	10.53
Matt 6:34	9.105,	Mark 9:26	10.50	John 1:11	10.53
	9.106	Mark 9:49	7.8	John 1:29	8.56
Matt 7:12	6.54, 10.8	Mark 11:25	9.24,	John 3:5	9.32
Matt 7:22	8.75		10.30	John 3:8	10.13
Matt 7:22-23	8.66	Mark 12:30	7.28	John 4:13	6.20
Matt 7:23	8.75	Mark 12:31	7.28	John 4:38	9.47
Matt 8:21	7.41	Mark 16:15	6.20	John 5:46	7.8
Matt 9:6	8.34	Luke 1:74	9.63	John 6:51	6.47
Matt 12:36	7.58	Luke 2:29	6.53	John 6:57	7.7
Matt 12:44-45	7.20	Luke 3:38	9.3	John 7:6	6.62, 10.54
Matt 13:7	7.39	Luke 5:12-19	6.56	John 10:9	6.4, 7.14
Matt 13:17	7.7, 9.42	Luke 6:37-38	10.30	John 10:24	6.34
Matt 13:30	9.98	Luke 8:39	6.60	John 11:50	6.32
Matt 16:17	10.5	Luke 9:13	8.45	John 12:19	6.32
Matt 17:11	9.9	Luke 9:29-33	8.92	John 12:35	6.34, 9.96
Matt 18:6	6.57	Luke 9:60	7.41	John 14:2	9.98
Matt 18:9	6.57	Luke 10:27	7.28,	John 14:27	6.53
Matt 19:26	6.9		9.101, 10.8	John 15:12	10.7
Matt 19:28	6.9, 6.23,	Luke 10:41-42	6.61	John 15:15	10.52
	10.52	Luke 12:19	8.92	John 16:2	6.5
Matt 20:12	8.13	Luke 12:20	8.92	John 16:7	8.41
Matt 22:13	9.97	Luke 12:49	6.56	John 16:20	6.23,
Matt 22:19	7.28	Luke 13:25	8.35		8.88
Matt 22:37	7.28, 10.8	Luke 14:26	7.41	John 16:22	6.23,
Matt 23:3	6.10	Luke 14:33	8.45		8.88
Matt 23:6-7	8.80	Luke 16:12	8.12	John 18:36	8.12
Matt 23:15	6.4	Luke 16:23	9.101,	Acts 1:18	9.58
Matt 25:8	8.74		10.8	Acts 3:17-18	7.54
Matt 25:12	8.85	Luke 16:24	1.11	Acts 3:19	7.54
Matt 25:13	7.45	Luke 16:27-28	8.29	Acts 3:21	10.54
Matt 25:34	6.48	Luke 16:28	9.101,	Acts 4:19-20	7.53
Matt 25:35-36	6.9,		10.8	Acts 5:41	6.16
	6.48	Luke 17:21	8.41	Acts 7:51	7.53
Matt 25:41	9.97	Luke 18:19	9.46	Acts 7:60	7.54
Matt 25:44	6.48	Luke 22:53	6.62	Acts 9:16	9.54
Matt 25:44	6.48	Luke 22:61-62	8.30	Acts 13:46	7.11, 9.6

Scriptural Index